HOSEA'S GOD

ANCIENT ISRAEL AND ITS LITERATURE

Corrine L. Carvalho, General Editor

Editorial Board:
Susan Ackerman
Alphonso Groenewald
Shuichi Hasegawa
Annette Schellenberg
Naomi A. Steinberg

Number 48

HOSEA'S GOD

A Metaphorical Theology

Mason D. Lancaster

SBL PRESS
Atlanta

Copyright © 2023 by Mason D. Lancaster

All rights reserved. No part of this work may be reproduced or transmitted in any form or by any means, electronic or mechanical, including photocopying and recording, or by means of any information storage or retrieval system, except as may be expressly permitted by the 1976 Copyright Act or in writing from the publisher. Requests for permission should be addressed in writing to the Rights and Permissions Office, SBL Press, 825 Houston Mill Road, Atlanta, GA 30329 USA.

Library of Congress Control Number: 2023941763

For Susie

> In our stammering after a transcendent God we must speak,
> for the most part, metaphorically or not at all.
>
> —Janet Soskice, *Metaphor and Religious Language*

Contents

Acknowledgments — xi
Figures and Tables — xiii
Abbreviations — xv

1. Conceptualizing Yahweh with Metaphor Clusters: Introducing the Argument and Methods of This Study — 1

Part 1. Interactions within the Fifteen Metaphor Clusters of Hosea 4–14

2. Metaphors of Accusation — 31
3. Metaphors of Sentencing — 91
4. Metaphors of Redemption — 135

Part 2. Metaphor Patterns across Clusters

5. Affective Patterns — 161
6. Literary Patterns — 173
7. Rhetorical Patterns — 185

Part 3. Who Do You Say That I Am? A Metaphorical Theology of Hosea 4–14

8. An Aspective Constellation of Yahweh — 199
9. A Character Portrait of Yahweh — 209

10. Conclusion: Faithful beyond Death	227
Appendix: Graphs of the Distribution of Divine Metaphors, Themes, and Emotions in Hosea 4–14	233
Bibliography	235
Ancient Sources Index	265
Modern Authors Index	277

Acknowledgments

"The book of Hosea is complex and sophisticated, but ultimately everything revolves around gifts."[1] As Göran Eidevall asks of Hosea's metaphors, "How do you summarize a universe?"[2] so I wonder: How does one offer adequate acknowledgment in a universe where everything is a gift?

To my professional colleagues who gave invaluable feedback and encouragement along the way—Danny, Adam, Brad, Cooper, and Benjamin—thank you so very much for all you did that went and continues to go unseen. You have made this work so much better; I owe you each a great debt. To those at SBL Press who accepted this book and shepherded it to publication—especially the editorial board, Nicole L. Tilford, and Bob Buller—thank you.

I am also thankful for my extended family, especially Mom and Dad, and Mommy and Daddy, who selflessly, tirelessly, and freely gave of themselves in a variety of ways to help me get this project done. A special thanks to Miss Debbie—you are a gift. We could not have asked for someone better, and we could not have done it without you.

As much as I initially chafed at the reduction of my work time when you were born, Jaden, I grew to cherish our time together. After long hours in the exegetical weeds, time with you and your mother reminds me what is actually important in life. My greatest debt, though, is to my beautiful partner in crime. Susie, I know the toll these years have taken on you. As we sit together while I write this, there is no one with whom I would rather share this crazy journey. Thank you for your sacrifices and, moreover, for your constant love and encouragement. You are God's tangible expression

---

1. Eric J. Tully, *Hosea: A Handbook on the Hebrew Text*, BHHB (Waco, TX: Baylor University Press, 2018), x.

2. Göran Eidevall, *Grapes in the Desert: Metaphors, Models, and Themes in Hosea 4–14*, ConBOT 43 (Stockholm: Almqvist & Wiksell, 1996), 2.

(metaphor?) to me of his חסד. And finally, my great thanks are due to the Giver of all good and perfect gifts (ממני פריך נמצא).

Mason D. Lancaster
March 2022

Figures and Tables

Figures

2.1. Competing divine portraits of clusters 3–5	73–75
8.1. A constellation of metaphors for Yahweh in Hosea 4–14	204
A.1. Distribution of metaphors for God in Hosea 4:1–9:3	233
A.2. Distribution of metaphors for God in Hosea 9:4–14:10	234

Tables

3.1. Metaphor Time Frames and Their Positivity/Negativity in Hosea 10:10–12	115
5.1. Clusters Involving Betrayal, according to Metaphor Domain	165

Abbreviations

4Q78	Twelve Prophets[c]
4Q82	Twelve Prophets[g]
4Q167	pesher Hosea[b]
ÄAT	Ägypten und Altes Testament
AB	Anchor Bible
ABD	Freedman, David Noel, ed. *Anchor Bible Dictionary*. 6 vols. New York: Doubleday, 1992.
ABR	*Australian Biblical Review*
AcBib	Academia Biblica
ACEBTrSup	Amsterdamse Cahiers voor Exegese van de Bijbel en zijn Tradities: Supplement Series
ACT	Ancient Christian Texts
AIL	Ancient Israel and Its Literature
AnCrac	*Analecta Cracoviensia*
ANEM	Ancient Near Eastern Monographs
AOAT	Alter Orient und Altes Testament
AoF	*Altorientalische Forschungen*
AOTC	Apollos Old Testament Commentary
ArBib	The Aramaic Bible
ARCL	*Annual Review of Cognitive Linguistics*
ARM	Archives royales de Mari
ASV	American Standard Version
ATD	Das Alte Testament Deutsch
AUUWR	Acta Universitatis Upsaliensis: Women in Religion
BBB	Bonner biblische Beiträge
BBR	*Bulletin for Biblical Research*
BDB	Brown, Francis, S. R. Driver, and Charles A. Briggs. *A Hebrew and English Lexicon of the Old Testament*.
BerOl	Berit Olam
BETL	Bibliotheca ephemeridum theologicarum lovaniensium

BHHB	Baylor Handbook on the Hebrew Bible
BHQ	Schenker, Adrian, et al., eds. *Biblia Hebraica Quinta*. Fascicle 13: The Twelve Minor Prophets. Prepared by Anthony Gelston. Stuttgart: Deutsche Bibelgesellschaft, 2010.
BHRG	Merwe, Christo H. J. van der, Jackie A. Naudé, and Jan H. Kroeze. *A Biblical Hebrew Reference Grammar*. 2nd ed. London: T&T Clark, 2017.
BHS	Elliger, Karl, and Wilhelm Rudolph, eds. *Biblica Hebraica Stuttgartensia*. Stuttgart: Deutsche Bibelgesellschaft, 1983.
Bib	*Biblica*
BibInt	*Biblical Interpretation*
BibInt	Biblical Interpretation
BibJudStud	Biblical and Judaic Studies
BibThSt	Biblisch-theologische Studien
BIT	The Bible in Its Traditions
BJS	Brown Judaic Studies
BRLAJ	The Brill Reference Library of Ancient Judaism
b. Sanh.	Babylonian Talmud Sanhedrin
BSL	Biblical Studies Library
BTB	*Biblical Theology Bulletin*
BZ	*Biblische Zeitschrift*
BZAW	Beihefte zur Zeitschrift für die alttestamentliche Wissenschaft
CAT	Commentaire de l'Ancient Testament
CBQ	*Catholic Biblical Quarterly*
CBQMS	Catholic Biblical Quarterly Monograph Series
CEB	Common English Bible
CELCR	Converging Evidence in Language and Communication Research
CI	*Critical Inquiry*
CL	*Cognitive Linguistics*
ConBOT	Coniectanea Biblica: Old Testament Series
COS	Hallo, William W., and K. Lawson Younger, eds. *The Context of Scripture*. 4 vols. Leiden: Brill, 1997–2016.
CS	*Cognitive Semiotics*
CTAT	Barthélemy, Dominique. *Critique textuelle de l'Ancien Testament*. Vol. 3, *Ézéchiel, Daniel et les 12 Prophètes*. Göttingen: Editions universitaires, 1992.
CTR	*Criswell Theological Review*

CurBR	*Currents in Biblical Research*
DCH	Clines, David J. A., ed. *Dictionary of Classical Hebrew.* 9 vols. Sheffield: Sheffield Phoenix, 1993–2014.
DDD	van der Toorn, Karel, Bob Becking, and Pieter W. van der Horst, eds. *Dictionary of Deities and Demons in the Bible.* 2nd rev. ed. Leiden: Brill, 1999.
DOTPr	J. Boda, Mark, and J. Gordon McConville, eds. *Dictionary of the Old Testament: Prophets.* Downers Grove, IL: InterVarsity Press, 2012.
Dtn	Deuteronomic
DULAT	del Olmo Lete, Gregorio, and Joaquín Sanmartín. *A Dictionary of the Ugaritic Language in the Alphabetic Tradition.* Translated and edited by Wilred G. E. Watson. 3rd rev. ed. Leiden: Brill, 2003.
EA	El-Amarna tablets. According to the edition of Jørgen A. Knudtzon. *Die el-Amarna-Tafeln.* Leipzig, 1908–1915. Repr., Aalen: Zeller, 1964. Continued in Anson F. Rainey, *El-Amarna Tablets, 359–379.* 2nd rev. ed. Kevelaer: Butzon & Bercker, 1978.
EBR	Klauck, Hans-Josef, et al., eds. *Encyclopedia of the Bible and Its Reception.* Berlin: de Gruyter, 2009–.
ESV	English Standard Version
ETL	*Ephemerides theologicae lovanienses*
FAT	Forshungen zum Alten Testament
FCB	Feminist Companion to the Bible
FHN	*Frontiers in Human Neuroscience*
FOTL	Forms of the Old Testament Literature
FRLANT	Forschungen zur Religion und Literatur des Alten und Neuen Testaments
FSRT	Friedensauer Schriftenreihe: Reihe A, Theologie
GKC	Gesenius, Wilhelm. *Gesenius' Hebrew Grammar.* Edited by Emil Kautzsch. Translated by Arthur E. Cowley. 2nd ed. Oxford: Clarendon, 1910.
HALOT	Koehler, Ludwig, Walter Baumgartner, and Johann J. Stamm. *The Hebrew and Aramaic Lexicon of the Old Testament.* Translated and edited under the supervision of Mervyn E. J. Richardson. Electronic ed. Leiden: Brill, 1994–2000.
HAR	*Hebrew Annual Review*

HBAI	*Hebrew Bible and Ancient Israel*
HBM	Hebrew Bible Monographs
HBS	Herder's Biblical Studies
HBT	*Horizons in Biblical Theology*
HCP	Human Cognitive Processing
HCSB	Holman Christian Standard Bible
HMS	Hebrew Monograph Series
HOSSNME	Handbook of Oriental Studies: Section 1, The Near and Middle East
HSM	Harvard Semitic Monographs
HSS	Harvard Semitic Studies
IBHS	Waltke, Bruce K., and Michael O'Connor. *An Introduction to Biblical Hebrew Syntax.* Winona Lake, IN: Eisenbrauns, 1990.
ICC	International Critical Commentary
Int	*Interpretation*
IP	*Intercultural Pragmatics*
ISBL	Indiana Studies in Biblical Literature
JAJSup	Journal of Ancient Judaism Supplements
JAL	*Journal of Applied Linguistics*
JBL	*Journal of Biblical Literature*
JCP	*Journal of Cognitive Psychotherapy*
JETS	*Journal of the Evangelical Theological Society*
JHS	*Journal of Hellenic Studies*
JMP	*Journal of Medicine and Philosophy*
JNES	*Journal of Near Eastern Studies*
JNSL	*Journal of Northwest Semitic Languages*
Joüon	Joüon, Paul. *A Grammar of Biblical Hebrew.* Translated and revised by T. Muraoka. 2 vols. Rome: Pontifical Biblical Institute, 1991
JP	*Journal of Pragmatics*
JPR	*Journal of Psycholinguistic Research*
JQR	Jewish Quarterly Review
JR	*Journal of Religion*
JSem	*Journal for Semitics*
JSOT	*Journal for the Study of the Old Testament*
JSOTSup	Journal for the Study of the Old Testament: Supplement Series
JSS	*Journal of Semitic Studies*

JT	*Journal of Translation*
JTI	*Journal of Theological Interpretation*
JTS	*Journal of Theological Studies*
KAT	Kommentar zum Alten Testament
KHC	Kurzer Hand-Commentar zum Alten Testament
KTU	Dietrich, Manfried, Oswald Loretz, and Joaquín Sanmartín, eds. *Die keilalphabetischen Texte aus Ugarit*. Münster: Ugarit-Verlag, 2013. 3rd enl. ed. of *KTU: The Cuneiform Alphabetic Texts from Ugarit, Ras Ibn Hani, and Other Places*. Edited by Manfried Dietrich, Oswald Loretz, and Joaquín Sanmartín. Münster: Ugarit-Verlag, 1995 (= *CTU*).
Lam. Rab.	Lamentations Rabbah
LHBOTS	Library of Hebrew Bible/Old Testament Studies
LSPC	Lexington Studies in Political Communication
LXX	Septuagint
MAPW	Medicinal and Aromatic Plants of the World
ModTheo	*Modern Theology*
MS	*Metaphor and Symbol*
MT	Masoretic Text (as found in Codex Leningradensis, represented in *BHQ*)
NAC	New American Commentary
NASB	New American Standard Bible
NCB	New Century Bible
NET	New English Translation
NIB	Keck, Leander E., ed. *The New Interpreter's Bible*. 12 vols. Nashville: Abingdon, 1994–2004.
NICOT	New International Commentary on the Old Testament
NIDOTTE	VanGemeren, Willem A., ed. *New International Dictionary of Old Testament Theology and Exegesis*. 5 vols. Grand Rapids: Zondervan, 1997.
NIV	New International Version
NJPS	*Tanakh: The Holy Scriptures: The New JPS Translation according to the Traditional Hebrew Text*
NKJV	New King James Version
NRSV	New Revised Standard Version
NSBT	New Studies in Biblical Theology
OBO	Orbis Biblicus et Orientalis
OBT	Overtures to Biblical Theology

OTE	*Old Testament Essays*
OTG	Old Testament Guides
OTL	Old Testament Library
OTM	Oxford Theological Monographs
OTWSA	*Die Ou-Testamentiese Werkgemeenskap in Suid-Afrika* (= OTSSA: *Old Testament Society of South Africa*)
Pesiq. Rab.	Pesiqta Rabbati
Pesiq. Rab Kah.	Pesiqta of Rab Kahana
PG	Patrologia Graeca [= Patrologiae cursus completes: Series graeca]. Edited by Jacques-Paul Migne. 162 vols. Paris, 1857–1886.
PL	*Philosophy and Literature*
PMP	Princeton Monographs in Philosophy
Poet.	Aristotle, *Poetics*
Presb	*Presbyterion*
RB	*Revue biblique*
RBS	Resources for Biblical Study
Readings	Readings: A New Biblical Commentary
ResQ	*Restoration Quarterly*
RevExp	*Review and Expositor*
Rhet.	Aristotle, *Rhetoric*
RIPT	Routledge Innovations in Political Theory
RM	*Review of Metaphysics*
RPF	*Revista Portuguesa de Filosofia*
RSV	Revised Standard Version
SAA	State Archives of Assyria
SANER	Studies in Ancient Near Eastern Records
SAS	Series in Affective Science
SBLDS	Society of Biblical Literature Dissertation Series
SBLMS	Society of Biblical Literature Monograph Series
SBS	Stuttgarter Bibelstudien
SCS	Septuagint and Cognate Studies
SEÅ	*Svensk exegetisk årsbok*
SeptCS	Septuagint Commentary Series
SESI	Studies in Emotion and Social Interaction
SHBC	Smyth & Helwys Bible Commentary
SJOT	*Scandinavian Journal of the Old Testament*
SLTHS	Siphrut: Literature and Theology of the Hebrew Scriptures

SSN	Studia Semitica Neerlandica
StBL	Studies in Biblical Literature
STR	Studies in Theology and Religion
SubBi	Subsidia Biblica
SymS	Symposium Series
Syr.	Syriac
TD	*Theology Digest*
TDOT	Botterweck, G. Johannes, and Helmer Ringgren, eds. *Theological Dictionary of the Old Testament*. Translated by John T. Willis et al. 8 vols. Grand Rapids, 1974–1976.
Tg. Neb.	Targum of the Prophets
Them	*Themelios*
THOTC	Two Horizons Old Testament Commentary
ThTo	*Theology Today*
TOTC	Tyndale Old Testament Commentaries
TQ	*Theologische Quartalschrift*
UBL	Ugaritisch-biblische Literatur
UCOP	University of Cambridge Oriental Publications
UF	*Ugarit-Forschungen*
VT	*Vetus Testamentum*
VTSup	Vetus Testamentum Supplements
Vulg.	Vulgate
WAW	Writings from the Ancient World
WBC	Word Biblical Commentary
WMANT	Wissenschaftliche Monographien zum Alten und Neuen Testament
WSC	Wisconsin Studies in Classics
ZAW	*Zeitschrift für die alttestamentliche Wissenschaft*
ZTK	*Zeitschrift für Theologie und Kirche*

1
Conceptualizing Yahweh with Metaphor Clusters: Introducing the Argument and Methods of This Study

> The source of metaphor is the liberty of the mind among such words as there are.
>
> —Denis Donoghue, *Metaphor*

The God of Hosea has been an enigmatic and highly contested figure for centuries, largely due to the variety of Hosea's metaphors. Is Yahweh essentially a loving father (11:1) or one who will snap Israel's neck (10:2)? How can Hosea's deity be a lion who will tear his[1] people to shreds (5:14) and refreshing dew that will bring life to a languishing land (14:6)? Is he a kind farmer lifting the harness of the animal so the animal can eat (11:4) or a moth that will subtly but assuredly eat away at the fabric of Israel's existence (5:12)? Hosea's God has been variously characterized as the quintessential deity of doom or of compassion, of abuse or of self-giving generosity. How is a reader to make sense of such rapidly shifting depictions? Walter Brueggemann concludes that the narrative flow of this poetry depicts a God who is "a recovering agent of violence," replete with remorse and relapse.[2] The metaphoric variety has led other scholars, such as Francis Landy, to conclude simply that Hosea's language is "fractured, baffling, and claims a status verging on madness" and that God himself "lacks coherence" in the book.[3] Thus, amid the many advances since bibli-

---

 1. Since most metaphors for the deity reflect masculine gender, I will refer to God with masculine pronouns throughout the book.
 2. Walter Brueggemann, "The Recovering God of Hosea," *HBT* 30 (2008): 19, emphasis removed.
 3. Francis Landy, "In the Wilderness of Speech: Problems of Metaphor in Hosea," *Biblnt* 3 (1995): 56, 46.

cal and theological studies embraced metaphor around forty years ago, an area that continues to invite inquiry is how to make sense of the Hebrew Bible's tendency toward having multiple overlapping and at times conflicting metaphors for God, even within a single passage.

It turns out that this is not a new arena of confusion. The book of Hosea itself witnesses to a contest between conflicting interpretations of Yahweh, between which divine images should reign supreme. Hosea 6:1–3 quotes Israel's cultic elite who are confident in Yahweh's generosity. Bracketing that quotation are Hosea's rebuttals, challenging the priests' optimistic construal of Yahweh as a beneficial storm god. Hosea responds that they do not properly know Yahweh and instead offers opposing storm-god images for Yahweh.

It is no wonder that Jerome needed "much more" divine help with Hosea than with the other prophets, crying out to God, "Expound to us this parable."[4] From the days of ancient Israel to early Christian interpreters to modern Western scholarship, discerning a portrait of Hosea's God has been a perennial challenge. That is, the pluriform nature of biblical metaphors still presents challenges—and opportunities—to the reader. Who is the God of Hosea? This book aims to shed light on the question of Hosea's metaphorical portrait of Yahweh. The point of departure for my approach is the recognition that Hosea's divine metaphors are not evenly distributed but tend to cluster together into groups. This observation opens new vistas into the book's metaphoric presentation of Yahweh and communicative purpose.

The Shape of This Study: Questions, Thesis, and Contributions

One could think of the book's questions, thesis, and contributions as an hourglass. Many questions and their pluriform answers (the wide end at the top of an hourglass) lead to the primary thesis of the book regarding Yahweh's fidelity (the narrow middle of the hourglass), which in turn contributes to multiple larger conversations (the wide bottom of the hourglass).

The primary question driving this investigation is: Who is Yahweh according to the metaphors of Hos 4–14? Several additional questions are

---

4. Jerome, *Commentaries on the Twelve Prophets*, ed. Thomas P. Scheck, ACT (Downers Grove, IL: IVP Academic, 2017), 2:148.

pertinent. How does one respond to the hundreds of diverse—at times conflicting or paradoxical—metaphors for God in Hos 4–14? What, if anything, holds them together? How does any pluriform unity relate to the discourse's rhetorical purpose? How are Hosea's metaphors deployed to achieve their rhetorical purpose? What would cause such diverse metaphors to remain together in the final form? And what is one to make of all these metaphors—both individually and collectively—theologically? What kind of mosaic portrait of God emerges? What do all these metaphors say about Yahweh? The varied questions outlined above led me to a single conclusion. I will ultimately argue that Yahweh's enduring loyalty to Israel is the key to everything, the core of Hosea's portrait of God.

In order to address these questions in a way that offers new insight, I develop a new approach to metaphorical theology that brings metaphors into conversation with one another while respecting their diversity and considering their literary, rhetorical, and theological functions in light of the larger discourse. The remainder of this chapter outlines the parameters and initial methodology of my study, drawing especially from research on metaphor clustering. My approach is further developed throughout the book, drawing on insights from narratology on characterization (esp. part 2), and the ancient aspective approach (introduced in ch. 8 to shape part 3).

Part 1 applies the metaphor-clustering framework to an analysis of 103 divine metaphors across fifteen clusters. Each metaphor cluster is analyzed in isolation from the others in terms of their contributions to a portrait of Yahweh. In part 2, I turn to intercluster analysis, identifying patterns across the clusters of the book pertaining to divine emotions, literary development and inversion of metaphors, and the rhetorical purpose of the book, which is procuring Israel's return to Yahweh. Part 3 is where I attempt to bring all the threads together, offering an aspective constellation of Yahweh's diverse presentation in Hos 4–14, then identifying five divine characteristics arising from the metaphors under study. A conclusion summarizes the findings in each chapter and the central thesis at which I arrive, which concerns Yahweh's fidelity to Israel as essential to the Hosea's metaphorical presentation of God.

In pursuing this project, I hope to make contributions both methodological (a fresh *approach* to biblical metaphors) and exegetical/theological (a fresh metaphorical theology of Hosea). Furthermore, one of the broader implications of this study is that it demonstrates how metaphors affect worldviews, how the *contesting* or *changing* of those metaphors can destabilize and rebuild a social imagination, and thus how metaphors can influence the shape and ethics of a society.[5] This is, as we shall see, Hosea's goal in deploying such metaphors.

Let me turn now to explain my approach to the project.

Preliminary Matters Regarding Hosea

My investigation of divine metaphors focuses on the final form of Hos 4–14. The choice for the final form arose because, at base, metaphors have meaning within a given verbal and social context.[6] The *literary* context used for metaphor identification in this study is the final form of the book of Hosea, as presented in the MT (*BHQ*), because it is the earliest extant stable literary context available (anything earlier being hypothetical, fragmentary, and lacking consensus).[7] The *temporal* context of eighth-century

---

5. For an analysis of social imagination in modern societies, see, e.g., Charles Taylor, *Modern Social Imaginaries* (Durham, NC: Duke University Press, 2003); also Taylor, *A Secular Age* (Cambridge: Harvard University Press, 2007), 171–72. For modern examples of how metaphors shape this process, see George Lakoff, *Moral Politics: How Liberals and Conservatives Think*, 2nd ed. (Chicago: University of Chicago Press, 2002).

6. For instance, according to Raymond Gibbs Jr., "Metaphorical language also emerges from the interplay of the brain, bodies, and world, and must be ultimately explained as the product of an entire context-sensitive dynamical system." See Gibbs, "Metaphor, Language, and Dynamic Systems," in *The Routledge Handbook of Metaphor and Language*, edited by Elena Semino and Zsófia Demjén (Abingdon: Routledge, 2017), 60. The challenges to metaphor interpretation in Hosea are evident, given that modern readers are not part of Hosea's "language community," nor do they share its complex of associated commonplaces that are necessary to complete the enthymeme, i.e., "arguments in which the audience participates in forming the conclusion." See Thomas R. Burkholder and David Henry, "Criticism of Metaphor," in *Rhetorical Criticism: Perspectives in Action*, ed. Jim A. Kuypers, LSPC (Lanham, MD: Lexington, 2009), 99.

7. See Sungjin Kim, "Is the Masoretic Text Still a Reliable Primary Text for the Book of Hosea?," *BBR* 28 (2018): 34–64. An alternative approach is to interpret metaphors according to their redaction strata. E.g., Juan Cruz, *Who Is like Yahweh? A Study of Divine Metaphors in the Book of Micah*, FRLANT 263 (Göttingen: Vandenhoeck & Ruprecht, 2016). The choice for the MT as a base text does not preclude text-critical decisions resulting in departures from the MT (see Hos 4:10–11a; 6:2–3, 5c, 10; 10:10; 11:2, 3b).

Compositional theories of the book range from its being the product of ninth- and eighth-century prophecy (Gruber) to an original composition by Persian-Yehud literati (e.g., Trotter, Ben Zvi, Bos). See Mayer I. Gruber, *Hosea: A Textual Commentary*,

1. Conceptualizing Yahweh with Metaphor Clusters

Israel is the world within which the metaphors and their literary context are intended to be read and interpreted.[8]

My decision to focus on chapters 4–14 came about for several reasons. First, this study is interested in metaphorical *variety*. Hosea has a greater density of metaphors for God than any other book of the Bible,[9] yet these are not evenly distributed throughout the book. The first three chapters deal in relatively homogenous metaphorics concerning the sexual and marriage metaphor domains, supplemented with some agricultural imagery. Hosea 4–14, on the other hand, holds most of the book's metaphorical variety. The second reason is related to the first: Hos 4–14 has attracted comparatively little attention, largely because scholarship has demonstrated an "overwhelmingly myopic focus on the marriage metaphor in

---

LHBOTS 653 (New York: T&T Clark, 2017), 6; James M. Trotter, *Reading Hosea in Achaemenid Yehud*, JSOTSup 328 (Sheffield: Sheffield Academic, 2001); Ehud Ben Zvi, *Hosea*, FOTL (Grand Rapids: Eerdmans, 2005); James M. Bos, *Reconsidering the Date and Provenance of the Book of Hosea: The Case for Persian-Period Yehud*, LHBOTS 580 (London: Bloomsbury T&T Clark, 2013). For recent surveys of composition theories, see Bos, *Reconsidering the Date*, 21–30 (see 30 for an example of the lack of consensus); Brad E. Kelle, "Hosea 4–14 in Twentieth-Century Scholarship," *CurBR* 8 (2010): 324–32; Stuart A. Irvine, "Hosea," in *The Oxford Handbook of the Minor Prophets*, ed. Julia M. O'Brien (New York: Oxford University Press, 2021), 405–8.

  8. That is, regardless of one's view on the origin or compositional history of the book, the eighth century is the book's "intellectual horizon," from which it "never overtly departs." See Mark W. Hamilton, "History among the Junipers: Hosea 14:2–10 as Metahistoriography," *BZ* 63 (2019): 108; see also Nadav Na'aman, "The Book of Hosea as a Source for the Last Days of the Kingdom of Israel," *BZ* 59 (2015): 232–56; Irvine, "Hosea," 407–8. It is, in other words, the world of the text. The difficulty of the text of Hosea has occasioned speculation as to the dialectical northern origins of the text. We have not found instances in which a clear northern dialect makes a substantial difference for the reading of a metaphor. For more, see Yoon Jong Yoo, "Israelian Hebrew in the Book of Hosea" (PhD diss., Cornell University, 1999). Macintosh and Gruber are among commentators who affirm a northern dialect in Hosea. See Andrew A. Macintosh, *A Critical and Exegetical Commentary on Hosea*, ICC (London: Bloomsbury T&T Clark, 1997); Gruber, *Hosea*.

  9. Casper J. Labuschagne, "The Similes in the Book of Hosea," *OTWSA* 7 (1964): 64; James Luther Mays, *Hosea: A Commentary*, OTL (Philadelphia: Westminster John Knox, 1969), 7; Hans Walter Wolff, *Hosea*, trans. Gary Stansell, Hermeneia (Philadelphia: Fortress, 1974), xxiv; Paul A. Kruger, "Prophetic Imagery: On Metaphors and Similes in the Book Hosea," *JNSL* 14 (1988): 143, 150; Macintosh, *Critical and Exegetical Commentary*, lxiii; Sharon Moughtin-Mumby, *Sexual and Marital Metaphors in Hosea, Jeremiah, Isaiah and Ezekiel*, OTM (Oxford: Oxford University Press, 2008), 49–50.

Hos 1–3, often to the exclusion of serious engagement with other parts of the book."[10] Commensurate attention to the metaphors of Hos 4–14 is overdue. Third, attending to the substantial discussions of Hos 1–3 (necessary for developing a truly exhaustive Hosean theology) would make this volume unmanageably long. Fourth, the marital and agricultural imagery of Hos 1–3 is echoed in 4–14 (esp. chs. 4, 10, and 14), so one could argue that a metaphorical theology of Hos 4–14 thus includes aspects of 1–3 and is therefore relatively representative of the book as a whole, though admittedly such a project bypasses many of the important scholarly discussions of Hos 1–3. Hence, my investigation focuses on the metaphorical portrait of Yahweh in Hos 4–14 specifically.

The metaphorical variety in Hosea is crucial to understanding the book's message. Indeed, the final verse explicitly demands that the reader "understand these things," things that center on Israel's God and are largely communicated figuratively.[11] The crucial observation that sets the trajectory of this investigation is that even within Hos 4–14, metaphors are not uniformly distributed. Hosea 5:10–6:5, for instance, involves fourteen metaphors for God, yet other passages of the same length, such as 4:2–10, lack any metaphors for Yahweh.[12] This raises several questions. Does Hosea evidence other such metaphor groupings? If so, why do metaphors tend to group together? Are there any patterns to their groupings? Why do they coalesce where they do?

To answer these and other questions and to further investigate Hosea's divine metaphors, metaphor research provides a number of useful tools and perspectives.

---

10. Kelle, "Hosea 4–14 in Twentieth-Century Scholarship," 315. The major exception in terms of longer work focused on metaphors in Hosea 4–14 is Eidevall, *Grapes in the Desert*.

11. I follow MT versification, and all translations are my own unless otherwise noted.

12. My initial observation that certain metaphor domains are introduced in tight proximity to one another in 5:8–6:6 and are then revisited and inverted throughout the remainder of the book was eventually published as Mason D. Lancaster, "Wounds and Healing, Dew and Lions: Hosea's Development of Divine Metaphors," *CBQ* 83 (2021): 407–24.

What Is a Metaphor, and What Does It Do?

Metaphor: Definition and Holistic Approach

The state of biblical scholarship is now such that an acquaintance with metaphor theory can usually be assumed. What follows is far from an overview of the whole field of metaphor research.[13] It is, more modestly, a brief description of the definitions and criteria used in this study.

According to the prevailing theory of metaphor from cognitive linguistics (namely, conceptual metaphor theory), people write and speak in metaphor because we first think in metaphors.[14] Metaphors are fundamentally conceptual and only secondarily linguistic.[15] A conceptual metaphor may be defined as "understanding one domain of experience (that is typically abstract) in terms of another (that is typically concrete)" or even more concisely as a "cross-domain mapping in thought."[16] (I do not follow

---

13. For an entrée into this vast field, see Mason D. Lancaster, "Metaphor Research and the Hebrew Bible," *CurBR* 19 (2021): 235–85; see also Jakub Mácha, "Metaphor in Analytic Philosophy and Cognitive Science," *RPF* 75 (2019): 2247–86. For an up-to-date compendium, mostly from a cognitive-linguistics perspective, see Semino and Demjén, *Routledge Handbook*. For concise summaries of major theories in relation to biblical studies, see, e.g., Hanneke van Loon, *Metaphors in the Discussion on Suffering in Job 3–31: Visions of Hope and Consolation*, BibInt 165 (Leiden: Brill, 2018), 4–32, particularly focused on cognitive accounts; Benjamin M. Austin, *Plant Metaphors in the Old Greek of Isaiah*, SCS 369 (Atlanta: SBL Press, 2019), 12–65, covering a broader swath of theories. For a philosophical and literary perspective by a biblical scholar, see Paul K.-K. Cho, *Myth, History, and Metaphor in the Hebrew Bible* (Cambridge: Cambridge University Press, 2019), 17–38.

14. George Lakoff and Mark Johnson, *Metaphors We Live By*, 2nd ed. (Chicago: University of Chicago Press, 2003), 3.

15. Contra Janet Martin Soskice, *Metaphor and Religious Language* (Oxford: Clarendon, 1985), 16.

16. The first definition comes from Zoltán Kövecses, "Conceptual Metaphor Theory," in Semino and Demjén, *Routledge Handbook*, 13, emphasis removed. The second definition comes from Gerard J. Steen, "Deliberate Metaphor Theory: Basic Assumptions, Main Tenets, Urgent Issues," *IP* 14 (2017): 3. For other conceptual metaphor theory definitions, see George Lakoff, "The Invariance Hypothesis: Is Abstract Reason Based on Image-Schemas?," *CL* 1 (1990): 39–74; Mark Turner, "Aspects of the Invariance Hypothesis," *CL* 1 (1990): 247–55; George Lakoff, "The Contemporary Theory of Metaphor," in *Metaphor and Thought*, ed. Andrew Ortony, 2nd ed. (Cambridge: Cambridge University Press, 1993), 203, 215–16, 228–29; Lakoff, "The Neural Theory of Metaphor," in *The Cambridge Handbook of Metaphor and Thought*,

the practice of writing conceptual metaphors in small caps in this book.) A particular linguistic instantiation of a metaphor is called a metaphorical expression.[17] For the sake of simplicity this study will often use the term *metaphor* to refer to Hosea's textual metaphorical expressions.

Additionally, conceptual metaphor theory emphasizes the ordinariness of metaphor. Metaphor is not merely poetic flourish intentionally added to ornament speech. Rather, metaphor is embedded in everyday speech because it reflects the fundamental ways in which we conceptualize the world. Recent studies probe the metaphorical conceptualizations underlying everyday speech in the Bible.[18] For the purposes of this study, it is irrelevant whether Hosea's metaphors for God are intentional or poetic metaphors, as we are interested in Hosea's conceptualization of Yahweh.[19]

Conceptual metaphor theory is certainly the most well-known and probably the most used account of metaphor, but it is not the only theory.[20] In fact, as scholars recognize the limitations of conceptual metaphor theory and that no single theory is sufficient to account for the richness

---

ed. Raymond W. Gibbs Jr. (New York: Cambridge University Press, 2008), 26; Zoltán Kövecses, *Metaphor: A Practical Introduction*, 2nd ed. (New York: Oxford University Press, 2010), 130–32. For literary and theological perspectives, see Benjamin Harshav, *Explorations in Poetics* (Stanford, CA: Stanford University Press, 2007), 32–75; Soskice, *Metaphor and Religious Language*, 15.

17. See Lakoff, "Contemporary Theory of Metaphor," 209; Kövecses, "Conceptual Metaphor Theory," 16–17.

18. See, e.g., Nicole L. Tilford, *Sensing World, Sensing Wisdom: The Cognitive Foundation of Biblical Metaphors*, AIL 31 (Atlanta: SBL Press, 2017); Johan de Joode, *Metaphorical Landscapes and the Theology of the Book of Job*, VTSup 179 (Leiden: Brill, 2018).

19. That is, I focus on particular instances of communication as parts of the large conceptual systems behind them. See Beth M. Stovell, "'I Will Make Her Like a Desert': Intertextual Allusion and Feminine and Agricultural Metaphors in the Book of the Twelve," in *The Book of the Twelve and the New Form Criticism*, ed. Mark J. Boda, Michael H. Floyd, and Colin M. Toffelmire, ANEM 10 (Atlanta: SBL Press, 2015), 37–39. Doubtless many of Hosea's divine metaphors are "deliberate." On this emerging field, see Steen, "Deliberate Metaphor Theory."

20. In addition to multiple philosophical, literary, and rhetorical accounts, there is conceptual blending theory, career of metaphor theory, class-inclusion theory, conceptual metaphor and metonymy theory, and deliberate metaphor theory, among others. See Lancaster, "Metaphor Research and the Hebrew Bible"; Van Loon, *Metaphors in the Discussion*, 10–15.

of metaphor, the future of the field of metaphor research seems to be hybrid, integrative, or multidisciplinary accounts of metaphor.[21] I have tried to use an approach in this study that is holistic, both in terms of metaphor *theory* and in terms of attending to its *function* in the text. I adopt a holistic theory of metaphor in that I have incorporated conceptual, philosophical, linguistic, and rhetorical accounts of metaphor, as will be evident here and throughout. Next, I provide a brief account of metaphor's holistic function.

The Whole Power of Metaphor

Functionally speaking, metaphors have historically been considered in terms of their cognitive impact. But there are also long traditions—including among poets and philosophers—analyzing their impact on affect and volition. My approach is functionally holistic because I have tried to be aware of the cognitive, emotional, and volitional implications of metaphors on an ancient audience or even a modern reader. A brief outline of the multifaceted *function* and power of metaphor is crucial for the holistic metaphor analyses of this project. Accounting for metaphor's impact on thinking, feeling, and acting directly shapes my reading of Hosea's metaphors.

First, metaphors do not merely repeat what is known but introduce fresh knowledge or ways of knowing. They involve semantic ingenuity. "Metaphor, or something very much like it, is what renders possible and intelligible the acquisition of new knowledge."[22] This is true on the linguistic plane and on a deeply neurological level.[23] Since the semantic ingenuity of metaphor constitutes the major turn in metaphor studies in the past sixty years and is therefore well known, a few representatives from various

---

21. Raymond W. Gibbs Jr., "Why Do Some People Dislike Conceptual Metaphor Theory?," *CS* 5 (2009): 14–36; Mácha, "Metaphor in Analytic Philosophy," 2274–77. For examples of integrated accounts of metaphor, see, e.g., Raymond W. Gibbs Jr., *Metaphor Wars: Conceptual Metaphors in Human Life* (Cambridge: Cambridge University Press, 2017); Gibbs, "Metaphor, Language, and Dynamic Systems"; Steen, "Deliberate Metaphor Theory."

22. Hugh G. Petrie and Rebecca S. Oshlag, "Metaphor and Learning," in Ortony, *Metaphor and Thought*, 582; see also 580–84. On what and how exactly a reader/hearer "knows" after interpreting a metaphor, see also Josef Stern, *Metaphor in Context* (Cambridge: MIT Press, 2000), 316–17.

23. Lakoff, "Neural Theory of Metaphor."

disciplines should suffice to illustrate the point that metaphors can open novel ways of perceiving reality.[24] Philosopher Paul Ricoeur affirms "the power of metaphor to project and to reveal a world." That is, metaphors "redescribe reality."[25] As cognitive linguist George Lakoff and philosopher Mark Johnson put it, metaphor has "the power to define reality."[26] Because of this, theologian Janet Soskice notes, "A good metaphor may not simply be an oblique reference to a predetermined subject but *a new vision, the birth of a new understanding, a new referential access*. A strong metaphor compels *new possibilities of vision*."[27] This is profoundly the case for *theological* metaphors. Biblical scholar William Brown observes, "The power of the metaphor, moreover, lies in its ability (and its manipulability) to inspire new theological vision."[28]

Second, metaphors have the power to affect feelings. This fact has received comparatively little scholarly attention, as emotions—like metaphors—have historically been considered outside the realm of "serious" rational scholarship.[29] Recent researchers have rightly tried to keep these

---

24. For some recent work, see further Sam Glucksberg, *Understanding Figurative Language: From Metaphor to Idioms* (Oxford: Oxford University Press, 2001); Ted Cohen, *Thinking of Others: On the Talent for Metaphor*, PMP (Princeton: Princeton University Press, 2008).

25. Paul Ricoeur, *The Rule of Metaphor: Multi-disciplinary Studies of the Creation of Meaning in Language*, trans. Robert Czerny (Toronto: University of Toronto Press, 1981), 93, 7; see also Ricoeur, "The Metaphorical Process as Cognition, Imagination, and Feeling," *CI* 5 (1978): 143–59; Ricoeur, "Poetry and Possibility," in *A Ricoeur Reader: Reflection and Imagination*, ed. Mario J. Valdéz (Toronto: University of Toronto Press, 1991), 455.

26. Lakoff and Johnson, *Metaphors We Live By*, 157.

27. Soskice, *Metaphor and Religious Language*, 57–58, emphasis added; see also 48, 144.

28. William P. Brown, *Seeing the Psalms: A Theology of Metaphor* (Louisville: Westminster John Knox, 2002), 214.

29. Thomas Hobbes is representative when he includes metaphors among those "senseless and ambiguous words" that are "for nothing else but to insinuate wrong ideas, move the passions, and thereby mislead the judgment." See Mark Johnson, "Metaphor: An Overview," in *Encyclopedia of Aesthetics*, ed. Michael Kelly (New York: Oxford University Press, 1998), 2:209. The two quotations are Hobbes's, the first cited from *Leviathan*, part 1, ch. 5; the second from *Essay Concerning Human Understanding*, book 3, ch. 10. For a survey of views, see Amy C. Cottrill, "A Reading of Ehud and Jael through the Lens of Affect Theory," *BibInt* 22 (2014): 433–37.

aspects in better balance.³⁰ Emotions relate to metaphor in at least three different respects. Metaphors can (1) describe an emotional state, (2) reflect the feelings of the creator of the metaphor, and (3) cause the recipient to feel things.

Metaphors can be used to (1) describe the emotion itself. In English one might say he is "boiling over" with anger, or she is "green" with jealousy. In Hebrew, one's nose grows hot with anger (חרה אפי, Hos 8:5); God's wrath can be "poured out like water" (אשפוך כמים עברתי, Hos 5:10), or God can have a change of heart (נהפך עלי לבי, Hos 11:8).³¹

Additionally, a metaphor can (2) reflect the emotions of its creator regarding the target domain. "When metaphor is used to talk about 'something in terms of something else,' it seems that people choose that 'something else' so that it expresses how they feel about what they are saying."³² An important implication for our investigation is that when Yahweh chooses metaphors for Israel, it can indicate not only facts about Israel but how Yahweh *feels* about Israel. For instance, the metaphors of sexual promiscuity (זנה) in Hosea perhaps reflect, among other things, Yahweh's sense of shame by virtue of association to "his" promiscuous wife.³³ The farmer metaphors in Hos 10:11 reflect Yahweh's feelings of frustration and disappointment with Israel.³⁴

---

30. Among more recent work, see Zoltán Kövecses, *Metaphor and Emotion: Language, Culture, and Body in Human Feeling*, rev. ed., SESI 2 (Cambridge: Cambridge University Press, 2003); Kövecses, "Metaphor and Emotion," in Gibbs, *Cambridge Handbook of Metaphor*, 380–96. For recent overviews of the science of emotions, see David Sander and Klaus Scherer, eds., *Oxford Companion to Emotion and the Affective Sciences*, SAS (Oxford: Oxford University Press, 2009); Lisa Feldman Barrett, *How Emotions Are Made: The Secret Life of the Brain* (Boston: Houghton Mifflin Harcourt, 2017). On metaphors and emotion within biblical studies and a discussion of divine emotion, see ch. 5.

31. For some examples, see Alec Basson, "A Few Metaphorical Source Domains for Emotions in the Old Testament," *Scriptura* 100 (2009): 121–28.

32. Lynne Cameron, "What Is Metaphor and Why Does It Matter?," in *Metaphor Analysis: Research Practice in Applied Linguistics, Social Sciences and the Humanities*, ed. Lynne Cameron and Robert Maslen (London: Equinox, 2010), 5.

33. This shame is both an emotion and a social status. See further ch. 2, cluster 1.

34. See ch. 3, cluster 10.

A metaphor can (3) change the receiver's feelings.[35] This is a direct result of the previous point. The speaker intends hearers to share in the emotional evaluation of the target domain. Philosopher Ted Cohen affirms,

> *A principal ambition in the use of metaphor* ... is to induce others to *feel* as we do, and to do this by describing the objects of our feelings in a way which requires a special effort at comprehension on the part of others. When I offer you a metaphor I invite your attempt to join a community with me, an intimate community whose bond is our common feeling about something.[36]

This can occur in literature as well, as a reader is invited to relive the experiences of the characters.[37] This may indeed be true of Yahweh's emotions in the book of Hosea. Emotional reevaluation can happen *through* the conceptual semantic ingenuity of the metaphor, or *independently* of conscious rational processes. In conceptual metaphor theory, the cross-domain mapping of a metaphor consists of cognitive *and emotional* mapping: such metaphorical "image mapping allows us to map our *evaluation* of the source domain onto the target."[38] By "evaluation," Lakoff here refers to evaluations that are not primarily rational but affective, such as the recognition of beauty and the inspiration of awe. As Laura Otis observes, "The command to 'move on,' for instance, implies that life is a journey on which a person contemplating her pain is balking. Personal pains often have social causes, and orders to 'move on' not only humiliate sufferers; they delegitimize protests; they drown accusations in shame."[39] Having heard a metaphor, it is not simply that we *think* about the target differently but that we *feel* differently as well.

Third, there is the pragmatic or performative aspect of metaphor: its use or function in discourse. Metaphors can shape how people behave; they can have volitional impact. This occurs implicitly and explicitly. A few examples illustrate how this can happen implicitly or indirectly. One's everyday actions, if one thinks of life as "a full-contact sport," will be dif-

---

35. Laura Otis, *Banned Emotions: How Metaphors Can Shape What People Feel* (Oxford: Oxford University Press, 2019).
36. Ted Cohen, "Metaphor, Feeling, and Narrative," *PL* 21 (1997): 233, emphasis added.
37. Otis, *Banned Emotions*, 3; see also Cottrill, "Reading of Ehud."
38. Lakoff, "Contemporary Theory of Metaphor," 230, emphasis added.
39. Otis, *Banned Emotions*, 1.

ferent from if one thinks that "all the world's a stage."[40] How one feels and behaves while operating with the metaphor of sin as burden is different from a person assuming sin is debt.[41] Metaphors can even influence sensory perception: "Fishy smells induce suspicion, ... unburdening yourself of a secret lowers the estimation of the upward slant of hills."[42]

But speakers can also intentionally deploy metaphors for the explicit purpose of changing the behavior in others. This brings us to the art of persuasion—in many ways the conceptual home of metaphor in Western thought: rhetoric.[43] Because metaphors shape possibilities for behavior, they have long been recognized as a powerful means of persuasion: *change* the metaphor, and you can *change* someone's behavior.[44] Policies and actions

---

40. Burkholder and Henry, "Criticism of Metaphor," 98.

41. Gary A. Anderson, *Sin: A History* (New Haven: Yale University Press, 2010); see also Joseph Lam, *Patterns of Sin in the Hebrew Bible: Metaphor, Culture, and the Making of a Religious Concept* (New York: Oxford University Press, 2016).

42. George Lakoff, "Mapping the Brain's Metaphor Circuitry: Metaphorical Thought in Everyday Reason," *FHN* 8 (2014): 7; see also Lisa M. Lindeman and Lyn Y. Abramson, "The Mental Simulation of Motor Incapacity in Depression," *JCP* 22 (2008): 228–49; Somogy Varga, "Embodied Concepts and Mental Health," *JMP* 43 (2018): 241–60, esp. 248–50 for examples. For the broad implications of the embodied nature of cognition, see Francisco J. Varela, Evan T. Thompson, and Eleanor Rosch, *The Embodied Mind: Cognitive Science and Human Experience* (Cambridge: MIT Press, 1991); George Lakoff and Mark Johnson, *Philosophy in the Flesh: The Embodied Mind and Its Challenge to Western Thought* (New York: Basic, 1999); Zoltán Kövecses, *Where Metaphors Come From: Reconsidering Context in Metaphor* (New York: Oxford University Press, 2015); Barrett, *How Emotions Are Made*.

43. For the purposes of this study, *rhetoric* is defined as "the strategic use of communication, oral or written, to achieve specifiable goals." See Jim A. Kuypers and Andrew King, "What Is Rhetoric?," in Kuypers, *Rhetorical Criticism*, 4.

44. Aristotle provided the first detailed studies of metaphor in the Western tradition, doing so from the perspectives of rhetoric and poetics. See Aristotle, *Rhet.* 1404b–1411b; Aristotle, *Poet.* 1457b; see also Ricoeur, *Rule of Metaphor*, 9–43. Western philosophy continued to discuss metaphor primarily under the rubric of rhetoric from then until the 1960s. See Soskice, *Metaphor and Religious Language*, 1–14; Mark Johnson, "Introduction: Metaphor in the Philosophical Tradition," in *Philosophical Perspectives on Metaphor*, ed. Mark Johnson (Minneapolis: University of Minnesota Press, 1981), 4–8, for brief summaries of Greek thought on metaphor and rhetoric. For modern work on metaphor and rhetoric, see Wayne C. Booth, "Metaphor as Rhetoric: The Problem of Evaluation," in *On Metaphor*, ed. Sheldon Sacks (Chicago: University of Chicago Press, 1979), 47–70; Burkholder and Henry, "Criticism of Metaphor." As John L. Austin famously argued, all words *do*. See Austin, *How to Do Things with Words*,

around drug use, for instance, vary dramatically depending on how one characterizes the issue, whether as "a problem of addiction," a "symptom of social dysfunction," or a "war."[45] In these cases, Lakoff and Johnson recognize that "metaphor was not merely a way of viewing reality; it constituted a license for policy change and political and economic action." By changing one's perceptual field, "a metaphor may thus be a guide for *future* action."[46]

Likewise, the rhetorical function of metaphor has long been recognized by biblical scholars.[47] Two representatives will suffice to illustrate the point. Theologian Sally McFague, in one of the early influential works on metaphor, comments, "Good metaphors ... are implicitly revolutionary.... They shock and disturb; they upset conventions and expectations and in so doing have revolutionary potential."[48] Brueggemann similarly notices this prophetic-poetic rhetorical weaponry:

> The poet engages in the kind of guerrilla warfare that is always necessary on behalf of oppressed people. First, the hated one must be ridiculed and made reachable, then she may be disobeyed and seen as a nobody who claims no allegiance and keeps no promises. The big house yields no real life, need not be feared, cannot be trusted, and must not be honored.

2nd rev. ed., ed. James O. Urmson and Marina Sbisà (Cambridge: Harvard University Press, 1975). Recent metaphor scholarship has recognized this, increasingly attending to not only the *content* of metaphors but their *function* in communication as well. See, e.g., Zazie Todd and Graham Low, "A Selective Survey of Research Practice in Published Studies Using Metaphor Analysis," in Cameron and Maslen, *Metaphor Analysis*, 26–41, esp. 26–27; Lynne Cameron, "Metaphors and Discourse Activity," in Cameron and Maslen, *Metaphor Analysis*, 147–60; Steen, "Deliberate Metaphor Theory."

45. Burkholder and Henry, "Criticism of Metaphor," 101. They provide dozens more examples. For more on metaphor and politics, see, e.g., George Lakoff, *The Political Mind: A Cognitive Scientist's Guide to Your Brain and Its Politics* (New York: Penguin, 2009); Terrell Carver and Jernej Pikalo, eds., *Political Language and Metaphor: Interpreting and Changing the World*, RIPT 30 (London: Routledge, 2011); James Underhill, *Creating Worldviews: Metaphor, Ideology and Language* (Edinburgh: Edinburgh University Press, 2013); Andreas Musolff, "Metaphor and Persuasion in Politics," in Semino and Demjén, *Routledge Handbook*, 309–22.

46. Lakoff and Johnson, *Metaphors We Live By*, 156, emphasis added.

47. For an overview of the use of rhetoric and metaphor in biblical studies, see Brad E. Kelle, *Hosea 2: Metaphor and Rhetoric in Historical Perspective*, AcBib 20 (Atlanta: Society of Biblical Literature, 2005).

48. Sallie McFague, *Metaphorical Theology: Models of God in Religious Language* (Philadelphia: Fortress, 1982), 17; see also Moughtin-Mumby, *Sexual and Marital Metaphors*, 1, 269.

1. Conceptualizing Yahweh with Metaphor Clusters

When the Babylonian gods have been mocked, when the Babylonian culture has been ridiculed, and when the dethroned king is re-enthroned, then history is inverted.... *We ought not to underestimate the power of the poet. Inversions may begin in a change of language, a redefined perceptual field, or an altered consciousness.*[49]

Hosea deploys radical metaphors for Yahweh, in part because they have the power to create a novel set of possible futures. Brueggemann summarizes their effect:

What the poetry of Hosea—poetry that characterizes God—does is to load us with a world that is not available to us—and surely did not exist—until this utterance.... The imagined poetic world of Hosea creates alternative space in which Israel can live, if and when it is willing to forego either the certitude of *quid pro quo* or the narcotic of entitlement.[50]

Given that Hosea's metaphors concern a deity, the relationship between metaphors and behavior implies that metaphorical theology shapes ethics.[51] Metaphors create a new vision of reality, in which there are new possibilities for action. When considering Hosea's metaphors, then, it is crucial to account for how the metaphors would affect the behavior and volition of their recipients.

In sum, metaphors have the power to change how people think, feel, and act in the world in a variety of ways. Hosea intends its vision of God and Israel to persuade its audience to change their course of action and so change their future.[52]

Having outlined my understanding of an individual metaphor and its holistic function, we turn now to consider how *multiple* metaphors interact with each other, how and why they group together, and how to identify such clusters.

---

49. Walter Brueggemann, *The Prophetic Imagination*, 2nd ed. (Minneapolis: Fortress, 2001), 73–74, emphasis added. Notice that all three beginnings of inversion are the realm of metaphor.

50. Brueggemann, "Recovering God of Hosea," 7.

51. See Christopher J. H. Wright, *Old Testament Ethics for the People of God* (Downers Grove, IL: IVP Academic, 2013), 23–25, 46.

52. Andrew A. Macintosh, "Hosea and the Wisdom Tradition: Dependence and Independence," in *Wisdom in Ancient Israel: Essays in Honour of J. A. Emerton*, ed. John Day, Robert P. Gordon, and Hugh G. M. Williamson (Cambridge: Cambridge University Press, 1995), 125.

Metaphors Move in Families: Identifying and Analyzing Clusters

"A metaphor," as Ricoeur observes, "never comes alone. One metaphor calls for another and all together they remain alive thanks to their mutual tension and the power of each to evoke the whole network."[53] "Metaphorical meaning," therefore, "feeds on the density of imagery released by the poem."[54] Philosopher Josef Stern notes that "metaphors move in families." That is, the interpretation of a given metaphor "is sensitive to the networks to which its vehicle is presupposed to belong (in that context).... The content of a metaphor in a context is highly dependent on and sensitive to the other elements in the various complexes in which it figures."[55] Adele Berlin recognizes this phenomenon in relation to biblical poetry, claiming that "to understand the Bible's use of imagery is to perceive the *network of relationships* in the biblical text and in the view of the world that it represents. Therein lies the meaning of the biblical message."[56]

Metaphor theorists have noted that metaphors are rarely evenly distributed through a text but instead group together. They have termed this phenomenon "metaphor clustering" and have recently begun to study clusters in real-world spoken and written discourse.[57] Their perspectives offer a helpful set of tools for identifying and analyzing these families in which metaphors move. In order to identify a metaphor cluster, one must first be able to identify a metaphorical expression. This has proven more difficult than many high school English students have assumed. In what

---

53. Paul Ricoeur, "Biblical Hermeneutics," *Semeia* 4 (1975): 94. Kruger claims this is a *conscious* strategy in Hosea. See Paul A. Kruger, "The Divine Net in Hosea 7:12," *ETL* 68 (1992): 132–36, esp. 134.

54. Ricoeur, *Rule of Metaphor*, 214.

55. Stern, *Metaphor in Context*, 316–17. This warrants assigning interpretive significance to the slightest shifts between metaphors (317).

56. Adele Berlin, "On Reading Biblical Poetry: The Role of Metaphor," in *Congress Volume: Cambridge, 1995*, ed. John A. Emerton, VTSup 66 (Leiden: Brill, 1997), 35, italics mine. This is especially the case due to the similarities between the functions of metaphor and parallelism. See also Berlin, *The Dynamics of Biblical Parallelism*, 2nd ed. (Grand Rapids: Eerdmans, 2007), 99–102; Nancy Louise Rogers, "Poetic Revelation: The Relationship between Parallelism and Metaphor in Biblical Hebrew Poetry" (PhD diss., Fordham University, 2010); Robert Alter, *The Art of Biblical Poetry*, rev. ed. (New York: Basic, 2011), 10, 17.

57. For a few earlier studies, see Lynne Cameron and Juurd H. Stelma, "Metaphor Clusters in Discourse," *JAL* 1 (2004): 108.

follows, then, I will first provide criteria to identify metaphorical expressions in the text. Next, I discuss some aspects of evaluating the strength of a figurative expression. Then we turn to criteria for identifying and analyzing metaphor clusters, and finally explore why metaphors cluster in the first place.

Identifying Metaphorical Expressions

In order to identify clusters of metaphors, one must first be able to identify a metaphor. I try to be as precise and objective as possible in the identification of metaphors, while realizing that ambiguity is the poet's playground.

Debate on metaphor identification has raged for centuries. A simple criterion for identifying a metaphor is whether an expression brings together two disjunctive domains of experience.[58] (Consistent with contemporary metaphor theories, this includes similes.)[59] Sometimes it can be quite difficult to identify those domains and determine whether they are sufficiently disjunctive to be metaphorical. Thankfully, metaphor researchers have developed a more precise process.

A group of scholars known as the Pragglejaz group offers such an approach, called metaphor identification procedure. In this process, one

---

58. This is consistent with understanding metaphor as *the mapping itself* of one domain of experience onto another domain of experience (see Lakoff, "Contemporary Theory," 206–7; Kövecses, "Conceptual Metaphor Theory," 14).

59. E.g., see Ricoeur, *Rule of Metaphor*, 248; Soskice, *Metaphor and Religious Language*, 59; Lynne Cameron and Robert Maslen, "Identifying Metaphors in Discourse Data," in Cameron and Maslen, *Metaphor Analysis*, 110–11; Susan E. Haddox, *Metaphor and Masculinity in Hosea*, StBL 141 (New York: Lang, 2011), 47–49; Joseph Lam, "The Metaphorical Patterning of the Sin-Concept in Biblical Hebrew" (PhD diss., University of Chicago, 2012), 59–62; Gerard J. Steen, "Identifying Metaphors in Language," in Semino and Demjén, *Routledge Handbook*, 75.

Hosea prefers similes for Yahweh (ואני מוסר לכלם [5:2], if nominal, may be the exception). Perhaps this was to avoid risking idolatrous misinterpretations (Labuschagne, "Similes in the Book," 76; Kruger, "Prophetic Imagery," 149; Moughtin-Mumby, *Sexual and Marital Metaphors*, 51–53). Verbal metaphors, of course, are exceptions because they cannot be used with comparative כ (e.g., in Hos 4:16, God "feeds them" [ירעם] as a shepherd). In these cases, "it seems that Hosea was not afraid of being misunderstood and had other reasons to employ similes frequently." See Bernhard Oestreich, *Metaphors and Similes for Yahweh in Hosea 14:2–9 (1–8)*, FSRT 1 (Frankfurt: Lang, 1998), 30. This is especially true in appropriation of metaphors frequently associated with other deities (e.g., see discussion on 14:9).

first reads the whole discourse. Second, one identifies the lexical units of the expression in question. Third, one analyzes each lexical unit by (a) determining its meaning in context, then (b) asking whether there is a more basic or concrete sense of that lexical unit. "Basic meanings tend to be more concrete [what they evoke is easier to imagine, see, hear, feel, smell, and taste]; related to bodily action; more precise (as opposed to vague); [or] historically older."[60] If there is a more concrete contemporary meaning, the analyst then (c) determines whether "the contextual meaning contrasts with the basic meaning but can be understood in comparison with it."[61] Fourth and finally, if there is a contrast and comparison with a more basic meaning, the analyst marks the expression as metaphorical.

I will use this operationalized definition to identify metaphorical expressions in this study. That is, metaphorical words or phrases "have one meaning in the context and another, different, meaning which is more basic in some way, usually more physical or more concrete than the contextual meaning."[62] This operational definition of metaphor will capture "words and phrases that are *potentially* metaphorical."[63] For the purposes of this study, and consistent with the metaphor identification procedure

---

60. Peter Crisp et al., "MIP: A Method for Identifying Metaphorically Used Words in Discourse," *MS* 22 (2007): 3. The first (longer) bracket is original, the second ("[or]") is mine. See also Cameron and Maslen, "Identifying Metaphors in Discourse Data"; Gerard J. Steen et al., "Pragglejaz in Practice: Finding Metaphorically Used Words in Natural Discourse," in *Researching and Applying Metaphor in the Real World*, ed. Graham Low et al., HCP 26 (Amsterdam: Benjamins, 2010), 165–84; Steen, "Identifying Metaphors in Language"; Gerard J. Steen et al., *A Method for Linguistic Metaphor Identification: From MIP to MIPVU*, CELCR 14 (Amsterdam: Benjamins, 2010). When analyzing according to usage, as here, it is necessary that the more basic meaning be still available in contemporary usage (Steen et al., *Method for Linguistic Metaphor Identification*, 75). אף, e.g., displays within contemporary Biblical Hebrew both meanings of "nose" (more basic) and "anger"; therefore "anger" can be regarded as a metaphorical expression. The use of this approach in Biblical Hebrew is complicated by the fact that these modern tools for metaphor identification have been primarily worked out with English examples, using appropriate dictionaries (Steen, "Identifying Metaphors in Language," 85), yet Biblical Hebrew lexicography is considerably more ambiguous. Very little work has been done in applying these tools to languages beyond English, and to my knowledge they have never been used in Biblical Hebrew or any other ancient Near Eastern language.

61. Crisp et al., "MIP," 3.
62. Cameron and Maslen, "Identifying Metaphors in Discourse Data," 102.
63. Cameron and Maslen, "Identifying Metaphors in Discourse Data," 102.

approach, it is immaterial whether the creator or audience would have recognized expressions as metaphorical.[64] The key question for an expression's inclusion in this study is, Is this a metaphor that contributes to the characterization of Yahweh in Hos 4–14?[65]

While I will use this method of metaphor identification in the following investigation, it is appropriate to acknowledge its limitations. For one, it is heavily dependent on individual lexical units, which sounds similar to early metaphor theories that saw the word as the locus of metaphor. The solution to this is to "locate the notion of incongruity and indirectness not in word use but at the level of concepts and referents."[66] Sometimes, therefore, a metaphorical expression may be identified using the simpler criterion mentioned above, of an expression that brings together two disjunctive domains of experience.

Another limitation of the metaphor identification procedure approach is that texts require readers, and metaphorical expressions require readerly construal. The metaphoricity or literalness of a given phrase may be ambiguous, as in the phrases "no man is an island" or "he lives in a glass house."[67] This mitigates the reliability of the metaphor identification procedure criteria in isolation. Metaphorical construal takes a certain level of native-speaker intuition and a knowledge of the context of the utterance. This is significantly more difficult in the case of modern interpreters wrestling with metaphors of an ancient society in an ancient language, for which there are no native speakers to consult. While every effort will be made to responsibly handle the expressions in Hosea, interpretive certainty is unobtainable.

Additionally, the metaphor identification procedure process operates on the assumption of binary categories: either an expression is metaphorical, or it is not. The reality of metaphor deployment is more complex than this suggests. So while metaphor identification procedure is a helpful operation that I adopt, additional perspectives are necessary to account for the

---

64. Steen et al., "Pragglejaz in Practice," 175.

65. This can include metaphors for Israel that imply something about Yahweh (see more below). See also Brigitte Seifert, *Metaphorisches Reden von Gott im Hoseabuch*, FRLANT 166 (Göttingen: Vandenhoeck & Ruprecht, 1996), 252–54. Some potential metaphors for Yahweh are excluded as too thin or weak (see n. 71, below).

66. Steen, "Identifying Metaphors in Language," 83; see also Cameron and Maslen, "Identifying Metaphors in Discourse Data," 105–8; Steen et al., "Pragglejaz in Practice."

67. See the discussion and examples in Joseph Lam, "Metaphor in the Ugaritic Literary Texts," *JNES* 78 (2019): 41–44.

spectrum of metaphoricity that one finds in Hosea. Once expressions have been identified as metaphorical, their relative strength must be evaluated.

Evaluating Metaphoric Strength and Contribution

Not all metaphors are created equal; certain metaphors are more arresting than others. Toward the beginning of the modern philosophical interest in metaphor, Max Black recognized this fact, creating categories of strong and weak metaphors.[68] Strong metaphors are those that are both emphatic and resonant. Emphatic metaphors are those in which only *this* source domain will do. They are not "'expendable,' 'optional,' 'decorative,' [or] 'ornamental'" but are "intended to be dwelt upon for the sake of their unstated implications."[69] Resonance is the degree to which those implications can be elaborated, unfolded, extended. Resonant metaphors are "relatively rich in background implications" and "support a high degree of implicative elaboration."[70] More recently, Paul Avis notes, "'Literal' and 'metaphorical' are merely limit concepts on a sliding scale of imaginative investment."[71] Consequently, certain metaphors are likely to contribute more substantially to Hosea's characterization of Yahweh. I have already noted that the husband metaphor has been a myopic focus of scholarship, yet who remembers that Yahweh is also pictured as a fowler (7:12)?

---

68. Max Black, "More about Metaphor," in Ortony, *Metaphor and Thought*, 19–41.

69. Black, "More about Metaphor," 26. No doubt some will take issue with Black's implication that any metaphor can be merely "ornamental." Despite the assumptions of some, Black—and Richards before him—recognized the ubiquity of metaphor in everyday language. There seems to me to be some resemblance between Black's account here and that of deliberate metaphor theory (see Steen, "Deliberate Metaphor Theory").

70. Black, "More about Metaphor," 26.

71. Paul Avis, *God and the Creative Imagination: Metaphor, Symbol and Myth in Religion and Theology* (London: Routledge, 1999), 102. See also David Aaron's suggestion of a spectrum of metaphoricity in *Biblical Ambiguities: Metaphor, Semantics and Divine Imagery*, BRLAJ 4 (Leiden: Brill, 2001), esp. 30. For reflections on the theological import of such a spectrum for god-talk, see Soskice, *Metaphor and Religious Language*, 118–41. For a survey of how three biblical theologians deal with the "yes" and "no" of metaphors for God, see Matthew R. Schlimm, "Different Perspectives on Divine Pathos: An Examination of Hermeneutics in Biblical Theology," *CBQ* 69 (2007): 678–90. Schlimm argues that Heschel emphasizes discontinuity between God and humanity, Fretheim tries to find a middle ground, and Brueggemann emphasizes the continuity of the metaphors.

1. Conceptualizing Yahweh with Metaphor Clusters

My categorization of metaphors must therefore account for the relative strength of an expression's depiction of Yahweh.

For the sake of simplicity, a three-point scale will be used. A score of 1 means the expression is a weak metaphor. It is common, simple, and not resonant, such as God being a fowler (7:12).[72] A score of 2 refers to an expression that may be a common metaphor with a strong claim about God (e.g., "God is king") or an expression that is uncommon but also does not make a strong claim about Yahweh. This frequently includes metaphors for Israel that only imply things of God (e.g., Hos 4:16a: "Israel is stubborn, like a stubborn calf"). A score of 3 means the metaphor is both more metaphorical than most other expressions and is strong according to Black's definition (i.e., it is emphatic and resonant). Hosea 5:12, in which God is a moth (עָשׁ), is an example of this: it is a unique metaphor for God in the Hebrew Bible, and it is highly suggestive.

A more complex example is the lion metaphors. A stock metaphor for kings and deities (by default scored as 1) is given new life by being extended into a miniature metaphorical narrative with terrifying detail (5:14–15), which is subsequently intensified (13:7–8) and inverted (11:10). These extended uses of the stock metaphor make a significant contribution to Hosea's presentation of Yahweh and thus warrant a higher rating—2 or 3 depending on contextual usage.

Because metaphors for *Israel* that imply something about Yahweh are included in this study on metaphors for *God*, the directness of each metaphor is also identified in part 1. *Direct* means it is a metaphor for Yahweh;

---

72. Certain metaphorical expressions are not included because their contribution to a metaphorical portrayal of Yahweh is too thin for a project of this scope. E.g., there are interesting patterns conceptualizing relationship in terms of proximity or distance. In Hos 5:6, Israel cannot find Yahweh because he has *withdrawn* from them (וְלֹא יִמְצָאוּ חָלַץ מֵהֶם). Conversely, Israel is invited to *return* to Yahweh (שׁוּבָה [12:7]; וְאַתָּה בֵּאלֹהֶיךָ תָשׁוּב) יִשְׂרָאֵל עַד יְהוָה אֱלֹהֶיךָ [14:2]; passim), but their deeds prevent them from traversing the path back to Yahweh (לֹא יִתְּנוּ מַעַלְלֵיהֶם לָשׁוּב אֶל אֱלֹהֵיהֶם [5:4]). This relational-distance conception may reflect a conception of sin as waywardness. Sin is also conceptualized as debt (4:9; see Lam, *Patterns of Sin*). For more on the ancient Near Eastern "seeking and (not) finding" myths and their inversions in Hosea, see Eidevall, *Grapes in the Desert*, 248–52; for an alternate interpretation of the immanence and transcendence of Yahweh in Hosea, see Seifert, *Metaphorisches Reden*, 256–59. On the use of Hosea's Assyria-Egypt motif to denote distance from Yahweh, see Yisca Zimran, "The Prevalence and Purpose of the 'Assyria-Egypt' Motif in the Book of Hosea," *JSOT* 46 (2021): 3–23.

indirect means it is a metaphor for something else that implies something about Yahweh.

A relative weightiness can therefore be determined for the contributions of metaphorical expressions explored in chapters 2–4. In chapter 8, the relative weight of whole source domains can be established. Having identified individual metaphorical expressions, one is then in a position to identify metaphor clusters.

Identifying and Analyzing Clusters

I adopt and modify for Hosea Lynne Cameron and Juurd Stelma's method for identifying clusters.[73] Each instance of a metaphorical expression is counted individually, even if multiple consecutive expressions reflect the same metaphorical domain.[74] For example, the extended discourse around sexual promiscuity in Hos 4:10–15 includes four metaphorical *expressions*, even though they share a single metaphorical *domain*. The second step is to graph the occurrence of metaphorical expressions across the span of Hos 4–14. Similar to prior studies surveyed by Cameron and Stelma, a line graph maps the total number of metaphorical expressions (y axis) against the total cumulative number of verses in the text (x axis). More illuminating for the data set in Hosea is a bar graph mapping the total number of metaphorical expressions within three verses. This makes clusters easily identifiable (see appendix). A cluster is defined for this study as having an *average* of at least three metaphors within three continuous verses, equivalent to a score of 1 on the bar graph.[75] The maximum metaphoric density in the book reaches a score of 3, at Hos 6:2.

---

73. For a survey of methods of identifying clusters and problems in previous studies, see Cameron and Stelma, "Metaphor Clusters in Discourse," 111–18.

74. There are a few cases (e.g., Hos 14:6–8) in which a set of metaphors for Israel implies a uniform metaphor for God by association (e.g., a farmer). These were counted as a single metaphor for God.

75. This corresponds roughly to the threshold Cameron and Stelma used, who count by intonation unit ("Metaphor Clusters in Discourse," 119), though Cameron and Maslen note that "written texts can also be prepared for metaphor identification by being segmented by sentence or clause, if that seems appropriate or if software constraints demand it" ("Identifying Metaphors in Discourse Data," 101). Verses were chosen as a heuristic equivalent to intonation units. Maslen writes that clusters can be simply identified by underlining metaphorical expressions and noting where they are more common. "A more quantitative approach," however, "is setting a density threshold

1. Conceptualizing Yahweh with Metaphor Clusters

Admittedly, such an approach requires "stat[ing] how one is managing to count what is essentially uncountable."[76] Every effort has been made to objectively identify clusters, but—given the nature of Hosea as a literary text—poetic and structural features at times impressed a hermeneutical force on cluster delineation and metaphorical analysis.

In light of these ambiguities and subjective decisions in metaphor analysis, Graham Low and Zazie Todd's five guidelines are instructive. Metaphor analysis involves "recognizing that metaphoricity can be complex, indeterminate and unstable; admitting the problems and treating one's solutions as compromises; knowing what the compromises entail; telling the reader how/why one arrived at conclusions; and admitting the limitations of one's conclusions."[77] While the definition of or criteria for clusters could be reformulated, resulting in slightly different identifications of clusters in Hosea, I do not think this would significantly change the interpretations presented here.

As noted above, it is the *interactions* between the metaphors—their relationships, contrasts and similarities, ingenuity and opaqueness, mutual clarifying and obscuring functions—that make a passage meaningful. Once clusters are identified, therefore, the interactions between the individual metaphors within each cluster must be analyzed, a crucial step not always taken in biblical studies.[78] Sometimes these networks clarify the meaning of their metaphors through overlapping entailments, including minor semantic variation.[79] Other times, the proximity of jarringly discor-

---

"markedly greater than the transcript average," as I have sought to do here. See Robert Maslen, "Working with Large Amounts of Metaphor Data," in Cameron and Maslen, *Metaphor Analysis*, 191.

76. Graham Low and Zazie Todd, "Good Practice in Metaphor Analysis," in Cameron and Maslen, *Metaphor Analysis*, 225.

77. Low and Todd, "Good Practice," 218.

78. Examples of notable exceptions are Alison Ruth Gray, *Psalm 18 in Words and Pictures: A Reading through Metaphor*, BibInt 127 (Leiden: Brill, 2014); Antje Labahn and Danilo Verde, eds., *Networks of Metaphors in the Hebrew Bible*, BETL 309 (Leuven: Peeters, 2020). The latter volume became available too late to be well integrated into the current monograph.

79. Note, e.g., the overlapping entailments of the four metaphors in Hos 13:3, or the five in 13:7–8. On overlapping entailments, see Lakoff and Johnson, *Metaphors We Live By*, 89–105; Kövecses, *Metaphor: A Practical Introduction*, 121–33; Kövecses, "Conceptual Metaphor Theory," 15. For a lexical-semantic account of metaphor clusters and meaning, see Gray, *Psalm 18 in Words and Pictures*, 28–33. On discourse

dant metaphors can challenge readers. Additionally, the metaphors may reside on differing conceptual planes (be they temporal, causal, speaker, or belief-related conceptual planes).[80]

Extensive guidelines for the interpretive process were produced and followed.[81] But as Hans-Georg Gadamer persuasively argued, the rigorous application of a "scientific" method cannot guarantee "accurate" interpretation of literature.[82] The test of a methodology such as that presented here is whether it illuminates the text. Sometimes one perspective is especially beneficial in elucidating the metaphoric interactions of a passage, and for other clusters a different perspective is more helpful.[83] Melissa Gregg and Gregory Seigworth rightly ask, "Isn't theory—any theory with or without a capital T—supposed to work this way? Operating with a certain modest methodological vitality rather than impressing itself upon a wiggling world like a snap-on grid of shape-setting interpretability?"[84]

---

coherence among diverse metaphors, see George Lakoff and Mark Turner, *More than Cool Reason: A Field Guide to Poetic Metaphor* (Chicago: University of Chicago Press, 1989), 86–89, 140–59; Lakoff and Johnson, *Metaphors We Live By*, 9–13, 87–105; Kövecses, *Metaphor*, 285–89. For analyses of coherence among mixed metaphors by a variety of means, see, e.g., Michael Kimmel, "Why We Mix Metaphors (and Mix Them Well): Discourse Coherence, Conceptual Metaphor, and Beyond," *JP* 42 (2010): 97–115; Andrea L. Weiss, "From 'Mixed Metaphors' to 'Adjacent Analogies': An Analysis of the Poetry of Hosea," in *Built by Wisdom, Established by Understanding: Essays on Biblical and Near Eastern Literature in Honor of Adele Berlin* (Bethesda: University Press of Maryland, 2013), 127; Lance R. Hawley, *Metaphor Competition in the Book of Job*, JAJSup 26 (Göttingen: Vandenhoeck & Ruprecht, 2018), 28–42, 62–66.

80. Kimmel, "Why We Mix Metaphors."

81. I have not included those guidelines in this volume, but for a helpful visual model similar to my own, see Gray, *Psalm 18 in Words and Pictures*, 33.

82. Hans-Georg Gadamer, *Truth and Method*, 2nd rev. ed., trans. Joel Weinsheimer and Donald G. Marshall (London: Continuum, 2004), 1–161; see also Jean Grondin, *Introduction to Philosophical Hermeneutics*, trans. Joel Weinsheimer (New Haven: Yale University Press, 1997), 108.

83. This is true of interpretive steps (e.g., comparing the metaphorical imagery to ancient iconography) and of metaphor theories (e.g., conceptual metaphor theory, poetic perspectives, rhetorical criticism).

84. Melissa Gregg and Gregory J. Seigworth, "An Inventory of Shimmers," in *The Affect Theory Reader*, ed. Melissa Gregg and Gregory J. Seigworth (Durham, NC: Duke University Press, 2010), 4.

Why Metaphors Cluster

Having defined metaphor, holistically explored its functions, and provided criteria to identify and analyze metaphors and clusters, let us finally ask the question: *Why* do metaphors coalesce in certain places and not others?

Cameron rightly notes, "Using metaphor as a research tool involves understanding what people *do* with metaphors, as well as which metaphors they use."[85] Lakoff and Johnson similarly claim that "the most important thing to bear in mind" when analyzing the coherence of multiple metaphors "is the role of purpose."[86] While scholars have noted *that* metaphors move in families, they have only recently started to explore *why* metaphors group together at certain places in a discourse. Several recent studies on metaphor clusters share three common conclusions relevant to this study: metaphor clusters occur at rhetorically significant locations in a discourse, they occur in order to aid listeners' comprehension of difficult topics, and they are often inextricably and intricately connected to other metaphors in the discourse.

According to Daniel Corts and Kristina Meyers, metaphor clusters are more likely than other figurative language to be (1) coherent, (2) novel, and (3) topically central.[87] Clusters are *produced*, though, due only to their tendency to be coherent and topically central, not due to their novelty.[88] Other studies confirm that topical centrality is a crucial feature of clusters. Cameron and Stelma conclude, "Metaphor clusters occur when some *intensive interactional work linked to the overall purpose of the discourse is being carried out*."[89] Michael Kimmel likewise observes that metaphor

---

85. Cameron, "Metaphors and Discourse Activity," 160, emphasis added.

86. Lakoff and Johnson, *Metaphors We Live By*, 97.

87. Daniel P. Corts and Kristina Meyers, "Conceptual Clusters in Figurative Language Production," *JPR* 31 (2002): 393. Cameron and Stelma confirm in their own research that clusters tend to be "novel" and "topically central" ("Metaphor Clusters in Discourse," 113, 134).

88. Corts and Meyers, "Conceptual Clusters," 406. By "coherent," they mean that the metaphors derive from the same conceptual metaphor, but they grant that not all clusters demonstrate this feature (393). Cameron and Stelma found that clusters "very seldom" arose from a shared conceptual metaphor ("Metaphor Clusters in Discourse," 132; see also 114). Lakoff and Johnson note that metaphors can be "coherent" even when not deriving from the same conceptual metaphor (*Metaphors We Live By*, 95; see also Kimmel, "Why We Mix Metaphors"), as is the norm in Hosea.

89. "Metaphor Clusters in Discourse," 134, emphasis added. See also Lynne Cam-

clusters occur "where the action is."[90] In other words, clusters tend to occur in places central to the rhetorical purpose of the discourse. Consequently, rhetorical strategy or communicative purpose must be a key consideration for metaphor analysis.

The *reason* this happens is the second point relevant to our study. Metaphors are an effective tool to help listeners understand another point of view, because they by nature help listeners to see things in a fresh way. The accumulation of multiple novel metaphors helps to crystallize the new point of view—in a sense by triangulating onto the intended aspects, thereby ruling out unintended ones.[91] This is especially important in the case of overcoming alterity, in presenting one's view to another who does not share it,[92] as Hosea does. Hence, the more abstract the topic, the more frequently clusters occur.[93] Kimmel notes that clusters are frequently "used to shed light on complex and unfamiliar subject matters."[94] Hosea's many metaphors, sometimes in tension with one another, are clustered in order to describe what is essentially indescribable.[95]

Third, Kimmel also finds that clusters are an "attention-grabbing and thus a relevance-producing device." This makes them highly efficient

---

eron, "Confrontation or Complementarity? Metaphor in Language Use and Cognitive Metaphor Theory," *ARCL* 5 (2007): 107–35; Lynne Cameron, "Metaphor and Talk," in Gibbs, *Cambridge Handbook of Metaphor*, 197–211.

90. Kimmel, "Why We Mix Metaphors," 98.

91. This is done through the accumulation of overlapping entailments between metaphors, as mentioned in n. 78, above.

92. Cameron and Stelma, "Metaphor Clusters in Discourse," 133–34.

93. Cameron and Stelma, "Metaphor Clusters in Discourse," 113; Maslen, "Working with Large Amounts," 191.

94. Kimmel, "Why We Mix Metaphors," 98.

95. From the perspective of metaphor studies, see Lakoff and Johnson, *Metaphors We Live By*, 89, 95, 105. From the perspective of ancient Near Eastern god-talk, see Michael B. Hundley, "Here a God, There a God: An Examination of the Divine in Ancient Mesopotamia," *AoF* 40 (2013): 68–107; see also ch. 8 of this volume. From the perspective of biblical scholars, see Walter Brueggemann, "Preaching a Sub-version," *ThTo* 55 (1998): 199; Brent A. Strawn, *What Is Stronger Than a Lion? Leonine Image and Metaphor in the Hebrew Bible and the Ancient Near East*, OBO 212 (Göttingen: Vandenhoeck & Ruprecht, 2005), 272; Andrea L. Weiss, "Motives behind Biblical Mixed Metaphors," in *Making a Difference: Essays on the Bible and Judaism in Honor of Tamara Cohn Eskenazi*, ed. David J. A. Clines, Kent Harold Richards, and Jacob L. Wright, HBM 49 (Sheffield: Sheffield Phoenix, 2012), 326; Weiss, "From 'Mixed Metaphors,'" 127.

and effective for discourse. They "connect and dynamize discourse." That is, they "extend, reject, limit or elaborate" previously used metaphors—an extension of the idea that metaphors never move alone but travel in families.[96] This facet of metaphor clustering is especially important when considering Hosea's dynamic reusage of metaphor domains, hence the intercluster analyses of part 2.

It is noteworthy that these studies, though analyzing different kinds of discourses, arrive at similar conclusions. They agree that metaphor clusters occur at rhetorically significant parts of a discourse, aid in describing complex or abstract topics, and are integrally connected to other metaphors throughout the discourse. Robert Maslen summarizes Cameron and Stelma's findings—that metaphors "tend to be produced more frequently where speakers are dealing with themes which are difficult, either conceptually or in terms of the dynamics between speakers"—then infers: "Metaphor clusters can therefore point to moments in a discourse which are worth investigating more closely."[97] I think this is certainly the case with Hosea. Clusters are a crucial tool in considering Hosea's rhetorical strategies to conceptualize Yahweh in a new way for Hosea's audience. More closely investigating these specific instances of the deity's figuration will open new windows into the communicative purposes and functions of the book as a whole.

Conclusion

This book is about exploring the complex and contested presentation of God found in the metaphors of the final form of Hos 4–14. In this chapter I have introduced the shape of my argument and the tools, perspectives, and criteria used therein. I noticed early on that Hosea's metaphors are not evenly distributed but tend to cluster together in certain places. As shown above, clusters tend to be crucial to the communicative purpose of the discourse, aid in comprehension of difficult or abstract topics and in overcoming alterity, and connect and dynamize a wider network of metaphors throughout the discourse. Clusters therefore warrant closer examination for opening windows into important aspects of the discourse as a whole.

---

96. Kimmel, "Why We Mix Metaphors," 98.
97. Maslen, "Working with Large Amounts," 191.

Adopting a holistic understanding of metaphor that attends to cognitive, affective, and volitional implications as described above, I attempt in part 1 to explore 103 metaphors identified among fifteen clusters in Hos 4–14 in as far as they contribute to a portrait of Yahweh. In part 2, I account for intercluster patterns, focusing especially on emotive, literary, and rhetorical patterns. Part 3 synthesizes these findings in two ways: an aspective constellation of Yahweh and a fivefold character portrait of Yahweh. Among other things, I conclude that Yahweh's fidelity to Israel undergirds the book's metaphoric presentation of God in almost every respect and that such commitment will transcend even Israel's inevitable death.

In a society facing increasingly overt antagonism and vitriol, how can metaphors be used to overcome alterity? How can new images for God be used, particularly among spiritual and religious communities, to increase understanding, to change worldviews, to reshape priorities and values, to confront injustices, to improve our communities? The ancient text of Hosea provides a number of strategies for doing just that. Perhaps some could be revived for a new day.

PART 1

Interactions within the Fifteen Metaphor Clusters of Hosea 4–14

Metaphorical language, especially in Hosea, is often fractured, baffling, and claims a status verging on madness. In Hosea, it seeks mimetically both to depict social and political entropy, and to interpret it, thus reconstructing and repairing its world.
—Francis Landy, "In the Wilderness of Speech"

Part 1 applies the theoretical and practical tools outlined in chapter 1 to analyze how fifteen metaphor clusters in Hos 4–14 contribute to the portrayal of Yahweh. Part 2 will trace metaphor development across the book. In other words, part 1 examines the *intra*cluster metaphoric interactions, while part 2 examines *inter*cluster interactions.

The book of Hosea is organized into three cycles (1:2–3:5, 4:1–11:11, 12:1–14:9), and each cycle progresses through three stages, from initial accusation of Israel's covenant crimes (4:1–8:14, 12:1–15), to sentencing and consequences appropriate to their conviction (9:1–11:7, 13:1–14:1), to the possibility of future redemption (11:8–11, 14:2–9).[1] The analyses of metaphor clusters have therefore been organized into three chapters for the sake of conceptual coherence, each corresponding to a stage of Hosea's metaphorical lawsuit against Israel: metaphors of accusation, sentencing, and redemption.[2]

---

1. With only slight modification, I follow Tully's account of the structure of the book (*Hosea*, 2–3).

2. This means that only cluster 12 is not in the order it appears in Hosea—it is discussed after cluster 14. An alternative threefold rubric is Laldinsuah's "responsibility, chastisement, and restoration." See Ronald Laldinsuah, *Responsibility, Chastisement, and Restoration: Relational Justice in the Book of Hosea* (Carlisle: Langham Monographs, 2015). The two ריב metaphors (4:1, 12:3) are not analyzed because they are not

For most clusters analyzed below, metaphors are first examined individually, then the interactions among metaphors within a cluster are analyzed. In some clusters (e.g., clusters 3, 4, and 5, which comprise a supercluster, and 6, 11, and 13), individual metaphor analyses are skipped. This was done because the metaphoric interactions are too dense to be separated, because the metaphors are minor repetitions of previous metaphors, or due to space restrictions.

---

part of a cluster, but they are very significant for understanding the structure of the book and its metaphorical presentation of Yahweh. On the three cycles of Hosea, see, among many, Wolff, *Hosea*, xxix–xxxi; Jörg Jeremias, *Der Prophet Hosea*, ATD 24/1 (Göttingen: Vandenhoeck & Ruprecht, 1983), 18–20; Gerald Paul Morris, *Prophecy, Poetry and Hosea*, JSOTSup 219 (Sheffield: Sheffield Academic, 1996), 115–19; Ben Zvi, *Hosea*, 4; Tully, *Hosea*, 2–3; Irvine, "Hosea," 399–402 (includes survey and critiques). On metaphors at the seams of these three cycles, see Gary W. Light, "Theory-Constitutive Metaphor and Its Development in the Book of Hosea" (PhD diss., Southern Baptist Theological Seminary, 1991), 200; Thomas Worth Walker, "The Metaphor of Healing and the Theology of the Book of Hosea" (PhD diss., Princeton Theological Seminary, 1997), 173, 189–90. On "verbal interweaving" creating the patterns of these cycles, see Morris, *Prophecy, Poetry and Hosea*, 110–31. Some divide the book in two: Hos 1–3 and Hos 4–14. See, e.g., Mays, *Hosea*, 15–17, though chs. 4–11 and 12–14 are distinct subsections; Francis I. Andersen and David Noel Freedman, *Hosea: A New Translation*, AB 24 (Garden City, NY: Doubleday, 1980), 57; Eidevall, *Grapes in the Desert*; Gruber, *Hosea*, 7–12. Part of the reason there is no consensus on the book's structure is its tendency toward fragmentation (see Grossberg) and a heavily aspectival presentation (see ch. 8 of this study). See Daniel Grossberg, *Centripetal and Centrifugal Structures in Biblical Poetry*, SBLMS 39 (Atlanta: Scholars Press, 1989). Hence, the units identified above, especially their subunits, should be understood as centered sets rather than bounded sets. That is, the stages of each cycle (that is, accusation, sentencing, redemption) are identified in terms of their *relative* emphasis compared to others, but their boundaries are not sharp and their contents do not follow a consistent pattern. Additionally, the balance between the three categories changes among the two cycles under consideration here. Cycle 2 (4:1–11:11) emphasizes accusation with a large portion of sentencing, while the redemption category is given only four verses out of eight chapters. Yet cycle 3 (12:1–14:9) has almost an entire chapter (14:2–9)— out of only three chapters—that builds to a crescendo of Israel's restoration.

2
Metaphors of Accusation

The first stage of Hosea's cyclical lawsuit (4:1, 12:3; see 2:4) is that of accusation or indictment. The metaphors in this category tend to emphasize specific transgressions within Israel's general failure to observe the covenant (see 4:1–2, 6:7, 8:1).

Cluster 1: Hosea 4:10–16

4:10c–11a   Indirect, 3
כי את יהוה עזבו לשמר זנות
because they abandoned Yahweh to commit to whoring[1]

4:12c   Indirect, 3
כי רוח זנונים התעה
because a spirit of whoredom led [them] astray

4:12d   Indirect, 3
ויזנו מתחת אלהיהם
and they whored away from their God[2]

4:15a[3]   Indirect, 3
אם זנה אתה ישראל

---

1. On the inclusion of זנות from 4:11, see LXX; Syr.; Tully, *Hosea*, 94; Eidevall, *Grapes in the Desert*, 60.

2. DeGrado renders 4:12c–d well: "*For a spirit of horniness leads them astray, and they cheat on their god.*" See Jessie DeGrado, "The Qdesha in Hosea 4:14: Putting the (Myth of the) Sacred Prostitute to Bed," *VT* 68 (2018): 10, emphasis original.

3. Many scholars think that the verses that mention Judah are later glosses (Macintosh lists 1:7; 3:5; 4:5, 15; 5:5; 6:11; 9:4; 10:11; 11:10; 12:1, 3). Since this study

If/Though you, Israel, are a whore …⁴

4:16a   Indirect, 2
כי כפרה סררה סרר ישראל
For Israel is stubborn, like a stubborn calf.

4:16b   Direct, 3
עתה ירעם יהוה ככבש במרחב
[Will/Can/Should] Yahweh now pasture them like a lamb in the open space?⁵

This unit is dominated by language of sexual promiscuity and cultic activity, with only two metaphors outside that domain, both in 4:16, related to animal husbandry.

The Extended Frame of Reference of Sexual Promiscuity (4:10–15)

The metaphors in this pericope constitute an extended frame of references that interacts meaningfully with a mostly literal broader unit (vv. 10–19) via the shared theme of sexual promiscuity.⁶ The question of which expres-

---

is on the final form, comment is made only here on this first alleged gloss, not for subsequent instances. See Macintosh, *Critical and Exegetical Commentary*, lxxi–lxxii; Gruber, *Hosea*, 27–31.

4. LXX deals with the awkward syntax by reading אם זנה with the end of 4:14, thus "and the people who had understanding were embracing a prostitute" (καὶ ὁ λαὸς ὁ συνίων συνεπλέκετο μετὰ πόρνης). On the scribal misunderstanding and grammatical issues of LXX, see W. Edward Glenny, *Hosea: A Commentary Based on Hosea in Codex Vaticanus*, SeptCS (Leiden: Brill, 2013), 98.

5. It is common to read the verb as modal (*BHRG* §19.3.5) and the phrase as a rhetorical question assuming a negative answer (most English versions). See Mays, *Hosea*, 76; Wolff, *Hosea*, 72, 91; Jeremias, *Prophet Hosea*, 64, 72; Eidevall, *Grapes in the Desert*, 64; Macintosh, *Critical and Exegetical Commentary*, 165–67; Marvin A. Sweeney, *The Twelve Prophets*, BerOl (Collegeville, MN: Liturgical Press, 2000), 1:51; J. Andrew Dearman, *The Book of Hosea*, NICOT (Grand Rapids: Eerdmans, 2010), 120. Alternatively, it could be understood as an imminent future (LXX; Vulg.; Syr.; NKJV, NJPS).

6. On extended frames of reference, see Harshav, *Explorations in Poetics*, 32–75. Christina Bucher concludes that the verb זנה, when referring figuratively to apostasy, should be rendered with some form of "promiscuous." See Bucher, "The Origin and Meaning of ZNH Terminology in the Book of Hosea" (PhD diss., Claremont Graduate School, 1988), 162. For discussions of the metaphorics of the word in contexts of metaphorical adultery,

2. Metaphors of Accusation

sions are metaphorical is linked to the questions of the existence of cultic prostitution as an ancient institution and of the activities referred to in this passage (esp. 4:13–14). There are four basic proposals for explaining the language of sexual promiscuity in the unit.

The classic explanation draws heavily on the supposed existence of the ancient practice of cultic prostitution.[7] It is alleged that prostitution was practiced as part of cultic activity to procure favorable results from fertility deities.[8] Some proponents claim that this passage reflects literal cultic prostitution (e.g., 4:13–14) as well as Hosea's metaphorical extension of it to present Israel's spiritual whoring from Yahweh (e.g., 4:10c–11b).[9] This interpretation may be rejected out of hand in light of the total lack of hard evidence and the broad consensus that no such practice ever existed in the ancient Near East.[10]

---

see Phyllis A. Bird, "'To Play the Harlot': An Inquiry into an Old Testament Metaphor," in *Gender and Difference in Ancient Israel*, ed. Peggy Day (Minneapolis: Fortress, 1989), 75–94; Julie Galambush, *Jerusalem in the Book of Ezekiel: The City as Yahweh's Wife*, SBLDS 130 (Atlanta: Scholars Press, 1992), 27–31; Peggy Day, "The Bitch Had It Coming to Her: Rhetoric and Interpretation in Ezekiel 16," *BibInt* 8 (2000): 236 n. 12. For overview treatments of this metaphor domain in Hosea (usually focusing on chs. 1–3), see Marie-Theres Wacker, "Hosea," in *Feminist Biblical Interpretation: A Compendium of Critical Commentary on the Books of the Bible and Related Literature*, ed. Luise Schottroff and Marie-Theres Wacker, trans. Martin Rumscheidt (Grand Rapids: Eerdmans, 2012), 371–85.

7. This view reigned among interpreters of the previous 150 years (see DeGrado, "Qdesha in Hosea 4:14," 8 n. 1). Among recent commentators, see Wolff, *Hosea*, esp. 85–88; Andersen and Freedman, *Hosea*, 370; Jeremias, *Prophet Hosea*, 70–71; Seifert, *Metaphorisches Reden*, 138–42, though she says 4:12c–d is metaphorical; Macintosh, *Critical and Exegetical Commentary*, 157–58; Dearman, *Book of Hosea*, 166.

8. A subset of this view posits a fertility goddess being part of the original formulation of this passage, as evidenced by the residual feminine suffixes of 4:17–19. E.g., Grace I. Emmerson, "Fertility Goddess in Hosea 4:17–19," *VT* 24 (1974): 492–97; Christian Frevel, *Aschera und der Ausschließlichkeitsanspruch YHWHs*, BBB 94.1 (Weinheim: Beltz Athenäum Verlag, 1995), 1:298–317; Frédéric Gangloff and Jean-Claude Haelewyck, "Osée 4,17–19: Un marzeah en l'honneur de la déesee 'Anat?," *ETL* 71 (1995): 370–82; Marie-Theres Wacker, "Traces of the Goddess in the Book of Hosea," in *A Feminist Companion to the Latter Prophets*, ed. Athalya Brenner, FCB 8 (Sheffield: Sheffield Academic, 1995), 221–23.

9. Wolff, *Hosea*, 82–88. Childs distinguishes these interpretations diachronically: "harlotry" was originally literal (referring to cultic prostitution), but in the later Judean context that lacked cultic prostitution, it was construed metaphorically. See Brevard S. Childs, *Introduction to the Old Testament as Scripture* (Philadelphia: Fortress, 1979), 379.

10. Select treatments of this widely held view include Julia Assante, *Prostitutes*

The remaining three views deny the existence of cultic prostitution in the ancient world. First, Mayer Gruber claims that all of 4:10–19 should be read literally as referring to *noncultic* sexual promiscuity. He claims that the passage indicts male religious pilgrims for engaging in noncultic, adulterous prostitution, facilitated by inebriation, while away from their families and on their pilgrimage to religious activity and festivals.[11] A second alternative view is to read the whole passage metaphorically, reflecting the conceptual metaphor "covenant is a marriage,"[12] referring to apostasy. Karin Adams, for instance, posits that "the actual subject of this text [4:13–14] is the commission of (nonsexual) acts of religious apostasy by female Israelites, which included a group of female cult functionaries (קדשות) whose role was considered non-Yahwistic, and hence objectionable, by Hosea."[13] A third alternative is to read the passage as involving

---

and Courtesans in the Ancient World, ed. Christopher A. Faraone and Laura McClure, WSC (Madison: University of Wisconsin Press, 2006); Christine Stark, *"Kultprostitution" im Alten Testament? Die Qedeschen der Hebräischen Bibel und das Motiv der Hurerei*, OBO 221 (Göttingen: Vandenhoeck & Ruprecht, 2006), esp. 218; Stephanie Lynn Budin, *The Myth of Sacred Prostitution in Antiquity* (New York: Cambridge University Press, 2008), esp. 14–47 on the ancient Near East; Christl M. Maier, "Myth and Truth in Socio-historical Reconstruction of Ancient Societies: Hosea 4:11–14 as a Test Case," in *Thus Says the LORD: Essays on the Former and Latter Prophets in Honor of Robert R. Wilson*, ed. John J. Ahn and Stephen L. Cook, LHBOTS 502 (New York: T&T Clark, 2009), 256–72; DeGrado, "Qdesha in Hosea 4:14"; Phyllis A. Bird, *Harlot or Holy Woman? A Study of Hebrew Qĕdēšah* (University Park, PA: Eisenbrauns, 2019). Though ancient Near Eastern evidence is lacking to support the notion of ritual sex for the procurement of agricultural fertility by the fertility gods (though see Charpin), ancient Near Eastern evidence can support the occasional existence of normal "prostitution that was profitable to, and at times organized by, the temple and its administration." See Karel van der Toorn, "Prostitution, Cultic," *ABD* 5:510; Dominique Charpin, *La vie méconnue des temples mésopotamiens* (Paris: Les Belles Lettres, 2017), 158.

11. See esp. Gruber, *Hosea*, 212–26. For the ancient Near Eastern iconographic evidence for the ancient "nexus of inebriation and sexuality," see the Old Babylonian clay plaque (Louvre AO 16681) in Jerrold S. Cooper, "The Job of Sex: The Social and Economic Role of Prostitutes in Ancient Mesopotamia," in *The Role of Women in Work and Society in the Ancient Near East*, ed. Brigitte Lion and Cécile Michel, SANER 13 (Berlin: de Gruyter, 2016), 214.

12. Karin Adams, "Metaphor and Dissonance: A Reinterpretation of Hosea 4:13–14," *JBL* 127 (2008): 298.

13. Adams, "Metaphor and Dissonance," 295. See also Alice A. Keefe, *Woman's Body and the Social Body in Hosea*, JSOTSup 338 (Sheffield: Sheffield Academic, 2001), 100–102, who argues that קדשות and זנות refer to male priests.

both literal noncultic sexual promiscuity and a metaphorical, spiritual sense of sexual unfaithfulness.[14]

David Aaron rightly characterizes the impasse when he notes, "In the scholarship of biblical thought, no issue pits literalism against metaphor as powerfully as that of idolatry."[15] The issue need not be either/or but can be both/and. Though *cultic* prostitution is a scholarly myth, the passage could still refer to *noncultic* literal sexual activity. But in Gruber's exuberance to reject cultic prostitution and reread the passage literally, he overlooks passages that should be read metaphorically. I find the final position most compelling: the passage demonstrates a productive vacillation between the literal and metaphorical.[16] The Israelites engaged in literal sexual promiscuity (similar to what Gruber describes), but the prophet takes up the language of their experience to redescribe their relationship to Yahweh metaphorically.

There are four metaphorical expressions of sexual promiscuity in the passage: 4:10c–11a, 12 (x2), and 15.[17] Hosea 4:10c–11a is fruitfully polyvalent; it can be read metaphorically or literally, and it certainly does contribute to a portrait of Yahweh.[18] Since allegiance to Yahweh entails ethical obligations, Israel's literal sexual activity is proof of abandoning Yahweh. The previous two lines (4:10a–b) also suggest a literal reading. On the other hand, the metaphorical other spouse to whom Israel ran after abandoning Yahweh could be structured as זנות—prostitution embodied.[19] That Israel is "led astray" by a "spirit of whoredom" (כי רוח זנונים התעה, 4:12c)[20] suggests a metaphorical reading due to the possessive רוח. The

---

14. A variety of authors argue for an interweaving of literal and metaphorical in this verse, though their interpretations vary. See Bird, "'To Play the Harlot,'" 83; Eidevall, *Grapes in the Desert*, 58–63; Sweeney, *Twelve Prophets* 1:45–51; Moughtin-Mumby, *Sexual and Marital Metaphors*, 61–66, 72–75; James E. Miller, "A Critical Response to Karin Adams's Reinterpretation of Hosea 4:13–14," *JBL* 128 (2009): 503–6; DeGrado, "Qdesha in Hosea 4:14"; Joshua N. Moon, *Hosea*, AOTC 21 (London: Apollos, 2018), 88. Miller bases his claim on the existence of cultic prostitution.

15. Aaron, *Biblical Ambiguities*, 125.

16. Certainty here remains elusive; an entirely metaphorical reading is possible.

17. For more extensive discussion of the metaphorics of 4:10–15 than space permits, see Eidevall, *Grapes in the Desert*, 58–63.

18. On its polyvalence, see Ben Zvi, *Hosea*, 105–6.

19. Andersen and Freedman identify זנות as "the covenant code of Baal" (*Hosea*, 363).

20. Gruber points out that רוח in 4:19 is an epicene noun, capable of functioning

next line favors a metaphorical reading, because it structures the relationship with Yahweh in terms of a domain that can be understood in different contexts in more concrete terms (ויזנו מתחת אלהיהם, 4:12d). Eidevall claims that 4:12 is the single "undebatable" metaphor in the unit.[21] Finally, the identification of the whole of Israel as a single (male) prostitute (אם זנה אתה ישראל, 4:15) must be read metaphorically. Further support for the metaphoricity of these expressions is the fact that similar metaphoric language is used elsewhere in the Hebrew Bible to describe illicit worship of other deities.[22]

The remaining four instances of זנה language in the unit (4:13, 14 [2x], 18) and נאף in verses 13–14 suggest a nonmetaphorical sense.[23] This literal/figurative interweaving is further supported by the observation that Hosea uses sexual and marital promiscuity language both literally and

---

as grammatically masculine or feminine, so it can here be the subject of the masculine התעה (*Hosea*, 239–40).

21. Eidevall, *Grapes in the Desert*, 61. Seifert also argues that 4:12c–d is metaphorical and much of the context is literal, though she bases this on cultic prostitution (*Metaphorisches Reden*, 138–42).

22. E.g., Lev 20:5; Deut 31:16; Judg 2:17; 8:27, 33; Jer 3:1–9; Ezek 16; 23. The language is also used of Israel's illegitimate political relationships (Isa 23:17; Ezek 23:5, 11–12). The distinction between religious and political unfaithfulness should not be overplayed (e.g., 1 Kgs 11:1–3, 9–10); both are deviations from the relationship of exclusive loyalty to Yahweh. On these themes, see further Renita J. Weems, *Battered Love: Marriage, Sex, and Violence in the Hebrew Prophets* (Minneapolis: Fortress, 1995); Moughtin-Mumby, *Sexual and Marital Metaphors*. For the use of whoredom language in an ancient Near Eastern treaty, see Wolff, *Hosea*, 143; Eidevall, *Grapes in the Desert*, 61–63; Kelle claims that "there are no ancient Near Eastern texts that describe religious or political misbehavior with the metaphor of adultery or fornication" (*Hosea 2*, 99). On marriage in the Old Testament with regard to the marriage metaphor in Hosea, see Gale A. Yee, "Hosea," in *Women's Bible Commentary*, 3rd rev. and updated ed., ed. Carol A. Newsom, Sharon H. Ringe, and Jacqueline E. Lapsley (Louisville: Westminster John Knox, 2012), 301–2; Kelle, *Hosea 2*.

23. Stark identifies 4:13–14 as the only instance of the whoring motif in Hos 4–11 lacking a high level of abstraction in the metaphor and concludes they should be read literally (*"Kultprostitution" im Alten Testament?*, 182–83, 211–12; see also Bird, "'To Play the Harlot,'" 83; Eidevall, *Grapes in the Desert*, 59 n. 46). Moon explains the identification of the women as consistent with Lev 21:9 (*Hosea*, 87). In Hos 4:18, the other three clauses seem to be literal descriptions, though the textual challenges make certainty unattainable (see n. 47, below).

2. Metaphors of Accusation

metaphorically elsewhere.[24] The interpretive significance of this interweaving is revisited below.

Marriage is the fundamental domain of experience that structures Yahweh's relationship to his wayward people here, cultic and covenantal failure is the target domain, and the notion of a covenant between Israel and Yahweh forms the conceptual link between the source and target domains.[25] Hosea employs the familiar covenantal image of marriage to

---

24. That Israel was indicted for literal adultery is affirmed by the clear usage of the נאף root in 4:2 and perhaps in 7:4, while a metaphorical sense of sexual promiscuity occurs in 5:3, 4; 6:10; 8:9; 9:1. This is further supported by Hos 1–3, in which a concrete human relationship involving sexual unfaithfulness (2:4, 6, 7; 3:3) is used metaphorically to structure the relationship between Yahweh and Israel (e.g., 1:2, 3:1).

25. The idea that marriage is the fundamental domain of experience is contra Eidevall, who identifies the basic metaphor as that of disloyal vassal to suzerain (*Grapes in the Desert*, 75–76). This is mistaken because the vassal-suzerain relationship is itself structured in terms of marital unfaithfulness. It is true that metaphorical language of אהב, זנה, and/or אתנן does not necessitate that God is *husband*. See Richtsje Abma, *Bonds of Love: Methodic Studies of Prophetic Texts with Marriage Imagery (Isaiah 50:1–3 and 54:1–10, Hosea 1–3, Jeremiah 2–3)*, SSN (Assen: Van Gorcum, 1999), 3. Professional prostitutes, almost by definition, do not usually have husbands and therefore are not directly a part of the marriage domain.

Nonetheless, God-as-husband is the most natural reading for two reasons. First, זנה language can indicate sexual promiscuity in general (not necessarily prostitution), so it is not incompatible with a person being married (Bird, "'To Play the Harlot,'" 76–80; see also Andersen and Freedman, *Hosea*, 157; Adams, "Metaphor and Dissonance," 300–304). Second, Hos 1–3 combines the husband metaphor with that of sexual promiscuity, picturing God as husband to the sexually promiscuous wife Israel (see, e.g., Ezek 16:31–32). This functions as a theological introduction to interpret the sexual promiscuity metaphors throughout the book. See Mark J. Boda, *A Severe Mercy: Sin and Its Remedy in the Old Testament*, SLTHS 1 (Winona Lake, IN: Eisenbrauns, 2009), 297; Wacker, "Hosea," 374). That is the shocking point of the metaphor: a *wife* is cheating on her husband (technically נאף), to the extent that it can be characterized by זנה (Bird, "'To Play the Harlot,'" 88–89). Understanding the sexual promiscuity language to refer to religious apostasy has been the standard interpretation through the history of reception (see Pentiuc et al.) and is not uncommon among modern scholars (e.g., Bird, "'To Play the Harlot,'" 83; Eidevall, *Grapes in the Desert*, 63; Macintosh, *Critical and Exegetical Commentary*, esp. 167–68; Sweeney, *Twelve Prophets* 1:49; Moughtin-Mumby, *Sexual and Marital Metaphors*, 68; Dearman, *Book of Hosea*, 162–64). See Eugen J. Pentiuc et al., eds., *Hosea: The Word of the Lord that Happened to Hosea*, BIT 3 (Leuven: Peeters, 2017), 134–37. Kelle argues that the prostitution metaphors of Hos 2 refer to Israel's foreign policies (*Hosea 2*). Keefe argues that the female adultery metaphor refers to structural violence resulting from economic processes (see *Woman's Body*, though elsewhere

help the Israelites comprehend the less concrete reality of their covenantal obligations and relationship to their deity.[26] Just as sexual unfaithfulness to a spouse breaks their covenantal relationship, so aberrant worship breaks Israel's relationship with God. Worshiping other gods (or worshiping Yahweh *as* another god) is like cheating on a husband.

Gruber claims, "The issue of idolatry is totally absent from the text of Hos. 4."[27] Yet in this very chapter one finds the statement that חבור עצבים אפרים ("Ephraim is bound to images," 4:17), the trees under which sexual activity occurs (אלון ולבנה ואלה, 4:13) are overwhelmingly associated with cultic aberrations (see 2 Kgs 16:4; 17:10–12; Jer 2:19–20, 23, 26–28; 3:6–10, 13),[28] and the context is religious (ועל הגבעות, על ראשי ההרים יזבחו יקטרו, Hos 4:13). Furthermore, the language of sexual promiscuity in Hos 4 echoes that of Hos 1–3, which clearly links religious apostasy with sexual promiscuity (also 5:3–4, 6:10, 9:1).[29] Mark Boda rightly claims that "Israel's apostasy from Yahweh, presented in chaps. 1–3 through the image of

---

she affirms cultic apostasy as the referent). See Alice A. Keefe, "Hosea," in *The Prophets: Fortress Commentary on the Bible Study Edition*, ed. Gale A. Yee, Hugh R. Page Jr., and Matthew J. M. Coomber (Minneapolis: Fortress, 2016), 824–25. The Israelites may not have viewed idolatry in the same terms as moderns (see Aaron, *Biblical Ambiguities*, 125–55). Hosea nonetheless sees Baal worship as mutually exclusive with Yahweh worship (Samaria's calf [עֶגְלֵךְ] is no god [ולא אלהים הוא] in 8:6). The phrase *marriage metaphor* is used as a heuristic summary without—heeding Moughtin-Mumby's warning—any assumptions of a preexisting story line as background to the individual metaphorical expressions or of homogeneity in its use among various prophets (*Sexual and Marital Metaphors*, 7–8), though Gray suggests it is more accurately a "marriage *model*" (*Psalm 18 in Words and Pictures*, 14). On the notion of a deity being the husband of a worshiping community in the ancient Near East, see Martti Nissinen, *Prophets and Prophecy in the Ancient Near East*, WAW 12 (Atlanta: Society of Biblical Literature, 2003), 120–22 (§§86–87); see also Martti Nissinen and Risto Uro, eds., *Sacred Marriages: The Divine-Human Sexual Metaphor from Sumer to Early Christianity* (Winona Lake, IN: Eisenbrauns, 2008); Moon, *Hosea*, 20. For a more extensive treatment of the covenantal background of the metaphors in Hosea, see my discussion of the legal metaphors in 5:1 and 5:5 below.

26. Keefe, "Hosea," 824.
27. Gruber, *Hosea*, 220.
28. Gruber translates עצבים as "images" without further comment but then seems to commend Ginsberg's rejection of עצבים as a scribal error, "incongruent" with the context of drinking. They emend to "lechers" or "lovers" (Gruber, *Hosea*, 235).
29. The betrayal in 5:7 likely derives from the marital domain (see below). Sexual promiscuity language can also suggest political infidelity (perhaps 8:9–10). Loyalty to Yahweh means absolute loyalty in all spheres of life, including the religious, political,

2. Metaphors of Accusation

the wayward wife, dominates the prophet's imagination" in Hos 4–14.[30] In this passage, therefore, "Israel's apostasy is like whoredom."[31] Indeed, רוח זנונים (4:12, 5:4) "characterizes the power of apostasy as an overwhelming force which comes upon the people from the outside."[32]

The effect of this comparison is to provoke shame. Drawing on the shame associated with such illicit yet intimate bodily activity, and the association between honor/shame and ancient Near Eastern covenantal contexts, this metaphor associates "religious pluralism with sexual pollution, disgust, and shame."[33] This has two implications, one for Israel and one for Yahweh.

As especially highlighted recently among masculinist studies such as that of Susan Haddox, the use of the sexual promiscuity (זנה, נאף) source domain promotes a sense of shame among the audience and male leaders, especially when the whole nation is identified as a male prostitute (4:15).[34]

---

and beyond (see ch. 9 below for more). That is why they can occur in sequential indictments (e.g., 8:1–14, 9:1–9).

30. Boda, *Severe Mercy*, 297.
31. Wolff, *Hosea*, 82.
32. Wolff, *Hosea*, 85.
33. Thomas Staubli, "Disgusting Deeds and Disgusting Gods: Ethnic and Ethical Constructions of Disgust in the Hebrew Bible," *HBAI* 6 (2017): 461 n. 16. On the association between honor/shame and ancient Near Eastern covenantal contexts, see Saul M. Olyan, "Honor, Shame, and Covenant Relations in Ancient Israel and Its Environment," *JBL* 115 (1996): 201–18. On shame more generally, see Johanna Stiebert, "Shame and Prophecy: Approaches Past and Present," *BibInt* 8 (2000): 255–75; Stiebert, *The Construction of Shame in the Hebrew Bible: The Prophetic Contribution*, LHBOTS 346 (London: Sheffield Academic, 2002); Paul A. Kruger, "On Emotions and the Expression of Emotions in the Old Testament: A Few Introductory Remarks," *BZ* 48 (2004): 218–20; Tchavdar S. Hadjiev, "Honor and Shame," *DOTPr*, 333–38. Shame can have external and objective aspects as well: social pressure and a loss of status, respectively (Hadjiev, "Honor and Shame," 336). One can therefore engage in socially shameful behavior without subjectively experiencing shame (e.g., see Jer 6:15, 8:12). Cooper mentions the lack of scholarly consensus as to whether Mesopotamians would have felt shame around the occupation of prostitution ("Job of Sex," 210). The Hebrew Bible, though, treats this activity with uniform disdain. See, e.g., the associated language of "defilement" (טמא) in Gen 34:4, 5, 13; Num 5:13; Ezek 18:11 and here in Hos 5:3; 6:10 (see Gruber, *Hosea*, 249–50).
34. Weems, *Battered Love*, 68–69; Susan E. Haddox, "(E)Masculinity in Hosea's Political Rhetoric," in *Israel's Prophets and Israel's Past: Essays on the Relationship of Prophetic Texts and Israelite History in Honor of John H. Hayes*, ed. Megan Bishop Moore and Brad E. Kelle, LHBOTS 446 (New York: T&T Clark, 2006), 188–89;

The metaphor restructures Israel's religious infidelity in more physical, emotional, and personal terms. The problem is not merely that of superficial procedural errors; Israel's behavior is deeply and personally shameful (see קלון in 4:7, 18). Shame is thus used for social control: to elicit a change in behavior into conformity with Yahweh's stipulations.[35] In other words, "by bringing attention to the disgrace the prophet hopes for repentance."[36] Tchavadar Hadjiev summarizes the mechanics of this process: "While in judgment Israel is objectively shamed by Yahweh [e.g., in 4:1], internalizing this shame [e.g., in 4:10–15] can lead to realization of the inherent shamefulness of sin and thus can bring about repentance."[37]

The vacillation between literal and metaphoric and the polysemy of phrases such as 4:10c–11a are intentional and powerful means of persuasion. The power of metaphor, after all, arises from its grounding in embodied experience.[38] The poet dances between the literal and metaphorical, using the bodily experiences of the Israelites to reframe their perception of their relationship to the deity. The profoundly embodied experience of sexual activity is played on to restructure their conception of their relationship to Yahweh. The sexual promiscuity metaphor may have been chosen because the preexisting illicit sexual practices enabled the metaphor to connect with Hosea's audience more powerfully than if they were faithful monogamous spouses.

The second implication is that Israel's view of Yahweh is likewise restructured.[39] That is, Yahweh is publicly shamed by virtue of association

---

Haddox, *Metaphor and Masculinity in Hosea*, 69–70; Hadjiev, "Honor and Shame," 337; Yee, "Hosea," 303.

35. See Lyn M. Bechtel, "Shame as a Sanction of Social Control in Biblical Israel: Judicial, Political, and Social Shaming," *JSOT* 16 (1991): 47–76.

36. Moon, *Hosea*, 44.

37. Hadjiev, "Honor and Shame," 335; see also Bird, "'To Play the Harlot,'" 89; Stiebert, *Construction of Shame*, 81, 170; this is the main argument of Haddox, though she avoids the term "repentance" (*Metaphor and Masculinity in Hosea*, 164).

38. See p. 13 n. 41, above.

39. For a concise overview of the implications of the marital metaphor for Yahweh and male leaders in terms of provision, fidelity, and reproduction and their rhetorical effects, see Haddox, "(E)Masculinity," 184–89. Also in support of this position are Bird, "'To Play the Harlot,'" 77; Carole R. Fontaine, "Hosea," in *A Feminist Companion to the Latter Prophets*, ed. Athalya Brenner, FCB 8 (Sheffield: Sheffield Academic, 1995), 54; Gale A. Yee, "The Book of Hosea," *NIB* 7:207–11; Victor H. Matthews, "Honor and Shame in Gender-Related Legal Situations in the Hebrew Bible," in *Gender and Law in*

with Israel's failure. In a society of high corporate identity, an individual's identity is always connected to one's associations with others. The shame or honor of an individual affects the shame or honor of those with whom they are in relationship. The shame of the promiscuous wife, for instance, was "contagious within a household in the ANE."[40] Israel's public and shameful act of betrayal therefore reflects poorly on Yahweh, bringing his name into disrepute because "YHWH's own honour is at stake in his binding himself to his people."[41]

In 4:1, Yahweh is the wronged victim of a crime, who is taking judicial action to prosecute the wrong. In 4:10–15, Yahweh is the victim of *relational betrayal*. "Marriage and family constitute the most intimate bonds among the human species. Thus the power of the harlotry metaphor comes in its ability to evoke betrayal in personal terms."[42] Yahweh has been abandoned, forsaken (את יהוה עזבו, 4:10) for someone else.[43] Yahweh was the good husband who did nothing wrong to deserve such heartache (see 2:9–10), which leads to anger.[44]

---

the Hebrew Bible and the Ancient Near East, ed. Bernard M. Levinson, Victor H. Matthews, and Tikva Frymer-Kensky, JSOTSup 262 (Sheffield: Sheffield Academic, 1998), 104–8; Haddox, *Metaphor and Masculinity in Hosea*, 69–70; Joshua N. Moon, "Honor and Shame in Hosea's Marriages," *JSOT* 39 (2015): 335–51; Keefe, "Hosea," 824; contra Tchavdar S. Hadjiev, "Adultery, Shame, and Sexual Pollution in Ancient Israel and in Hosea: A Response to Joshua Moon," *JSOT* 41 (2016): 221–36.

40. Moon, *Hosea*, 41.
41. Moon, *Hosea*, 43 (see 41–43).
42. Dearman, *Book of Hosea*, 368.
43. Haddox stresses that the "other husband" is not named, thereby putting the focus on Yahweh as the one abandoned (*Metaphor and Masculinity in Hosea*, 64–65).
44. This is of course the claim of the text of Hosea. For important contemporary ethical considerations and critical readings of these metaphors, including the inappropriate reuse of this perspective by abusers, see, among the vast literature on the topic, Susan Brooks Thistlethwaite, "Every Two Minutes: Battered Women and Feminist Interpretation," in *Feminist Interpretation of the Bible*, ed. Letty M. Russell (Philadelphia: Westminster, 1985), 96–107; Weems, *Battered Love*; David R. Blumenthal, *Facing the Abusing God: A Theology of Protest* (Louisville: Westminster John Knox, 1993); Yvonne Sherwood, *The Prostitute and the Prophet: Hosea's Marriage in Literary-Theoretical Perspective*, LHBOTS 212 (Sheffield: Sheffield Academic, 1996); Marie-Theres Wacker, *Figurationen des Weiblichen im Hosea-Buch*, HBS 8 (Freiburg: Herder, 1996); Rut Törnkvist, *The Use and Abuse of Female Sexual Imagery in the Book of Hosea: A Feminist Critical Approach to Hos 1–3*, AUUWR 7 (Uppsala: Uppsala University Library, 1998); Keefe, *Woman's Body*; Carol J. Dempsey, *The Prophets: A Liberation-Critical Reading* (Minneapolis: Fortress, 2000); Gerlinde Baumann, *Love and Violence:*

The metaphor highlights the passivity of Yahweh in contrast to the active treachery of his wife[45] and the shame that Israel's actions bring on him. "The real shock of the book" is "the portrayal of a God who feels justly wounded."[46] The shame of this metaphor is intended to indict the male leadership by exposing Israel's sin, provoke the people to reexamine their own culpability in the breakdown of their relationship with Yahweh, and spur them to acting rightly.

The Stubborn Cow and the Exacerbated Shepherd (4:16)

Hosea 4:16 contains this cluster's only metaphors outside the domain of sexual promiscuity that contribute to a characterization of Yahweh.[47] Yahweh is implicitly pictured as an owner of a cow that refuses to do as it is told, then as a shepherd who questions whether he should continue caring for his sheep. The rhetorical question containing the shepherd metaphor demonstrates the reasonableness of Yahweh's judgment. The implied answer is as follows: "If Israel is that stubborn, *of course* there is nothing Yahweh can do but leave Israel to their own devices!" The next verse displays the same two-step logic as 4:16 (indictment of behavior,

---

Marriage as Metaphor for the Relationship between Yhwh and Israel in the Prophetic Books, trans. Linda M. Maloney (Collegeville, MN: Glazier, 2003); Gale A. Yee, *Poor Banished Children of Eve: Woman as Evil in the Hebrew Bible* (Minneapolis: Fortress, 2003); Julia M. O'Brien, *Challenging Prophetic Metaphor: Theology and Ideology in the Prophets* (Louisville: Westminster John Knox, 2008), 63–75; Moughtin-Mumby, *Sexual and Marital Metaphors*; Stuart Macwilliam, *Queer Theory and the Prophetic Marriage Metaphor in the Hebrew Bible* (Sheffield: Equinox, 2011); Susanne Scholz, "Reading the Minor Prophets for Gender and Sexuality," in *The Oxford Handbook of the Minor Prophets*, ed. Julia M. O'Brien (New York: Oxford University Press, 2021), 299–312.

45. Contra Haddox, who claims that "YHWH is consistently portrayed as active … and is not acted upon" (*Metaphor and Masculinity in Hosea*, 141).

46. Dearman, *Book of Hosea*, 368.

47. Some argue that 4:17–19 involves Asherah imagery (see n. 8, above), and 4:19 may evoke storm-god imagery polemically appropriated from Baal. Because of the textual difficulties and speculation involved in finding any metaphorical claims about Yahweh in those verses, they will not be addressed here (see Eidevall, *Grapes in the Desert*, 65–67). The metaphor identification procedure approach stipulates that such utterances be discarded for consideration (Steen et al., "Pragglejaz in Practice," 173–74; Steen, "Identifying Metaphors in Language," 80).

2. Metaphors of Accusation

then consequence). The close of 4:17 is the explicit answer to the rhetorical question in 4:16: Israel will be left alone (הנח לו).[48]

The switch from the cow to lamb metaphor highlights different elements of Israel's national character and relation to Yahweh. The first highlights Israel's active stubbornness. The second highlights their need for Yahweh's provision. The first pictures Yahweh as an owner who does not receive the benefits he expects from his animal (obedience in accomplishing a task in the field), while the second pictures Yahweh as actively choosing to not provide for the needs of his animal.[49] Yahweh has a purpose for Israel with corresponding expectations, but these are not being realized. Yahweh is frustrated by Israel's stubborn refusal to live their national life in accordance with the mutual agreement stipulating the terms for their relationship (i.e., the ברית whose violation is indicted).

This juxtaposition of metaphors may provoke a behavioral change in two simultaneous ways. First, Israel may have perceived their religious activities and national politics as conforming to Yahweh's intentions (8:2). Hosea names the truth: these activities are *not* in conformance to Yahweh's intentions, and Israel's refusal to change their behavior ("return to Yahweh") is *stubborn*. Second, the sheep metaphor functions as an implicit threat that Israel will no longer receive what they need (see 2:11–15). The response implicitly suggested by these metaphors is clear: stop being stubborn and ignoring Yahweh's/Hosea's warning. Instead, they must demonstrate complete allegiance through appropriate deeds in order to receive the necessary nourishment for continued national life from their divine shepherd.

Analyzing Their Interaction

Why add the cow and sheep metaphors to a unit primarily concerned with sexual promiscuity (both literal and metaphorical)? Why call Israel a prostitute (4:15) then immediately a cow and a lamb (4:16)? One axis on which their interaction turns is that of obligation within relationship. In the ancient world, there was an expectation that wives and herd animals could recognize their rightful master (*baal*) and that they would remain

---

48. This interpretation of הנח לו is reflected in, e.g., NRSV; Wolff, *Hosea*, 72; Macintosh, *Critical and Exegetical Commentary*, 167; Gruber, *Hosea*, 48.

49. See Labuschagne, "Similes in the Book," 67–68, who interprets the metaphor switch as God fattening up the calf for the slaughter of his judgment.

loyal to that master. A spouse was obliged to remain sexually faithful to their spouse. A cow was obliged to do the work its owner commanded. Reciprocally, a shepherd was obliged to feed his sheep.

Yet in each metaphor, the obligation is ignored. First, one spouse (Israel) cheats on the other (Yahweh), then the cow (Israel) stubbornly refuses to obey the master (Yahweh). These images are then juxtaposed to the image of the sheep, which adopts the cheating and disobedient characteristics of the preceding promiscuous spouse and stubborn cow. If a covenant is essentially about mutual loyalty and obligations, a complete breakdown has occurred. As with an ancient Near Eastern treaty in general, so this "covenant ends only through persistent disobedience that mocks the commitment at the heart of the covenant."[50] Israel's disloyalty broke the covenant, so Yahweh questions whether he is still obliged to uphold his commitments to Israel. The shepherd asks of his composite cheating-and-disobedient *sheep*, How can I fulfill my relational obligations after you have so heartlessly disregarded your obligations to me?[51] The answer is clear: Israel's behavior as cheating wife and heifer has absolved Yahweh the shepherd of any obligation to care for Israel as a nation.

Cluster 2: Hosea 5:1–7

5:1d Indirect, 2
כי לכם המשפט
For the verdict[52] is for you

5:2b Direct, 3
ואני מוסר לכלם
And I am the punishment/chastisement/correction[53] for them all

---

50. Richard S. Hess, *The Old Testament: A Historical, Theological, and Critical Introduction* (Grand Rapids: Baker Academic, 2016), 142.

51. See Pierre van Hecke, "Conceptual Blending: A Recent Approach to Metaphor Illustrated with the Pastoral Metaphor in Hos 4,16," in *Metaphor in the Hebrew Bible*, ed. Pierre van Hecke, BETL 187 (Leuven: Leuven University Press, 2005), 215–31.

52. משפט can have the sense of a judicial decision (verdict) or a sentence (see *HALOT*, 651; Deut 16:18; 19:6; 21:22; 25:1; 1 Kgs 3:28; 2 Kgs 25:6; Jer 26:11, 16; Ezek 18:8).

53. The strangeness of this attribution has occasioned many emendations and translations. Wolff, for example, follows Oort and *BHS* in emending to מְיַסֵּר and renders as "but I am the chastiser of all of you" (*Hosea*, 94). Tully suggests an emenda-

2. Metaphors of Accusation

5:3c–d   Indirect, 3

כי עתה הזנית אפרים נטמא ישראל
For now you, O Ephraim, have whored;[54] Israel has defiled itself.

5:4b–c   Indirect, 3

כי רוח זנונים בקרבם ואת יהוה לא ידעו
For a spirit of whoredom is among them, but *Yahweh* they do not know

5:5a   Indirect, 2

וענה גאון ישראל בפניו
And the arrogance of Israel testifies against them[55]

5:7a   Direct, 3

ביהוה בגדו
Yahweh they have betrayed

---

tion to מוֹסֵר ("fetters"; *Hosea*, 115; also suggested in *BHS*). *BHQ* does not suggest an emendation. The MT is retained because it is sensible, though admittedly unusual. The alternative metaphor "fetters" would suggest slightly—not fundamentally—different implications for Yahweh.

Many English versions understand it as a verbal participle or translate the noun periphrastically (e.g., "but I will punish all of them," [NRSV]). Others interpret nominally ("taskmaster" [*HALOT*, 557], "reprover" [NJPS], "I was the correction for them all" [Goldingay], "I am [a force for] discipline to all of them" [Macintosh, *Critical and Exegetical Commentary*, 178], "teacher" [παιδευτὴς; LXX]). See John Goldingay, *The First Testament: A New Translation* (Downers Grove, IL: InterVarsity Press, 2018), 851.

54. Some detect a semantic difference between the *qal* and the *hiphil* stems of זנה (e.g., NJPS; Wolff, *Hosea*, 94; Moughtin-Mumby, *Sexual and Marital Metaphors*, 64–65; Gruber, *Hosea*, 250). The *hiphil* may be emphatic, though it need not be in 4:10 (Wolff, *Hosea*, 82).

55. This interpretation rests on the choice of ענה I (to answer, reply) as the root rather than ענה II (to be wretched), its collocation with בפני, and the legal context of the utterance. In support, see *HALOT*, 852; Kevin J. Cathcart and Robert P. Gordon, *The Targum of the Minor Prophets*, ed. Martin McNamara, ArBib 14 (Collegeville, MN: Liturgical Press, 1997), 39 n. 8; and virtually all English translations. LXX and Tg. Neb. understand it as ענה II, rendering as καὶ ταπεινωθήσεται ἡ ὕβρις τοῦ Ισραηλ εἰς πρόσωπον αὐτοῦ and וימאך יקר ישראל ואנון חזן, respectively; so also ibn Ezra; NJPS; see Macintosh, *Critical and Exegetical Commentary*, 185, though he supports ענה I. There may be intentionality to this ambiguity, as the sense of "be brought low" (ענה II) would be juxtaposed to the subject of the verb, the *pride* of Israel (גאון־ישראל), and its more basic sense of "height."

5:7b   Indirect, 3
כי בנים זרים ילדו
For they have borne illegitimate[56] children

Hosea 5 marks a clear beginning to a new unit, thrice calling Israel, particularly its leadership, to attention. Unsurprisingly, this section begins with a judicial verdict (המשפט), one of two legal metaphors (5:1, 5). The most unique metaphor in the cluster is that of the disciplinarian (5:2b). In addition, two metaphors (5:3, 4) pick up the sexual promiscuity theme from Hosea 4. The final verse provides a summary accusation and the proof and consequences of Israel's duplicity.

The Legal Metaphors (5:1, 5)

These metaphors extend the legal framework instituted in 4:1. Though 4:1 is not part of a cluster and is therefore not considered for independent analysis, it is very significant for the structuring of Hosea and therefore merits a few comments here regarding the themes that 5:1–5 continues.

Hosea 4:1 institutes a legal framework for the proceedings, which will unfold across 4:1–11:11 and will then be repeated in 12:1–14:9.[57] That is, it metaphorically structures one domain of experience (Israel's relationship to Yahweh) by mapping it onto another, more familiar, domain (legal proceedings). Yahweh calls for a legal case (ריב; 4:1, 12:3; see 2:4) against Israel, then summarizes their transgressions as a modern attorney might

---

56. E.g., *HALOT*, 279; LXX; NRSV; Andersen and Freedman, *Hosea*, 395; contra Eidevall, *Grapes in the Desert*, 73. On the wordplay of זר with other occurrences in Hosea, see Moughtin-Mumby, *Sexual and Marital Metaphors*, 71–72; Dearman, *Book of Hosea*, 177–78.

57. Richelle recently described the "well-known theme of dispute (ריב)" in 4:1–3 as "a point of agreement between most exegetes" (my trans.). See Matthieu Richelle, "Structure littéraire et interprétation en Osée 4," *RB* 121 (2014): 6. I do not presuppose a technical form of "covenant lawsuit" or a *Sitz im Leben*. See Michael DeRoche, "The Reversal of Creation in Hosea," *VT* 31 (1981): 400–409; DeRoche, "Yahweh's *Rîb* against Israel: A Reassessment of the So-Called 'Prophetic Lawsuit' in the Preexilic Prophets," *JBL* 102 (1983): 563–74; Dwight R. Daniels, "Is There a 'Prophetic Lawsuit' Genre," *ZAW* 99 (1987): 339–60. I seek only to unfold the implications of this metaphor in its own literary context. As Ben Zvi observes, "v. 1 served to evoke or play with common images associated with legal proceedings that existed in the world of knowledge of the readership" (*Hosea*, 111–12).

2. Metaphors of Accusation

make opening remarks in a case (4:1): Israel lacks honesty/faithfulness/ truthfulness (אמת), loyal love (חסד), and a knowledge of God (דעת אלהים). Specific indictments are given in 4:2, then the universal consequences of Israel's violent transgressions are outlined in 4:3.[58]

The question naturally arises: On what basis is a legal case being prosecuted? Hosea, a "remarkably 'covenantal' text," suggests that the relationship between Yahweh and Israel has been structured by a preexisting covenant (ברית) that includes legal stipulations and consequences—many commentators rightly see in the next verse (4:2) allusions to the Decalogue.[59] Though the introductory ריב patterns in 4:1 and 12:3 (see 2:4) do not mention a ברית, the term ברית appears in 6:7 and 8:1. Both indicate that Israel/Ephraim has violated preexisting conditions of a created (nonnatural) relationship between them and Yahweh. Hosea 12:2 indicts Ephraim for making covenants with Assyria and (implicitly) with Egypt, presumably rather than being faithful to the covenant with Yahweh. Finally, 2:20 envisions a new covenant in "that day," which results in universal peace and flourishing. This will be inaugurated with, among other

---

58. See further Katherine Murphey Hayes, *"The Earth Mourns": Prophetic Metaphor and Oral Aesthetic*, AcBib 8 (Atlanta: Society of Biblical Literature, 2002); Jeffrey H. Hoffmeyer, "Covenant and Creation: Hosea 4:1–3," *RevExp* 102 (2005): 143–51; Melissa T. Loya, "'Therefore the Earth Mourns': The Grievance of the Earth in Hosea 4:1–3," in *Exploring Ecological Hermeneutics*, ed. Peter L. Trudinger and Norman C. Habel, SymS 46 (Atlanta: Society of Biblical Literature, 2008), 53–62.

59. Harold Fisch, *Poetry with a Purpose: Biblical Poetics and Interpretation* (Bloomington: Indiana University Press, 1988), 138. McKenzie calls covenant "the most important theme in Hosea." See Steven L. McKenzie, "Exodus Typology in Hosea," *ResQ* 22 (1979): 100. E.g., Andersen and Freedman claim that the initial list of five infinitive absolutes "reads like an excerpt from the Decalogue" (*Hosea*, 337). See also Walter Brueggemann, *Tradition for Crisis: A Study in Hosea* (Richmond, VA: John Knox, 1968), 38–43; Wolff, *Hosea*, 67–68; Heinz-Dieter Neef, *Die Heilstraditionen Israels in der Verkündigung des Propheten Hosea*, BZAW 169 (Berlin: de Gruyter, 1987), 196–209; Macintosh, *Critical and Exegetical Commentary*, 130; contra Eidevall, *Grapes in the Desert*, 53. See also Douglas Stuart, *Hosea–Jonah*, WBC 31 (Grand Rapids: Zondervan, 2014), xxxii–xl, for the covenantal stipulations, some of which overlap with Hosea. "The predominant sense of ברית in Biblical Hebrew is an elected, as opposed to natural, relationship of obligation established under divine sanction." See Gordon P. Hugenberger, *Marriage as a Covenant: Biblical Law and Ethics as Developed from Malachi*, BSL (Grand Rapids: Baker, 1994), 171. On the consensus of the antiquity of the covenant concept and a substantial bibliography, see Olyan, "Honor, Shame, and Covenant Relations," esp. 201–2.

things, the very elements named in 4:1 as lacking in the land: חסד, אמת, and אלהים דעת (2:21–22). The final form of Hosea, then, assumes a preexisting set of stipulations that structures a nonnatural relationship between Israel and Yahweh. The inference that the ריב is a legal indictment for the breaking of God's covenant with Israel is therefore reasonable.[60] It is the violation of these stipulations that is being metaphorically prosecuted in the book.

What then does 4:1 contribute to a portrait of Yahweh that is echoed and extended by 5:1–5? Two things may be highlighted. First is the multivalent legal role that Yahweh assumes. Yahweh is pictured as a legal prosecutor and accuser. In the ancient world, this role would have commonly been taken by the victim of a crime or someone closely related to the victim, rather than a professional role hired by the victim.[61] Since Hosea does not posit a pantheon among which Yahweh might have relatives, and since Yahweh is consistently presented as the victim of Israel's transgressions in the book, it appears to be the case that Yahweh is presented as the victim of a crime prosecuting his own case. This of course has parallels to ancient suzerains prosecuting a case against vassals.[62] Yahweh is also pictured as judge, further underscoring his role as suzerain. While typically an ancient Near Eastern deity would call together other deities as witnesses, Yahweh calls no witnesses. Hosea's polemic asserts that there are no other legitimate deities who could function as witnesses.[63] To this composite legal image—victim/suzerain, prosecutor/accuser, judge, and

---

60. So also Jeremias, *Prophet Hosea*, 60–61; Francis Landy, *Hosea*, Readings (Sheffield: Sheffield Academic, 1995), 53–54; Macintosh, *Critical and Exegetical Commentary*, 130–31; Sweeney, *Twelve Prophets* 1:43; James D. Nogalski, *The Book of the Twelve: Hosea–Jonah*, SHBC (Macon, GA: Smyth & Helwys, 2011), 73–75; Gruber, *Hosea*, 186–90; Moon, *Hosea*, 75–76.

61. For the semantics of the term ריב, see Edwin M. Good, "Hosea 5:8–6:6: An Alternative to Alt," *JBL* 85 (1966): 278.

62. Despite denying the presence of allusions to the Decalogue and the legal background of 4:1, Eidevall concludes that "the discourse in Hos 4:1–5:7 can be read as a three-fold *rîb* (controversy) between a suzerain and his vassals" (*Grapes in the Desert*, 76). For an analysis of Hos 4 in light of Neo-Assyrian treaties, see Martti Nissinen, *Prophetie, Redaktion und Fortschreibung im Hoseabuch: Studien zum Werdegang eines Prophetenbuches im Lichte von Hos 4 und 11*, AOAT 231 (Kevelaer: Butzon & Bercker, 1991).

63. Seifert, *Metaphorisches Reden*, 148. Hosea need not have affirmed monotheism; this claim is consistent with henotheism.

2. Metaphors of Accusation

jury—executioner will shortly be added. This multilayered metaphor therefore pictures Yahweh in *both* active (accuser, prosecutor, judge) and passive (victim of a crime) roles.

The second aspect of the ריב metaphor from 4:1 to be highlighted here is its entailments regarding Yahweh's justice. Before Yahweh, wrongs will not go unseen or unpunished. Israel, in turn, is to realize that they have violated the agreement and will be held accountable; judgment is coming. If Israel thought they were safe, that their foreign alliances were avenues of hope and security, or that their cultic activities sufficiently conformed to Yahweh's expectations of their relationship, the triple-ריב pattern (2:4, 4:1, 12:3) that structures the three cycles of Hosea disabuses Israel of such illusions.

Returning to the legal metaphors of 5:1 and 5:5, one finds that these metaphors confirm the contributions of 4:1 that the book is concerned with identifying transgressions of expected norms in order to return the people to obedience to those norms. They also indicate that the indictment/accusation stage of prosecuting a ריב is still in view. The crimes are still being listed; guilt is still accumulating. The punishment is yet to be declared in full. The ultimate verdict of this trial, though, is already clear: Israel is guilty.

Hosea 5:1 opens with a threefold call for specific leaders to pay attention; 5:1d clarifies that the verdict is especially for them. While all Israel bears responsibility for their sin, the leaders have a special burden of responsibility for leading Israel into sin (see 4:9a). They are not bystanders watching Hosea indict others; they are not exempt. Rather, the priests and the household of the king stand accused alongside the house of Israel. Hosea declares, "*This* verdict is for *you all!*"

Hosea 5:5a underscores that this verdict is *justified*; the accusations are correct.[64] Israel's actions testify against them in a court of law. These actions are denoted by the phrase "the pride of Israel" (גאון ישראל).[65] The judicial metaphor indirectly underscores the metaphorization of Yahweh as the victim of a crime and prosecutor of a ריב in a legal context.

In sum, these metaphors communicate that Israel, and especially its leadership, cannot escape Yahweh's indictment. The accusation is accurate (5:5) and the verdict is for them (5:1). Yahweh is pictured as

---

64. The phrase recurs in 7:10a; see discussion of 6:5c below.
65. It is difficult to determine the referent of the phrase; see Macintosh, *Critical and Exegetical Commentary*, 186–87, for the options.

clear-sighted and justified in his placing the greatest responsibility and guilt on Israel's leadership.

Yahweh as Disciplinarian (5:2)

As the most novel image in this unit, the metaphor of Yahweh as מוסר merits more attention. מוסר is a noun derived from יסר,[66] a verb meaning "to teach, instruct," and, by extension, "to discipline or chastise." The noun has to do with discipline, training, instruction, and correction (e.g., Isa 26:16, 53:5, Jer 2:30, Ps 50:19, Prov 1:2). It is a strange attributive moniker to place in a predicate nominative clause with אני, and this strangeness should be retained in any interpretation of the phrase. A translation such as "I am their chastisement" is preferable.[67]

The phrase should be understood metaphorically, as מוסר can be taken in a more concrete and basic sense, such as with a parent or teacher providing verbal instruction or physical correction. It is, in Black's terms, a very strong metaphor.[68] A few observations evince its strength. First, this is the only metaphor in the unit overtly about Yahweh. Significantly, this may be the only nominal metaphor for God in Hosea, as Hosea almost entirely favors similes for Yahweh, perhaps to guard against perceived idolatrous interpretations.[69] Second, as a true literary metaphor (not a simile), its attributive distance to Yahweh is minimized. God is not *like* a disciplinarian; he *is* one. Third, it is not spoken by Hosea or the people but by Yahweh himself.[70] Yahweh himself claims that he is a disciplinarian to *all* of the people of Israel. Finally, the source domain is quite unusual.[71]

---

66. Contra Bernhard Duhm, *Die zwölf Propheten, in den Versmassen der Urschrift übersetzt* (Tübingen: Mohr Siebeck, 1910), and Arnold B. Ehrlich, *Randglossen zur Hebräischen Bibel*, vol. 5 (Leipzig: Hinrichs, 1912) (see Macintosh, *Critical and Exegetical Commentary*, 180); Jeremias, *Prophet Hosea*, 73.

67. See n. 53, above.

68. Black, "More about Metaphor," 25-26; see pp. 20-22, above.

69. See p. 17 n. 58, above.

70. Kimchi thinks Hosea is the subject (Macintosh, *Critical and Exegetical Commentary*, 180). Yahweh is the preferable subject because (1) the following context also makes more sense with Yahweh as the subject; (2) Hosea would be speaking on behalf of Yahweh rather than himself; and (3) מוסר should be understood as "disciplinarian," "taskmaster," or "punisher," which makes little sense if Hosea is the subject.

71. In the entire Hebrew Bible, Ezek 5:15 seems to be the only other instance of this word personified with a pronoun. Other than Hos 5:2, it is never applied to Yahweh.

As a strong metaphor, it is emphatic and resonant. Such figures are "intended to be dwelt upon for the sake of their unstated implications."[72] As it is resonant, one can draw implications from the parent domain, the teacher domain, and/or the king/suzerain domain and take each in a different direction.[73] The precise source domain remains uncertain. While it is unclear whom Yahweh is pictured as, it remains clear what Yahweh will do. He takes on the responsibility of personally punishing Israel.

As with other metaphors in this context, this threat of punishment evokes fear and opens the possibility of a changed course of action into obedience to Yahweh's ways. This is its rhetorical purpose. Israel cannot think that Yahweh offers only empty threats. They have now been told that Yahweh disapproves of their actions and will be the one to apply punishment.

It is important to observe that the verb is not פקד but יסר. This is not punishment for its own sake but *discipline* deployed for *correction* and *instruction*.[74] The personal nature of this punishment retains the hope that it may correct Israel's errant path and enable them to walk in Yahweh's instructions (see 14:10). Israel's penchant for stumbling in those ways (4:5, 5:5, 14:2) and regarding Yahweh's instructions as foreign (8:12), however, tempers any such hope.

The Sexual Promiscuity Metaphors (5:3, 4)

These two metaphors resume the sexual promiscuity domain from a few verses earlier (cluster 1). Hosea 5:4b–c seems a strong candidate for metaphorical usage because of its use of the construct phrase רוח זנונים and its parallelism with not knowing *Yahweh*.[75] Hosea 5:3c–d is less sure, though a metaphorical reading is preferable, because the subject is the

---

72. Black, "More about Metaphor," 26.

73. Wolff says, "The root יסר belongs to the language of instruction in the family; it especially denotes the father's instruction of his son" (*Hosea*, 99). While it is frequently used in these contexts, it is used in enough other contexts that the father domain cannot be assumed here.

74. Wolff, *Hosea*, 99; Macintosh, *Critical and Exegetical Commentary*, 181. While Gruber affirms these aspects of the noun, he reverses the order (*Hosea*, 246–47). In his view, Yahweh first teaches Israel, and this eventually gives way to punishment. The restorative purpose of the punishment is absent.

75. Recall that Eidevall claims that this phrase in 4:12 is the "only undebatable case of metaphorical usage of 'whoredom' language" in that unit (see n. 21, above).

entire nation (אפרים) and Israel as a whole is declared as defiled in the parallel clause.⁷⁶

These two metaphors emphasize the claims of 4:10–15, but their unique contributions to the presentation of Yahweh are minor. Hosea 5:3 is similar to 4:15a in that it personifies the entire nation as whoring. It extends this in the next clause by naming the ritual consequences of this behavior: Israel has become ceremonially unclean (נטמא ישראל). They are no longer welcome in the presence of God; they are endangered, since nothing unclean can enter Yahweh's presence. Hosea 5:4 repeats the whole clause of 4:12c, only substituting בקרבם for התעה. This switch internalizes Israel's problem further. It is not only an *external* spirit that can lead them astray (4:12c). Now the problem is internal; it is *within* them (בקרבם).

This passage extends the sexual metaphor further with a double use of ידע. Yahweh declares that he has known Ephraim (אני ידעתי אפרים, 5:3), yet due to the spirit of whoredom within them (כי רוח זנונים בקרבם), manifest in evil deeds that prevent their return to Yahweh (לא יתנו מעלליהם לשוב אל אלהיהם), the people do not know Yahweh (ואת יהוה לא ידעו, 5:4). This may be suggestive of sexual intercourse within the marital domain, with the sad implication that "the people no longer desire such a relationship, but rather prefer to engage in 'prostitution.'"⁷⁷

A Betrayed Spouse and Illegitimate Children (5:7)

The target domain of Israel's relationship to Yahweh is restructured by means of the embodied experience of betrayal. The phrase ביהוה בגדו is metaphorical because the verb can be understood in more concrete and historically older ways,⁷⁸ such as marital perfidy.

The brevity of the metaphor and the semantic range of the verb make determining the source domain difficult. The verb בגד denotes human relationships in which one fails to fulfill one's obligations to another.⁷⁹ This

---

76. Most interpreters read 5:3c–d metaphorically. The tight parallelism suggests that the sexual promiscuity language and not knowing Yahweh (idolatry, apostasy, cultic and political unfaithfulness) are in fact the same thing (on the "binocular vision" of parallelism, which can function akin to metaphor; see p. 16 n. 55, above). Gruber is a recent example of a continued literal reading of this passage (*Hosea*, 249).

77. Moughtin-Mumby, *Sexual and Marital Metaphors*, 70.

78. See p. 18, above.

79. Seth Erlandsson, "בגד," *TDOT* 1:470.

2. Metaphors of Accusation 53

occurs in marital contexts (e.g., Jer 3:8, 20 [see also 3:11, 5:11]; Mal 2:14, 16), familial or household contexts (e.g., Exod 21:8, Jer 12:6, Ps 73:15), political contexts (e.g., Judg 9:23, Ps 59:6), or among friends (Lam 1:2; perhaps implying lovers).[80] Usually in the Old Testament, Yahweh is the object of the verb.[81] It stands to reason that these Yahwistic uses draw on the concrete human instances for their meanings.

Scholars often prefer the marital domain as the background for Hos 5:7a, though a political domain is possible.[82] The marital domain is the most likely background for this metaphor, because (1) בגד is used elsewhere in prophetic contexts that make the marital metaphor explicit (Jer 3:8, 20; Mal 2:11), and (2) metaphors drawing on the marriage domain are common in Hosea, even in the immediate context (5:3–4, 7b).

Definitively determining a single source domain, however, is unnecessary for understanding the metaphor. The metaphor works, regardless of whether a marriage or a political alliance or any other human relationship is envisioned as the background. The verb suggests intentional duplicity under the guise of benevolence, "the hint of ruthlessly purposeful deception."[83] One does not easily forget an experience of betrayal; it leaves deep and permanent wounds. Hosea draws on that visceral experience of human treachery to shatter Israel's self-deceptive illusion of being in good standing with Yahweh and to reshape the nation's interpretation of their place before the deity.

Indictments of divine betrayal elsewhere in the Old Testament usually refer to breaking the covenant through idolatry. Likely Hosea, too, conceives of covenant breaking as treachery, evidenced by idolatry along with social and political disobedience.[84] The immediately preceding verses character-

---

80. Erlandsson suggests the four semantic domains of marriage, covenant, created order, and human agreements ("בגד"). The verb is also frequently used in an absolute sense, without an object (e.g., 1 Sam 14:33, Isa 24:16, Ps 25:3).

81. Robin Wakely, "בגד," *NIDOTTE* 1:582; Erlandsson, "בגד," 470.

82. Mays, *Hosea*, 84; Andersen and Freedman, *Hosea*, 395; Macintosh, *Critical and Exegetical Commentary*, 191; Dearman, *Book of Hosea*, 176; Pentiuc et al., *Hosea*, 152; Tully, *Hosea*, 122. Eidevall points out that the plural verb בגדו would be strange for a (monogamous) marriage metaphor; he prefers the political domain (*Grapes in the Desert*, 72–73). Macintosh acknowledges the possibility of the political domain but prefers the marital (*Critical and Exegetical Commentary*, 191).

83. Moughtin-Mumby, *Sexual and Marital Metaphors*, 71; see also Tully, *Hosea*, 122.

84. See discussion of Hos 6:7 below, which has the only other occurrence of בגד in the book (שם בגדו בי), referring to the place at which they transgressed the

ize this idolatrous betrayal in personal detail. They have whored with others so much that they have irreparably estranged themselves from their true husband; their actions are so perverse as to prohibit them (לא יתנו מעלליהם) from returning to Yahweh (5:3b–4a). Though he knows them (5:3a), they do not know him (5:4) and probably never truly have.[85] They have forgotten who Yahweh is and what Yahweh is like (see 2:15, 4:6, 8:14, 13:6).

The image of a sexually unfaithful spouse continues into 5:7b.[86] The illegitimate children of 5:7b are the consequences of their promiscuity (5:3–4) and the proof of their betrayal claimed in 5:7a: ביהוה בגדו כי בנים זרים ילדו.[87] Whatever the historical referent of the metaphor,[88] the intent is clear: Israel should have been producing legitimate and faithful offspring, but instead Israel's unfaithfulness to Yahweh has borne illegitimate and unfaithful children. Hosea 5:7b extends the picture of the shamed husband to one whose illegitimate children serve as a public reminder of his shame to all who see them.

Analyzing Their Interaction

In the middle of the unit is a set of sexual promiscuity metaphors (5:3–4), bracketed by judicial metaphors (5:1, 5) and the statement that Yahweh

---

covenant (עברו ברית). See also Hos 4:1–3, 6:8–10, 8:1, 9:9–10. See also Wakely, "בגד," 588; Erlandsson, "בגד," 471–72; Jeremias, *Prophet Hosea*, 76.

85. Significantly, the book *never* says that Israel knows (though they *claim* to, 8:2) or has known God, though they will in the future (2:22).

86. So Mays, *Hosea*, 84; Andersen and Freedman, *Hosea*, 395; Jeremias, *Prophet Hosea*, 77; Seifert, *Metaphorisches Reden*, 144; Dearman, *Book of Hosea*, 176; Bo H. Lim and Daniel Castelo, *Hosea*, THOTC (Grand Rapids: Eerdmans, 2015), 125–26; Moon, *Hosea*, 103; Tully, *Hosea*, 122. Eidevall reads 5:7a as a political metaphor, which he believes continues in 5:7b (*Grapes in the Desert*, 72–73).

87. The כי does not indicate that 5:7b causes 5:7a but "describes the outcome of that treachery" (Tully, *Hosea*, 122; see also Sweeney, *Twelve Prophets* 1:58). See also the "children of promiscuity" (ילדי זנונים) in 1:2 (so also Sweeney, *Twelve Prophets* 1:58; Dearman, *Book of Hosea*, 176).

88. Suggested referents include literal children through intermarriage with non-Israelites or cult prostitutes (Wolff, *Hosea*, 101), children of marital unions who are thought of as the gifts of Baal (Seifert, *Metaphorisches Reden*, 144, entertains both possibilities), or the deposing of the current priests (Gruber, *Hosea*, 255–56; see Hos 4:6), but it more likely refers metaphorically to creating a new generation of idolaters (Jeremias, *Prophet Hosea*, 77: "children of Baal"; Eidevall, *Grapes in the Desert*, 73; Seifert, *Metaphorisches Reden*, 144; Macintosh, *Critical and Exegetical Commentary*, 191; Glenny, *Hosea*, 105; Moon, *Hosea*, 103).

2. Metaphors of Accusation

will be the one to personally exact the corrective punishment (5:2). Hosea 5:7 concludes 5:1–6 by summarizing the accusations of 5:1–5 in 5:7a, providing the proof (5:7b), and naming the consequences (5:7c).

The sexual promiscuity metaphors highlight the pain, shame, and anger that Yahweh experiences, and the disciplinarian metaphor highlights the personal nature of Yahweh's punishment. It is *Yahweh's* hand that does the striking. The responsibility to punish Israel is neither assigned to an intermediary nor relinquished as a pointless obligation. Neither is it merely something Yahweh will *do* (a verb); it is—more fundamentally—something Yahweh *is* (a noun). Yahweh alone determines when, how much, and to what end the punishment will be deployed.

The betrayal metaphor (5:7a) denotes the *fundamental problem* with Israel's promiscuous actions, and the *reason*[89] Yahweh has withdrawn from them (חלץ מהם, 5:6; see 5:15) and will bring punishment: they have forsaken their promised obligations to Yahweh. In other words, betrayal in 5:7a is the basic problem *beneath* the sexual promiscuity metaphors (5:3–4, 7b) and the substance of the accusations in the courtroom scene established by the legal metaphors (5:1, 5). Robin Wakely's comments on Jer 3:11 equally befit Hosea: Israel's religion "consisted of maintaining the outward shows of orthodox Yahwism while acting contrary to the demands of Yahweh's covenant. While expecting her divine husband to fulfil all his marital commitments, she had no intention of fulfilling hers."[90] Or as Eric Tully comments on Hos 5:7, "They have acted treacherously because their 'piety' has been manipulative and nothing more than a ruse to enable their unfaithfulness."[91]

Israel should stand in fear, because the consequence of their behavior is that Yahweh is now entitled to end the relationship and punish his betrayer.[92] In the marriage metaphor, wife-Israel risks divorce from her provider and guardian. In the political metaphor, Israel risks being destroyed and deposed by the suzerain's invading army. Either way, Israel's future is at risk. The metaphor closes off certain courses of action for Israel.

---

89. LXX inserts ὅτι at the beginning of 5:7 (see Glenny, *Hosea*, 104–5); many English translations include "because" or "for" (CEB, ESV, NASB, NJPS, NKJV, NRSV); see also Abraham ben Meïr Ibn Ezra, *The Commentary of Rabbi Abraham Ibn Ezra on Hosea*, trans. Abe Lipshitz (New York: Sepher-Hermon, 1988), 58; Gruber, *Hosea*, 254–55.

90. Wakely, "בגד," 587.

91. Tully, *Hosea*, 122.

92. Recall Hess's comment above (n. 50).

Israel can no longer continue with the status quo into a future of provision and protection in an idyllic relationship with their sovereign deity. Rather, Israel ought to tremble as Yahweh contemplates his response to such betrayal. Yahweh, for the first time explicitly in Hosea, is characterized as the *betrayed one*. Similar to the sexual promiscuity metaphors, Yahweh is the victim of relational depravity for which no human would stand. How will God respond?

The answer is that Yahweh will not stand by idly. The final clause (5:7c) indicates the outcome of Israel's behavior in 5:1–7b: "Now the New Moon [festival] will devour them [along] with their portions [of land]" (עתה יאכלם חדש את חלקיהם; 5:7c).[93] While details of the passage are unclear, what is generally agreed on is that the punishment for their betrayal is destruction of their land (חלקיהם), which provides for all their needs.[94] The destruction is probably by an invading army that takes them into exile (see Hos 8:8–14, 9:3), reflecting the Deuteronomic covenant curses for treaty violation (e.g., Deut 28:49–57).[95] Fittingly—in Hosea the punishment often fits the crime—the new moon festival may have involved a "confrontation with idolatry,"[96] as exemplified in Psalm 81: "Blow the trumpet at the new moon, at the full moon, on our festal day.... There shall be no strange god among you; you shall not bow down to a foreign god" (vv. 4, 10 NRSV). The association of the new moon festival with the blowing of the trumpets

---

93. In support of this rendering, and for ancient Near Eastern background, see Othmar Keel, *Goddesses and Trees, New Moon and Yahweh: Ancient Near Eastern Art and the Hebrew Bible*, JSOTSup 261 (Sheffield: Sheffield Academic, 1998), 104–9, esp. 105.

94. עתה often indicates the beginning of a declaration of punishment or judgment in Hosea (2:12; 7:2; 8:8, 10, 13; 10:2). אכל often denotes judgment as well (2:14, 4:10, 7:9, 8:14, 9:3, 11:6, 13:8).

Emendation (see *BHS*) is unnecessary (see *CTAT*, 519–21; *BHQ*, 59*), but some despair of a solution (e.g., Wolff, *Hosea*, 95, who follows the LXX). The MT is supported by other versions (Aquila, Symmachus, Theodotion, Vulg.; Tg. Neb. paraphrases); Syr. omits; LXX reads ἐρυσίβη ("blight," "mildew," or "locusts"). If one reads את as the preposition "with," rather than as the direct object marker, the MT is viable. חדש specifically refers to the new moon festival, not "month" in general (Gruber, *Hosea*, 256–57; see also Macintosh, *Critical and Exegetical Commentary*, 192).

95. Jeremias, *Prophet Hosea*, 77. Tg. Neb. may recognize the Dtn reference, as it inserts additional commentary to clarify: "They have dealt faithlessly with *the Memra of* the Lord, for they have *brought up* children *of the daughters of the nations. Now I shall bring against them nations, month by month, who shall plunder the produce of their land*" (Cathcart and Gordon, *Targum Minor Prophets*, 39).

96. Moon, *Hosea*, 103.

(as reflected in Ps 81:4) facilitates a segue from Hos 5:7 to the next textual unit, which begins with the blowing of the trumpets (תקעו שופר) as a warning, perhaps of this invading army (5:8). The truly "catastrophic loss," however, is not destruction of the land, but the withdrawal of Yahweh (ולא ימצאו חלץ מהם, 5:6c).[97] This marks the decisive end of the relationship.[98]

Supercluster: 5:10–6:7

This unit is the most significant metaphor cluster in the book of Hosea. It has the greatest density of metaphors for God as well as some of the most innovative and daring. It is a supercluster because it is a unified dialogue with a metaphor density well above the required threshold for a cluster, which nonetheless involves three distinct clusters, differentiated by speaker. The limits of this supercluster (5:10–6:7) roughly coincide with a textual unit. An influential article by Albrecht Alt in 1919 identified 5:8–6:6 as a unit composed of five oracles originating from Hosea's preaching during the Syro-Ephraimite War of 733–732 BCE (see 2 Kgs 15:23–17:6; Isa 7).[99] Since then, scholarship on this unit has been primarily concerned with positing emendations and determining the historical events behind the text. Unfortunately, this has meant that the metaphors have received little attention.

Cluster 3: Hosea 5:10–15

There are five metaphors for God in this passage, one of which extends into a miniature poetic narrative (5:14–15). Hosea 5:13, though not itself a metaphor for God, is influenced by the surrounding metaphors such that it makes an implicit metaphorical claim about Yahweh.

5:10b   Indirect, 3
עליהם אשפוך כמים עברתי

---

97. Moon, *Hosea*, 103.

98. Jeremias points out that, though Israel is constantly seeking Yahweh (pointing to the imperfect verb in 5:6a: ילכו לבקש), Yahweh's withdrawal is decisive (the perfect verb in 5:6b: חלץ מהם) (*Prophet Hosea*, 76–77; similarly Tully, *Hosea*, 121).

99. Albrecht Alt, "Hosea 5,8–6,6: Ein Krieg und seine Folgen in prophetischer Beleuchtung," in *Kleine Schriften zur Geschichte des Volkes Israel* (Munich: Beck, 1953), 2:163–87. For an updated reconstruction of the Syro-Ephraimite War, incorporating biblical and extrabiblical evidence, see Kelle, *Hosea 2*, 181–99.

on them I will pour out like water my rage

5:12a   Direct, 3
ואני כעש לאפרים
Yet I am like a moth[100] to Ephraim

5:12b   Direct, 3
וכרקב לבית יהודה
and like rottenness to the house of Judah

5:13   Indirect, 2
וירא אפרים את חליו
ויהודה את מזרו
וילך אפרים אל אשור
וישלח אל מלך ירב
והוא לא יוכל לרפא לכם
ולא יגהה מכם מזור
Ephraim saw his sickness,
and Judah his sore.
So Ephraim went to Assyria,
and sent to the Great King.[101]

---

100. Common translations of עש include "moth" (עש I [*HALOT*, 895; *DCH* 6:615–16]; ESV, NASB, NIV, NET; Landy, *Hosea*, 76; Eidevall, *Grapes in the Desert*, 83–84; see Ps 29:12; Job 13:28 is the only other place עש occurs with רקב), "maggots" (NRSV), "pus" (*HALOT*, 895 [עש II]; *DCH* 6:616 [עש VI]; Mays, *Hosea*, 85; Wolff, *Hosea*, 104; Jeremias, *Prophet Hosea*, 78; Eidevall, *Grapes in the Desert*, 83–84; Seifert, *Metaphorisches Reden*, 157), or "rot" (HCSB, NJPS). LXX and Syr. found the word challenging, rendering it as "trouble" or "confusion." For a discussion of the difficulties, see Macintosh, *Critical and Exegetical Commentary*, 207.

Often arguments for "rot" appeal to synonymous parallelism with רקב; Rudolph argues for "pus" because "moth" presupposes Israel is a garment, though the context concerns sickness of the body. See Wilhelm Rudolph, *Hosea*, KAT 13/1 (Stuttgart: Mohn, 1966), 123–24. Given Hosea's propensity for diverse and contrasting images, I do not find these arguments convincing. The common meaning of עש is "moth," it co-occurs with רקב in Job 13:28, and this fits with the variety of images depicting a variety of destructive means at Yahweh's disposal.

101. Some claim this is a proper name ("King Jareb"; LXX) or place (Syr.). More likely, "Great King" refers to the king of Assyria (see 2 Kgs 18:19; so *CTAT*, 524–26; *BHQ*, 59–60*; Pentiuc et al., *Hosea*, 159; Macintosh, *Critical and Exegetical Commentary*, 209–10; Tully, *Hosea*, 131). The phrase recurs in Hos 10:6.

2. Metaphors of Accusation

But he is unable to heal you,
and he will not heal your sore.

5:14a   Direct, 2
כי אנכי כשחל לאפרים
For I am like a lion against Ephraim

5:14b–15a   Direct, 3
וככפיר לבית יהודה אני
אני אטרף ואלך אשא ואין
מציל אלך אשובה אל מקומי
and like a young lion[102] against the house of Judah.
I'm the one who will tear and go; I will carry away and there is none who can deliver [you from me].
I will go, I must[103] return to my place[104]

This cluster uniformly presents Yahweh as an angry and destructive presence. The metaphoricity of most expressions in this passage is self-evident, and most are strong metaphors. They are unusual, emphatic, and resonant.[105] The metaphors of 5:12, for instance, are "shockingly bold and abrasive, even for Hosea."[106] The stock metaphor of God as lion[107] takes on

---

102. On the two lion terms, see Strawn, *Stronger Than a Lion?*, 304–10, 322–25.

103. The cohortative may indicate resolve (Arnold and Choi; *IBHS* §34.5.1) or result ("I will go so that I may return"), or there may be no semantic difference from the preceding *yiqtol*. See Bill T. Arnold and John H. Choi, *A Guide to Biblical Hebrew Syntax* (New York: Cambridge University Press, 2003), 65.

104. Some think the lion metaphor ends in 5:14 and that 5:15a refers to Yahweh (no longer a lion) returning to his temple (see Isa 26:21, Jer 7:12, Mic 1:3); e.g., Macintosh, *Critical and Exegetical Commentary*, 214–15; see also Good, "Hosea 5:8–6:6," 279. Hosea 5:15 functions as a hinge verse (Mays, *Hosea*, 92; Eidevall, *Grapes in the Desert*, 89), without necessitating an end to the lion metaphor until after מקומי (e.g., Wolff, *Hosea*, 116; Andersen and Freedman, *Hosea*, 411; Seifert, *Metaphorisches Reden*, 161).

105. Black, "More about Metaphor," 25–26; see also pp. 20–22, above. God is compared to a moth (עש I) only here and in Ps 39:12. Nowhere else is God compared to רקב, nor the pouring of his rage to water. These are apparently unique divine metaphors in the Bible and perhaps in the ancient Near East.

106. Mays, *Hosea*, 90.

107. Lions of various kinds are used to conceptualize deities, nations, and kings. See Seifert, *Metaphorisches Reden*, 158–59; Othmar Keel, *The Symbolism of the Biblical World: Ancient Near Eastern Iconography and the Book of Psalms*, trans. Timo-

new life as it transforms a standard image into a terrifying miniature story of being ripped apart and dragged away without hope (5:14b–15a). In Isa 5:29–30, the lion is a nation far away (גוים מרחוק). In Hos 5:14, Yahweh inverts the trope of a foreign nation being the terror to Israel and is himself the terror. None, not even Assyria, can rescue (ואין מציל).

In terms of contributions to divine characterization, 5:10b emphasizes the emotional life of Yahweh, while the rest point to Yahweh's catastrophic power. The precise implications intended by 5:10b are hard to identify. Given the uniqueness and brevity of the metaphor, and the lack of any clear background,[108] perhaps this metaphor should be read on its own terms. When water is poured out, it envelops everything it touches, whether for blessing (e.g., crops) or destruction (e.g., the global flood). In an interesting twist, it is not destruction that is characterized as כמים but Yahweh's *emotion*: עברתי ("my rage"). "The image is one of a continuous stream of fury, soaking the people and the land."[109] Yahweh is not emotionally detached from Israel's betrayal (in 5:7); the greed of Judah's leaders (5:10a) has not left Yahweh unmoved. Yahweh is furious; his anger at their avarice and treachery will soon overflow. When it does, no part of Israel will be left untouched. The leaders of Judah will be submerged in Yahweh's rage.

The other four metaphors identify Yahweh as a threat, though with differing nuances. The two metaphors of 5:12 demonstrate a subtle kind of destruction. As a moth slowly and quietly eats away at a garment (Isa 51:8, Ps 39:12, Job 13:28), so God can subtly destroy the nation; as rottenness gradually eats away from the inside, so God will undermine the nation from within.[110] These metaphors characterize Yahweh as a "destructive

---

thy J. Hallett (Winona Lake, IN: Eisenbrauns, 1997), 82–86; Strawn, *Stronger Than a Lion?*; Yisca Zimran, "The Notion of God Reflected in the Lion Imagery of the Book of Hosea," *VT* 68 (2018): 149–67.

108. Andersen and Freedman suggest the global "flood tradition" as background (*Hosea*, 408); Wolff suggests "the rushing waters of the torrential winter rains" (*Hosea*, 114). This metaphor occurs nowhere else. When Yahweh's wrath is poured out *like* something, it is usually like fire (Jer 7:20, 44:6, Lam 2:4, Ezek 21:36). Other entities characterized as כמים include the glory of Yahweh (Isa 11:9, Hab 2:14) and justice (משפט, Amos 5:24). On the biblical conceptual metaphor of "emotion is a fluid in a container," see Basson, "Metaphorical Source Domains," 123–24.

109. Haddox, *Metaphor and Masculinity in Hosea*, 127.

110. Eidevall, *Grapes in the Desert*, 84.

immanence."[111] On the other hand, God can also—like a lion—act as an external force to decisively and violently ravage the nation. Any glimmer of hope is dashed when Yahweh confirms that no deliverer exists who can save them (ואין מציל, 5:14), just as there is no healer in 5:13. Yahweh the lion victoriously returns to its place (5:15a). He awaits Israel seeking him out, but he is never sought (see 7:10, 10:12). Or, paradoxically, he is not found when sought because he withdraws (5:6).[112]

Since God presents himself in the immediately surrounding verses (5:12, 14) as an afflictive presence, the illness and healing metaphors of 5:13 take on suggestive connotations. God is the *cause* of their health problems. As none can deliver from Yahweh (5:14), so none can heal the wounds Yahweh inflicts (5:12, 14–15; 6:1). Hosea 5:13 underscores the futility of seeking another healer, since Yahweh is Israel's only proper healer.[113] God as healer will be analyzed in its more explicit form in 14:5.[114]

Hosea 5:13 also demonstrates, for the first time overtly in Hos 4–14, that Yahweh contends not only with other deities for the devotion of his people but with other nations as well.[115] Yahweh is betrayed by religious

---

111. Landy, *Hosea*, 76.

112. Fisch, *Poetry with a Purpose*, 141–44; Landy, *Hosea*, 78; Eidevall, *Grapes in the Desert*, 248–52.

113. A deity can be both a healer and the cause of illness (see, e.g., Deut 32:39). Haddox points to the curses of the Esarhaddon Succession Treaty, where the god Gula, "the great physician," will bring sickness. See *Metaphor and Masculinity in Hosea*, 208–9 n. 61, citing Simo Parpola and Kazuko Watanabe, *Neo-Assyrian Treaties and Loyalty Oaths*, SAA 2 (Winona Lake, IN: Eisenbrauns, 1988), 48. This is also true of Marduk (Hamilton, "History," 111, citing *Ludlul bēl nēmeqi* in COS 1.153:487).

114. For more on God as the cause of their illness, and on ancient Near Eastern sickness, medicine, and healing practices, see Walker, "Metaphor of Healing," 18–42, esp. 74–101; Seong-Hyuk Hong, *The Metaphor of Illness and Healing in Hosea and Its Significance in the Socio-economic Context of Eighth-Century Israel and Judah*, StBL 95 (New York: Lang, 2006), 33–89, esp. 50–53; JoAnn Scurlock, *Sourcebook for Ancient Mesopotamian Medicine*, WAW 36 (Atlanta: SBL Press, 2014). Katherine Southwood points out the associations of illness with social stigma. See Southwood, "Metaphor, Illness, and Identity in Psalms 88 and 102," *JSOT* 43 (2018): 230. Perhaps this metaphor also entails shame, extending that implication from cluster 1.

115. See 7:11, 8:9, 10:13; Eidevall, *Grapes in the Desert*, 86; Seifert, *Metaphorisches Reden*, 261. See Jer 30:12–17 for similar metaphors of healing from Yahweh and wounds symbolizing iniquities and the "illnesses of empire." See Walter Brueggemann, "The 'Uncared for' Now Cared for [Jer 30:12–17]: A Methodological Consideration," *JBL* 104 (1985): 420.

apostasy but also by political disloyalty (see 8:9–10),[116] as Israel relies on the strength of other nations instead of on their God (see 14:4). Yahweh will not tolerate dependence on other suzerains.[117]

This cluster shows that God is extremely angry and the cause of Israel's present lack of health. Consequently, danger is imminent and destruction is certain. The Lord has a few strategic options for *how* to cause their devastation (e.g., moth or lion), but whenever and however he chooses to take action against Israel, it will be decisive. There can be no doubt that the intended response (perlocutionary force) to these metaphors is terror that leads to repentance.[118] The pericope ends in an implicit nonmetaphorical invitation to repentance: Yahweh waits *until* Israel recognizes their guilt and truly seeks Yahweh (עד אשר יאשמו ובקשו פני בצר להם ישחרנני).[119] Even as the devouring lion, "YHWH's withdrawal can thus be interpreted as part of a divine strategy to provoke repentance."[120]

---

116. Most commentators agree that 8:9–10 refers to political alliances. See also William L. Moran, "Ancient Near Eastern Background of the Love of God in Deuteronomy," *CBQ* 25 (1963): 77–87; Peggy Day, "A Prostitute Unlike Women: Whoring as Metaphoric Vehicle for Foreign Alliances," in Moore and Kelle, *Israel's Prophets and Israel's Past*, 167–73, esp. 169 for ancient Near Eastern data.

117. Eidevall, *Grapes in the Desert*, 87 n. 50; Zimran, "Notion of God," 166; see further pp. 215–17 ("The Exclusive Sovereign"), below.

118. Walter J. Houston, "What Did the Prophets Think They Were Doing? Speech Acts and Prophetic Discourse in the Old Testament," *BibInt* 1 (1993): 167–88; see further ch. 7, below (esp. p. 191).

119. יאשמו should be understood as *acknowledging* or *feeling* guilt. See NJPS, NRSV; *HALOT*, 95–96; *DCH* 1:414; Andersen and Freedman, *Hosea*, 416; Jacob Milgrom, *Leviticus 1–16*, AB 3 (New Haven: Yale University Press, 1998), 339; Gruber, *Hosea*, 279–80. Seeking Yahweh diligently (ישחרנני) or truthfully (as in Hos 12:7, 14:2–3) contrasts to Israel's current practice of seeking Yahweh duplicitously (e.g., 7:14a, 8:2). Seeking to avoid speculating on internal psychological processes in ancient repentance, Lambert renders "till they are utterly destitute on account of their guilt." See David Lambert, *How Repentance Became Biblical: Judaism, Christianity, and the Interpretation of Scripture* (Oxford: Oxford University Press, 2015), 80. For a critique, see Dennis T. Olson, "Emotion, Repentance, and the Question of the 'Inner Life' of Biblical Israelites: A Case Study in Hosea 6:1–3," in *Mixed Feelings and Vexed Passions: Exploring Emotions in Biblical Literature*, ed. F. Scott Spencer, RBS 90 (Atlanta: SBL Press, 2017), 167.

120. Eidevall, *Grapes in the Desert*, 90; see also Mays, *Hosea*, 92; Seifert, *Metaphorisches Reden*, 161; Macintosh, *Critical and Exegetical Commentary*, 214–15; Emmanuel O. Nwaoru, *Imagery in the Prophecy of Hosea*, ÄAT 41 (Wiesbaden: Harrassowitz, 1999), 73.

Cluster 4: Hosea 6:1–3

Here the characterization of Yahweh shifts dramatically. Excepting two brief allusions to 5:14–15 in 6:1 (טרף and יד), the portrait in these three verses is overwhelmingly positive and hopeful—a stark contrast to the assured devastation and rage of the preceding six verses.[121]

The shift in perspective reflects a shift in speaker. In 5:10–15, Yahweh is the speaker. Hosea 6:1 begins with two first-person-plural volitive verbs, invitations to go and return to Yahweh (לכו ונשובה), which mirror Yahweh's desire to go and return (אלך אשובה, 5:15). The verses are an invitation to the people spoken by a cultic representative, designed to appease the deity without making cultic, sociopolitical, or ethical changes, and lacking any acknowledgment of guilt (contra the demand in 5:15).[122] Harold Fisch notes that the lines (6:1–3) are "too smooth.... It is all a good deal too pat," which suggests "that we need only go through the motions of 'seeking God' and the reward is 'in the bag.'"[123] The ancient world was a highly religious context. As M. Daniel Carroll R. notes, "The

---

121. For a more detailed explication of my understanding of the rhetorical dynamics between 6:1–3 and 6:4–6, see Mason D. Lancaster and Adam E. Miglio, "Lord of the Storm and Oracular Decisions: Competing Construals of Storm God Imagery in Hosea 6:1–6," *VT* 70 (2020): 634–44.

122. Much debate surrounds who is speaking in these verses. For surveys of views concerning the identity of the speaker, see Macintosh, *Critical and Exegetical Commentary*, 216–19; Ben Zvi, *Hosea*, 134–35; Felipe Fruto Ramirez, "A Love like a Morning Mist: Hosea 5:15–6:6," *Landas* 27 (2013): 107–8. Some understand 6:1–3 to be the words of Hosea inviting a return to God, whether in the present (Eidevall, Garrett, Moon) or future (Yee [through a postexilic redactor], Macintosh). See Eidevall, *Grapes in the Desert*, 93; Duane A. Garrett, *Hosea, Joel*, NAC 19A (Nashville: Holman Reference, 1997), 156; Moon, *Hosea*, 114; Gale A. Yee, *Composition and Tradition in the Book of Hosea: A Redaction Critical Investigation*, SBLDS 102 (Atlanta: Scholars Press, 1987), 146–52; Macintosh, *Critical and Exegetical Commentary*, 217. Ramirez understands the invitation to be the people's genuine desire, which is accepted by Yahweh ("Love like a Morning Mist," 128). In support of the view held here, see LXX and Tg. Neb., which introduce 6:1 with plural forms of "saying" (λέγοντες, יימרון), indicating 6:1–3 is the response of the people; Edmond Jacob, "Osée," in *Osée, Joël, Abdias, Jonas, Amos*, CAT 11a (Neuchâtel: Delachaux & Niestlé, 1965), 51–52; Wolff, *Hosea*, 116–17; Jeremias, *Prophet Hosea*, 84; Landy, *Hosea*, 78–81; Seifert, *Metaphorisches Reden*, 161–64, 258; Ben Zvi, *Hosea*, 145; Boda, *Severe Mercy*, 299–301; Gruber, *Hosea*, 287.

123. Fisch, *Poetry with a Purpose*, 150; see also Alt, "Hosea 5,8–6,6," 185; Good, "Hosea 5:8–6:6," 280; Olson, "Emotion, Repentance, and the Question," 162, 166–67.

mere fact, therefore, that Israel mouths proper jargon is no proof of a true commitment to change."[124] William Harper summarizes that Israel had "a conception of Yahweh so false and an idea of repentance so inadequate as to make the whole action a farce."[125]

As such, the liturgical cry is rejected by Yahweh in 6:4–6 because their loyalty (חסד) is ephemeral.[126] Like the fleeting dew (6:4), it does not last. Instead, Yahweh reiterates his desires for lasting חסד ("commitment") and דעת אלהים ("acknowledgment of God" [6:6]). The prayer shows that "the people remain trapped in a religiosity that believes it can bend God to its will."[127] These are the metaphors that the people use of God.

6:1b   Direct, 2
כי הוא טרף
because he has mauled,[128]

6:1b   Direct, 2
וירפאנו
but he will heal us;

6:1c   Direct, 2
יך
he struck,[129]

6:1c   Direct, 2
ויחבשנו

---

124. M. Daniel Carroll R., "The Prophetic Denunciation of Religion in Hosea 4–7," *CTR* 7 (1993): 34.
125. William R. Harper, *A Critical and Exegetical Commentary on Amos and Hosea*, ICC (Edinburgh: T&T Clark, 1905), 281.
126. Lambert thinks the request is rejected because it is late, not disingenuous (*How Repentance Became Biblical*, 80–81).
127. Seifert, *Metaphorisches Reden*, 164, my trans.
128. See Macintosh, *Critical and Exegetical Commentary*, 216, for "mauled."
129. The shortened prefix form is often assumed to be an error (see Syr.), and is emended in a variety of ways, usually by adding a prefix *wāw*, thus converting to a past tense *wayyiqtol* (see BHS). But the MT can be retained (BHQ, 60*; LXX; Vulg.) and read as a completed (if preterite from *yaqtul*; Tully, *Hosea*, 137) or repetitive (if imperfective aspect *yiqtol*) striking in the past (*BHRG* §§19.3.3, 19.3.6; *IBHS* §31.2.b) or into the present (*BHRG* §19.3.4; *IBHS* §31.3.b).

2. Metaphors of Accusation

but he will bind us up.

6:2a   Direct, 2

יחינו מימים

He will revive us on the second day;

6:2b–6:3a   Direct, 2

ביום השלישי יקמנו ונחיה לפניו ונדעה

on the third day he will raise us, so that we might live before him and know him.[130]

6:3b   Direct, 2

כשחר נכון מוצאו

Like the dawn his coming forth is assured;

6:3c   Direct, 2

ויבוא כגשם לנו

and he will come like early rain to us,

6:3d   Direct, 2

כמלקוש יורה ארץ

as the late rain which waters the land.

The first six metaphors (6:1–3a) concern the domains of wounds and healing. Of those, two (יד ... כי הוא טרף) demonstrate the people's awareness of Yahweh as a lion who strikes them, while the remaining four express their confidence that Yahweh will be their healer or reviver. The next three metaphors invoke meteorological imagery to reflect Israel's certainty of Yahweh's life-giving presence.

The collocation יקמנו ונחיה in 6:2 has long been a *crux interpretum*. This study understands the word pair to describe resurrection from the dead.[131] The notion may have its roots in the dying-and-rising-god motif

---

130. For the inclusion of ונדעה, ignoring the MT's *silluq*, see *BHS*; Tully, *Hosea*, 137–38.

131. Bertrand Casimis Pryce, "The Resurrection Motif in Hosea 5:8–6:6: An Exegetical Study" (PhD diss., Andrews University, 1989), esp. 301–7; John Day, *Yahweh and the Gods and Goddesses of Canaan*, JSOTSup 265 (London: Sheffield Academic, 2002), 116–22; Dearman, *Book of Hosea*, 193–94; Moon, *Hosea*, 115. Others argue

in the ancient world, if such a tradition existed.[132] The hermeneutical move of this prayer is to appeal to a god who has himself died and risen, on the assumption that the deity then has the power to do the same for the nation. The prayer is thus a self-condemnation: the people do not think rightly of Yahweh, who was not a dying-and-rising deity, but in terms of Baal, who was.[133]

---

the word pair refers strictly to healing, not resurrection—e.g., Rudolph, *Hosea*, 135; Mays, *Hosea*, 95; Wolff, *Hosea*, 117; Michael L. Barré, "New Light on the Interpretation of Hosea 6:2," *VT* 28 (1978): 129–41; Graham I. Davies, *Hosea*, OTG 25 (Sheffield: Sheffield Academic, 1993), 161; Macintosh, *Critical and Exegetical Commentary*, 222. Every other occurrence of the two verbs together (2 Kgs 8:1; 13:21; Isa 26:14, 19; Job 14:12, 14) unambiguously refers to resurrection from the dead, except for Gen 43:8, where the construction is different. Indeed, "no healing context has been found in the Hebrew Bible where these paired verbs are employed" (Pryce, "Resurrection Motif," 302). On resurrection as an extension of healing because life and death reside on a spectrum, see Barré, "New Light," 137; Pryce, "Resurrection Motif," 42–43, 306.

132. E.g., Klaas Spronk, *Beatific Afterlife in Ancient Israel and in the Ancient Near East*, AOAT 219 (Neukirchen-Vluyn: Neukirchener, 1986), 276; Marjo Christina Annette Korpel, *A Rift in the Clouds: Ugaritic and Hebrew Descriptions of the Divine*, UBL 8 (Münster: Ugarit-Verlag, 1990), 319–20; Day, *Yahweh and the Gods*, 117–18, 122; Gruber, *Hosea*, 283. The concept can rely on this tradition without verbal correspondence; dying-and-rising-god traditions never use the word pair חיה and קום or their cognates (Barré, "New Light," 137). Others deny this background in Hosea (e.g., Mays, *Hosea*, 95; Eidevall, *Grapes in the Desert*, 93–94). Smith denies the existence of the tradition altogether. See Mark S. Smith, *The Origins of Biblical Monotheism: Israel's Polytheistic Background and the Ugaritic Texts* (New York: Oxford University Press, 2003), 104–31, esp. 120–30.

133. See n. 132, above. As the first, but certainly not the last, comparison between Baal and Yahweh in Hos 4–14, a few comments are in order about the comparative use of Baal or storm gods with respect to Hosea and my presuppositions behind such comparisons. On the legitimacy of using Ugaritic material on Baal for elucidating prophetic indictments, see Paul Layton Watson, "Mot, the God of Death, at Ugarit and in the Old Testament" (PhD diss., Yale University, 1970), 225–27, 243; Edward L. Greenstein, "The God of Israel and the Gods of Canaan: How Different Were They?," in *Proceedings of the Twelfth World Congress of Jewish Studies: Jerusalem, July 29–August 5, 1997; Division A: The Bible and Its World*, ed. Ron Margolin (Jerusalem: World Union of Jewish Studies, 1999), 47–58. On the association of certain traits with a central conception of a deity, despite variation in divine ideas over time and space, see Mark S. Smith, *God in Translation: Deities in Cross-cultural Discourse in the Biblical World* (Grand Rapids: Eerdmans, 2008); Spencer L. Allen, "The Splintered Divine: A Study of Ištar, Baal, and Yahweh Divine Names and Divine Multiplicity in the Ancient Near East" (PhD diss., University of Pennsylvania, 2011); Aren M. Wilson-Wright, *Athtart:*

To what does the resurrection metaphor refer? The target domain is uncertain. Some argue that it refers to covenant renewal.[134] Others think

---

The Transmission and Transformation of a Goddess in the Late Bronze Age, FAT 2/90 (Tübingen: Mohr Siebeck, 2016).
  Some have argued that Hosea's allegation of a Baal cult contravenes the historical and biblical (2 Kgs 10:28) evidence. E.g., Jeffrey H. Tigay, *You Shall Have No Other Gods: Israelite Religion in the Light of Hebrew Inscriptions*, HSS 31 (Atlanta: Scholars Press, 1986); Tigay, "Israelite Religion: The Onomastic and Epigraphic Evidence," in *Ancient Israelite Religion: Essays in Honor of Frank Moore Cross*, ed. Patrick Miller, Paul Hanson, and S. Dean McBride (Philadelphia: Fortress, 1987), 157–94; Kelle, *Hosea 2*, 137–52, which includes a survey of views; Lim and Castelo, *Hosea*, 52–53; Irvine, "Hosea," 408. In response, see Andrew King, "Did Jehu Destroy Baal from Israel? A Contextual Reading of Jehu's Revolt," *BBR* 27 (2017): 309–32; see also J. Andrew Dearman, "Baal in Israel: The Contribution of Some Place Names and Personal Names to an Understanding of Early Israelite Religion," in *History and Interpretation: Essays in Honour of John H. Hayes*, ed. M. Patrick Graham, William P. Brown, and Jeffrey K. Kuan, JSOTSup 173 (Sheffield: JSOT, 1993), 173–91; Dearman, "Interpreting the Religious Polemics against Baal and the Baalim in the Book of Hosea," *OTE* 14 (2001): 9–25; John Day, "Hosea and the Baal Cult," in *Prophecy and the Prophets in Ancient Israel*, ed. John Day, LHBOTS 531 (New York: T&T Clark, 2010), 202–24; Dearman, *Book of Hosea*, 349–52. For a summary of the three main views on the nature of Hosea's Baal polemic, see Abma, *Bonds of Love*, 195–202. The view taken here is what Abma calls the "revised" view (variants held by Lemche, Jeremias, Lang, and Abma), in which the book represents an intra-Israelite theological clash between those who worship a Baalized Yahweh versus Hosea's more distinct Yahwistic theology. Two additional views may be added: Keefe thinks "Baal" and "lovers" in Hos 1–2 refer to socioeconomic systems (*Woman's Body*, 122–34), while Kelle argues they refer to foreign alliances (*Hosea 2*; so also Irvine, "Hosea," 409–10). On the religion that Hosea attacks, see Paul A. Kruger, "Yahweh and the Gods in Hosea," *JSem* 4 (1992): 81–97; Jörg Jeremias, "Der Begriff 'Baal' im Hoseabuch und seine Wirkungsgeschichte," in *Ein Gott allein? JHWH-Verehrung und biblischer Monotheismus im Kontext der israelitischen und altorientalischen Religionsgeschichte*, ed. Walter Dietrich and Martin A. Klopfenstein (Freiburg: Universitätsverlag, 1994), 441–62; Seifert, *Metaphorisches Reden*, 243–50, esp. 247–50; Dany Nocquet, *Le "livret noir de Baal": La polémique contre le dieu Baal dans la Bible hébraïque et l'ancien Israël* (Geneva: Labor et Fides, 2004), 278–81, 287, 297–99. On Yahweh as not a dying-and-rising deity, see Alberto R. W. Green, *The Storm-God in the Ancient Near East*, BibJudStud 8 (Winona Lake, IN: Eisenbrauns, 2003), 280.
  134. John Wijngaards, "Death and Resurrection in Covenantal Context (Hos 6:2)," *VT* 17 (1967): 226–39; Jerzy Chmiel, "Un kérygme prophétique ou une liturgie de repentance en Osée 6,1–6?," *AnCrac* 15 (1983): 99–104. Barré allows that this "*may*" be a possible "secondary" or "applied" level of meaning ("New Light," 136, emphasis original).

it describes restoration after exile.[135] If 5:10–15 suggests exile through the images of death and destruction and 6:1–3 does not mention guilt or covenant (though see 6:7), perhaps restoration from exile is the more likely referent. This metaphor's contribution to a portrait of Yahweh, however, does not depend on a firm decision. Yahweh is the one with power over death, who can raise the nation back to life, whether into renewed covenantal life or restoration from exile.

The final three metaphors (6:3) express the people's total confidence in the assurance and manner of God's coming to them. The basis of the people's hope is their confidence that Yahweh's presence among them will be a good thing. Yahweh will not be far off (contra 5:6, 15) but will certainly come to them, just as dependably as the sun rises each morning. When Yahweh comes, his coming will not be in devastation and judgment (contra 5:8–15) but as refreshing showers (כגשם) and late seasonal rains that water the earth (כמלקוש יורה ארץ).

Israel's metaphors used to describe Yahweh reflect a highly baal-ized conception of deity. Most aspects of Israel's description of Yahweh—Yahweh's ability to heal in 6:1–2 (on the basis of being a dying-and-rising god), and the ascription of meteorological terms to Yahweh in 6:3[136]—are reminiscent of Baal mythology. That the book explicitly attacks Baal throughout suggests that the metaphors are appropriations of Baal attributes. But the people's appropriation is not polemical.[137] They are so thoroughly com-

---

135. Andersen and Freedman, *Hosea*, 418–20; Pryce, "Resurrection Motif"; Eidevall, *Grapes in the Desert*, 95; Day, *Yahweh and the Gods*, 117.

136. "In Ugarit Ba'lu is the absolute master of all types of precipitation" (Korpel, *Rift in the Clouds*, 611). On storm, thunder, and cloud imagery for Baal, see James S. Anderson, *Monotheism and Yahweh's Appropriation of Baal*, LHBOTS 617 (London: T&T Clark, 2015), 86–88. For the common association between storm gods and sun gods of justice such as Shamash (see 6:5), see Lancaster and Miglio, "Lord of the Storm," 639–41. Baal was "the great healer [rp'u] among the gods" (Korpel, *Rift in the Clouds*, 332). See also Manfried Dietrich and Oswald Loretz, "Baal RPU in KTU 1.108; 1.113 und nach 1.17 VI 25-33," *UF* 12 (1980): 171–82; Wolfgang Herrmann, "Baal," *DDD*, 135; Anderson, *Monotheism and Yahweh's Appropriation of Baal*, 90–92. See, e.g., *KTU* 1.17.VI.30 (= *COS* 1.103:343–57). On Baal's ability to raise the dead, see *KTU* 1.10.I.10; 1.21.II.6, though both are unreliable. Baal's healing ability was no doubt connected to his role as a fertility god.

137. Contra Anderson, *Monotheism and Yahweh's Appropriation*, 81, who reads 6:1–3 as the words of Hosea/Yahweh and therefore as a polemical appropriation.

promised that they can conceive of deity only in terms of Baal.¹³⁸ Based on iconographic evidence, Othmar Keel and Christoph Uehlinger comment that in Hos 6:3

> Yahweh's appearance is connected directly with sunrise and rain, which means that Yahweh is portrayed in the same role in which Baalshamem is depicted, against whom or against whose local representations the book of Hosea directs so vigorous a polemic.... Ultimately, the reason appears to have had much more to do with the fact that the two gods were nearly indistinguishable in eighth-century Israel, fulfilling the same functions and roles and being conceived of using the same categories.¹³⁹

Their argument can be sustained with the specification that the two deities were indistinguishable *to the people and their priests* (who are speaking in 6:1–3), but not to Hosea. Hosea recognizes the difference and does *not* conceive of them in the same categories, apart from instances of polemical appropriation. This distinction between Hosea's and the people's perceptions explains *both* halves of Keel and Uehlinger's seemingly paradoxical observation: Hosea can mount such a vigorous polemic, and the two gods were apparently indistinguishable in 6:1–3 and in that material culture.

Cluster 5: Hosea 6:5–7

6:5a   Direct, 3
על כן חצבתי בנביאים
Therefore I have hewn [them] using¹⁴⁰ the prophets;

---

138. Jeremias, *Prophet Hosea*, 86; Fisch, *Poetry with a Purpose*, 150–51; Seifert, *Metaphorisches Reden*, 258.

139. Othmar Keel and Christoph Uehlinger, *Gods, Goddesses, and Images of God in Ancient Israel*, trans. Thomas H. Trapp (Minneapolis: Fortress, 1998), 261.

140. Some take בנביאים as the object of the verb (LXX; Syr.; ibn Ezra; Gruber, *Hosea*, 291; NJPS; see also GKC §119.k; *IBHS* §11.2.5.f). Others, as here, take it as the instrumental means of the verb (Tg. Neb.; Rashi; Wolff, *Hosea*, 105; Jeremias, *Prophet Hosea*, 79; Ben Zvi, *Hosea*, 146; Seifert, *Metaphorisches Reden*, 150; Eidevall, *Grapes in the Desert*, 98; Macintosh, *Critical and Exegetical Commentary*, 230; NRSV, JPS; see also GKC §119.o; *IBHS* §11.2.5.d). חצב appears to never require a ב on the object, though a ב is used instrumentally in Isa 10:15. Note also the parallelism with the next clause and Yahweh using instruments (see Landy, *Hosea*, 75). Hosea 12:11 (וביד

6:5b   Direct, 3

הרגתים באמרי פי

I have killed them with the words of my mouth.

6:5c   Direct, 3

ומשפטי כאור יצא [141]

And my verdict goes forth like light

6:7a   Indirect, 2

והמה כאדם עברו ברית

Yet like [the city of] Adam,[142] they transgressed a covenant;

6:7b   Direct, 3

שם בגדו בי

there they betrayed me.

הנביאים אדמה) may echo this idea, if אדמה is "I will bring destruction" (NRSV; דמה III; see Hos 4:5, 6; 10:7, 15) rather than "I spoke parables" (CEB, NJPS, RSV; from דמה I).

141. MT reads ומשפטיך אור יצא; reflected in Vulg.; NJPS; Macintosh, *Critical and Exegetical Commentary*, 230–33. The modified word division (כ prefixed to אור instead of suffixed to ומשפטי) is reflected in LXX; Tg. Neb.; Syr.; BHS; CTAT, 526–27; BHQ, 60*; and most commentaries and translations.

142. אדם is a location (NRSV), perhaps the place mentioned in Josh 3:16. Using six locative terms, Hos 6:7–10 explicitly identifies this betrayal with historical and geographical specifics. Mays refers to this passage as a "geography of treachery" (*Hosea*, 99). For a suggestion of the historical background to the events related in this verse, see Macintosh, *Critical and Exegetical Commentary*, 237–39. Emendation to באדם is unnecessary. The כ still indicates comparison but refers to the inhabitants of the town collectively (see BHQ, 60*), hence "they [Hosea's contemporaries?], like [the town/inhabitants] of Adam, transgressed a covenant." Referring obliquely to the place name would be consistent with Hosea's pattern of citing a location as a trigger alluding to a historical tradition, then reworking the alluded tradition. See Cooper Smith, "The 'Wilderness' in Hosea and Deuteronomy: A Case of Thematic Reappropriation," *BBR* 28 (2018): 256. There are other viable interpretations (see NJPS), but a reference to the primordial Adam of Genesis is unlikely (though an early view; see Lam. Rab. 4.1; b. Sanh. 38b[2]). For surveys of views, see Macintosh, *Critical and Exegetical Commentary*, 236–37; Gruber, *Hosea*, 295–97. In support of the man of Genesis, see Brian C. Habig, "Hosea 6:7 Revisited," *Presb* 42 (2016): 4–20. Whether read as person or place, the verse indicates that "Israel has been a covenant violator from the very beginning" (Lim and Castelo, *Hosea*, 136).

2. Metaphors of Accusation

Hosea counters Israel's vision of God with Yahweh's pointed rebuttal. Yahweh asks, "What am I to do with you?" (מה אעשה לך) because—turning the people's meteorological metaphors against them—their חסד is like the morning clouds and evaporating dew (כענן בקר וכטל משכים הלך, 6:4). Yahweh outlines what he truly desires: loyal commitment (חסד) and proper acknowledgment (ודעת אלהים, 6:6). In 6:5, Yahweh deploys three metaphors of his own in stark contrast to those of 6:1–3. *Because* of Israel's actions (על כן), the deity will cut down (חצבתי) the people through the prophets (בנביאים) and kill them with his word (באמרי פי). The light metaphor signals that Yahweh's actions will be vindicated as a fair treatment of a rebellious people.[143] Notably, all three metaphors of 6:5, as well as the images in 6:4, reflect storm-god imagery, but of a very different sort from in 6:1–3.[144] The metaphors highlight divine aspects of violence and justified judgment, resulting in death and suffering.

Hosea 6:7 combines two previous metaphorical concepts: breaking a covenant (עברו ברית, echoing the ריב in 4:1) and betrayal (בגדו בי, echoing ביהוה בגדו in 5:7). One finds explicit correlation of what was previously only assumed: to betray Yahweh (6:7b) *is* to break a ברית (6:7a).[145] That mutual agreement is presumably Yahweh's תורה referred to elsewhere (the notions of betrayal and covenant have been explored at length above).[146] The two metaphors of 6:7 underscore the *reason* for the terrifying pictures

---

143. This reading of the metaphor (Davies, *Hosea* [1993], 169; see also Eidevall, *Grapes in the Desert*, 98) is based on the similar metaphor in Ps 37:6: והוציא כאור צדקך ומשפטך כצהרים. Light is used as a metaphor to justify the actions and oracle of Judge Yahweh (Lancaster and Miglio, "Lord of the Storm," 641).

144. Lancaster and Miglio, "Lord of the Storm."

145. 4Q167 (Pesher Hosea[b]) 7–8 affirms this interpretation of עברו ברית when it interprets 6:7a as עזבו את אל ו[י]לכו בחוקות, "*they abandoned God* and followed the laws of …" (remainder of phrase missing).

146. See also 8:1, where the terms are combined in so-called synonymous parallelism (יען עברו בריתי ועל תורתי פשעו); see 4:6, 8:12. Wolff clarifies that "this disclosure of Yahweh's will [תורה] … is not a presupposition of the covenant, but a consequence of it" (*Hosea*, 138). Macintosh grants that his assumption that 6:7 "speaks of Yahweh's covenant with Israel" "is far from certain" (*Critical and Exegetical Commentary*, 237). The first-person suffixes (תורתי, בריתי) and the following clause (שם בגדו בי) confirm that regardless of *which* covenant is in view, it is necessarily a covenant *with Yahweh*. Yahweh is the one betrayed in the breaking of this covenant (so Wolff, *Hosea*, 121–22; Andersen and Freedman, *Hosea*, 439; Davies, *Hosea* [1993], 171–72; Eidevall, *Grapes in the Desert*, 105; Sweeney, *Twelve Prophets* 1:84–87; see also Neef, *Heilstraditionen*, 142–55; Nissinen, *Prophetie*, 199–202).

of Yahweh in 5:10–15 and 6:4–6. Yahweh is judge, jury, and executioner in response to Israel's fickle betrayal outlined in 6:4–6.[147]

Analyzing Their Interaction

Despite the internal consistency of divine portrayals within each of the three clusters, the first and third stand in striking contrast to the second, resulting in two mutually exclusive pictures of Yahweh and Israel.[148] The difference in portraits is explained by the shift in speakers: the second unit resides on a different speaker conceptual plane from the other two, therefore on a distinct belief-related conceptual plane as well.[149] One view (clusters 3 and 5) is Hosea's, the other (cluster 4) Israel's. The two competing metaphorical claims are as follows:

1. Hosea: Yahweh's equitable judgment means death for Israel, because Israel is prone to betray Yahweh with their unethical behavior (politically, religiously, socially).
2. Israel: Yahweh may have once struck Israel, but Yahweh will dependably restore Israel (without a meaningful change in their behavior?).

These competing characterizations are illustrated in the three panels of figure 2.1: Competing divine portraits of clusters 3–5 (pp. 73–75).

In Hosea's conception, there is no mention of hope of restoration; judgment is fair and imminent. In Israel's conception, there is no mention of culpability or a meaningful change in their behavior; restoration is imminent. Notably, the invitation (6:1–3) and Yahweh's response (6:4–6) both use storm god imagery, but of very different kinds.[150]

---

147. Good argues for a lawsuit metaphor for the whole unit (5:8–6:6; see "Hosea 5:8–6:6").
148. Contra Seifert, who thinks that the metaphors or the third cluster replace those of the first (*Metaphorisches Reden*, 164). She thinks 6:4–6 presents Yahweh "in einer menschlichen Weise," worrying whether his people will recognize him. Seifert draws too sharp a distinction between these metaphors and those of 5:12–14. Though different, they offer a consistent characterization.
149. Kimmel, "Why We Mix Metaphors."
150. It has long been argued that Yahweh was originally conceived of as a storm god. Surveying a variety of views are Karel van der Toorn, "Yahweh," *DDD*, 910–19, esp. 916; Thomas Römer, *The Invention of God*, trans. Raymond Geuss (Cambridge:

2. Metaphors of Accusation   73

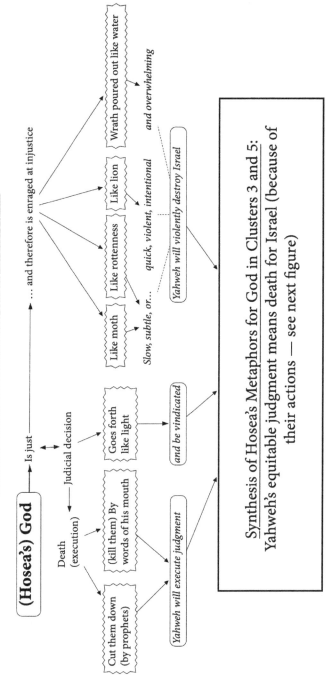

Hosea's Metaphors for Israel in Clusters 3 and 5

Israel

Leaders → Like boundary-movers

- Sick, without a healer
- Is oppressed
- Is crushed
- Like ephemeral dew
- Like morning clouds → **Israel's loyalty (חסד)**

Because חסד is fleeting, God will NOT restore (as Israel imagines)

- Deceitful
- Self-seeking
- Disloyal (to Yahweh)
- Israel suffers from its behavior (namely…)
- Israel is prone to betrayal

Religiously (=idolatry), and… politically

Synthesis of Hosea's Metaphors for Israel: Israel is prone to betray Yahweh with its unjust and unethical behavior (politically, religiously, socially)

2. Metaphors of Accusation 75

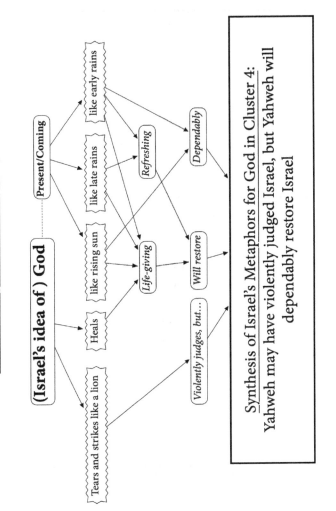

Why include conflicting images? Israel's words are a foil to Hosea's words, highlighting the vast distance between Hosea's ideas about God and Israel's:[151]

> Hosea's message is that YHWH is not the storm god who will bring life and abundance, but the storm god who will bring decisive judgment on false religiosity. In other words, the prophetic rejoinder is as if to say: "You think that I am a storm god who caters to your well-being (Hos 6:1–3)? No, I am the storm god who brings clear and certain oracles, and in the present circumstances that means judgment (Hos 6:4–6)."[152]

Yahweh subverts the people's storm-god metaphors by replacing them with different storm-god metaphors in order to condemn their worldview. This is necessary because Hosea, according to Andrew Macintosh, "was convinced that wrong perceptions of reality, of the way things were, would lead inevitably to the demise and ruin of his people and nation."[153] Whether the prophet thought this or not, metaphor scholars confirm that it is generally true that metaphors shape worldview, and worldview shapes actions.[154]

Hosea's inclusion of opposing divine portraits, then, is designed to bring about a change of action. The conflicting portrayals bring into sharp relief the difference between Israel's perception of reality and Hosea's (and Yahweh's) in the hopes that it will reorient Israel away from their dangerous ideas about Yahweh.[155] The people do not know Yahweh or their standing before Yahweh, nor the extent of their present danger. Hosea's perspective emphasizes Yahweh's judgment and Israel's

---

Harvard University Press, 2015), 32–34. Regardless of Yahweh's conceptual origins, he is portrayed here according to storm-god imagery (Lancaster and Miglio, "Lord of the Storm").

151. Nwaoru, *Imagery in the Prophecy*, 76; see also Luis Alonso Schökel, *A Manual of Hebrew Poetics*, SubBi 11 (Rome: Pontifical Biblical Institute, 1988), 174–76.

152. Lancaster and Miglio, "Lord of the Storm," 643–44.

153. Macintosh, "Hosea and the Wisdom Tradition," 125.

154. See pp. 12–14, above.

155. See Willem Boshoff, "Who Let Grain, Grapes and Olives Grow? Hosea's Polemics against the Yahwists of Israel," in *Religious Polemics in Context: Papers Presented to the Second International Conference of the Leiden Institute for the Study of Religions (LISOR) Held at Leiden, 27–28 April, 2000*, ed. Theo L. Hettema and Arie van der Kooij, STR 11 (Assen: Van Gorcum, 2004), 266.

2. Metaphors of Accusation

culpability for the rhetorical purpose of provoking repentance through terror or shame.

Cluster 6: Hosea 6:10–7:1

6:10   Indirect, 2

בבית ישראל ראיתי שעוריה שם זנות לאפרים
נטמא ישראל

In the house of Israel, I have seen something horrible:[156] there is the fornication of Ephraim;
Israel has become unclean.

6:11a   Direct, 2

גם יהודה שת קציר לך

Judah, too: he has appointed a harvest for you[157]

7:1a–c   Direct, 2

כרפאי לישראל ונגלה עון אפרים ורעות שמרון

When I would heal[158] Israel, the iniquity of Ephraim is exposed, and the evils of Samaria

Additions to previous sexual promiscuity metaphors include that here the metaphor is localized (שם, בבית ישראל) and the shameful uncleanness (נטמא) is underscored (see 5:3); it is identified as "something horrible" (שעוריה).[159] In 6:11a, Yahweh is pictured for the first time (but not the last) as a farmer, but this farmer is not benevolent

---

156. *Qere*; *ketiv* is שעריריה.

157. NJPS and Gruber understand Judah to be the subject and Israel the referent of "you"; hence it is not a metaphor for God (*Hosea*, 302–3). Most read as above.

158. Parallel with בשובי שבות עמי in 6:11b, כרפאי should be read as a temporal infinitive and adopts a modal sense in context (an "unfulfilled wish" according to Macintosh, *Critical and Exegetical Commentary*, 250). The ב in 6:11b indicates that action occurs at the same time as the main clause (Tully, *Hosea*, 152; *IBHS* §36.2.2b), while the כ in 7:1a indicates that "the temporal clause occurs immediately before the main clause" (Tully, *Hosea*, 153; *IBHS* §36.2.2b).

159. See Staubli, "Disgusting Deeds and Disgusting Gods."

or passive. Using a common metaphor (see Isa 17:5–6, Jer 51:33, Joel 4:12–14), farmer-Yahweh has appointed a harvest. It is not only the Northern Kingdom that receives his wrath; the Southern Kingdom will also be judged.[160]

The healing metaphor is reintroduced (from Hos 5:13–6:2) in 7:1a–c. For the first time, Yahweh identifies himself as a healer (previously, Assyria was *not* a healer, and the people assumed Yahweh would be their healer), yet it is not possible for Yahweh to heal Israel at this time. His healing (and restoration, 6:11b) is prevented by the referent of the metaphorical wound: the moral depravity and treachery of the nation (see 14:5), which continues to fester.

Analyzing Their Interaction

One of the interesting interactions in this cluster is the use of metaphors to coordinate logical consequences with temporal horizons. Metaphors in previous clusters tend to share the same temporal plane, *realis* state, and category of prophetic speech (i.e., indictment, punishment, or restoration). Here, though, metaphors with different planes, states, and categories intermingle. First comes a repetition of *indictment*, naming the evil of Israel's *past* deeds ("fornication," 6:10). The temporal plane and category of prophetic speech shift to a statement of *future punishment*, where Yahweh is the farmer who has set a time to cut down the crops (6:11). Finally, in 7:1, the possibility of forestalling the punishment is foreclosed. The *realis* state shifts to *irrealis* (the modal "would" of the infinitive with ב prefix), and the category of speech straddles restoration and punishment. The possibility of restoration is briefly entertained, but ultimately punishment rules the day.[161]

This cluster reflects Hosea's message in interaction with the people's changing expectations. He repeats his accusation and the inevitable consequence of punishment. As they wonder whether the prophet's message can be forestalled by their change of mind but not behavior (see Jer 18:8, Ezek 18:21), Hosea preempts their speculation with a clear answer in the nega-

---

160. Andersen and Freedman, *Hosea*, 443; Eidevall, *Grapes in the Desert*, 107; contra Stuart, who interprets the harvest as eschatological deliverance (*Hosea-Jonah*, 112).

161. It is also possible to read the infinitives and the main clause as futures (e.g., Tully, *Hosea*, 141).

2. Metaphors of Accusation

tive. God has considered the possibility of healing and restoring the people, but their sin springs up again and prevents him doing so (7:1; see 7:13b). The people are fixated on deception and betrayal. They are incapable of changing to avoid punishment (5:4, 11:7). If there is restoration, it will be on the other side of a necessary harvest. In a switch of metaphors, "like a skilled physician [Yahweh] must expose the wound and express from it all the pus and rottenness.... Only when the nation's guilt is exposed and the moral depravity to which ... they have stooped is acknowledged (v. 2) does healing become possible."[162]

Cluster 7: Hosea 7:8–8:1

7:8   Indirect, 2

אפרים בעמים הוא יתבולל
אפרים היה עגה בלי הפוכה

Ephraim is among the nations; he is mixed up.[163]
Ephraim has become an unturned cake.

7:10a   Indirect, 2

וענה גאון ישראל בפניו

The arrogance of Israel testifies against them

7:11a–b   Indirect, 2

ויהי אפרים כיונה פותה אין לב

Ephraim has become like a gullible dove, thoughtless

7:12a–b   Direct, 1

כאשר ילכו אפרוש עליהם רשתי

When they go [to Assyria; see 7:11d], I will spread my net over them;

7:12c   Direct, 1

כעוף השמים אורידם

like a bird of the sky, I will bring them down

---

162. Macintosh, *Critical and Exegetical Commentary*, 251.
163. Or "Ephraim: with the nations he is mixed" (Tully, *Hosea*, 157).

7:12d   Indirect, 1
איסרם כשמע לעדתם
I will discipline them according to the report of their assembly

7:13b   Direct, 3
שד להם כי פשעו בי
devastation is theirs, for they rebelled against me!

7:13c–d   Direct, 2
ואנכי אפדם והמה דברו עלי כזבים
And *I* would redeem[164] them, but *they* utter lies against me.

7:15a   Direct, 2
ואני יסרתי
But I, I trained—

7:15b   Direct, 2
חזקתי זרועתם
I strengthened their arms

7:16b   Indirect, 2
היו כקשת רמיה
They have become like a slack bow.

8:1c   Direct, 3
יען עברו בריתי
because they transgressed my covenant,

8:1d   Direct, 3
ועל תורתי פשעו
and revolted against my instruction.

---

164. Reading as a modal expressing desire and possibility (Macintosh, *Critical and Exegetical Commentary*, 279, following Rashi, ibn Ezra, and Kimchi; Dearman, *Book of Hosea*, 157; Tully, *Hosea*, 174; see *IBHS* §31.4.h). Some take this verb as a past-tense *yiqtol* (LXX; Gruber, *Hosea*, 327), referring to the exodus out of Egypt (see Hos 11:1; 12:10, 14; 13:4). Others assume a question (Harper, *Amos and Hosea*, 305; Wolff, *Hosea*, 104).

2. Metaphors of Accusation

This cluster is a combination of previous metaphors reused with and without modification, as well as strong new metaphors. It is also the longest cluster in the book.[165] Certain themes recur within the cluster, so the metaphors will be analyzed in six groups according to themes.

Judge of the Self-Condemned (7:10)

Hosea 7:10a is a verbatim repetition of a phrase from 5:5. The only difference is that in 5:6 the people seek Yahweh but will not find him; here they do not even bother seeking.[166]

The Fowler (7:12a)

Hosea 7:12a provides a stock metaphor of a bird being caught by a fowler. It extends the "Israel is a bird" metaphor from 7:11, but the two expressions are deployed to different ends and so should be treated separately.[167] The metaphorical scene in 7:12a has two parts: Yahweh the bird catcher throws a net over Israel the bird, then brings the bird down. This is a common metaphor for punishment across millennia throughout the ancient Near East. In a treaty, for instance, if the vassal is disobedient, the witnessing deity will bring the vassal down like a bird. Esarhaddon wishes, "May Šamaš clamp a bronze bird trap over you, (your sons and your [daught]ers); may he cast you into a trap from which there is no escape, and never let you out alive."[168] In the Mari letters, the god Dagan speaks to Babylon through a prophet about giving them over to Zimri-Lim: "I will bring you down like a bird with a net."[169] Yahweh uses similar threats against Israel in Ezekiel 12:13, 17:20, 32:3. Keel concludes that

---

165. Since the supercluster of 5:10–6:7 is technically three separate clusters due to different speaker conceptual planes.
166. Eidevall, *Grapes in the Desert*, 118.
167. So Eidevall, *Grapes in the Desert*, 119; contra Rudolph, *Hosea*, 150–51; Mays, *Hosea*, 109; Jeremias, *Prophet Hosea*, 99.
168. Esarhaddon's Succession Treaty in Parpola and Watanabe, *Neo-Assyrian Treaties and Loyalty Oaths*, 58 (line 649).
169. ARM 13.23.9–10. See Keel for more on ancient net types, hunting with nets, and the description of battles and victories using nets (*Symbolism of the Biblical World*, 89–92); Eidevall, *Grapes in the Desert*, 119 nn. 97–99.

"the net is a symbol of absolute sovereignty and control, and of ultimate world dominion."[170]

In addition to the fact that this metaphor was common in political contexts across the ancient Near East, its literary context in Hosea concerns politics and foreign alliances. Yahweh brings a net down on Israel "when they go" (כאשר ילכו, 7:12a) to Assyria (אשור הלכו, 7:11b), just as a suzerain would threaten a vassal making alternative political alliances.

From this, Eidevall deduces that "v 12 portrays YHWH as a king taking punitive measures against his own people." Eidevall's claim is not strictly true, though. He is similarly eager to deduce from the sexual promiscuity metaphors that Yahweh is a king.[171] There, as here, if subject A is described metaphorically as M (where M happens to be a source domain commonly applied to subject B), that does not mean *A is B*. A is still M. The double vision of this redeployment of a metaphor may color how one sees A *also* in terms of B, but A is still fundamentally characterized by M, the metaphorical source domain itself.

The metaphor portrays Yahweh (A) *as a fowler* (M). Though Hosea uses a metaphor (M) from political contexts (involving kings), this does not mean that God (A) is a king (B). In the ancient Near Eastern quotations above, it is, strictly speaking, the *deity* who is likened to a fowler, not the king.[172] Haddox notes, "Part of the effectiveness of this imagery is the contrast it shows between the power and wisdom of the hunting gods and the weakness of the humans, who are completely at the mercy of the gods."[173] She notes that the imagery "show[s] YHWH as unremittingly active and powerful" (like a true ancient Near Eastern male), while attacking the masculinity, and even humanity, of Hosea's elite audience.[174] Because the metaphor is used of deities and not kings, one wonders why Yahweh should be understood as a metaphorical king. Furthermore, politics and kingship are not the only contexts in which this metaphor is used. It is also used for judgment of enemies (e.g., Ps 9:16) or to describe their malicious actions (e.g., Pss 31:5, 35:7, 57:7). In lieu of any explicit evi-

---

170. Keel, *Symbolism of the Biblical World*, 90.
171. Eidevall, *Grapes in the Desert*, 61–63. See n. 25, above.
172. Even when the king Eannatum throws a net over the people of Umma, the net belongs to the god Enlil (Keel, *Symbolism of the Biblical World*, 89).
173. Haddox, *Metaphor and Masculinity in Hosea*, 107.
174. Haddox, *Metaphor and Masculinity in Hosea*, 109.

dence to the contrary, it is better to understand the metaphor as "Yahweh (the deity) is a fowler" rather than "Yahweh (further metaphor: the king) is a fowler." While Yahweh may also be seen in suzerain-like terms, the emphasis should be on the metaphor itself, which pictures Yahweh as a fowler, not a suzerain.[175]

Eidevall nonetheless grasps the essence of the fowler metaphor, saying that it "focuses unambiguously on the helplessness of small birds."[176] Israel may think they are successfully navigating the waters of international diplomacy, but in reality, Yahweh declares, Israel is nothing but an unsuspecting bird about to be trapped. Yahweh—not Israel, nor Assyria—exercises ultimate world dominion. Israel's attempts at manipulating their own political destiny cannot escape his gaze. Bird-Israel is at the mercy of fowler-Yahweh, whose hunting is decisive, whose nets are inescapable. Israel's enemy is not ultimately Assyria or any other political entity but Yahweh.[177]

Training and Support (7:12d, 15a–b [x2])

The metaphors of 7:12b and 7:15a (x2) have vague source domains. The metaphorical expressions involve discipline/training (איסרם, 7:12b; יסרתי, 7:15; both from √יסר) and strengthening their arms (חזקתי זרועתם). Possible source domains include military trainer, wisdom teacher, or parent (as an extension of wisdom teacher).[178] Because the source domains are so ambiguous, little weight should be placed on any single source domain. The sense of the metaphor is clear enough: Yahweh has taught and supported Israel and will punish them because they spurned that training and support (see 8:12, 11:1–4).

The context in which these metaphors are deployed contributes to the emotional picture of Yahweh's relationship with Israel. The two metaphors in 7:15 are followed by Israel's response to Yahweh's generous care and provision: "but *against me* they plot evil" (ואלי יחשבו רע). This pattern

---

175. If Yahweh is pictured implicitly here as a suzerain, this only underscores other metaphors that picture Yahweh as suzerain (such as three unambiguous cases in this cluster: 7:13, 8:1 [x2]).
176. Eidevall, *Grapes in the Desert*, 119.
177. Kruger, "Divine Net in Hosea 7:12," 135.
178. Eidevall, *Grapes in the Desert*, 121. See the excursus on discipline and training in Dearman, *Book of Hosea*, 159–60.

occurs twice more in context. Yahweh's consideration of redemption in 7:13 is followed by their response: "but *they* speak lies *against me*" (והמה דברו עלי כזבים). In 7:14, they do not genuinely cry out to Yahweh (ולא זעקו אלי בלבם). Three times in these verses, Yahweh's past actions are contrasted with Israel's responses, and all three times the implication is that Yahweh is unjustly spurned.[179] The metaphors underscore the imbalance in the relationship and the deeply personal nature of Israel's rebellion, which provokes God's anger and discipline. Jörg Jeremias states that in 7:13-16, "personal categories are employed that, in a theological way, point Yahweh out as the person directly affected by the offenses."[180] In 7:15, one can almost hear the mournful frustration of a selfless instructor rejected by their child or pupil. All the years of equipping Israel for a life of flourishing are met not only with heartless rejection but with the active plotting of evil against God.

The Rejected Suzerain (7:13a, 8:1c–d [x2])

Three metaphors picture Yahweh as a suzerain over a vassal who has rebelled (פשע, 7:13a, 8:1b]) and broken their mutual agreement (עברו בריתי, 8:1b). These are the only two occurrences of the "political" verb פשע in Hosea.[181] The verb is used frequently for vassal kings in rebellion against suzerains (e.g., 1 Kgs 12:19; 2 Kgs 1:1; 3:5, 7; 8:20, 22). By metaphorical extension, it is frequently used in the prophets of Israel's rebellion against Yahweh (Isa 43:27; 66:24; Jer 2:8, 29; 3:13; 33:8; Ezek 2:3; Zeph 3:11; Lam 3:42; see the noun in Amos 2:4, 6; 3:14; 5:12) and of other nations transgressing Yahweh's rule (Amos 1:3, 6, 9, 11, 13; 2:1 in noun form). In Isaiah 1:2 Israel is characterized as a rebellious child, but even then "children" may reflect the standard metaphorical term for a vassal.

Each expression has its own nuance. In Hos 7:13a, Yahweh says the people have rebelled "against me" (בי), so Yahweh decrees destruction on

---

179. Note the frequent fronting of the pronouns or prepositional phrases, emphasizing the contrast between God and Israel, and that it is *against God* whom they plot and speak.

180. Jeremias, *Prophet Hosea*, 92, my trans. Wolff claims, "Hosea regards the sum total of Israel's transgressions as a personal attack upon Yahweh, especially upon his love" (*Hosea*, 128; see also 129).

181. Jeremias, *Prophet Hosea*, 104. The substantive פשעים occurs in 14:10.

them (שד להם).[182] In 8:1d, they have revolted not against Yahweh himself but against his instruction (ועל תורתי). Hosea 8:1c augments this picture of a rebellious vassal by including the only explicit occurrence in Hosea of a ברית with Yahweh ("*my* covenant," בריתי), which Israel has transgressed (עברו). This aspect of suzerain imagery is obliquely pictured in 4:1 (the ריב) and 6:7 (ברית), but here it is explicitly affirmed to damning effect. It is because of their breach of this agreement that the invading army approaches (8:1c).[183] If one recalls the terrifying descriptions found in treaty curses[184] and takes seriously Yahweh's threat, these metaphors should result in abject terror.

The Redeemer (7:13c)

This metaphor constitutes the first use of the ransom/redeem domain (ואנכי אפדם). The verb describes taking or buying something back from another master. A person can redeem someone or something from legal, economic, political, or cultic obligations, or from death (Lev 27:29; see Hos 13:14).[185] By extension, the term can be synonymous with "save," as one

---

182. The tone is that of a lament oracle (the verse starts with אוי). The main clause שד להם lacks a verb, but contextually it is reasonably Yahweh's decree of punishment.

183. The sounding of a trumpet (אל חכך שפר) was often associated with the warning of an incoming army (see Hos 5:8). The נשר was a symbol of destruction in treaty curses, usually of an incoming army (Mays, *Hosea*, 115; Eidevall, *Grapes in the Desert*, 128, esp. n. 16; Sweeney, *Twelve Prophets* 1:85; Stuart, *Hosea–Jonah*, 130; see Deut 28:26, 49; Jer 48:40, 49:22). Tg. Neb. understands it this way: "Like *a swooping* eagle *a king will come up with his armies and encamp against the Sanctuary* of the Lord" (Cathcart and Gordon, *Targum Minor Prophets*, 45). Emmerson, on the other hand, argues that the verse should be emended and read as a cultic/prophetic proclamation to the house of the Lord. See Grace I. Emmerson, "Structure and Meaning of Hosea 8:1–3," *VT* 25 (1975): 700–710.

184. Lev 26:14–39; Deut 28:15–69 (see Stuart, *Hosea–Jonah*, xxxii–xl); Parpola and Watanabe, *Neo-Assyrian Treaties and Loyalty Oaths*, e.g., Esarhaddon's Succession Treaty, §§37–56 (lines 414–93 on pp. 45–49); Kenneth A. Kitchen and Paul J. N. Lawrence, *Treaty, Law and Covenant in the Ancient Near East: Part 1. The Texts*, vol. 1 (Wiesbaden: Harrassowitz, 2012).

185. See, e.g., the categories in *HALOT*, 912. For responsibilities of a family redeemer, see Frank Moore Cross, *From Epic to Canon: History and Literature in Ancient Israel* (Baltimore: Johns Hopkins University Press, 2000), 5; Philip King and Lawrence Stager, *Life in Biblical Israel* (Louisville: Westminster John Knox, 2002), 38–39; Christopher J. H. Wright, *The Mission of God: Unlocking the Bible's Grand Narrative* (Downers Grove, IL: IVP Academic, 2006), 265–67.

can be redeemed from enemies (Job 6:23).[186] Here Yahweh is pictured as a "kinsmen-redeemer."[187] At the very least, Yahweh is pictured as someone *capable* of redeeming Israel; whether he does so is yet to be determined.

Yahweh claims that he has *considered* taking Israel back from their oppressive masters (whether political or spiritual). But because of Israel's actions, God will not follow through (see Hos 7:1a). He *would* redeem them, but *they* uttered lies against him.[188] Yahweh is a kinsmen-redeemer who will not redeem his family member because the family member has treated him so reprehensibly. As a metaphor from the household domain, this expression may elicit more acute emotional reactions than other metaphors. The elder male family member was supposed to watch over his family. This one, though, has been slandered and betrayed, so he no longer feels the obligation to fulfill his duties. The normal familial safety net is now absent.

Three Metaphors about Useless Israel (7:8, 11, 16)

Perhaps the most unique contribution of this cluster to the characterization of Yahweh is in the least likely place: three vague and seemingly random metaphors for Israel with no obvious relation to Yahweh.

In a creative play on the baking and oven metaphors of 7:4–7, 7:8 describes Ephraim as "an unturned cake" (אפרים היה עגה בלי הפוכה), with the implication that it is burnt on one side and uncooked on the other. It is, therefore, a useless exception to what cakes are supposed to be; it is inedible.[189] As Andrew Dearman states, "No one starts the process of cooking

---

186. In Exodus, Leviticus, and Numbers, the term is used literally of people and animals. In Deuteronomy, however, it is used exclusively metaphorically, always referring to Yahweh's rescue of the nation from Egypt (7:8, 9:26, 13:6, 15:15, 21:8, 24:18).

187. NJPS renders the term as a noun: "For I was their Redeemer." If the word, as in Job 6:23, means "deliverance from physical danger" (Wolff, *Hosea*, 127; also Davies, *Hosea* [1993], 189–90), it is not a metaphor—or at least it is a *very* weak one. Eidevall seems to read it this way, as he passes over the phrase without elaboration (*Grapes in the Desert*, 120). Neither do the commentaries surveyed identify this as a metaphor.

188. Tully, *Hosea*, 174. Note the clause-initial, and therefore contrasting, pronouns.

189. Mays, *Hosea*, 108; Davies, *Hosea* [1993], 187; Eidevall, *Grapes in the Desert*, 116; Sweeney, *Twelve Prophets* 1:80; David Allan Hubbard, *Hosea*, TOTC (Downers Grove, IL: InterVarsity Press, 2009), 147. Others claim that the picture suggests Israel's return to Yahweh is still lacking (Wolff, *Hosea*, 126), or that Israel is "crusty toward Yahweh" (Stuart, *Hosea–Jonah*, 121), hasty in foreign policy (Gruber, *Hosea*, 321), or

pancakes with such a result in mind."¹⁹⁰ Extending the notion of uselessness in light of the association between baking and sexuality, Haddox claims this metaphor pictures Ephraim as "squishy" and "impotent," thus emasculating the male leadership.¹⁹¹

In 7:11a, Ephraim is a gullible and thoughtless dove (ויהי אפרים כיונה פותה אין לב). Eidevall argues, contrary to many interpreters, that doves are presented in the Old Testament and ancient Near Eastern literatures as wise creatures. This dove, then, is not a stereotypical dove but an anomaly.¹⁹² Among other abilities, doves are good navigators. Yet Ephraim could not make up its mind in foreign policy, whether it should go after Egypt or Assyria (מצרים קראו אשור הלכו, 7:11b). The nation does not know the dangerous effects of its foreign policy (7:9; see 4:14). Dove-Ephraim is a useless example of the species, an exception to the norm.

Finally, in 7:16, the people are likened to a slackened bow (היו כקשת רמיה). A bow only works properly if the string is taut. A slackened bow is incapable of achieving the reason for which it exists.¹⁹³

In all three metaphors, the portrayal of the source domain is that it does not live up to its only purpose. It is a failed version of its kind. All

---

lazy and inept (Paul). See Shalom M. Paul, "The Image of the Oven and the Cake in Hosea VII 4–10," *VT* 18 (1968): 118.

190. Dearman, *Book of Hosea*, 157.
191. Haddox, "(E)Masculinity," 195.
192. Eidevall, *Grapes in the Desert*, 118–19.
193. Wolff, *Hosea*, 128; Jeremias, *Prophet Hosea*, 101; Eidevall, *Grapes in the Desert*, 122; Macintosh, *Critical and Exegetical Commentary*, 288; Stuart, *Hosea–Jonah*, 124; Tully, *Hosea*, 178. The bow is also a common ancient Near Eastern symbol for sexual potency, hence a *slack* bow figures sexual impotency. See Shalom M. Paul, "The Shared Legacy of Sexual Metaphors and Euphemisms in Mesopotamian and Biblical Literature," in *Sex and Gender in the Ancient Near East: Proceedings of the 47th Rencontre Assyriologique Internationale*, ed. Simo Parpola and Robert M. Whiting (Helsinki: University of Helsinki Press, 2002), 489–98; Kitchen and Lawrence, *Treaty, Law and Covenant* 1:945. The taut bow also symbolized military readiness, and the slack bow was associated with dead or defeated enemy soldiers. Both connotations feminize the enemy as examples of "failed masculinity." See Cynthia R. Chapman, *The Gendered Language of Warfare in the Israelite-Assyrian Encounter*, HSM 62 (Winona Lake, IN: Eisenbrauns, 2004), 57; see 50–58, plates on 173–76; Haddox, "[E]Masculinity," 196–99; Claudia D. Bergmann, "We Have Seen the Enemy, and He Is Only a 'She': The Portrayal of Warriors as Women," *CBQ* 69 (2007): 664–68. Haddox suggests that this makes sense of the textual problem of the previous line (ישובו לא על), making it an "[im]potency image: 'They return, not "up"—they are like a slack bow!'" ("[E]Masculinity," 199).

three metaphors characterize the nation of Israel as useless (so also 8:8–9, 9:16, 10:1).[194] This implies that Yahweh has expectations for Israel—that he chose Israel for a purpose. Yet Israel fulfills neither. God's chosen instrument is worthless.[195]

What are Yahweh's expectations for Israel in these cases? The answer revolves around what is widely agreed to be the topic of 7:8–16: international politics.[196] The three metaphors in question are tightly bound to language of foreign policy. In the unturned-cake metaphor, Israel is or will be mixed among the nations (אפרים בעמים הוא יתבולל, 7:8a) and is ignorant that foreigners devour her strength (אכלו זרים כחו והוא לא ידע גם שיבה זרקה בו והוא לא ידע, 7:9). In the dove metaphor, Israel vacillates between foreign alliances (מצרים קראו אשור הלכו, 7:11b). In the bow metaphor, their leaders will bear the consequences of failed foreign policy as they fall by the sword (7:16).[197] Yahweh's expectations of allegiance involve cultic or religious loyalty (4:10–19 and elsewhere) but also political loyalty. The "illusory and godless foreign policy" of depending on other nations for safety and security is, according to Yahweh, treasonous.[198]

Analyzing Their Interaction

These metaphors intensify and nuance previous images of Yahweh—for example, as the suzerain who is coming to punish his rebellious vassal (7:10, 12a, 13; 8:1 [x2]). This is appropriate, since this is the last cluster

---

194. In Hos 8:8c, Israel is ככלי אין חפץ בו, "a useless vessel" (NRSV) or "like an object that no one wants" (Goldingay, *First Testament*, 853; see Jer 48:38). Hosea 8:9b describes Ephraim as a lonely wild ass (פרא בודד לו). Wild asses are of course herd animals (see Dearman, *Book of Hosea*, 172), so one traveling alone is likewise an exception to the norm. Wolff says that 8:9a "explains Israel's worthlessness among the nations" (*Hosea*, 143).

195. Compare the metaphorics of Jeremiah's sign-acts, where this is made explicit (לא יצלח לכל [Jer 13:7, 10]).

196. E.g., Wolff, *Hosea*, 125; Jeremias, *Prophet Hosea*, 97; Eidevall, *Grapes in the Desert*, 114; Macintosh, *Critical and Exegetical Commentary*, 267; Dearman, *Book of Hosea*, 157; Gruber, *Hosea*, 322. In Hos 8:8, Israel is explicitly identified as an "unwanted" vessel among the international community (נבלע ישראל עתה היו בגוים ככלי אין חפץ בו); see 5:13, 8:9, 10:6, 12:2.

197. Gruber interprets the verse as describing a failed diplomatic mission to Egypt (*Hosea*, 332–34; see also 53).

198. Jeremias, *Prophet Hosea*, 92, my trans.

2. Metaphors of Accusation

in the initial indictment section (4:1–8:14) of the second cycle of Hosea (4:1–11:11). What is new in this cluster in its divine characterization is Yahweh's expectations for Israel and Israel's inability to meet them. Yahweh has sought to do good for Israel, train and support them, and enable them to prevail (7:12b, 15 [x2]). But Israel has failed and is useless (7:8, 11, 16), though their ultimate failure was not returning to Yahweh (7:10). Yahweh is disappointed, since he is not getting a return on his investment. Consequently, switching metaphors, the suzerain is returning to collect payment: he will punish the useless/disobedient vassal (7:10, 12a, 13; 8:1 [x2]).

In addition to Yahweh's expectations for Israel, one gathers from this cluster a sense of God's justice (retribution; e.g., 8:1), his rebuffed generosity (7:13–15), and his claim to absolute sovereignty.[199] Emotionally, there is more of the same: Yahweh's pain of betrayal (7:13–15), Yahweh's anger in response to that betrayal, his desire for recompense, and his lament and curse on the nation (7:13). The emotions uniquely prominent in this cluster are disappointment and frustration with Israel.

An explicit admonition to return is absent in this entire unit of accusation (4:1–8:14), but the ultimate ideal response, of course, would be to turn away from their political and religious dealings and turn back to Yahweh. Alas, such a return is absent (7:10). Consequently, there is more of the same rhetorical purpose: Hosea aims to convince Israel's leadership of their guilt and culpability, convince them of the futility of their alternative options (e.g., foreign alliances, other deities and cultic practices), and make them hopeless. "Accusations ... assail the audience again and again with well-known facts of their guilt elucidated by appropriate metaphors."[200] The effect of this relentless indictment is that

> this text [6:7–7:16] takes the reader on a journey which leads towards "the heart of darkness." The metaphor and similes in this text are like scattered annotations from an expedition with the aim of exploring what is hidden beneath the surface of the contemporary culture. What is disclosed is evil: criminality, hatred, and apostasy. The statement in 6:10a, "I have seen a horrible thing," seems to summarize the text's perspective.[201]

---

199. Recall Keel's comment above that "the net is a symbol of absolute sovereignty and control, and of ultimate world dominion" (*Symbolism of the Biblical World*, 90).
200. Wolff, *Hosea*, 129; see also 130.
201. Eidevall, *Grapes in the Desert*, 124.

Indeed, such a statement seems to summarize not only that passage's perspective but the essence of the accusation sections of Hosea. From indictments of crimes, Hosea turns to announce the consequences of Israel's covenant disobedience.

3
Metaphors of Sentencing

After a defendant has been convicted of a crime, a sentence is announced—the consequences of disobedience. The clusters discussed in this chapter announce to Israel their impending doom. Additionally, they display a progression—perhaps, more accurately, a descent. The first cluster claims that because of Israel's unfaithfulness, the sources of sustenance to which they have turned instead of Yahweh will fail to provide for them. The final clusters announce to Israel the ultimate repercussion for their failures: a death sentence of terrifying proportions.

Cluster 8: Hosea 8:14–9:2

8:14a Direct 2
וישכח ישראל את עשהו
Israel has forgotten his maker

9:1b Indirect, 2
כי זנית מעל אלהיך
for you have whored away from your God,

9:1c Indirect, 3
אהבת אתנן על כל גרנות דגן
you have loved a prostitute's wage[1] on all threshing floors of grain.

---

1. Apparently אתנן, which could mean "gift," is uniquely associated with prostitutes. See Deut 23:19; Isa 23:17–18; Ezek 16:31, 34, 41; Mic 1:7; Wolff, *Hosea*, 149; Jeremias, *Prophet Hosea*, 112; Seifert, *Metaphorisches Reden*, 144; Macintosh, *Critical and Exegetical Commentary*, 337; Yoo, "Israelian Hebrew," 49; Tully, *Hosea*, 205.

9:2a   Indirect, 2

גרן ויקב לא ירעם

Threshing floor and wine vat[2] will not pasture/feed[3] them

Hosea 9:1 marks the transition from indictment to sentencing.[4] Strong metaphors are clustered at this rhetorically significant point as Hosea mixes metaphors for father, husband, and shepherd to proclaim the consequences for Israel's transgressions. The first three metaphors in this cluster summarize the indictment (8:14 as a conclusion to 8:1–14; 9:1 [x2] as a transition into v. 2). The final metaphor (9:2) begins the declaration of consequential punishment.

Israel's Maker (8:14a)

As a conclusion to the indictment phase (4:1–8:14) in this second cycle, Israel is accused of forgetting their maker (וישכח ישראל את עשהו). עשה is a common verb with a wide semantic domain. Lexical study of the verb, per the metaphor identification procedure approach to identifying metaphor, is inconclusive in determining whether this is metaphorical or what its source domain is. More helpful is a study of the term *maker* in other prophetic literature, especially Isaiah, where it is a prominent theme (see esp. 51:13, 54:5). Marc Zvi Brettler concludes that in Isaiah, *maker* means

---

2. The term seems to denote a vat or pressing machine. It could be an oil press, winepress, or wine vat (*HALOT*, 429). While the last is preferable, reading as "oil press" would not significantly change the interpretation, because oil was also identified as one of Baal's gifts (2:7) and associated with the fertility of the land.

3. Some emend to ידעם, following LXX, οὐκ ἔγνω αὐτούς ("did not know them"; see *BHS*). Others read רעה II, meaning "befriend" (Wolff, *Hosea*, 149; Jeremias, *Prophet Hosea*, 112; Seifert, *Metaphorisches Reden*, 144–45), or רעה III, meaning "pay attention to" (Macintosh, *Critical and Exegetical Commentary*, 339–40). MT should be retained and identified as רעה I (Tg. Neb., Vulg.; Syr.; *CTAT*, 559–60; *BHQ*, *64; Glenny, *Hosea*, 134; Gruber, *Hosea*, 371–72; Tully, *Hosea*, 207).

4. With many commentators (e.g., Davies, *Hosea* [1993], 214; Macintosh, *Critical and Exegetical Commentary*, 335; Hubbard, *Hosea*, 165). This is the beginning of the second phase (declaration of judgment, 9:1–11:7) of the book's second cycle (4:1–11:11). Cluster 8 technically straddles two textual units: the indictment (4:1–8:14) and the declaration of punishment in light of that indictment (9:1–11:7). As noted, structural features of Hosea have been considered when determining the limits of clusters, but these textual divisions are centered rather than bounded sets. Preference has been given to the feature of clustering over divisions between textual units.

"father." "However, the image is not merely biological—rather, the biological relationship has implications—as a result of involvement in creating a child, a father is expected not to abandon that child."[5] In Hos 8:14, the accusation is the inverse. Father-Yahweh has been faithful to his child; it is the son who has *forgotten* his father. Inverting this again, Yahweh will now *remember* Israel's iniquity (עתה יזכר עונם, 8:13; see Isa 27:11).[6] Hence, "no matter what they have made, the charge of forgetting the divine *maker* can only lead to disaster."[7]

Partner to the Prostitute (9:1b)

This metaphor revisits the prominent Hosean theme of sexual promiscuity as a metaphor for Israel's relationship to Yahweh.[8] It is one of the clearest metaphorical uses of the domain: Israel has "gone a-whoring away from" (זנית מעל) their God.[9] Two similar statements occur in Hosea:

כי זנה תזנה הארץ מאחרי יהוה
For the land has grossly whored away from Yahweh (1:2)

ויזנו מתחת אלהיהם
And they whored away from their God (4:12)

In all three verses, Israel is the subject (metonymically the "land" in 1:2) of the verb זנה, and God/Yahweh is the object of a preposition. Differences include the prepositions and the shift from the more distant third person in 1:2 and 4:12 to the more personal and direct second-person confrontation in 9:1. Though all three prepositions are translated above as "away

---

5. Marc Zvi Brettler, "Incompatible Metaphors for YHWH in Isaiah 40–66," *JSOT* 23 (1998): 112; see also 111–14; similarly Davies, *Hosea* [1993], 210; Macintosh, *Critical and Exegetical Commentary*, 332 (Deut 32:6). Isaiah 27:11 (על כן לא ירחמנו עשהו) may evoke *motherly* connotations for the term due to the collocation of עשהו and רחם.

6. So also Tully, *Hosea*, 204. This is related to two motifs in Hosea: the theme of reversal (see esp. pp. 177–84 below) and language in the semantic domain of knowing, forgetting, and remembering (e.g., "knowledge of God").

7. Dearman, *Book of Hosea*, 176, emphasis original.

8. So virtually all commentators, except for Gruber (*Hosea*, 369).

9. Mays, *Hosea*, 124.

from,"[10] Tully suggests that the preposition מאחרי in 1:2 puts the "emphasis on the break in relationship," מתחת in 4:12 emphasizes the "lack of submission," and מעל in 9:1 has to do with (lack of) proximity (note NRSV's *"departing* from"). Historically, "this sense might be motivated by the context of going away into captivity (see v. 3). In other words, because they chose to leave YHWH on their terms (in idolatry), now they will be forced to leave him on his terms (in captivity)."[11] Linguistically, the phrase creates "associations of separation, estrangement, and even unfaithfulness."[12] Theologically, divine distance is death for Israel.[13] The possible interpretations and implications of 9:1b are considered along with 9:1c below.

Partner to the Prostitute Who Pays (9:1c)

This metaphorical expression extends 9:1b by adding specificity: Israel has *loved* the fees received for their sexual promiscuity in all the places associated with the harvest festival (כל גרנות דגן).[14] The term אתנן recalls its cognate in Hos 2:14, which identifies Israel's fees with products of agricul-

---

10. LXX translates all with ἀπό (adding ὄπισθεν in 1:2). For this sense of מעל, see *HALOT*, 827, 8a.
11. Tully, *Hosea*, 208.
12. Moughtin-Mumby, *Sexual and Marital Metaphors*, 63.
13. Seifert, *Metaphorisches Reden*, 146.
14. This specification of loving the fees received for sexual promiscuity adds to Hosea's prior use of the metaphor and is a modification of the trope in standard ancient Near Eastern treaty curses. Assur-nerari V's treaty with Mati'-ilu (ca. 754 BCE) involves the curse (§13, ll. 9–10): "may Mati'-ilu become a prostitute, his soldiers women, // may they receive [a gift] in the square of their cities like (any) prostitute" (Kitchen and Lawrence, *Treaty, Law and Covenant* 1:945). For Assur-nerari V it is a curse for the vassal to become a prostitute. For Hosea, far from being a curse to Israel, they *loved it!* The oracles of Hos 9:1–9 may have originated at the autumnal harvest festival, Sukkoth, celebrating the bounty of the land. So most commentators, e.g., Jeremias, *Prophet Hosea*, 115; Sweeney, *Twelve Prophets* 1:119–20; Dearman, *Book of Hosea*, 178. The oracle may have been delivered at Bethel or Samaria, perhaps in "the breathing space in the years after the crisis of 733" (Mays, *Hosea*, 125), or it may be a later reflection by the prophet on those events (Macintosh, *Critical and Exegetical Commentary*, 335–38). Gruber thinks 9:1d–2 is from two different festivals: Passover or Pentecost, and Sukkoth (*Hosea*, 370). Hosea 9:1–9 suggests that this may have been a syncretism of the festival outlined in the Torah and other Canaanite fertility rites. On the significance of the threshing floor, see Macintosh, *Critical and Exegetical Commentary*, 339.

3. Metaphors of Sentencing 95

tural fertility. Israel's "pay, which [her] lovers have given [her]" (אתנה המה לי אשר נתנו לי מאהבי, 2:14 NRSV), is her vine and fig (גפנה ותאנתה). Further specified there is the lover from whom Israel has received these gifts: Baal/s (2:7, 9–10, 15, 18; 9:10), a natural associate of the fertility/harvest festivals.[15] Macintosh summarizes that on the threshing floors "was nurtured the carefree preoccupation with immediate self-gratification which led Israel to forget Yahweh and promiscuously to attribute the immediate blessings of harvest to her (*sic*) appreciative lovers, the Baals (cf. 2.7, EV 5)."[16] Hosea has transitioned from addressing political unfaithfulness to Yahweh (8:1–14) to cultic unfaithfulness (9:1–9).[17]

Not only has the nation cheated on husband-Yahweh by being sexually promiscuous, but they have *loved* the fees they received in exchange. Israel was supposed to love Yahweh, but instead Israel has loved the gifts more than the giver (see 2:10).

Bad Shepherds (9:2a)

A smooth transition from 9:1 is provided by the catchword גרן. If one retains the MT and reads the verb as רעה I, with the meaning of "feed" (as a shepherd), the metaphor in this passage is clear.[18] Israel has chosen replacement shepherds—namely, threshing floor and wine vat. But these shepherds have abandoned Israel. Israel is now functionally a sheep without a shepherd, in that the false shepherds fail to provide. This "bold metaphor" drips with irony.[19] The very sources of nourishment and merriment for the people (threshing floors and wine vats) are unable to supply their sustenance (see יכחש בה, 9:2b). This may be seen as a veiled critique of Baal, the deity directly responsible for the bounty of the wine press and threshing floor.

---

15. In 8:9 the term *lover* probably denotes political entities, while in Hos 2 and here it is a deity or deities.
16. Macintosh, *Critical and Exegetical Commentary*, 339. The "(*sic*)" is original.
17. Mays, *Hosea*, 125–26; Jeremias, *Prophet Hosea*, 115; Seifert, *Metaphorisches Reden*, 146; Macintosh, *Critical and Exegetical Commentary*, 338; Tully, *Hosea*, 207; Tg. Neb. adds, "You have loved *to worship idols* on every threshing floor of corn" (Cathcart and Gordon, *Targum Minor Prophets*, 48). Gruber entertains the possibility that this could be addressed to hotel owners who receive fees from prostitutes paying to use the hotel with their clients during the festivals (*Hosea*, 373–74).
18. See n. 3, above.
19. Davies, *Hosea* [1993], 214.

That threshing floor and wine vat are *not* Israel's proper and sufficient shepherd implies that Israel must have another (divine) shepherd. One senses a mild contrast to two similar metaphors in the book. In 4:16, shepherd-Yahweh chooses *not* to feed his wayward sheep. In 13:5–8, shepherd-Yahweh not only forsakes sheep-Israel but in fact becomes various predators to mangle Israel. Here, Hosea deploys the metaphor not so much in threat (as in the other two passages) but to awaken Israel to their *need* and to indict Israel for abandoning their true shepherd.

Analyzing Their Interaction

Two points may be made regarding the interactions in this cluster. The first relates to their differences, the second to similarities.

This cluster juxtaposes three metaphors for Yahweh: father (8:14), husband (9:1 [x2]), and shepherd (9:2). It is not uncommon to mix these metaphors. For example, Isaiah 54:5 combines the father and the husband metaphors, saying "for your husband is your maker" (כי בעליך עשיך) or "He who made you will espouse you" (NJPS). Psalms 95:6–7 and 100:3 combine the maker and shepherd metaphors. Brettler is right that "as metaphors they could work side by side to fill in different aspects of this relationship" between Yahweh and Israel.[20]

Highlighted aspects of the relationship may include the father's (biologically derived) lifelong obligation of fidelity, willfully forgetting (i.e., abandoning) one's father, the husband's obligation to protection even at the cost of his life, the possibility of being transferred to another shepherd for provision, who may be unable to feed the sheep.

In terms of similarities, the idea of provision may be an overlapping entailment of all three source domains. While perhaps not the focus of the father metaphor in this passage (the obligation to fidelity is the focus), it is nonetheless a commonplace that fathers provided for their children in the ancient Near East. Husbands, likewise, provided for their wives. Wife-Israel has gone after other husbands (Hos 2:9, 18) and other lovers (2:7, 9, 14–15; 8:9) and enjoyed their gifts and fees (2:14; 9:1), but they are unable to provide for her. The final metaphor is clear: the false shepherds of fertility rites, deities, and harvests cannot ultimately provide. Their gifts, understood broadly across the book, may encompass all the ben-

---

20. Brettler, "Incompatible Metaphors," 111.

efits of Israel's religious and political treachery. But the material provision and political security sought through these false shepherds will fail Israel (יכחש בה, 9:2b). The following verse (9:3) declares the consequences of their unfaithfulness: exile.

Cluster 9: Hosea 9:15–10:2

9:15b   Direct, 3
כי שם שנאתים
indeed, there I began to hate[21] them

9:15d   Direct, 3
על רע מעלליהם מביתי אגרשם
Because their actions are evil, I will drive them from my house—

9:15e   Direct, 3
לא אוסף אהבתם
I will not continue to love them.

9:16a   Indirect, 2
הכה אפרים
Ephraim will be[22] struck,

9:16b   Indirect, 2
שרשם יבש
their root is dried up,

9:16c   Indirect, 2
פרי בלי יעשון
they do/will not bear fruit.

9:17c   Indirect, 2
ויהיו נדדים בגוים
So they shall become wanderers among the nations

---

21. "The *qatal* is inchoative, stating that the events at Gilgal triggered the change in YHWH's attitude toward Israel" (Tully, *Hosea*, 231; see BHRG §19.2.2.e).

22. "The VS word order in this clause indicates that the verb is *irrealis* and expresses a prophetic prediction" (Tully, *Hosea*, 232).

10:1a   Indirect, 2
גפן בוקק ישראל
Israel is a ravaged[23] vine

10:1b   Indirect, 2
פרי ישוה לו
its fruit resembles[24] it.[25]

10:2c   Direct, 3
הוא יערף מזבחותם
He will break their altars.

---

23. The derivation and meaning of בוקק has been disputed since the ancient versions. For overviews, see esp. Rudolph, *Hosea*, 191; Macintosh, *Critical and Exegetical Commentary*, 383–85; Gerhard Tauberschmidt, "Polysemy and Homonymy in Biblical Hebrew," *JT* 14 (2018): 36–37. It may be a positive description from בקק II ("luxuriant," "proliferative"; see Arabic *baqqa*, "to be [or cause to be] plentiful"), in which case it is a *hapax*. In support of בקק II are LXX; Theodotion; Syr.; Vulg.; Paul Humbert, "En marge du dictionnaire hébraïque," *ZAW* 62 (1949): 200; Andersen and Freedman, *Hosea*, 547; Cornelis van Leeuwen, "Meaning and Structure of Hosea X 1–8," *VT* 53 (2003): 370; Glenny, *Hosea*, 144; Tully, *Hosea*, 237; most commentaries and English translations. Alternatively, it may be a negative description from בקק I ("ravaged," "wasted"; see Arabic *bāqa[w]*, "to ill-treat," contra *BDB*). In support of בקק I is primarily the Jewish tradition: Tg. Neb.; Aquila; Symmachus; Rashi; ibn Ezra; Kimchi; ibn Janāḥ; Macintosh, *Critical and Exegetical Commentary*, 383–85; Gruber, *Hosea*, 401–2; Moon, *Hosea*, 166–70; KJV, NJPS; see Nah 2:3, 11. In support of *both* meanings as a double entendre are Sweeney, *Twelve Prophets* 1:103; Stuart, *Hosea–Jonah*, 157; Lim and Castelo, *Hosea*, 162–63; Gruber, *Hosea*, 402.

24. The meaning of the verb is debated. Like בקק, it can be read positively ("yields its fruit"; so LXX; Syr.; Vulg.; NRSV; most commentators; see Tully, *Hosea*, 127) or negatively (its fruit "is like it" [i.e., ravaged]; so NJPS; or "whose fruit fails it" [Macintosh, *Critical and Exegetical Commentary*, 383]), or as a double entendre (Sweeney, *Twelve Prophets*, 1:103; Lim and Castelo, *Hosea*, 163). שוה has to do with resemblance or equivalence, frequently with a ל, as here, indicating the thing compared (see Isa 46:5). This favors the negative interpretation supported by most Jewish interpreters. See Rabbi Matis Roberts, *Trei Asar: The Twelve Prophets; A New Translation with a Commentary Anthologized from Talmudic, Midrashic, and Rabbinic Sources* (Brooklyn, NY: Mesorah, 1995), 1:96.

25. "It" renders the ambiguous לו. The ל indicates the object of resemblance, and the ו refers to the vine. If the verb is rendered "bears fruit," then לו is often understood to mean "for him," meaning for Yahweh (e.g., Andersen and Freedman, *Hosea*, 547), or as reflexive possessive (e.g., "its fruit," NRSV).

3. Metaphors of Sentencing 99

Some clusters are clear in their presentation of Yahweh. This is not one of them. The cluster is fraught with lexical difficulties fundamental to the interpretation of the metaphors, ambiguous source domains, and two possible double entendres. Yahweh may be a head of household (father, husband, host?) in 9:15d–e, 17c; is likely a farmer or vineyard owner in 9:16 and 10:1; and may be someone offering or killing an animal (sacrificial?) in 10:2.

Like the previous cluster, this one straddles two textual units within the section declaring punishment (9:1–11:7). Whereas 9:1–9 is primarily about the fertility cult resulting in a failed provision of food, 9:10–17 is about the fertility cult resulting in the failed provision of children.[26] Hosea 10:1–8 addresses the larger picture, claiming that "all important institutions in Israel will come to an end," with a focus mainly on the cult[27] but also the monarchy.

Disowning Israel (9:15, 17)

Four phrases contribute to this metaphor and echo a previous phrase outside the cluster. Constituting the center of this metaphor are the claims that Yahweh drives Israel from his house (מביתי אגרשם, 9:15d) and no longer loves them (לא אוסף אהבתם, 9:15e). What does this make Yahweh? Suggestions include that Yahweh is a husband divorcing his unfaithful wife, that Yahweh is a father disowning his rebellious son, that Yahweh is a host rejecting his guest, that Yahweh is a suzerain dealing with a rebellious vassal, or that it is not a metaphor but refers to the temple.[28] There is no way to know whether

---

26. Tully, *Hosea*, 220. Interpretations suggesting a polemic against Baal in this cluster have little foundation, as Baal's fertility powers were primarily associated with agricultural fertility, not human fertility. See Martin J. Mulder and Johannes C. de Moor, "בעל," *TDOT* 2:188; Herrmann, "Baal," 135.

27. On the coherence of this unit, demonstrated in a four-level concentric structure focusing on the idolatrous calf of 10:5–6, see Leeuwen, "Meaning and Structure," 377; Jeremias, *Prophet Hosea*, 127; Eidevall, *Grapes in the Desert*, 155. The translation "all important institutions in Israel will come to an end" comes from Eidevall, *Grapes in the Desert*, 158.

28. Yahweh is a husband divorcing his unfaithful wife: Harper, *Amos and Hosea*, 339; Mays, *Hosea*, 136; Andersen and Freedman, *Hosea*, 545; Jeremias, *Prophet Hosea*, 125; Macintosh, *Critical and Exegetical Commentary*, 377; Hubbard, *Hosea*, 178; Dearman, *Book of Hosea*, 256–57; Nogalski, *Hosea–Jonah*, 135–36; Glenny, *Hosea*, 142; Lim and Castelo, *Hosea*, 160–61. Yahweh is a father disowning his rebellious son: Laurie J.

the metaphor of 9:15 is based primarily on the family domain or whether it derives from suzerainty discourse, which itself is based on the family domain. As with the sexual promiscuity metaphors of 4:10–15 and others, preference is given here to the metaphor itself (i.e., the family domain), while acknowledging the possibility that this has political overtones due to common usage.

Both גרש and שנא can function as technical terms for divorce and for disowning a son, and both can be used in covenant-breaking contexts.[29] Though Eidevall entertains the possibility of the marital domain, he ultimately prefers the parental domain. He points out that the closest lexical parallels to Hos 9:15 are found in Judges 11:7, where Jephthah describes how his half-brothers drove him out of his father's house:[30] ותגרשוני מבית אבי (Judg 11:7); מביתי אגרשם (Hos 9:15). The two verses share the verb גרש, the preposition מן, and the object of the preposition בית. Since it is quite unlikely that Yahweh is pictured in Hosea as a half-brother, the most natural alternative is that he is a father. The following phrase (9:15f) describes the leaders of the nation as "stubborn" (סררים), suggesting that Israel's leaders are stubborn sons who deserve to be disowned (or worse; see בן סורר in Deut 21:18–21).[31] The passage pictures the "people and their leaders as sons who are disinherited by the divine parent."[32]

Braaten, "Parent-Child Imagery in Hosea (Marriage, Legitimacy, Adoption, Disownment)" (PhD diss., Boston University, 1987), 309–10; Eidevall, *Grapes in the Desert*, 154, who also suggests (n. 49) the image of driving a servant out of the house (see Gen 21:10). Yahweh is a host rejecting his guest: Hubbard, *Hosea*, 178. Yahweh is a suzerain dealing with a rebellious vassal: Norbert Lohfink, "Hate and Love in Osee 9:15," *CBQ* 25 (1963): 417; Stuart, *Hosea–Jonah*, 153–54; Lim and Castelo, *Hosea*, 160–61. That it is not a metaphor but refers to the temple: Ben Zvi, *Hosea*, 192.

29. Alejandro F. Botta, "Hated by the Gods and Your Spouse: Legal Use of שנא in Elephantine and Its Ancient Near Eastern Context," in *Law and Religion in the Eastern Mediterranean: From Antiquity to Early Islam*, ed. Anselm C. Hagedorn and Reinhard G. Kratz (Oxford: Oxford University Press, 2013), 117–18. On גרש and שנא as technical terms for divorce and for disowning a son, see Braaten, "Parent-Child Imagery in Hosea," 40–41; Sweeney, *Twelve Prophets*, 1:101–2; Kelle, *Hosea 2*, 64–78. See Lev 21:7, 14; 22:13; Num 30:10; Deut 24:1–4; Ezek 44:22.

30. Eidevall, *Grapes in the Desert*, 154 (see Judg 11:2).

31. So also Braaten, who acknowledges that the verbs can be used for divorce but that their wide lexical ranges mean that context is crucial in determining the precise image ("Parent-Child Imagery in Hosea," 40–41, 310). He bases his interpretation of this verse on certain redactional assumptions about "original" verses of Hosea—an assumption not shared here.

32. Eidevall, *Grapes in the Desert*, 154.

3. Metaphors of Sentencing

Two other phrases are suggestive and allusive. At Gilgal, Yahweh began to hate Israel (שנאתים, 9:15b).[33] The correlation between *hating* Israel (9:15b) and no longer *loving* Israel (9:15e) is plain. The verb שנא has a semantic range spanning action, bodily experience, and emotion.[34] It occurs often as a technical term in both divorce- and adoption-related ancient Near Eastern legal contexts that indicate "a cessation of the relationship and the distantiation of the parties."[35] In Hos 9:15, the verb denotes the act (because of the collocation of גרש) of formally ending the relationship, with the implication of disinheritance.[36]

As a subtle extension of the disowned-son metaphor, 9:17a notes that Yahweh rejected them (ימאסם), and 9:17c predicts Israel will become wanderers among the nations (ויהיו נדדים בגוים). Surely this refers to exile,[37] but it may suggest a metaphorical extension of the husband or father driving Israel out of the house. "In a twist, Israel has √נדד ("wandered") from YHWH (7:13), so now they will be wanderers (נדדים) among the nations."[38] Macintosh claims 9:17 is a "device to bring them back in repentance."[39]

---

33. Gilgal could refer to the first stop after the people crossed over the Jordan into the land (Josh 4:19), Saul's disobediences in 1 Sam 10:8; 13:4, 8–9; 15, or events contemporary with Hosea. If either of the first two options is correct, it indicates that Israel has been disobedient since the beginning (see Hos 6:7). גלגל can also refer to a generic stone structure or location, in which case the referent here would be indeterminable. For surveys of interpretations, see Else K. Holt, *Prophesying the Past: The Use of Israel's History in the Book of Hosea*, JSOTSup 194 (Sheffield: Sheffield Academic, 1995), 68–73; Macintosh, *Critical and Exegetical Commentary*, 375–77; Sweeney, *Twelve Prophets*, 1:101; Gruber, *Hosea*, 394–95.

34. Françoise Mirguet, "What Is an 'Emotion' in the Hebrew Bible? An Experience That Exceeds Most Contemporary Concepts," *BibInt* 24 (2016): 450.

35. Botta, "Hated by the Gods," 125. Botta argues that it is strictly a technical term for divorce at Elephantine, though Nutkowicz argues that it is an emotional term there. See Hélène Nutkowicz, "Concerning the Verb *śnʾ* in Judaeo-Aramaic Contracts from Elephantine," *JSS* 52 (2007): 211–25.

36. Mirguet, "What Is an 'Emotion,'" 450. See NJPS; Tully, *Hosea*, 230–31; Deut 21:15, 22:13, 24:3.

37. Lohfink, "Hate and Love"; Wolff, *Hosea*, 167; Emmerson, "Structure and Meaning," 708; Davies, *Hosea* [1993], 230; Eidevall, *Grapes in the Desert*, 154; Glenny, *Hosea*, 143.

38. Tully, *Hosea*, 234.

39. Macintosh, *Critical and Exegetical Commentary*, 382; so also Rudolph, *Hosea*, 189.

While either the divorced wife or disowned son is possible, the difference between the two metaphors is not great. The force of the metaphor is that Yahweh is a head of household disowning and rejecting a member of the family due to unfaithfulness or rebellion. Yahweh rejects the former object of his love and cuts all obligations of care and inheritance. If Yahweh is a husband, this marks a decisive end to the story of their relationship so far. Israel has been unceasingly promiscuous. If Yahweh is a father, he has contravened the natural inclination of his filial obligations (see above on 8:14) and has cut off his offspring in the face of such recalcitrant disobedience. Either way, Israel's sin has driven Yahweh to a deeply emotional response: he will no longer love them; rather, he hates them.[40] This emotional response leads Yahweh to institute relational distantiation: Israel is disowned.

The Disappointed Farmer (9:16, 10:1)

Two verses in this cluster picture Israel as a plant. The first is clear; the second is anything but. Hosea 9:16 pictures Israel as a plant whose root is withered up (יבש) and therefore will not bear fruit (פרי בלי יעשון). The fruit likely refers to the children of whom Israel will be deprived (see 9:11–14, 16b/e).[41] Consequently, the plant will be struck down (הכה). Yahweh is the agent in context (9:12, 14, 15, 16e) and therefore is the farmer who puts the axe to the root of the withered tree.[42] As an inversion of 9:10, where Yahweh was surprised by finding a cultivated vine in the wilderness, Yahweh here expresses his disappointment at the failed plant and his decision to remove it.

The next unit presents a metaphor using the same domain, but it is unclear whether Israel is pictured positively as a flourishing vine (e.g., NRSV) or negatively as a ravaged vine (e.g., NJPS). Most translations and

---

40. This is not to suppose that אהב and שנא have the same emotional sense as their English translations (see Botta, "Hated by the Gods," 116). For some of the complicating factors, see Ellen van Wolde, "Sentiments as Culturally Constructed Emotions: Anger and Love in the Hebrew Bible," *BibInt* 16 (2008): 1–24; Mirguet, "What Is an 'Emotion.'"

41. Eidevall, *Grapes in the Desert*, 154; Tully, *Hosea*, 232. Ben Zvi thinks it refers specifically to the "male side of that failed process" of conception (*Hosea*, 189).

42. Robert D. Bergen, "Calling Forth Yahweh's Curses: Hosea's Judgment of Israel in 8:1–10:15," *CTR* 7 (1993): 47; Ben Zvi, *Hosea*, 191; Stuart, *Hosea–Jonah*, 154; Tully, *Hosea*, 232; Eidevall, *Grapes in the Desert*, 155.

interpreters construe the metaphor positively. This study takes the minority position of reading it negatively for lexical and contextual reasons.

These divergent readings hinge on the meanings of two verbs.[43] בוקק should be derived from בקק I ("wasted"). Many scholars, however, posit a *hapax* homonym (בקק II) meaning "flourishing" (see LXX, εὐκληματοῦσα). The following verb, ישוה, carries the sense of resemblance (NJPS), though commentators advocating the positive reading render it along the lines of "yields" (NRSV). The suffix of the following לו refers to the vine; that is, the fruit resembles its vine.[44]

The context can be read in support of either position. The time frames of the verbs and the contextual imagery, however, favor a negative reading of the metaphors in 10:1a–b. For the first two verbs, the present time frame is a more natural reading than the past (בוקק, attributive participle in a verbless clause, and ישוה, *yiqtol*), while the next two indicate completion (הרבה and היטיבו, both *qatal* forms). This may support a reading in which Israel *is currently* ravaged (10:1a–b) despite their past proliferation (10:1c–f).[45] It is difficult to imagine that Hosea would affirm that Israel is *currently* a flourishing vine that produces fruit for Yahweh, when the rest of the book seems to suggest otherwise.[46]

In terms of contextual imagery, Dearman notices a pattern amid the nearby plant images (9:10, 13; 10:1), in which there is an initial affirmation of fertility followed by indictment.[47] Dearman suggests that this pattern favors a positive reading of 10:1a–b (initial affirmation), since 10:1c–f is clearly an indictment. He fails to mention an even nearer plant metaphor (9:16) that pictures Israel as a plant in poor health.[48] The nearer plant metaphor should more strongly influence the interpretation of 10:1a–b,[49] so that 10:1 continues the negative imagery of 9:16.

---

43. See nn. 23 and 25, above, esp. Macintosh, *Critical and Exegetical Commentary*, 383–88.

44. See n. 25, above.

45. See esp. ibn Janāḥ's comments in Macintosh, *Critical and Exegetical Commentary*, 385 (see 9:10).

46. The positive reading of the metaphor is forced to place 10:1a–b in the past frame despite these syntactical considerations: Israel was fruitful but squandered their resources on idolatry (e.g., Tully, *Hosea*, 237–38).

47. Dearman, *Book of Hosea*, 261.

48. Hosea 10:12 also implies this, as Israel the farmer is commanded to bear the fruit they have so far been unable to produce (see below).

49. Though for differences between them, see Hubbard, *Hosea*, 181.

The decision between metaphor readings may come down to choosing between an established Hebrew root or a proposed *hapax* for בוקק.[50] While Arabic cognate and contextual data can be found to support either reading of the metaphor, the clear meaning of בקק I as "ravaged" is preferable to positing a new homonym with an opposite meaning.[51] Hosea had words available to unambiguously describe Israel as a vine that grows profusely (סרח, Ezek 17:6; פרה, Isa 32:12, Ezek 19:10) but instead used a word otherwise meaning "ravaged." The interpreter should, by default, be sympathetic to the possibility that בוקק is a double entendre, given Hosea's propensity for such devices.[52] But if בוקק derives from בקק I, then no homonym exists and a double entendre is impossible.

How is one to interpret this difficult metaphor? Israel has squandered their early prosperity on idolatrous practices (Hos 10:1c–f; see 9:10, 13). The metaphors of 10:1a–b indicate that those idolatrous practices resulted in Israel's current withering and infertility. They can only produce "damaged goods."[53] Their idols promised fecundity, but this has been replaced by "barrenness and death."[54] In their flourishing was the seed of their ravaging.[55]

Most declarations of judgment emphasize what Israel should have done but did not or what they did do but should not have. This metaphor, however, emphasizes their *inability to do anything*. Israel is a malnourished, brittle, rotten vine. Such vines cannot fix themselves. Their situation is hopeless. The only solution is for the farmer to cut it down. Farmer-Yah-

---

50. Scholars' preferences correlate strongly with their era: early and medieval rabbinic sources tend to read בקק I, while most modern commentators derive the verb from בקק II.

51. Gruber discusses the phenomenon of Semitic homonyms with opposite meanings (*Hosea*, 401–2). See also Robert Gordis, "Studies in Hebrew Roots of Contrasted Meanings," *JQR* 27 (1936): 33.

52. See, e.g., Morris, *Prophecy, Poetry and Hosea*. On the possibility that בוקק is a double entendre, see Stuart, Gruber, Sweeney, and Lim and Castelo in n. 23, above. Haddox notes that "the translations are not necessarily at odds. Plants that grow profuse foliage sometimes do not fruit, expending their energy on growth rather than reproduction" (*Metaphor and Masculinity in Hosea*, 123).

53. Lim and Castelo, *Hosea*, 162.

54. J. Gordon McConville, "Hosea, Book of," *DOTPr*, 347. For more on fertility and sterility in Hosea, see Eidevall, *Grapes in the Desert*, 243–46; Alice A. Keefe, "Hosea's (In)Fertility God," *HBT* 30 (2008): 21–41; Moughtin-Mumby, *Sexual and Marital Metaphors*, 53–54.

55. This is true regardless of whether one reads 10:1a–b positively or negatively (see Mays, *Hosea*, 139; Macintosh, *Critical and Exegetical Commentary*, 388).

weh, by implication, is again frustrated with and disappointed in Israel, despite its initial promise (see 9:10).⁵⁶ Perhaps Yahweh is also angry and feels betrayed by this squandering of resources.⁵⁷ Either way, the plant must be struck down: punishment is inevitable.

Snapping the Neck (10:2c)

If 9:15 and 9:17 are unclear as to their source domains, and 9:16 and 10:1 are unclear as to the positive or negative tone of the metaphor for lexical reasons, 10:2 is unclear as to whether anything can be extrapolated to characterize Yahweh. The metaphor hinges on an exceptional use of a single term. In this regard, it is the perfect example of the appropriateness of the metaphor identification procedure approach. The verb יַעֲרֹף (10:2c) is a denominative of the noun עֹרֶף. The noun means "neck," and the verb *always* refers literally to breaking a neck. Hosea 10:2 is the single exception and so is clearly metaphorical.⁵⁸

The subject of the verb is not stated. Some take this as Israel, but Yahweh is preferable, especially with the contrastive הוּא as subject.⁵⁹ Yahweh metaphorically snaps the neck of the altars, thus picturing the altars as animals.

The question, then, is who does this make Yahweh? The options are, in order of decreasing specificity: a priest, the offeror of a sacrifice, or someone who kills an animal by breaking its neck (not for sacrifice). The

---

56. The image of Israel as a vine is frequent throughout the prophets, though this specific image of a ravaged vine appears to be unique. Macintosh points to Isa 5:1–7; 27:2; Jer 2:21; 12:10; Ezek 15:2–6; 17:6–10; see also Ps 80:9–10 (*Critical and Exegetical Commentary*, 387). See also Isa 27:3 for God as farmer of Israel; Ezek 19:10–14.

57. See Hubbard, *Hosea*, 181.

58. LXX misses the metaphor, translating κατασκάψει; so also Syr. The noun occurs thirty-three times in the Old Testament. The verb occurs in Exod 13:13; 34:20; Deut 21:4, 6; Isa 66:3; Hos 10:2.

59. Ernst Sellin, *Das Zwölfprophetenbuch: Hosea–Micha*, KAT 12/1 (Leipzig: Deichert, 1929), 103; Wolff, *Hosea*, 174; Andersen and Freedman, *Hosea*, 553; Dearman, *Book of Hosea*, 194; Stuart, *Hosea–Jonah*, 156; Tully, *Hosea*, 239; virtually all English translation except NJPS. Tg. Neb. inserts an instrumental "enemy" (סנאה) as subject. For the subject as Israel, see, e.g., D. Karl Marti, *Das Dodekapropheton*, KHC 13 (Tübingen: Mohr Siebeck, 1904), 78; NJPS. Alternatively, Rashi, ibn Ezra, Kimchi, and Macintosh understand the referent to be the "heart" (לֵב) in 10:2a (see Macintosh, *Critical and Exegetical Commentary*, 388).

answer hinges on the subjects and contexts used elsewhere for the verb (and noun) עָרַף.

Scholars often claim that the verb is usually found in cultic contexts or even that it is a technical term for sacrifice.[60] Given the "natural close association of altars and slaughter,"[61] perhaps Yahweh is the offeror of the sacrifice or even a priest.

The evidence, however, does not support the claim that עָרַף is a technical term for sacrifice. Though occurring twice in a cultic context, עָרַף is used to describe the breaking of an animal's neck that is *not* redeemed (Exod 13:13, 34:20). Other instances are a heifer killed by a wadi (Deut 21:4, 6) and a dog killed as a simile for unacceptable sacrifice (Isa 66:3). This exhausts all occurrences of the verb. None occur on an altar, and most are not acceptable sacrifices (excepting Deut 21:4, 6). The noun occurs thirty-three times with similar results (Lev 5:8 is the only exception). It is used in the common descriptor of Israel as a stiff-necked people (קְשֵׁה עֹרֶף), a metaphor that of course has nothing to do with being a sacrificial animal.[62] Moreover, a priest is never the subject of the verb, nor, with one exception (Lev 5:8), the one doing the breaking when the noun occurs. This suggests it is unlikely that Yahweh is pictured as a priest offering a sacrifice, or perhaps even that the altars are conceptualized as sacrifices.[63] The emphasis of the metaphor is that "the destruction of the altars is likened to the execution of an animal."[64] The clearest characterization of Yahweh is as an executioner.[65]

Consequently, "a satirical effect is achieved. Instead of serving as places for animal sacrifices, the altars will be treated as animals bound for slaughter."[66] In another of Hosea's inversions, the place of Israel's idolatrous

---

60. Davies, *Hosea* [1993], 235; Tully, *Hosea*, 239. On the verb as usually found in cultic contexts, see, e.g., Hubbard, *Hosea*, 182.

61. Stuart, *Hosea–Jonah*, 160.

62. The noun עֹרֶף is used metaphorically (22x) more often than literally (11x) in the Old Testament to denote the rebellious people or their turning their backs on Yahweh.

63. If they are, it is overtly as animals unacceptable in the official cult (Jacob, "Osée," 74; Wolff, *Hosea*, 174).

64. Dearman, *Book of Hosea*, 194.

65. So also Moon, *Hosea*, 170.

66. Eidevall, *Grapes in the Desert*, 156. The specification that the four horns of the altar are broken (Wellhausen, Wolff, Tully; see Amos 3:14) is unnecessary (Jacob, "Osée," 74; Rudolph, *Hosea*, 192–93; Leeuwen, "Meaning and Structure," 371; Macin-

slaughter will itself be slaughtered by Yahweh. Appropriate to this section declaring Israel's punishment (Hos 9:1–11:7) and echoing previous metaphors, Yahweh is the unassailable executioner. As a helpless animal dies by the quick work of an expert killer, so the altars (and by extension the cultic apparatus of Israel)[67] are helpless before Yahweh. Cornelis van Leeuwen suggests a subtle possibility for a further wordplay: perhaps Yahweh's snapping the neck of the altars is further figurative of Yahweh snapping the neck of this stiff-necked people.[68]

Analyzing Their Interaction

While other clusters are clear and consistent, this cluster is full of ambiguities. This analysis discusses contrasts between the metaphors, then similarities. It concludes with brief speculations on the reason for these ambiguities.

The first contrast is between the referents of the infertility metaphors. In 9:16, the image of fruit refers to children, while in 10:1 it refers to material prosperity. This difference serves a single purpose: all aspects of the future societal flourishing that Israel hoped to procure apart from Yahweh will end.

Another contrast is in the implications and nuances of each metaphor for Yahweh. Father, farmer, and executioner have different emotional reverberations, relational implications, and entailments. Father-Yahweh *disinherits* son-Israel. Farmer-Yahweh is *disappointed* with fruitless-vine-Israel. Executioner-Yahweh *kills* animal-Israel's cult.

There are differences in personal relevance and consequences. The first has significant relational and emotional implications (everyone has a father). It is terrifying and personal because it withholds livelihood and community inclusion. The second is of more relational distance (a plant/vine being an inert object). The executioner, the third image, is terrifying in its violence and finality, but there is no personal relationship.

There are a few points of similarity. With a negative reading of 10:1a, all the metaphors are starkly negative; many are images of barrenness. With the exception of 10:1a–b, the metaphors are pictures of the future,

---

tosh, *Critical and Exegetical Commentary*, 391). See Julius Wellhausen, *Die kleinen Propheten*, 4th ed. (Berlin: de Gruyter, 1963), 124; Wolff, *Hosea*, 174; Tully, *Hosea*, 239.

67. Davies, *Hosea* [1993], 235; Stuart, *Hosea–Jonah*, 160.
68. Leeuwen, "Meaning and Structure," 371.

consistent with the fact that this cluster is in the sentencing phase (9:1–11:7) of the second cycle of Hosea (4:1–11:11).[69] Many of the metaphors share entailments of death, suffering, and destruction.

The metaphors share the same conceptual planes in many respects. Because Hosea speaks on behalf of Yahweh, the metaphors are on the same speaker and belief-related conceptual planes. Most reside on the same temporal conceptual plane (future). Only on the causal conceptual plane is there a significant difference, if one holds that the disowning-father metaphors are the logical cause of the other metaphors in the cluster. Israel is destroyed *because* they are disowned.

There are two reasons for the ambiguous divine characterization in this cluster. One is that this section focuses on Israel, not Yahweh. The emphasis is on who Israel is and what they will suffer. A second reason is the destabilizing effect such ambiguity for Yahweh has on Israel. These shifting lines and ambiguous characterizations of Yahweh could have the effect of making Israel unsure of who God is. As soon as Israel thinks they have understood Yahweh, he shifts. Yahweh is not who they think he is. Is God knowable?

Cluster 10: Hosea 10:10–12

10:10a   Indirect, 1
באותי ואסרם
I will discipline[70] them as I desire[71]

---

69. עתה is often used in Hosea to begin a verdict of punishment in light of accusation (2:12; 5:7; 8:8, 13). NRSV rightly renders עתה יאשמו (10:2b) as "now they must bear their guilt." NJPS has "now he feels his guilt," but the *yiqtol* could equally be construed as "now he *will* feel his guilt" (i.e., now that punishment is poured out, he will feel the hurt). On the meanings of אשם, see p. 62 n. 119, above.

70. One might expect איסרם(ו) (see *BHS*), but it is unnecessary to emend in order to derive from root יסר (*BHQ*, 66*; Tully, *Hosea*, 254).

71. Lit. "[It is] in my desire [that] I will discipline them" (see Macintosh, *Critical and Exegetical Commentary*, 414; GKC §165a for the *waw* as a purpose clause). Many, following the LXX (ἦλθεν παιδεῦσαι αὐτούς), interpret this construction as "when I come" or the like. NRSV; Wolff, *Hosea*, 178; Andersen and Freedman, *Hosea*, 565–66, derive the verb from אתה, "to come." The MT makes sense as rendered (*CTAT*, 578; *BHQ*, 66*; Jeremias, *Prophet Hosea*, 132; Macintosh, *Critical and Exegetical Commentary*, 414; Sweeney, *Twelve Prophets* 1:108; Tully, *Hosea*, 251, 254).

10:11a　　　　Indirect, 2
ואפרים עגלה מלמדה אהבתי לדוש
Yet Ephraim [was][72] a trained heifer who loved[73] to thresh

10:11b　　　　Direct, 3
ואני עברתי על טוב צוארה
And I noticed[74] her good neck

10:11c　　　　Direct, 3
ארכיב אפרים
I would have harnessed[75] Ephraim

10:11d　　　　Indirect, 2
יחרוש יהודה
Judah would have plowed

---

72. The clause lacks a verb. The time frame could be present tense, in which case Ephraim is portrayed as the cow who was and *is still* trained but now refuses to work.

73. Most take this as a *qal* participle. Eidevall explains the *yôd* as *yôd compaginis* (*Grapes in the Desert*, 159 n. 86; see GKC 90k–m). Andersen and Freedman explain this as a *qal qatal* first-person common singular, with Yahweh as subject (*Hosea*, 567).

74. Many believe MT is "unintelligible" (Andersen and Freedman, *Hosea*, 567) and emend (adding another על, supposedly dropped by haplography) or revocalize to "I laid a yoke upon" (e.g., Rudolph, *Hosea*, 200; Mays, *Hosea*, 144; Andersen and Freedman, *Hosea*, 567; Stuart, *Hosea-Jonah*, 165–66). This metaphor is common in ancient Near Eastern imperial language (e.g., see Gen 27:40, 1 Kgs 12:4–14; EA 257: 12–19; 296: 30–35; COS 2.114C:273–74, 2.118A:293–94 [lines 72–78], 2.118E:296–97 [lines 90–112a], 2.119B:302–3). However, the verb עבר is never used to describe the placing of a yoke on an animal (Tully, *Hosea*, 256), and there is "no evidence in text or vrss." for an additional על (*BHQ*, 67*; see *CTAT*, 582–83). See ואעבר עליך in Ezek 16:8. Yahweh "passed by" the neck of this cow, implying he *noticed* the goodness of the neck for service (see n. 87, below).

75. The *hiphil* may mean "causing to mount," presumably in preparation for plowing. See Sigmund Mowinckel, "Drive and/or Ride in OT," *VT* 12 (1962): 285; *HALOT*, 1233; Andersen and Freedman, *Hosea*, 567–68; Sweeney, *Twelve Prophets* 1:109–10; contra NRSV ("but I will make Ephraim break the ground"). The *yiqtol* forms here and in 10:11d–e can be rendered as futures and/or jussives indicating future judgment. They are often understood as past-tense modals (e.g., Wolff, *Hosea*, 179–80). The word order indicates an *irrealis* mood, describing what Yahweh would have done (intended to do) with this new heifer (Tully, *Hosea*, 257).

1 0:11e   Indirect, 2
ישדד לו יעקב
Jacob would have harrowed for himself

10:12e[76]   Direct, 3
עד יבוא וירה צדק לכם
until he [Yahweh] comes and rains[77] righteousness on you.

Hosea 10:1–15 is a unit (sometimes subdivided between vv. 8, 9), whose topic comingles cult and monarchy. A prominent theme of the chapter is war,[78] and the passage suggests that problems with cult and monarchy *cause* the war and the end of the monarchy. The farming metaphors suggest a different set of causal relationships, in which Israel's returning to fulfill their purpose results in Yahweh's returning for their flourishing (10:12).

Disciplinarian (10:10a)

The first metaphor, that of disciplining (יסר), is common yet vague as to its source domain. Metaphorical expressions using this verb were treated in cluster 2 (Hos 5:2) and cluster 7 (Hos 7:12, 15) and so need not be extensively revisited. Briefly, the possible source domains include a military trainer, wisdom teacher, judge, or parent (as an extension of wisdom

---

76. Some consider the verse postexilic (e.g., Marti, *Das Dodekapropheton*, 84; Yee, *Composition*, 144–45, 152–53, 228–29).

77. Some derive the verb from ירה III ("to teach"): Vulg.; Syr.; Jerome, *Commentaries on the Twelve Prophets* 2:230; Mays, *Hosea*, 173; NJPS. Some follow LXX (ἕως τοῦ ἐλθεῖν δικαιοσύνης ὑμῖν) and suppose a *Vorlage* of פרי (Wellhausen, *Die kleinen Propheten*, 18, 126; Sellin, *Das Zwölfprophetenbuch*, 105, 109; Wolff, *Hosea*, 180). The plural verb in 4Q Twelve Prophets^g (4Q82) is probably simply an error from MT (בוא וירו צדק; see *BHQ*, 67*). On the other hand, "rain" (ירה II) fits the context of farming and agricultural productivity, echoes Hos 6:3, and has a similar parallel in Joel 2:23 (see Jer 5:24). וירה should be considered original and derived from ירה II (so *BHS* 67*; *HALOT*, 436; ibn Ezra; Rudolph, *Hosea*, 201; Andersen and Freedman, *Hosea*, 568–69; Jeremias, *Prophet Hosea*, 132, 135–36; Macintosh, *Critical and Exegetical Commentary*, 421–24; Stuart, *Hosea–Jonah*, 165–66; Tully, *Hosea*, 259). Some say this is an intentional double entendre (Rashi; Jacob, "Osée," 77; Sweeney, *Twelve Prophets* 1:110; Ben Zvi, *Hosea*, 221–22). Pentiuc et al. say that the verb is polysemous, with a basic sense of "cast in a direction," which generated various interpretations (*Hosea*, 253–54).

78. Wolff, *Hosea*, 188; Jeremias, *Prophet Hosea*, 133; Ben Zvi, *Hosea*, 224.

teacher).[79] One source domain Eidevall does not consider, which Marvin Sweeney suggests, is that of the farmer: "The verb 'chastise' [יסר] is used for the training or guidance of animals as well as for human instruction."[80] This source domain commends itself above the others, given the immediately following metaphors about cows and farming. As with previous uses of the verb, "the passage points to YHWH's efforts to use punishment as a means to train Israel in proper conduct; it is not used as a means to announce Israel's final destruction."[81]

Two elements add to the previous יסר metaphors in characterizing Yahweh. The first is the expression באותי. The verb has an emotional sense to it, indicating that Yahweh *longs* to punish Israel for the sake of their correction.[82] At this point, Yahweh does not regret the need to discipline Israel; he does not vacillate (as, perhaps, in 6:4, 11:8a–d). Second, a *reason* is given for this punishment. Nations will come against them and bind them *for their double iniquity* (לשתי עונתם).[83] The referent is unclear. While in canonical terms the two golden calves of the Northern Kingdom suggest themselves (1 Kgs 12:28–30), that view is often rejected.[84] The context consistently suggests that the reasons for Israel's eventual destruction are cultic aberrations (specifically the calf of Samaria in Hos 10:5; see 10:1–2, 6, 8, and "Bethel" in 10:15) and trusting in armies (10:13) and political

---

79. Eidevall, *Grapes in the Desert*, 121, 159; Wolff, *Hosea*, 184; p. 83 n. 178, above.
80. Sweeney, *Twelve Prophets* 1:109.
81. Sweeney, *Twelve Prophets* 1:109.
82. Sweeney, *Twelve Prophets* 1:108.
83. Qere (LXX; Syr.; Vulg.; followed by most modern translations). *Ketiv* is לשתי עינתם ("for two/double their springs"; though NJPS renders the *ketiv* as "furrows"; so also *CTAT*, 582). For discussion, see Macintosh, *Critical and Exegetical Commentary*, 414–17; Gruber, *Hosea*, 427–30.
84. There is no consensus on the referent of the "double sins." Most connect the phrase to Gibeah in 10:9, perhaps referring to the events recorded in Judg 19–20. The phrase could mean "Gibeah's former sin is doubled by Gibeah's present guilt" (Wolff, *Hosea*, 184); it could refer to the wicked policies of Judah and Ephraim, to which they have held since Gibeah (Macintosh, *Critical and Exegetical Commentary*, 415); to two idols, or more likely to the events and consequences of Gibeah (both Andersen and Freedman, *Hosea*, 566; see Gruber, *Hosea*, 430); to the "then and now" of their sin, or its extremity, or it could be a textual corruption of "suffer double for her sins (see Isa 40:2)" (all three suggestions Stuart, *Hosea–Jonah*, 169). See further Patrick M. Arnold, "Hosea and the Sin of Gibeah," *CBQ* 51 (1989): 447–60; Mark S. Smith, *Where the Gods Are: Spatial Dimensions of Anthropomorphism in the Biblical World* (New Haven: Yale University Press, 2016), 58–68.

solutions (10:15). Perhaps those are the double iniquities: aberrant cult and politics. Gibeah (10:9) may function as a representative example of those more general tendencies. Regardless, Yahweh delights to punish Israel *because* he is angry about their unfaithfulness.

Frustrated and Disappointed Farmer (10:11)

The main interpretive question is whether this metaphor is negative or positive. If emended to yield an image of yoking an animal, the image could be a negative picture of subjection, echoing the image of a suzerain yoking a vassal.[85] Emendation, however, is unnecessary.[86] The MT presents a positive image of Yahweh being pleasantly surprised at the potential usefulness of an animal as he passes by.[87] Hence, the image represents a historical retrospective concerning Israel's initial "election to service."[88] Yet the rest of the verse demonstrates that this positive beginning did not last.

The contribution of this set of metaphorical expressions to the characterization of Yahweh revolves around high expectations giving way to grave disappointment. Jeremias summarizes the position well, noting that Yahweh had "the highest hopes" for this chosen animal's ability to serve him well. "The verse speaks to God's high expectations of the young beast, not at the ideal beginning time, as 9:10 is." Rather, "the focus is entirely on the salvific future, on the usefulness of the pictured animal for long-term goals: tilling cultivated land."[89] These hopes proved unfounded. Israel failed in its destiny, leaving Yahweh disappointed, frustrated, and angry, hence the farmer's conclusion that the cow was a *"futile labor of love."*[90]

---

85. So Davies, *Hosea* [1993], 242–43; Glenny, *Hosea*, 148. A negative reading is also possible without emendation (NRSV).

86. See n. 74, above.

87. So most interpreters, e.g., *CTAT*, 583; Wolff, *Hosea*, 185; Jeremias, *Prophet Hosea*, 132–34; Eidevall, *Grapes in the Desert*, 159–61; Macintosh, *Critical and Exegetical Commentary*, 419–20; Stuart, *Hosea–Jonah*, 169; Tully, *Hosea*, 257.

88. Wolff, *Hosea*, 185. Andersen and Freedman interpret it as referring to the present time (*Hosea*, 567). Hosea's historical retrospectives (using metaphors) often give way to present indictment (e.g., 9:10, 11:1–4).

89. Jeremias, *Prophet Hosea*, 134, my trans.; see Macintosh, *Critical and Exegetical Commentary*, 419.

90. Seifert, *Metaphorisches Reden*, 215, my trans., emphasis original.

Raining Righteousness (10:12e)

The domain of agricultural productivity continues in 10:12, but the characters shift. In 10:12a–d, Israel, formerly the cow, becomes the farmer.[91] The first four lines of the verse do not contribute to a characterization of Yahweh. The final line, however, holds the surprise twist that Yahweh, formerly the farmer, now brings rain. That is, Yahweh is the storm god who rains not only water but, metaphorically, righteousness.[92]

Thomas Worden notices the similarities of this passage to Ugaritic myths: "In order to secure the resurrection and return of Baal Anat 'reaps' Mot and 'sows' him; Šapaš is set over *the furrows of the earth* to help Anat seek for Baal."[93] Whether Hosea polemicizes against a discrete deity similar to the one at Ugarit, or whether *Baal* is a catchall term for unacceptable (even allegedly Yahwistic) cultic practices, the moniker *Baal* draws on a storm-god figure.[94] When Yahweh is characterized as the one who brings rain (and righteousness), Hosea is polemically appropriating a fundamental aspect of the rival deity attacked throughout the book.[95] The metaphor denotes "the nation's need to persist in its acknowledgement that Yahweh, and not Baal, is the guarantor of the success of its vocation and endeavour (see 2.10, EV 8)."[96]

It is noteworthy that 10:12a–d is the first of only three explicit invitations to (re)turn to and/or seek Yahweh in the book (see 12:7, 14:2–4).[97] This call to return is formulated exclusively in metaphorical language, while the other two are relatively more literal in using the term שוב. Hence,

---

91. See Mays, *Hosea*, 184; Moon, *Hosea*, 176.

92. צדק may refer to deliverance from warfare and its consequences. See *HALOT*, 1005; Felipe Fruto Ramirez, "The Parable of the Heifer in Hosea 10:11–13," *Landas* 28 (2014): 109; Stuart, *Hosea–Jonah*, 170.

93. Thomas Worden, "The Literary Influence of the Ugaritic Fertility Myth on the Old Testament," *VT* 3 (1953): 296, emphasis original.

94. On the comparative use of Ugaritic material, see p. 66 n. 133, above.

95. So also Rudolph, *Hosea*, 204; Moon, *Hosea*, 176. Jeremias notes that this is a bold promise in light of the Canaanite ideas of the people expressed in 6:1–3 (*Prophet Hosea*, 135). Wolff rejects the connection to Baal because he emends the MT (see n. 77, above). Most other commentaries or monographs do not connect this metaphor to Baal.

96. Macintosh, *Critical and Exegetical Commentary*, 423.

97. Not all scholars see this exclusively as a present command for repentance (see Wolff, *Hosea*, 188; Jeremias, *Prophet Hosea*, 135; Stuart, *Hosea–Jonah*, 170).

the rhetorical strategy of this metaphorical expression is different from most other metaphors. While other metaphors share with this verse the ultimate purpose of provoking a return to Yahweh, their method is often to terrify Israel to return. Here, the method is to use hope to woo Israel.

Analyzing Their Interaction

The first metaphor in the cluster is weak. Training and discipline are fairly common metaphors in the Bible and ancient Near East (and occur elsewhere in Hosea), and the source domain remains vague. The core of this cluster is the set of farming and agriculture metaphors. Considered together, they form an extended frame of reference, with a narrative progression.[98]

The cluster begins with Yahweh's emotional longing to chastise the people in the near future (10:10a). The metaphors sharply shift to a historical retrospective. The relationship between the discipline and farming metaphors is causal: Yahweh will discipline Israel because they have failed to be useful to Yahweh, as elucidated in the farming narrative. Ephraim is described as a heifer that loves to thresh, probably freely walking around on the grain without a yoke, perhaps eating grain as she goes (10:11a). The farmer is absent. The farmer walks by the cow and notices that her neck seems strong. She has the potential for other types of work involving a yoke as well (10:11b). The farmer states his intentions for her future (10:11c–e): harnessing her so she might productively work the field. It is significant that three terms for God's northern and southern people are included (אפרים, יהודה, יעקב).[99] Both nations are viewed as a whole entity with a shared purpose: to faithfully serve God. The metaphorical narrative is not explicit that cow-Israel fails to fulfill farmer-Yahweh's purposes, but the context implies it.

The farming metaphor is given a provocative twist at the end, as Israel becomes the farmer and Yahweh becomes the storm god who brings not only rain but salvation. The first three imperatives of 10:12 picture Israel as the farmer who is to accomplish the agricultural productivity intended but unfulfilled by the metaphors in 10:11. The people are commanded to bear the fruit they have been unable to produce. In the final metaphor of the cluster, Yahweh reenters the picture as the reward for Israel's faithful

---

98. Harshav, *Explorations in Poetics*, 32–75; see Ramirez, "Parable of the Heifer."
99. On claims of יהודה being a redaction, see p. 31 n. 3, above.

service. But Yahweh is no longer the farmer. Israel is the farmer now, and God is the all-important and uncontrollable rain (or the clouds that bring the rain, or the god that brings both). The farmer can only do so much; if it does not rain, his efforts are fruitless. The hopeful future image of the final metaphor serves as an incentive to respond to the imperatives of 10:12 and fulfill the unfulfilled purposes of Yahweh of 10:11. It also foreshadows the hopeful end of the cycle (11:8–11).

There are interesting patterns in this cluster regarding time frame and the positivity or negativity of the metaphor in relation to their rhetorical use.

Table 3.1: Metaphor Time Frames and
Their Positivity/Negativity in Hosea 10:10–12

Verse	Time Frame	Positive/Negative Image
10:10a	Present or near future	Negative
10:11	Past	Positive
10:12e	Future	Positive

Hosea 10:10a and 10:12e function as motivational bookends to the metaphorical narrative of 10:11. The first is negative, a threat, in the present or near future (10:10a), while the second is a positive motivation in the future (a reward, 10:12e). In the middle is an image from the past, the positive image of the initially promising but eventually disappointing cow (10:11). This functions to accuse and motivate. Biblical memory is the actualization of the past in the present to chart a course for the future.[100] The cluster is a rhetorically complex, multifaceted attempt at motivating Israel to change. It spans time frames, multiple rhetorical strategies (threatening, 10:10a; wooing, 10:12e; and allowing the audience to respond to their implicit failure in the story, 10:11),[101] positive and negative metaphors, and metaphors partaking of different entailments within the same metaphorical domain and applied to different target domains. The rhetorical importance of this unit (esp. 10:12) as an implicit motivation and explicit call to repentance cannot be overstated.

---

100. A phrase borrowed and modified from Jeffrey D. Arthurs, *Preaching as Reminding: Stirring Memory in an Age of Forgetfulness* (Downers Grove, IL: IVP Academic, 2017).

101. See further pp. 190–94 ("Eight Strategies of Metaphor Deployment"), below.

Cluster 11: Hosea 11:1–4

11:1a Direct, 3
כי נער ישראל ואהבהו
When Israel was a boy, I loved him,

11:1b Direct, 3
וממצרים קראתי לבני
and out of Egypt[102] I summoned my son

11:2a–b Indirect, 2
קראו להם כן הלכו מפני // הם
They [also] summoned them, so they went away from me[103]

11:3a Direct, 2
ואנכי תרגלתי לאפרים
Yet I taught(?)[104] Ephraim

11:3b Direct, 2
קחם על זרועתיו
I took them in my arms[105]

---

102. Understanding the ablative sense of מן (NRSV) rather than the temporal ("ever since"; NJPS). See Wolff, *Hosea*, 190; Tully, *Hosea*, 268.

103. This difficult textual decision involves three variables. The first clause may be an "unmarked comparative clause" (Joüon §174e; so LXX; Syr.). Second, the first verb may become first-person, hence an original כקראי (so LXX; *BHS*; NRSV). Third, I read a different word division (הם לבעלים יזבחו // הלכו מפני) from the MT הלכו מפניהם, reading the final pronoun as "away from *me*" (LXX; Syr.; NRSV; Nissinen, *Prophetie*, 233; Tully, *Hosea*, 269). Tg. Neb. and Vulg. reflect MT.

104. תרגלתי is a *hapax*. On the morphology and history of interpretation, see Jeremy Hutton and Safwat Marzouk, "The Morphology of the tG-Stem in Hebrew and Tirgaltî in Hos 11:3," *JHS* 12 (2012): 1–41; see also Macintosh, *Critical and Exegetical Commentary*, 442–43; Yoo, "Israelian Hebrew," 134–36. Hutton and Marzouk decline to offer a meaning but reject a causative sense and therefore reject the meanings "I taught to walk" and "I led" (37). Tully admits that the question is currently indissoluble and that "taught" must suffice for now (*Hosea*, 271).

105. All ancient versions, followed by most modern translations and commentators, render the third-person verb קחם and the suffix on זרועתיו as first-person. It is unclear whether this reflects a different *Vorlage* or an attempt to make sense of the MT (see *CTAT*, 589–93; *BHQ*, 68*; Macintosh, *Critical and Exegetical Commentary*,

3. Metaphors of Sentencing

11:3c   Direct, 2
ולא ידעו כי רפאתים
Yet they did not realize that I [was the one that] healed them

11:4aA   Direct, 3
בחבלי אדם אמשכם
With cords of a man[106] I was drawing them

11:4aB[107]   Direct, 3
בעבתות אהבה
With ropes of love [I was drawing them]

11:4b   Direct, 3
ואהיה להם כמרימי על על לחיהם
And I was to them like one who lifts the yoke [which was] on their jawbones[108]

441–44; Tully, *Hosea*, 271–72), but it is equally unclear how the verb could be construed as anything other than first-person in context. Macintosh suggests that it could be an unusual form of a *qal* infinitive absolute (*Critical and Exegetical Commentary*, 443). Perhaps this is why many English translations render as a gerund.

106. The phrase is challenging, as is its parallel 11:4aB. אדם may indicate "the way the action is performed" (i.e., "humanely"; Eidevall, *Grapes in the Desert*, 172 n. 43). See Joy Philip Kakkanattu, *God's Enduring Love in the Book of Hosea: A Synchronic and Diachronic Analysis of Hosea 11:1–11*, FAT 2/14 (Tübingen: Mohr Siebeck, 2006), 58–60. They could refer to cords of human agency, meaning the prophets (Tg. Neb. 11:2-3). See Dwight R. Daniels, *Hosea and Salvation History: The Early Traditions of Israel in the Prophecy of Hosea*, BZAW 191 (Berlin: de Gruyter, 1990), 67.

107. The poetic line is broken here because it involves two discrete metaphorical expressions in parallel, the second (11:4aB) with ellipsis of the verb אמשכם.

108. See Macintosh (*Critical and Exegetical Commentary*, 446–49) for this interpretation (see also Dearman, *Book of Hosea*, 204) and a refutation of the images of placing the yoke *onto* the jaw (so NJPS; Rudolph, *Hosea*, 208) and of a parent lifting the child to the cheek, based on emendation (see *BHS*; so NRSV; Mays, *Hosea*, 154–55; Wolff, *Hosea*, 191, 199–200; Braaten, "Parent-Child Imagery in Hosea," 293; Seifert, *Metaphorisches Reden*, 184–86, 191–93; Kakkanattu, *God's Enduring Love*, 60–62). LXX interprets most of 11:3-4 negatively (Glenny, *Hosea*, 154–55).

11:4c   Direct, 3
ואט אליו אוכיל
in order that I might give him food.[109]

This cluster opens the final segment of the 4:1–11:11 cycle. Chapter 11 begins with this historical retrospective highlighting Yahweh's initial care for the nation and the nation's early and constant rejection of Yahweh (11:1–4) and proceeds to a declaration of judgment (11:5–7), then ultimately to compassion and victory (11:8–11).[110] As an intermediate summary chapter, Hosea 11 reflects in nuce the pattern of accusation, judgment, and restoration found across all three cycles of the book.[111] The chapter has little in the way of historical specificity, except for the reference to the exodus tradition in 11:1.[112]

Hosea 11:1–4 is one of the longest nearly continuous stretches of metaphors for Yahweh in the book.[113] Hosea 11:2c–d are the only literal lines.

---

109. ואט is an apocopated *hiphil yiqtol* first-person common singular from the root נטה, where the *waw* indicates purpose (see *BHQ*, 68*; *HALOT*, 693 ["extend, bestow"]; Macintosh, *Critical and Exegetical Commentary*, 447; Tully, *Hosea*, 274). אוכיל is understood as a noun meaning "food" (Macintosh, *Critical and Exegetical Commentary*, 445, 447; contra Tully, *Hosea*, 274–75). On the unreliability of the LXX in this instance, see Morris, *Prophecy, Poetry and Hosea*, 87–88 n. 57; Heinz-Dieter Neef, "Der Septuaginta-Text und der Masoreten-Text des Hoseabuches im Vergleich," *Bib* 67 (1986): 206.

110. See Macintosh, *Critical and Exegetical Commentary*, 436. On internal markers of cohesion, see Ben Zvi, *Hosea*, 228–30; Jopie Siebert-Hommes, "'With Bands of Love': Hosea 11 as 'Recapitulation' of the Basic Themes in the Book of Hosea," in *Unless Some One Guide Me ... Festschrift for Karel A. Deurloo*, ed. Janet W. Dyk et al., ACEBTrSup 2 (Maastricht: Uitgeverij Shaker, 2001), 168. Siebert-Hommes argues that the chapter is organized in a four-step chiasm. The historical retrospective continues prior themes from Hosea, though more intensely (Wolff, *Hosea*, 193; Macintosh, *Critical and Exegetical Commentary*, 436).

111. Tully, *Hosea*, 266. Siebert-Hommes argues that Hos 2 and 11 present the most basic claims of the book ("'With Bands of Love'").

112. Ben Zvi, *Hosea*, 232–33, 238; Kakkanattu, *God's Enduring Love*, 62–63. Tully thinks that the second and third references to Egypt are metonymic for captivity (*Hosea*, 266; alternatively, see Seifert, *Metaphorisches Reden*, 262). Macintosh dates 11:6 to 724 BCE (*Critical and Exegetical Commentary*, 454). On the possible historical referents of the metaphors, see Neef, *Heilstraditionen*, 88–95; Daniels, *Hosea and Salvation History*, 68.

113. Also note clusters 13 (Hos 13:5–8) and 15 (Hos 14:4–9). Cluster 7 is a longer cluster but involves many metaphors for Israel and literal statements.

3. Metaphors of Sentencing 119

The unit is full of textual difficulties,[114] resulting in entirely different metaphors. In 11:3–4, for instance, it is debated whether God is pictured as a farmer or a parent. While the source domain may be debated, the sense of the metaphor is clear: the images portray provision and care.

The Good Parent (11:1–3)

The first metaphor (11:1) is that of a parent and a son. It declares that Yahweh loved, or began to love, Israel in his "youth," identified as Israel's time in Egypt. As a parent summons a child, Yahweh called Israel out of Egypt. This may mark the beginning of the relationship, which signals adoption.[115] Ancient kings were often sons of the gods, either adopted or nursed from birth by a goddess.[116]

The gender of the parent is not specified in 11:1–4. Some suggest that Yahweh is pictured as a mother at various places throughout the chapter, such as suckling a newborn infant in verse 3, in accordance with other ancient Near Eastern monarchical depictions.[117] In the case of Hosea, however, the arguments for overt mother imagery go beyond the limits of the natural construal of the textual evidence.[118] The specific metaphor

---

114. In addition to the translation footnotes above, see esp. Seifert, *Metaphorisches Reden*, 183–93; Kakkanattu, *God's Enduring Love*, 12–30, 138–80.

115. Mays, *Hosea*, 153; Wolff, *Hosea*, 198; Andersen and Freedman, *Hosea*, 577; Braaten, "Parent-Child Imagery in Hosea," 295–308; Nissinen, *Prophetie*, 238–39; Janet L. R. Melnyk, "When Israel Was a Child: Ancient Near Eastern Adoption Formulas and the Relationship between God and Israel," in Graham, Brown, and Kuan, *History and Interpretation*, 251, 253; Duane Andre Smith, "Kinship and Covenant in Hosea 11:1–4," *HBT* 16 (1994): 41–53; Eidevall, *Grapes in the Desert*, 168.

116. See Wolff, *Hosea*, 198; Manfred Weippert, "Die Bildsprache der neuassyrischen Prophetie," in *Beiträge zur prophetischen Bildsprache in Israel und Assyrien*, OBO 64 (Göttingen: Vandenhoeck & Ruprecht, 1985), 71–78; Nissinen, *Prophetie*, 277–90; Eidevall, *Grapes in the Desert*, 175–76; Simo Parpola, *Assyrian Prophecies*, SAA 9 (Helsinki: Helsinki University Press, 1997), xxvi–xliv; Nicholas Wyatt, "Asherah," *DDD*, 100; Ben Zvi, *Hosea*, 233; Dearman, *Book of Hosea*, 279.

117. M. D. Goldman, "The Real Interpretation of Hosea XI.3," *ABR* 4 (1954): 91–92; Sweeney, *Twelve Prophets* 1:114. This often involves understanding תרגלתי in accordance with the Arabic root *rgl*, "to suck, quiet." For the suggestion that Yahweh is pictured as a mother at various places throughout the chapter, see Helen Schüngel-Straumann, "God as Mother in Hosea 11," *TD* 34 (1987): 3–8; Wacker, "Hosea," 380–82.

118. See Braaten, "Parent-Child Imagery in Hosea," 305–6; Siegfried Kreuzer, "Gott als Mutter in Hosea 11?," *TQ* 169 (1989): 123–32; Kakkanattu, *God's Endur-*

of adoption "conveniently circumvents the need for a birth-mother, and Yahweh is shown to be capable of every other maternal nurturing."[119]

Whereas previous metaphors emphasized Israel's usefulness and purpose, the emphasis here is on Yahweh's affection for Israel (אהב).[120] Yahweh's purposes may be implicit in summoning Israel out of Egypt, but this is not the emphasis of this metaphor. "Exodus … is translated into a metaphor which clothes the event with all the feeling and personal involvement that belong to a father's relation to a beloved child."[121] The emphasis of the divine-parent metaphor applied to Assyrian kings was on "the king's total dependence on his divine mother and the latter's ardent love for her child or creature."[122] The rhetorical purpose of this metaphor in 11:1 becomes clear in the contrast with 11:2—namely, to indict Israel. Though Yahweh was like a parent who loved the child (11:1), Israel spurned that affection (11:2).

The phrase קראו להם כן הלכו מפני (11:2a–b) is included in the list of metaphorical expressions because it may subtly extend the son metaphor and hint that Israel has become a rebellious son.[123] The next line (הם לבעלים יזבחו ולפסלים יקטרון, Hos 11:2c–d) may interpret the metaphor in 11:2a–b.[124] If so, the "they" who called (קראו) in 11:2a are the people of Moab who called the people of Israel (the rebellious son?) away from parent-Yahweh into Baal worship in 11:2c–d (see 9:10).[125]

---

ing Love, 61. Nissinen claims that the text uses *both* father and mother imagery. The image of breastfeeding is "if not the only possible one, at least quite plausible," though this could be interpreted as an animal or human mother (*Prophetie*, 271; similarly Nwaoru, *Imagery in the Prophecy*, 149). Seifert says God is neither mother nor father (*Metaphorisches Reden*, 198–202).

119. Melnyk, "When Israel Was a Child," 259. Ishtar, a female deity, tells Esarhaddon "I am your father and mother," thus exhibiting gender fluidity (Nissinen, *Prophets and Prophecy*, 116; see also 117 n. c).

120. The term may also connote covenantal or political relationships; see n. 40, above.

121. Mays, *Hosea*, 153.

122. Parpola, *Assyrian Prophecies*, xxvi.

123. Braaten, "Parent-Child Imagery in Hosea," 294; Melnyk, "When Israel Was a Child," 255–57. This theme of rebellious son (see Deut 21:18–21) echoes Hos 9:15 (see discussion there) and may be extended in 11:7–8 (see below).

124. On the metaphoric function of parallelism, see p. 16 n. 55, above.

125. Tully, *Hosea*, 269. See Num 25:1–5, which shares three lexemes (קרא, זבח, בעל) with Hos 11:2.

3. Metaphors of Sentencing

Hosea 11:3 includes three metaphorical clauses expressing Yahweh's gentleness and healing[126] and a fourth expressing Israel's ignorance of that care (ולא ידעו). These phrases can be read as part of the preceding parent metaphor or the following farmer metaphor.[127] The ambiguity is intentional and is revisited below.

The Good Farmer (11:3–4)

The ambiguous source domain of 11:3 comes more fully into the light in 11:4, where Yahweh is the farmer again.[128] Farmer-Yahweh pulls cow-Israel gently, humanely (בחבלי אדם אמשכם), and with great affection (בעבתות אהבה). Farmer-Yahweh is the one to remove the bit from the cow's mouth, taking her "away from the rigours of ploughing for rest and refreshment. Israel was not led by halters and ropes of coercion.... Rather, from the beginning, Yahweh acted with the gentleness and consideration" of a friend and "sought to draw his people into a relationship of friendship and familiarity."[129] The rhetorical purpose of this metaphor is the same as that of 11:1, implicit indictment. Though 11:4 is not followed by a claim about Israel's abandonment of God despite his care (as in 11:1), their betrayal is evident.

Analyzing Their Interaction

One of the interesting features of this chapter is the multiple instances of metaphoric ambiguity. This ambiguity raises several questions, which have been answered above. Does the parent metaphor continue into 11:2a? Yes. Is the source domain of 11:3 shepherd, farmer, or parent? The verse is intentionally polyvalent between farmer and parent as a transition to verse 4. Does 11:4 continue the parent metaphor, return to the parent metaphor, continue the

---

126. On healing in this passage, see Seifert, *Metaphorisches Reden*, 202–5; Walker, "Metaphor of Healing," 119–46; Daniël F. O'Kennedy, "Healing as/or Forgiveness? The Use of the Term רפא in the Book of Hosea," *OTE* 14 (2001): 458–74, esp. 463–64; Kakkanattu, *God's Enduring Love*, 54–57.

127. A third option is to interpret 11:3 as shepherd imagery (Eidevall, *Grapes in the Desert*, 174).

128. There is disagreement as to the source domain of the metaphor in 11:4. But assuming our text-critical and grammatical choices, 11:4 offers clearer textual indicators of a farmer source domain than those of 11:3. (Tg. Neb. explicitly adds that Yahweh was "like a farmer" [כאיכרא] in 11:4.)

129. Macintosh, *Critical and Exegetical Commentary*, 448.

farmer metaphor, or begin the farmer metaphor? It continues the farming aspect of the polyvalent metaphors in verse 3. Among the parent metaphors, is a gender identified? Not explicitly. Three further questions remain.

First, does the parent metaphor continue beyond the cluster into 11:7–8, where Yahweh vacillates about what to do about the rebellious son?[130] It is possible that 11:7–8, though it need not require a parent source domain, can meaningfully be read in light of 11:1 as suggestive of a further development in the parent's thinking and feeling.[131] It should be noted that anthropomorphic metaphors for God definitively end in 11:9 (כי אל אנכי ולא איש בקרבך קדוש).

Second, does this mean that the parent metaphor should be viewed as the dominant metaphor for the chapter?[132] This study identifies God as farmer in 11:4, and additional significant metaphors are discussed below. The parent metaphor should not be given undue significance as the overriding metaphor of the chapter to the exclusion or erasure of others. While significant, it serves its purpose alongside the other metaphors. This non-reductionistic approach respects the ancient aspective approach as well as the need for multiple metaphors to make a point.[133]

Abstruseness, though, should not be treated as a problem to be solved. The death of poetry is rigid analysis. The final question remains: *Why* is there metaphoric ambiguity? If our textual decisions are sound, and if these expressions were as ambiguous to original readers as to modern ones, then the ambiguity was intentional and productive. Benjamin Har-

---

130. So Wolff, *Hosea*, 194, 203; Seifert, *Metaphorisches Reden*, 211–15; Ben Zvi, *Hosea*, 228; Nogalski, *Hosea-Jonah*, 158–60; Yee, "Hosea," 306.

131. The standard ancient Near Eastern punishments involved in disowning a rebellious son were either disinheritance and/or being sold into slavery (Braaten, "Parent-Child Imagery in Hosea," 300–302). Possibly both punishments are pictured in 11:5–7: disinheritance in 11:6, slavery in 11:5.

132. E.g., Nogalski reads Hos 11:1–8 as constituting one continuous metaphor of God as father (*Hosea–Jonah*, 155–64).

133. Some continue the parent metaphor from 11:1–2 into 11:3–4 due to a preference for "contextual consistency" (Nogalski, *Hosea–Jonah*, 157), but this misses the significance of the aspective approach (see ch. 8 below; Macintosh, *Critical and Exegetical Commentary*, 448). Such diverse imagery is consistent with ancient Near Eastern deity depictions. E.g., "A Report of Prophecies: Mullissu-kabtat to Assurbanipal" has Ishtar as a nurse or mother to the king, who is then abruptly referred to as her calf (Nissinen, *Prophets and Prophecy*, 127–28, §92).

3. Metaphors of Sentencing

shav describes a similar phenomenon in a poem by T. S. Eliot, but his description applies to Hos 11:1–4:

> This imprecise, inexhaustible, demanding quality of unresolved poetic tensions has a powerful impact on the trained reader, quite unlike direct statements or explicit lexical (or transferred) meanings. What is certain here is not the solution to a relationship but the relationship itself between several frames of reference (as open constructs, to be filled from our world-experience); the material presented to the reader's imagination; as well as the possibilities for several specific, though undecided, solutions. Poetic texts provide us not definite meanings but approximations and open situations.[134]

One can sense in this cluster gradual shifts among domains with similar entailments, rather than abrupt transitions between starkly different domains. The parent metaphor in 11:1 is clear. Hosea 11:2 is *suggestive* of a parental theme but hardly transparent. Read right after the parent metaphor, it carries the reverberations of a mournful parent's call to a rebellious son. Read in isolation, or exclusively with 11:2c–d, it need have nothing to do with a parent metaphor. Similarly, one finds in 11:3 terms for a parent's care, and then the subsequent verse provides clearer instances of metaphorical expressions for a farmer's compassion.

Both the *ambiguity* of source domains and the *clarity* of metaphorical claims occur because of these shared entailments. Both parents and farmers are capable of caring for their charges. Both can exercise discipline, teach, feed, summon, hold in the arms, heal, and love.[135] The source domain may be unclear or polyvalent, but the claim of the metaphors is crystallized and widely recognized by scholars. Macintosh summarizes the common view that this cluster is about "[God's] consistent love and [Israel's] consistent ingratitude" since the beginning.[136] Yahweh was nothing but good to Israel from the start, despite Israel's subsequent rebellion.

The metaphors also highlight emotional aspects of Yahweh that have laid dormant. A common theme in previous clusters has been that of Israel's usefulness to Yahweh followed by disappointment. This cluster transitions to underscore God's generous love for Israel. The rhetorical

---

134. Harshav, *Explorations in Poetics*, 46.
135. Hosea 11:4a–b are the only exceptions. The mentions of cords, ropes, and a yoke on the jawbone favor the farmer metaphor. Arguments for the parent metaphor require textual emendation.
136. Macintosh, *Critical and Exegetical Commentary*, 436; see also Wolff, *Hosea*, 193.

function of these metaphors, however, is to emphasize the implicit betrayal in the relationship.[137] Israel thanklessly revolted against Yahweh's consistent care. Israel abandoned him as if Yahweh were an oppressive parent or farmer (see 11:4 NJPS). As with the phase it recapitulates (4:1–8:14), the rhetorical purpose of this cluster is implicit indictment: Israel deserves what is coming. It may also provoke the shame of a rebellious son.

Cluster 13: Hosea 13:5–8[138]

13:5   Direct, 3

אני ידעתיך במדבר בארץ תלאבות

It was *I* who knew [i.e., cared for][139] you in the pasture land, in a land of baking heat;[140]

13:6   Indirect, 2

כמרעיתם וישבעו שבעו וירם לבם על כן שכחוני

---

137. Note the emphatic word order and pronouns and that the subject vacillates between God and Israel. These features highlight the contrast between Yahweh's actions and Israel's response.

138. Hosea 13:10, 14 (2x) include expressions that some read as divine metaphors: "I will be your king" (13:10), "I will be your plagues … , I will be your sting" (13:14c-d; see Sweeney, *Twelve Prophets* 1:134; Gruber, *Hosea*, 546–49). Others see double entendres (Fisch, *Poetry with a Purpose*, 153; Landy, *Hosea*, 160, 162, 166; Morris, *Prophecy, Poetry and Hosea*, 92–93). The form is not the first-person singular of היה but either a variant of איה ("where" [so LXX]) or a term of derision (Macintosh, *Critical and Exegetical Commentary*, 537–38, 546–47). Macintosh provides the best explanation (537–38, 546; see *BHQ*, 71*; Dearman, *Book of Hosea*, 324; contra Heinz-Josef Fabry, "נחם," *TDOT* 9:354; Glenny, *Hosea*, 177–78). These verses are therefore not metaphorical and so are not included here. Even if a metaphor, 13:10 would not be part of a cluster.

139. It is often suggested on the basis of LXX and Syr. that ידעתיך be emended to רעיתיך, from root רעה, "to feed or shepherd" (*BHS*; NRSV; Wolff, *Hosea*, 220; Jeremias, *Prophet Hosea*, 159; Stuart, *Hosea–Jonah*, 200). It is more likely that the ancient versions are trying to bring out the sense of ידעתיך (see *HALOT*, 391: "take care of someone"; Tg. Neb.; *BHQ*, 71*; Neef, *Heilstraditionen*, 102; Landy, *Hosea*, 52; Eidevall, *Grapes in the Desert*, 196; Macintosh, *Critical and Exegetical Commentary*, 528–29; Tully, *Hosea*, 313).

140. For this translation, see Macintosh, *Critical and Exegetical Commentary*, 528–29. Or "a land of drought."

3. Metaphors of Sentencing

as they ate,[141] they were satisfied. When they were satisfied, their heart became proud, therefore they forgot me.

13:7a   Direct, 3
ואהי להם כמו שחל
So I became[142] to them like a lion

13:7b   Direct, 3
כנמר על דרך אשור
like a panther I will stalk beside the road.

13:8a   Direct, 3
אפגשם כדב שכול
I shall encounter them like a bear bereaved [of her cubs]

13:8b   Direct, 3
ואקרע סגור לבם
and I shall tear open their chest

13:8c   Direct, 3
ואכלם שם כלביא
and devour them there like a lioness

13:8d   Direct, 3
חית השדה תבקעם
as[143] a wild animal would mangle them[144]

---

141. Lit. "according to their pasturage."
142. A short form of first-person common singular היה; see 4Q78 (4QTwelve Prophets^c, ואהיה). The past tense is retained (Macintosh, *Critical and Exegetical Commentary*, 532; Moon, *Hosea*, 204, 207), but a future is possible in light of the following *yiqtol* verbs (NRSV; though Joüon §118s–t says this is "very rare"). The ingressive sense is preferred. In Hosea, poetic *wayyiqtols* frequently indicate the consequence of the preceding clause (e.g., 9:10; 12:5; 13:1, 6 [2x]; see Macintosh, *Critical and Exegetical Commentary*, 531). God becoming like a devouring animal is the natural result of their forgetting him. If Israel has behaved differently, Yahweh would have remained the shepherd and not become a predator (Seifert, *Metaphorisches Reden*, 181–82, 283 §17.2, 284 §21.5).
143. Implied comparative (Joüon §174e).
144. This translation is NRSV.

This is the first metaphor cluster in the declaration of punishment phase (13:1–14:1) of the third cycle (12:1–14:9).[145] The metaphors will be analyzed collectively, because of the density of similar metaphors.

Analyzing Their Interaction

The cluster is composed of two contrasting panels (one positive, one negative), differentiated by temporal plane and causal relationship. The first minicluster (13:5–6) is a historical retrospective referring to Yahweh's care for Israel in the wilderness period (13:4 refers to the beginning of the relationship in Egypt). It articulates the relationship between the people's being satisfied with the gifts of Yahweh and therefore forgetting the giver (see 2:15).[146] Deuteronomy uses similar language, where it refers to idolatry (Deut 6:10–15, 8:7–20, 11:15–17, 31:20, 32:15–18). The connection between idolatry and forgetting Yahweh is common in Hosea as well (Hos 2:10, 15, 19; see 13:1–2).[147] Rhetorically, this panel is an indictment intended to provoke shame at forgetting the source of their provision. This accusation of past failure provoking shame (13:5–6) gives way to a threatening declaration of impending punishment that provokes fear (13:7–8).

Hosea 13:7–8 is a minicluster of negative metaphors referring to the past or perhaps imminent future. God is compared to a lion (שחל), a leopard (נמר), a bear (דב), another type of lion (לביא),[148] and a generic wild animal (חית השדה). They share the entailment of danger. The differences are significant, as is the seminarrative progression. In the face of Yahweh's "raw power" and the inability of language to capture such realities, "one recourse is to multiply metaphors, even and especially in close proximity."[149] At first, Yahweh simply is a lion, without further description or action. Then leopard-Yahweh will crouch (אשור), ready to pounce,

---

145. For a form-critical analysis of the chapter, see Wolff, *Hosea*, 222–24.
146. See Macintosh, *Critical and Exegetical Commentary*, 531. Tully claims this is the central idea of the whole book (*Hosea*, 4).
147. Some scholars claim that Hosea influenced the later Dtn school (e.g., Wolff, *Hosea*, 226).
148. For these two types of lions, see Strawn, *Stronger Than a Lion?*, 311–19, 322–25.
149. Strawn, *Stronger Than a Lion?*, 272. See, e.g., an Old Aramaic treaty from Tell Sefire (ca. 773 BCE), which includes the lion, wolf, and panther in a curse (Kitchen and Lawrence, *Treaty, Law and Covenant* 1:931, §3, line 9). See further Strawn, *Stronger Than a Lion?*, 271.

3. Metaphors of Sentencing 127

alongside the path. Then bear-Yahweh is bereaved of her cubs (שכול) and therefore angry, hence it/she will confront Israel and rip open their chest cavity (ואקרע סגור לבם). Finally, lion-Yahweh will devour them (ואכלם), as a wild animal would tear them to shreds (תבקעם).

A wordplay initially alerts the reader to the double vision of these theriomorphic metaphors. It suggests that not only Yahweh and Israel but politics and war are in the background. Yahweh is said to "lurk" like a panther along the path (13:7b). The verb (אָשׁוּר) differs by only a *patakh* and a dagesh in the שׁ from the word for Assyria (אַשּׁוּר).[150] Phonically, the two are nearly indistinguishable. The image of leopard-Yahweh crouching, then, is suggestive of the *means* by which Yahweh's judgment is realized: God will use Assyria to tear them to shreds.[151] "The Assyrian threat has been lurking behind all these oracles, literally 'lying in wait' for Ephraim (5:13, 7:11, 10:6). That threat now reveals itself as an enraged animal, a leopard, a lion, a bear deprived of its whelps, ravaging the people of Israel with privy paw."[152]

Throughout the ancient Near East, leopards and lions picture both kings and deities in their strength and prowess.[153] Lion imagery was common in the eighth century, as Neo-Assyrian kings increasingly compared themselves to lions in battle, though never pictorially.[154] Their use of the metaphor emphasized predation: the dangerous threat to the victim.[155] Art from Iron IIC Phoenicia and Syria suggests that the deity-as-lion was viewed "as a creature that offered powerful protection." It may have been "especially dramatic and shocking" for Hosea to then picture Yahweh the

---

150. The versions misunderstood the wordplay, rendering as "on the road of [the] Assyrians" (κατὰ τὴν ὁδὸν Ἀσσυρίων [LXX]; similarly Syr.; Vulg.).

151. Irvine argues that this refers to Sargon in 720–719 BCE. See Stuart A. Irvine, "Relating Prophets and History: An Example from Hosea 13," in Moore and Kelle, *Israel's Prophets and Israel's Past*, 165.

152. Fisch, *Poetry with a Purpose*, 152; see Sweeney, *Twelve Prophets* 1:132.

153. Zimri-Lim, likened to the god storm god Addu, is said to be "the leopard of battle, // The powerful one who captures (his) adversary, // who utterly destroys (his) enemy." See "The Epic of Zimri-Lim" [A.3152+M.5665+], in *COS* 4.51:233. Similarly, Inanna/Ishtar is described as a "lion that stalks over the meadow" (Strawn, *Stronger Than a Lion?*, 209).

154. Strawn, *Stronger Than a Lion?*, 178–79. Pictorially, the norm is to show the king killing a lion, not *as* a lion.

155. Strawn, *Stronger Than a Lion?*, 207.

lion as turning to attack Israel.[156] The *bereaved* bear image further modifies this portrait: "YHWH's aggression ... is not simply the reflex action of a predator who kills to eat, but a rage over loss."[157]

Lion imagery is less common in Ugaritic material. While lion imagery is elsewhere commonly associated with storm gods, at Ugarit it is not associated with Baal but with Mot, the god of death.[158] For example, *KTU* 1.5.I.12b–15a reads,

tḥm. bn ilm mt.
hwt. ydd. bn il ġzr.
pnpš. npš. lbim thw

the message of Mot, the son of El;
the word of the beloved (son) of El, the hero
"My appetite is that of a desert lion"[159]

This association of lions with the Ugaritic god of death reflects a pattern throughout the chapter, beginning in the first verse. There, Israel incurs guilt through Baal and *dies* (ויאשם בבעל וימת). In consecutive words, one Ugaritic deity (Baal) gives way to another (Mot).[160] Israel suffers the same fate as Baal, the false god they worship: defeat at the hands of Death/Mot/Yahweh(?). In an ironic reversal, "Baal, the Canaanite god of fertility, brings Israel ultimately to her death."[161] The next verse (Hos 13:2) may be an "anti-Baal polemic" due to the rejection of the bull imagery.[162] At the end of the chapter, Yahweh is pictured as the one who sends the scorching east wind (13:15), associated at Ugarit with Mot. Baal was the storm god who brought rains, fertility, and satisfaction (as Yahweh does in 13:4–6), but

---

156. Keel and Uehlinger, *Gods, Goddesses, and Images*, 190. See Hos 11:10.
157. Dearman, *Book of Hosea*, 324.
158. Strawn, *Stronger Than a Lion?*, 206–7, 211.
159. Strawn's translation (*Stronger Than a Lion?*, 211); see Pardee in COS 1.86:265; Nicholas Wyatt, *Religious Texts from Ugarit: The Words of Ilimilku and His Colleagues* (Sheffield: Sheffield Academic, 1998), 116–17. See also *KTU* 1.4.VIII.17–20.
160. See Nah 1:3–5, where Yahweh usurps the functions of Baal and Mot (Korpel, *Rift in the Clouds*, 601–2).
161. Wolff, *Hosea*, 229. John F. Healey grants this as a possibility. See Healey, "Mot," *DDD*, 601.
162. Mark S. Smith, *The Early History of God: Yahweh and the Other Deities in Ancient Israel*, 2nd ed. (Grand Rapids: Eerdmans, 2002), 85.

Mot directed the parching east winds that wither the land.[163] Thus, thrice in chapter 13, in Ugaritic terms, Yahweh transitions from being pictured as the storm god of war to becoming the god of death itself. With the language of death in the forthcoming cluster (esp. 13:14), the picture becomes increasingly darker for Israel. Death is the central theme of the chapter. "As Ward has observed, 'the salient theological feature of the oracle' is Hosea's insistence that 'Yahweh is the Destroyer.' It is not Death (Māwet/Mot), 'an arbitrary power,' with whom Israel has to deal. Her 'cosmic battle' was with Yahweh, and Yahweh alone."[164] Far from merely recapitulating the previous cycle (4:1–11:11), the imagery of this cycle (12:1–14:9) is more somber.

Rhetorically, the second minicluster is an inversion of the shepherd imagery in the first. There is no deliverer besides Yahweh (13:4), so when he turns against them in judgment, there can be no hope (see 5:13–14, 13:9–10). Their only savior has become their executioner. "Behind the face of the leopard is Ehyeh ["I AM"] himself. It is he, the shepherd, who has become the devourer."[165]

Cluster 14: Hosea 13:14–14:1

13:14a   Direct, 3
מיד שאול אפדם
From the hand/power of the pit shall I ransom them?[166]

---

163. Watson, "Mot," 238, 252; Korpel, *Rift in the Clouds*, 599; Davies, *Hosea* [1993], 297; Landy, *Hosea*, 53; Day, *Yahweh and the Gods*, 121; Smith, *Early History of God*, 88. Fitzgerald contends that the east wind symbolizes the Assyrian army, though he grants that an echo of Mot in the Baal cycle is possible. See Aloysius Fitzgerald, *The Lord of the East Wind*, CBQMS 34 (Washington, DC: Catholic Biblical Association of America, 2002), 25–26.

164. Watson, "Mot," 251, citing James M. Ward, *Hosea: A Theological Commentary* (New York: Harper & Row, 1967), 223.

165. Fisch, *Poetry with a Purpose*, 152; similarly Rudolph, *Hosea*, 243; Wolff, *Hosea*, 227; Seifert, *Metaphorisches Reden*, 170–81; Macintosh, *Critical and Exegetical Commentary*, 534; Dearman, *Book of Hosea*, 323; Glenny, *Hosea*, 173; Gruber, *Hosea*, 538; Moon, *Hosea*, 207.

166. It is not uncommon to read 13:14a and 13:14b as rhetorical questions. For grammatical justification, see Tully, *Hosea*, 332. Goldingay renders "I could redeem/restore" (*First Testament*, 856).

13:14b[167]   Direct, 3
ממות אגאלם
From death shall I redeem them?

13:14e   Direct, 3
נחם יסתר מעיני
compassion[168] is hidden from my eyes.

14:1a-b   Indirect, 2
תאשם שמרון כי מרתה באלהיה
Samaria shall bear her guilt,[169] for she has rebelled against her God.

This cluster constitutes the nadir of the final section on judgment (13:1–14:1) in Hosea. These are the last words of doom; all that remains is an invitation to return to Yahweh and a picture of hopeful restoration. This cluster, then, summarizes the preceding thirteen chapters of mostly accusation and threat, and drives home the terrible consequences of Israel's actions.[170] The words heighten previous themes of the book. Hosea strains for the strongest expressions of language and paints as horrifying a picture

---

167. On the intriguing possibility of provocative metaphors for Yahweh in 13:14c–d, see n. 138, above.

168. The interpretation of נחם is largely responsible for diametrically opposed readings. Either "compassion" (NRSV) / "repentance" (ASV, KJV) is hidden from God's eyes, or "revenge" (NJPS; Andersen and Freedman, *Hosea*, 640) is far from God's thoughts. The literary context can support either. Landy, embracing the ambiguity, creatively suggests a possible meaning of "his triumph over death will never be revoked; for death there is no pity" (*Hosea*, 166). The most natural reading of the term is closer to the idea of compassion (Macintosh, *Critical and Exegetical Commentary*, 546–47; Gruber, *Hosea*, 549–50; Tully, *Hosea*, 333–34).

169. Wolff, Macintosh, and virtually all English translations understand the verb to denote the bearing of guilt, in the sense of "suffer the consequences of" (see *HALOT*, 95)—a slightly different nuance from in Hos 5:15 (see p. 62 n. 119, above; Wolff, *Hosea*, 222; Macintosh, *Critical and Exegetical Commentary*, 555). Gruber maintains it means "feel guilty" here, as in 5:15 (*Hosea*, 560). The metaphor of guilt as a burden to bear is not considered here (see Lam, *Patterns of Sin*). Others derive the verb from שמם ("to be desolate"; so LXX; Syr.; ibn Ezra; Stuart, *Hosea-Jonah*, 199; see discussions in Macintosh, *Critical and Exegetical Commentary*, 555, 557; Gruber, *Hosea*, 560).

170. Hosea 13 may thus reflect the last years of the Northern Kingdom (722–719 BCE; see Irvine, "Relating Prophets and History").

3. Metaphors of Sentencing   131

as possible in order to break through Israel's indifference. With 14:1, the gavel falls for the last time.

Nonredeemer (13:14a–b)

The words אפדם and אגאלם may evoke the imagery of a family member who would redeem them.[171] The lexeme גאל occurs only here in Hosea. פדה occurred in Hos 7:13, where it may suggest a family redeemer, or at least someone with the social capital to rescue Israel. Both 7:13 and 13:14 make the same claim, one through a declarative statement, the other through a rhetorical question: Yahweh *would* rescue Israel (7:13), or Yahweh had considered doing so (13:14), but in the end, Yahweh will *not*. In 7:13, the rescue is from destruction (שד); here, it is from the maw of death and the wasteland.

The next two lines may be questions that imply Yahweh's expectant welcome of death and Sheol to the people, as if Yahweh were to say, "I cannot wait for the plagues and destruction of death to finally arrive!"[172] Yahweh is pictured as the redeemer who has absolved himself of responsibility and given Israel over to the natural consequences of their actions: death. The only one who could save them (5:14; 13:4), their kinsmen-redeemer obligated to save, is now free from his obligations to them. The safety net has been withdrawn, and Israel has been handed over to death and oblivion.

No Compassion (13:14e)

The absolving of the divine kinsman's responsibilities is possible because compassion is hidden from his eyes. This is consistent with earlier declarations that Yahweh will no longer love the people (לא אוסף אהבתם, 9:15e), even though it seems to contradict the declaration that Yahweh's compassion is awakened and that Yahweh cannot give the people over to death (יחד נכמרו נחומי, 11:8f).[173] In 13:14, it is compassion that is muted, not

---

171. Perhaps the image is not merely evoked by the verb but is essential to its meaning. Cross suggests the verb גאל is often best translated as "to act as kinsman" (*From Epic to Canon*, 4).

172. So also Stuart, *Hosea-Jonah*, 207. For an alternative, see Macintosh, *Critical and Exegetical Commentary*, 546.

173. See pp. 168–71 ("Love and Hate") and 213–14 ("Passionate"), below.

judgment. At this moment, compassion does not factor into the calculus of Yahweh's decision about Israel's immediate future. This underscores the hopelessness of their situation. If Israel had hoped that Yahweh's mind might be changed (e.g., 11:8–9) to avoid destruction, the possibility is explicitly denied. Consistent with the other metaphors in the cluster, this metaphor has a sense of finality as it concludes and summarizes the punishment of God's lawsuit against Israel.

Yahweh versus the Rebel (14:1a–b)

Now that Yahweh no longer has an obligation to redeem Israel, and compassion is no more, Yahweh summarizes the immediate consequences for Israel: they shall bear the consequences of their guilt, because they have rebelled against their God (תאשם שמרון כי מרתה באלהיה, 14:1a–b). Their cities will be laid waste, and the people will suffer the worst consequences of war (14:1c–e). This is the final indictment and punishment of Israel in the book.

It is significant that among all the possibilities for Hosea's choice for a concluding metaphor to summarize Israel's fault, he chooses "rebel" (מרה). The word occurs only here in Hosea, although it is semantically similar to בגד (5:7, 6:7) and פשע (7:13, 8:1, 14:10). Because it occurs only here, it is difficult to discern whether a specific metaphorical domain is in view. Its usage elsewhere in the Old Testament is instructive. Unlike בגד, מרה does not frequently occur in political contexts, but it is used (along with סרר) of the rebellious son in Deut 21:18, 20. Though inconclusive, the usage of the verb may favor the familial domain of a rebellious son (as in Hos 9:15, 17) as more likely than that of a rebellious vassal (as with בגד in 5:7; 6:7).[174] The verb is often associated with Israel's rebellion in the wilderness (e.g., Num 27:14, Deut 9:7, Ezek 20:13, Ps 78:40). Along with the choice of the *qal* rather than the *hiphil*,[175] this suggests that disobedience is essential to Israel's nature. Considered together, the verse pictures Israel as a constitutionally rebellious son to father-Yahweh.

The metaphorics of the verb communicate that Yahweh and Israel are in a relationship with mutual obligations (presumably the covenant) and

---

174. Eidevall suggests, without further evidence, that since the city is pictured as a woman, מרה might suggest a rebellious maidservant (*Grapes in the Desert*, 203).

175. The *qal* is stative, while the *hiphil* means "*behave* rebelliously" (see *HALOT*, 632–33).

3. Metaphors of Sentencing

that Israel has violated those bilateral, relational obligations. Samaria, metonymic for the nation, *is* rebellious in her very nature. She can do nothing else, from the wilderness to the present. Thus, she must bear the consequences of her guilt (תאשם שמרון).

Analyzing Their Interaction

Three observations can be made about the interactions within this cluster. The first relates to their logical relationships; the second, to a common entailment; the third, to a possible polemical usage of metaphors.

Though Hos 13:14a–b was treated above primarily according to the declarative implications of the implied answer to the rhetorical question, it is significant that Yahweh again asks himself questions (see 11:8). This sets the stage for the progression within the cluster. This logic can be presented as follows:

1. Question: Should I be their kinsmen-redeemer? (13:14a–b)
2. Answer: No. Compassion will not factor into this decision. (13:14e)
3. Result: Samaria must bear the consequences of their actions. (14:1a)
4. Summary reason (כי): They have rebelled against their God. (14:1b)

Since Israel is described as ontologically rebellious (14:1b, מרתה *qal*; see 5:4; 9:10, 15; 10:9; 11:2, 7), "though the words of [ch. 13] v. 14 may repel us, 'this was the only honest conclusion to the logic of Hosea's theology of history.'"[176]

Second, there is a shared entailment between all three metaphors, namely, the rendering void of any obligation of Yahweh to protect or deliver Israel. Yahweh is the redeemer who will not redeem (13:14a–b; see 7:13); the one who hides compassion from his eyes (13:14e) and will not act for the benefit of the other because of pity; and the father, or suzerain, who has been betrayed by a rebel, thereby voiding the agreement of mutual obligation (14:1b). The hiding of compassion is the suppression of

---

176. Watson, "Mot," 251–52, quoting Ward, *Hosea*, 224.

emotion that might otherwise mitigate such an unbending correlation of deed and consequences.

Third, 13:14 may appropriate language and imagery from Canaanite deities yet also invert them in surprising ways. Scholars have noted similarities to the so-called Baal myth, in which Baal fights Mot, dies, then lives again as king. Some, interpreting 13:14 as positive declarations that Yahweh *will* rescue from death, conclude that Yahweh is presented in the role of Baal victoriously battling Mot. Worden, for example, concludes that "deliverance by Yahweh is described in terms reminiscent of Baal's delivery from Mot."[177]

This is not, strictly speaking, a correct reading of the parallel. It is the *people* who are battling Mot. Yahweh, the most high God (in the role of El), oversees the fight between Israel (= Baal) and Death (Mot).[178] Yahweh chooses *not* to intervene to rescue Israel from the deadly fight. Israel has so wed herself to her other husband Baal that she shall suffer the same consequences Baal did (see 2:18, 13:1). Hosea 13:14c–d (אהי דבריך מות אהי קטבך שאול) depicts the supreme God Yahweh summoning Mot to devour Yahweh's people. Even Death/Mot is the servant of Yahweh.[179] In this case, it shall be not only "like people, like priest" (4:9), but also "like people, like Baal"—given over to the ravages of Death itself (Mot). Will there be for Israel, as for Baal, a resurrection on the other side of death?[180]

---

177. Worden, "Literary Influence," 296; see Green, *Storm-God in the Ancient Near East*, 276 n. 232. Sweeney associates Yahweh in 13:12–14 with Baal only in regard to Baal's ability to grant fertility in childbirth (*Twelve Prophets* 1:133). Baal, however, was not associated with *human* fertility (see n. 26, above).

178. This puts the characters in different roles than in cluster 13, where Yahweh is cast in terms of Mot (13:7–8), though in 13:15 Yahweh is again cast in Mot-like images.

179. See John Goldingay, *Israel's Faith*, vol. 2 of *Old Testament Theology* (Downers Grove, IL: IVP Academic, 2006), 309.

180. Day suggests that the pattern of death and resurrection in Hos 13–14 "strongly suggests that the imagery of Israel's death and resurrection has been consciously appropriated from the Baal cult, against which the prophet is clearly polemicizing throughout his preaching." See John Day, "Baal," *ABD* 1:549.

4
Metaphors of Redemption

It turns out that there is hope for Israel, even after their death sentence has been carried out (Hos 13). That hope is rooted in the overturned heart of God (Hos 11), which results in nothing less than Israel's resurrection from the dead (Hos 14).

Cluster 12: Hosea 11:8–10

11:8e   Direct, 3

נהפך עלי לבי

I've had a change of heart[1]

---

1. Lit. "My heart/mind is changed/turned over." All three elements of this phrase have puzzled interpreters: the meaning of the *niphal* verb, לבב/לב as a subject, and the preposition על. The verb uses על six times (1 Sam 4:19, 2 Kgs 21:13, Job 30:15, Isa 60:5, Dan 10:8, Hos 11:8). הפך with לבב/לב as subject can mean "to change one's mind" (Exod 14:5, Ps 105:25) or to be remorseful (Lam 1:20; see Tully, *Hosea*, 280–81; see 1 Sam 10:9 and Ps 105:25 for לבב/לב as object). Exodus 14:5 is a close parallel, but Lam 1:20 (נהפך לבי בקרבי) is closer: it uses the *niphal* stem, has לב as a subject, and is followed by a prepositional phrase with a first-person singular suffix indicating the inner self of the speaker (בקרבי). The context of the phrase in Lam 1:20 indicates remorse: "See, O Lord, how distressed I am; // my stomach churns, // *my heart is wrung within me*, // because I have been very rebellious" (NRSV). על has different nuances from קרב, but על need not have an adversarial sense (i.e., "against me" per Mays, *Hosea*, 151; Wolff, *Hosea*, 193; Seifert, *Metaphorisches Reden*, 220), because it indicates "the personal subject of the motion upon whom, as it were, that emotion acts" (Macintosh, *Critical and Exegetical Commentary*, 459). See also J. Gerald Janzen, "Metaphor and Reality in Hosea 11," *Semeia* 24 (1982): 27–29. Interpretations differ by emphasizing either cognition (Mays; see Exod 14:5) or emotion (Macintosh, *Critical and Exegetical Commentary*, 458–59; Tully, *Hosea*, 267; NRSV; see Lam 1:20). See James Luther Mays, "Response to Janzen: 'Metaphor and Reality in Hosea 11,'" *Semeia* 24 (1982): 47. This may be a modern distinction not shared by ancient Israelites (see Mirguet, "What Is

11:8f   Direct, 3
יחד נכמרו נחומי
my compassion[2] is all warmed up

11:10a–b[3]   Direct, 2
אחרי יהוה ילכו כאריה ישאג
After Yahweh they shall follow;[4] like a lion he will roar.

11:10c–d   Direct, 2
כי הוא ישאג ויחרדו בנים מים

---

an 'Emotion'"). The phrase likely includes both aspects, related to one another causally: God feels remorse and so changes his mind about his course of action. In sum, the semiparaphrase "I've had a change of heart" (see Gruber, *Hosea*, 476; NJPS) captures the important features of the Hebrew (remorse resulting in changed plans) while retaining the ambiguity of the affective/cognitive balance. The choice for a *qatal* verb rather than a *yiqtol* suggests that the action is perceived as complete; Yahweh is no longer vacillating as in 11:8a–d (see Andersen and Freedman, *Hosea*, 588). This is consistent with 11:10–11, which pictures Yahweh's restoration of Israel, and hence is fitting for the end of the second cycle.

2. Some emend נחומי to רחמי (Wellhausen, *Kleinen Propheten*, 128; Marti, *Dodekapropheton*, 90; BHS; HALOT, 689 [contra HALOT, 1219]), but that is unnecessary (so HALOT, 1219 [contra HALOT, 689]; BHQ, 69*; Jacob, "Osée," 82; Rudolph, *Hosea*, 212; Wolff, *Hosea*, 193; Macintosh, *Critical and Exegetical Commentary*, 459; Kakkanattu, *God's Enduring Love*, 28–29). נחום can mean "compassion" (Isa 57:18; Zech 1:13; see נחם in Hos 13:14; HALOT, 689). For discussions of the term, see Jörg Jeremias, *Die Reue Gottes: Aspekte alttestamentlicher Gottesvorstellung*, 2nd ed., BibThSt 31 (Neukirchen-Vluyn: Neukirchener, 1997), 15–18, 52–59, 109–13; see also Seifert, *Metaphorisches Reden*, 221–22. Jeremias understands it to denote "self-restraint" (*Reue Gottes*, 110), but Seifert rejects this interpretation (*Metaphorisches Reden*, 221). For Wolff, the word denotes God's "remorse (over his wrathful intention to judge)," which "provokes and dominates him" (*Hosea*, 201). Gruber freely translates as "I experienced a feeling of empathy" and paraphrases as "a stirring of tenderness" (*Hosea*, 476, 480, respectively).

3. Hosea 11:10 is considered secondary by Grace I. Emmerson, *Hosea: An Israelite Prophet in Judean Perspective* (Sheffield: JSOT, 1984), 41–45; Seifert, *Metaphorisches Reden*, 218. For views, see Ben Zvi, *Hosea*, 232; Macintosh, *Critical and Exegetical Commentary*, 467–70. Note esp. Göran Eidevall, "Lions and Birds as Literature: Some Notes on Isaiah 31 and Hosea 11," *SJOT* 7 (1993): 78–81.

4. Eidevall suggests that the phrase אחרי יהוה ילכו pictures Yahweh as a shepherd and Israel as sheep who follow him (*Grapes in the Desert*, 181). I do not find this interpretation convincing.

4. Metaphors of Redemption

He is the one who[5] roars, sons[6] shall come trembling[7] from the sea [= west]

After seemingly relentless sentencing, God appears to pause for a moment of reflection to ask (11:8a–d): "What am I to do with you?" The divine self-response (11:8e) is that Yahweh's own heart has been overturned. This cluster contains some of the most profound things said about God's inner life in all of the Old Testament. Indeed, "the central importance of the words of this verse [11:8] has long been recognized."[8] Gerhard von Rad describes it as "an utterance whose daring is unparalleled in the whole of prophecy."[9] Barbara Leung Lai calls Hos 11:1–9 "a pathos-filled masterpiece of Hebrew poetry."[10] Joy Kakkanattu describes the chapter as "the hymn of the enduring love of God for Israel."[11]

The verses in this cluster contribute immensely to the affective characterization of Yahweh. The emphasis of this cluster is Yahweh's tremendous *feeling* for Israel. Hosea 11:8e–f are metaphors for God not in the sense of "God is X" but in the sense that they metaphorically describe God's internal experiences.

The relationships between judgment, forgiveness, and restoration are unclear. Is Yahweh's judgment coming (11:5–7) or not (depending on how one reads לא אעשה חרון אפי לא אשוב לשחת אפרים, 11:9)? What is the relationship between Israel's repentance and Yahweh's forgiveness? What

---

5. כי functions asseveratively, not temporally (Macintosh, *Critical and Exegetical Commentary*, 466; Tully, *Hosea*, 283–84; see Joüon §164b), and with an emphatic pronoun.

6. Some understand this as "*his* [i.e., Yahweh's] sons" (e.g., NRSV, NJPS; Macintosh, *Critical and Exegetical Commentary*, 466). They also could be Israel's sons (i.e., a later generation after the present one has died in exile [see Jer 31:17]; Andersen and Freedman, *Hosea*, 591–92). If they were Yahweh's sons, it is unclear whether Yahweh is supposed to be understood as a human parent (Hos 11:1) or as a lion with cubs (11:10b–c). Possibly God's people are *still* pictured as God's children at the beginning of their relationship (e.g., 11:1) and also into a hopeful future (11:10).

7. The verb could indicate fluttering (NJPS) like a bird, as in the next verse. This metaphor may suggest an inversion of the fowler metaphor of 7:11–12.

8. Macintosh, *Critical and Exegetical Commentary*, 460.

9. Gerhard von Rad, *Old Testament Theology*, trans. David M. G. Stalker (New York: Harper & Row, 1962), 1:145.

10. Barbara M. Leung Lai, "Hearing God's Bitter Cries (Hosea 11:1–9): Reading, "Emotive-Experiencing, Appropriation," *HBT* 26 (2004): 24.

11. Kakkanattu, *God's Enduring Love*, 100.

is the relationship between God's love and wrath? These questions cannot be answered conclusively within this pericope. Here I offer some initial observations that will be extended in chapters 5, 7, and 9.

The Change of Heart (11:8e–f)

Unquestionably the unique contribution of 11:8 is its emotive emphasis. As outlined in chapter 1, attending to the emotions within a metaphor, as well as those experienced by the reader, is crucial in metaphor construal. "Since metaphor has both informative and performative functions (an ability to communicate ideas and an ability to elicit a strong emotional response), one should account for both the speaker's intention in using metaphor and the reader/hearer's reception of it."[12]

After eight long chapters of wrath, where is God's compassion? Is there nothing but doom and anger for Israel? Nothing in the book compares to 11:8. If the phrases are understood in the present tense, they are the *only* metaphors in Hos 4–14 with positive implications for Yahweh *in the present*.[13] The text grants insight into the emotional wrestling of the parent who knows punishment is necessary for the corrective training of the child yet struggles with the anguish of inflicting it on the beloved son. God's heart "recoils" (נהפך, 11:8e) at the thought of permanently destroying Israel. He feels remorse over the necessity of punishment and so changes his mind regarding its finality.[14] At the same time, God's affections are stirred up (יחד נכמרו נחומי, 11:8f). The rare noun נחומי denotes "intense inner feelings."[15] לב is regularly used to describe emotions, with intensity "being the key behind these expressions" in 11:8.[16]

The Rescuing Lion (11:10)

The lion metaphor is a different term (אריה) than has been used before (כפיר, שחל, 5:14) and inverts the previous pictures. The image here denotes

---

12. Leung Lai, "Hearing God's Bitter Cries," 37.
13. Hosea 7:13c briefly entertains the *possibility* of Yahweh redeeming Israel in the present, but that possibility is denied when they speak lies against him (7:13d).
14. See nn. 1 and 2, above.
15. Fabry, "נחם," 354; see Mike Butterworth, "נחם," *NIDOTTE* 3:82.
16. Leung Lai, "Hearing God's Bitter Cries," 30; see 28–30, 38.

the victorious cry of a lion, which inspires awe mixed with trembling.[17] The power that terrifies Israel when deployed *against* them (5:14–15, 13:7–8) can now inspire confidence when deployed *for* them, although it remains intimidating.[18] The divine roar, which previously provoked fear, now draws the people to God.[19] As noted earlier, the lion image evokes a claim to sovereignty, perhaps even cosmic sovereignty.[20]

This is the first metaphor in Hos 4–14 deployed to inspire confidence in God. Most other metaphors have been negative, often designed to terrify. Even the positive metaphors (e.g., 11:1–4) are historical retrospectives that function to indict Israel. While God was kind in the past, Israel has failed God, and there is no longer a guarantee of his kindness. In fact, there has been every indication that it is *absent*. Yet here is an image depicting Yahweh as victorious *on behalf of God's people* (see Joel 4:16). The lion image gives way to a picture of Israel returning to their land as birds flutter home and settle in a nest, and a declaration that God will settle his people back in their homes (Hos 11:11). This image of ultimate restoration, resting on the victory and supremacy of God deployed for the benefit of God's people, inspires hope and confidence. It is designed to pull Israel back to Yahweh with expectancy rather than drive them back to God with threats.[21]

Analyzing Their Interaction

The major contribution of this cluster is its window into Yahweh's heart, as it were. With this characterization technique "the audience is forced to enter into Yahweh's inner life and join him in his decision."[22] This raises the

---

17. E.g., Strawn, *Stronger Than a Lion?*, 63–64; Kakkanattu, *God's Enduring Love*, 96; Pierre van Hecke, "'For I Will Be like a Lion to Ephraim': Leonine Metaphors in the Twelve Prophets," in *The Books of the Twelve Prophets: Minor Prophets, Major Theologies*, ed. Heinz-Josef Fabry, BETL 295 (Leuven: Peeters, 2018), 399–400. Tully understands it as a roar of eschatological judgment over God's enemies (*Hosea*, 266, 283).

18. Keel notes the dual function of lion imagery to denote threat and victory (*Symbolism of the Biblical World*, 86).

19. Eidevall, "Lions and Birds as Literature," 84.

20. See p. 62 n. 117, above.

21. Erich Zenger, "'Wie ein Löwe brüllt er …' (Hos 11,10): Zur Funktion poetischer Metaphorik im Zwölfprophetenbuch," in *"Wort Jhwhs, das geschah …" (Hos 1,1): Studien zum Zwölfprophetenbuch*, ed. Erich Zenger, HBS 35 (Freiburg: Herder, 2002), 42.

22. Dale Patrick, *The Rendering of God in the Old Testament*, OBT (Philadelphia: Augsburg Fortress, 1983), 24.

question, What is the relationship between the divine emotions in 11:8–9? How does God's desire for justice relate to his desire to love?[23] The context is often influential for one's interpretation of 11:8–9. Some maintain that divine wrath is given full expression without compassion in 11:9. Others interpret 11:8 as describing love's overthrow of justice. Three elements of 11:9, therefore, must be examined to elucidate the metaphors of 11:8 and the sense of 11:8–11.[24]

The first issue in 11:9 is the meaning of לא (2x). Some interpret לא as asseverative, translating לא אעשה חרון אפי לא אשוב לשחת אפרים as follows: "I will certainly act out my burning anger. I will certainly come back to destroy Ephraim."[25] This interpretation may be influenced by a concern to reconcile 11:9 with the historical reality of the destruction of the Northern Kingdom in 722 BCE.[26] John McKenzie describes how the asseverative reading of 11:9 is related to the next line (כי אל אנכי ולא איש): "His final choice is not the choice of love, but of anger. Like man, He destroys what He loves; unlike man, He does not do it because He is swept away by passion and self-love, but because His own integrity, His holiness, demands it, the same holiness which Os [Hosea] earlier saw as a restraint upon the divine anger."[27]

The majority, however, interpret לא as the negative particle. These scholars emphasize the triumph of God's love over God's justice. Brueggemann, for example, is representative:

---

23. The following discussion concentrates on Hos 11:8–11. For theological reflections, see pp. 168–71 ("Love and Hate") and 213–14 ("Passionate"), below; Steven J. Duby, "'For I Am God, Not a Man': Divine Repentance and the Creator-Creature Distinction," *JTI* 12 (2018): 149–69; Moon, *Hosea*, 189.

24. The final clause does not require a decision, as it is not determinative of the meaning of Hos 11:9. עיר should be understood as "wrath" (עיר II; so NRSV, NJPS; see Jer 15:8) given its context, not "city" (עיר I; so LXX). Yahweh will not come in (presumably ultimate) wrath. If "city" is preferred, the sense is that "the coming invasion will have its limits." See M. Daniel Carroll R., "Hosea," in *The Expositor's Bible Commentary*, rev. ed., ed. Tremper Longman III and David E. Garland (Grand Rapids: Zondervan, 2008), 8:287. Both readings support our interpretation of 11:9.

25. Andersen and Freedman, *Hosea*, 574; see also 589. See the much more common emphatic Ugaritic 'l II (*DULAT*, 45–46).

26. Macintosh has no such concern: "It must be said frankly that Hosea's estimate for Yahweh's graceful intervention was misplaced.... The final outcome was tragedy" (*Critical and Exegetical Commentary*, 462). For a response, see Moon, *Hosea*, 185–86.

27. John L. McKenzie, "Divine Passion in Osee," *CBQ* 17 (1955): 299, though see 297.

4. Metaphors of Redemption 141

> In these verses, YHWH asserts that Israel cannot be "given up" (handed over) to wrath and punishment as vv. 5–7 might indicate. The reason is that Israel is not like Sodom and Gomorrah, so easily rejected and given over to punishment.... YHWH internalizes the devastation of Israel, a devastation contained in YHWH's own life. The imagery of father–son in vv. 1–3 suggests a parent willing to endure the suffering deserved by the child, in order to shield the child. The final assertion of v. 9 shows YHWH breaking all old patterns of wrath. This "Holy One of Israel" violates all the conventional categories of divine wrath in radical commitment to Israel, a commitment most costly to YHWH.[28]

With most scholars, the asseverative "anger wins" reading should be rejected as an unnatural reading of the grammar and not fitting with the context. But the absolute "love wins" view should also be rejected as not accounting for the wider context of the verses. Rather, love and justice coexist.[29] Judgment *will* come (against the "love wins" view), but it is not the end of Israel's story (against the "anger wins" view).[30] God will not *totally* destroy Israel. This view is consistent with Israel's historical destruction, as the next two points show, because God does not come in uncontrolled fury to annihilate. His anger is restrained.

Second, that Yahweh will not execute his burning anger (לא אעשה חרון אפי, 11:9a) does not mean that he will never be angry. God is angry throughout the book. Rather, the phrase has a more technical sense. The verb חרה (the root of the nominal form חרון here) plausibly denotes anger that the subject has failed to contain, which overflows into "uncontrollable fury," leading to retribution for the cause of the anger.[31] In this verse, "the execution of Yahweh's anger means, for Hosea, the annihilation of Ephraim, i.e., the chosen people. That means the end of the Yahweh-Israel

---

28. Walter Brueggemann, "Symmetry and Extremity in the Images of YHWH," in *The Blackwell Companion to the Hebrew Bible*, ed. Leo G. Perdue (Malden, MA: Blackwell, 2001), 251.

29. M. Douglas Carew, "Hosea," in *Africa Bible Commentary: A One-Volume Commentary Written by Seventy African Scholars*, ed. Tokunboh Adeyemo (Grand Rapids: Zondervan, 2006), 1024.

30. McKenzie acknowledges that in the struggle within God between anger and love, ultimately love wins in the incarnation ("Divine Passion in Osee," 299). But "the only hope for Israel which Os [Hosea] can entertain is messianic and eschatological." Hence, "the historical Israel had to perish" (297). The claim made here is that *in Hosea's view* anger does not have the last word *for historical Israel*.

31. Van Wolde, "Sentiments as Culturally Constructed Emotions," 11–12.

relationship and the history of salvation."[32] This verse affirms that Yahweh will *not* execute his anger in this absolute way.

Third, 11:9b (לא אשוב לשחת אפרים) can be rendered either as "I will not (re)turn to destroy Ephraim" or "I will not again destroy Ephraim."[33] שחת specifically means to *totally destroy*. Significantly, the verb is used to describe the obliteration of Sodom and Gomorrah (Gen 13:10; 19:13, 14, 29). Admah and Zeboiim are associated with Sodom and Gomorrah in the Abraham story (Gen 14:2, 8; see Amos 4:11).[34] They are used with Sodom and Gomorrah as the archetypes of God's ability to obliterate a people as a consequence of covenant disobedience in idolatry (Deut 29:22–26).[35] Regardless of the rendering of לא אשוב, what is forestalled is absolute destruction, not judgment. Indeed, the very next verses (Hos 11:10–11) "are predicated on an exile that has scattered the people among the nations."[36]

In sum, the vision of Hos 11:9a–b is that God will execute judgment, but exile will not be the last word. Though Francis Andersen and David Freedman translate 11:9a–b differently, they arrive at a similar conclusion: "In Hosea's theology the divine compassion is expressed, not by deflecting or annulling just anger, but by restoration after the requirements of justice have been satisfied by inflicting the penalties for covenant violations."[37] Yahweh's relenting in 11:8–11 is a matter of degree: there will be destruction, but it will not be total.

---

32. Kakkanattu, *God's Enduring Love*, 86. Kakkanattu says that 11:9 "implies pardon and the interruption of the process of judgment" (87). Israel is not pardoned at this point, nor is judgment forestalled; yet the relationship will continue.

33. For "I will not (re)turn to destroy Ephraim" see, e.g., Emmerson, *Hosea*, 40; NJPS. For "I will not again destroy Ephraim" see, e.g., Tully, *Hosea*, 266; NRSV. A significant factor in deciding between these two readings is the date the passage was written. If written after the fall of Samaria in Judah, "again" may be preferable. If written before Samaria's fall, "(re)turn" is.

34. Just as God "overthrew" Sodom and Gomorrah (ויהפך את הערים האל [Gen 19:25]), so God's own heart is overthrown at the thought of treating Israel this way (נהפך עלי לבי [Hos 11:8]).

35. Deuteronomy 29:23 attributes this annihilation to God's חרי האף; see Hos 11:9a's חרון אפי.

36. Dale Patrick, *Redeeming Judgment* (Eugene, OR: Pickwick, 2012), 209. The image is perplexing because, of course, Israel would not have returned to the land from exile from the (Mediterranean) Sea/West (מים). Perhaps this is an image of returning from death or chaos, as symbolized by the sea.

37. Andersen and Freedman, *Hosea*, 590.

4. Metaphors of Redemption

The *reason* (כי) God does not respond to iniquity with absolute destruction, he declares, is that אל אנכי ולא איש בקרבך קדוש: "*God*—not man—am I;[38] the Holy One in your midst" (11:9c–d). This is often construed as the reason for God's overturned heart in 11:8.[39] The כי clause, however, is grammatically dependent on God's declaration that he will not come for annihilation. The implication is that "it is not God's repentance per se but rather God's commitment to his covenantal preservation of Israel that is rooted in the Creator-creature distinction in v. 9. That God remains faithful even after human infidelity is owing to the fact that he is God, not a fickle human partner."[40] God sets limits on his anger because he is divine and not human, and because the "ultimate aims" of God's judgment "are purification and restoration."[41] In other words, it is God's *constancy* toward Israel's ultimate good, not his *changing* (11:8), that is rooted in divinity.

Any description of God, even metaphors, is inadequate. The final resort is the *via negativa*, the apophatic affirmation that God does not respond to treachery with wrath and permanent destruction because he is ultimately *not* like anything any human has ever known.[42] This is God's only nonmetaphorical "I am/will be" claim in the book, and it is profoundly significant. Brigitte Seifert notes that the husband metaphor of Hos 1–3 "is ... relativized and transcended. YHWH is not like a husband but quite different" and furthermore that

> all other metaphors are now put in their place. Human language as such has reached its limits here. Even so, what awaits the people is still just visible beyond this limit: not ruin (שחת), not anger (חרון אף), not terror

---

38. The predicate is fronted to emphasize the contrast with איש.
39. E.g., Emmanuel Durand, "God's Holiness: A Reappraisal of Transcendence," *ModTheo* 34 (2018): 425.
40. Duby, "'For I Am God,'" 165, citing Carroll R., "Hosea," 286; Stuart, *Hosea-Jonah*, 181–83. Nonetheless, when God does repent, it is not as humans do. See Num 23:19, 1 Sam 15:29; R. Walter L. Moberly, *Old Testament Theology: Reading the Hebrew Bible as Christian Scripture* (Grand Rapids: Baker Academic, 2013), 130–32.
41. Carroll R., "Hosea," 286; see Zenger, "Wie ein Löwe," 42; Fredrik Lindström, "'I Am God and Not Human' (Hos 11,9): Can Divine Compassion Overcome Our Anthropomorphism?," *SJOT* 29 (2015): 135–51; Jer 10:24.
42. Soskice, *Metaphor and Religious Language*, 140; Seifert, *Metaphorisches Reden*, 263.

(עיר II), but unfathomable compassion, like people have never known (נחומים instead of רחמים).[43]

A cataphatic implication of this passage, according to Wallace Hartsfield, is that "when Yahweh breaks down and expresses love for Israel, despite the peoples' continued apostasy, Yahweh's love is *based not on unconditional but on compulsive love. Yahweh apparently cannot help himself because he is not mortal.*"[44] John Goldingay observes that "Yhwh's point is thus the reverse of the one often made when people suggest that Yhwh's holiness makes it is [*sic*] hard for Yhwh to forgive sin. For Yhwh, it is this holiness that makes it hard to punish sin.… The implication is that the instinct to love, comfort and tolerate is nearer the heart of Yhwh than the instinct to act in rage."[45] Such compassion is the "measure of God's deity and holiness."[46]

Far from describing the overthrow of justice by love, or even a transformation within God's existence, this passage is crucial for a portrait of Yahweh because it (with 14:5–9) affirms both compassion and justice, "twin aspects of the nation's God," which have been heretofore imbalanced in the book.[47] The overwhelming power of the Holy One's compassion

---

43. Seifert, *Metaphorisches Reden*, 225, my trans.
44. Wallace Hartsfield, "Hosea," in *The Africana Bible: Reading Israel's Scriptures from Africa and the African Diaspora*, ed. Hugh R. Page Jr. et al. (Minneapolis: Fortress, 2009), 168, emphasis added.
45. Goldingay, *Israel's Faith*, 2:164.
46. McConville, "Hosea, Book of," 349.
47. Macintosh, *Critical and Exegetical Commentary*, lxiii. Moon notes that "hope for YHWH's grace and continued love for Israel … may have loomed in the background" since Hos 2–3, "but we have heard very little of them since" (*Hosea*, 185). For describing the overthrow of justice by love, see, e.g., Mays, *Hosea*, 157; Wolff, *Hosea*, 201–3; Heinrich Groß, "Das Hohelied der Liebe Gottes: Zur Theologie von Hosea 11," in *Mysterium der Gnade: Festschrift für Johann Auer*, ed. Heribert Roßmann and Joseph Ratzinger (Regensburg: Pustet, 1975), 91; Jörg Jeremias, "'Ich bin wie ein Löwe für Efraim …' (Hos 5,14): … Aktualität und Allgemeingültigkeit im prophetischen Reden von Gott am Beispiel von Hos 5,8–14," in *"Ich will euer Gott werden": Beispiele biblischen Redens von Gott*, ed. Norbert Lohfink, SBS 100 (Stuttgart: Katholisches Bibelwerk, 1981), 95; Fisch, *Poetry with a Purpose*, 142; Seifert, *Metaphorisches Reden*, 220; Fabry, "נחם," 354; Leung Lai, "Hearing God's Bitter Cries," 42–43. For a transformation within God's existence, see, e.g., Janzen, "Metaphor and Reality"; Mays, "Response to Janzen."

(11:8–9)[48] gives way to a demonstration of another kind of overwhelming power deployed on their behalf: the victorious lion through whom the people are returned to their land from exile (11:10–11). These form a composite picture of the Holy One, who both is internally motivated to be *for* Israel and has the power to effect that *for*-ness into external reality. God is compassionate and strong.

Cluster 15: Hosea 14:4–9

This cluster, following the most overt invitation to repentance (14:2–4; see 10:12, 12:7), closes the third cycle and the book with a profound depiction of Israel's "resurrection."[49] The cluster contains six metaphorical expressions for Yahweh[50] and a host of images portraying Israel's flourishing (14:6b–8). The Israel images offer oblique implications for a portrait of Yahweh, considered in toto in the analysis of interactions.

14:4d   Direct, 3
אשר בך ירחם יתום
because[51] in you the orphan finds pity

14:5a[52]   Direct, 3
ארפא משובתם

---

48. Goldingay points out that this compassion is not unique to God's people, as God is not "the Holy One *of Israel*," but "the Holy One—period" (*Israel's Faith*, 2:164, emphasis original).

49. Chapters 6 and 7 below address the relationship of Israel's resurrection to their repentance, forgiveness, and prior judgment and the question of Hos 14's inversion of prior judgment. The present analysis is concerned with the metaphoric dynamics *within* the cluster.

50. The most comprehensive study of the metaphors for Yahweh in this passage identifies four: healing (14:5), love (14:5), dew (14:6), and tree (14:9; see Oestreich, *Metaphors and Similes*). This study finds additional metaphorical expressions, due to differences in methodology and definitions.

51. The relative particle seems unusual here but is frequently understood as causal (Theodotion; Tg. Neb.; Vulg.; Syr.; NJPS; Wolff, *Hosea*, 231–32; Tully, *Hosea*, 344; see Gen 30:18, 34:13, Josh 4:23, 1 Kgs 15:5, Jer 13:25, Eccl 4:9, 8:11; *HALOT*, 99; GKC §158b; Joüon §170e; *IBHS* §38.4a; *BHRG* §36.3.1.1.5.d). Alternatively it could be used absolutely, without an antecedent: "[You are the one] in whom the orphan finds pity" (LXX; Macintosh, *Critical and Exegetical Commentary*, 565; see Joüon §§145a, 158l; *IBHS* §19.3c).

52. Following Wellhausen, many claim all or parts of 14:5–10 are post-Hosean

I will heal their disloyalty

14:5b   Direct, 3
אהבם נדבה
I will love them freely

14:6a[53]   Direct, 3
אהיה כטל לישראל
I will be(come) like dew for Israel

14:6b–8   Indirect, 2

[The flora metaphors for Israel]

---

and do not reflect a *Hosean* metaphorical theology (Wellhausen, *Die kleinen Propheten*, 134). For surveys, see Walker, "Metaphor of Healing," 152–66; Judith M. Hadley, *The Cult of Asherah in Ancient Israel and Judah: Evidence for a Hebrew Goddess*, UCOP 57 (Cambridge: Cambridge University Press, 2000), 75–76; Ben Zvi, *Hosea*, 301. This consensus began to shift in the middle of the last century. See Eidevall, *Grapes in the Desert*, 208 n. 2; Roman Vielhauer, *Das Werden des Buches Hosea: Eine Redaktionsgeschichtliche Untersuchung*, BZAW 349 (Berlin: de Gruyter, 2007), 185–86; Guy Couturier, "Yahweh et les déesses cananéennes en Osée 14,9," in *Communion et réunion: Mélanges Jean-Marie Roger Tillard* (Leuven: Leuven University Press, 1995), 246–47. In support of 14:5–10 being original are, e.g., Rudolph, *Hosea*, 249–50; Wolff, *Hosea*, 234; Jeremias, *Prophet Hosea*, 169–70; Saul M. Olyan, *Asherah and the Cult of Yahweh in Israel*, SBLMS 34 (Atlanta: Scholars Press, 1988), 21; Graham I. Davies, *Hosea*, NCB (Grand Rapids: Eerdmans, 1992), 300–301; Couturier, "Yahweh et les déesses," 246–47; Frevel, *Aschera* 1:342; Macintosh, *Critical and Exegetical Commentary*, 558; Day, *Yahweh and the Gods*, 58–59. For an extensive analysis of the structure of the passage, see Oestreich, *Metaphors and Similes*, 45–55.

53. Hosea 14:5c contains the metaphorical phrase כי שב אפי ממנו ("for my anger has turned from them"), perhaps witnessing to the conceptual metaphor EMOTION IS AN OPPONENT (see Basson, "Metaphorical Source Domains," 124). It is metaphorical, because אף has a more basic meaning (i.e., "nose") than anger. However, the phrase is a stock expression (strength level 1; see Gen 27:45; Num 25:4; Isa 5:25; 9:11, 16, 20; 10:4; 12:1; Jer 2:35; 4:8; 23:20; 30:24; Jonah 3:9; Prov 24:18; 29:8; Dan 9:16; Ezra 10:14; 2 Chr 12:12), and its contribution to a *metaphorical* portrait of Yahweh is relatively minor and redundant. It is not considered for analysis here. See further Paul A. Kruger, "A Cognitive Interpretation of the Emotion of Anger in the Hebrew Bible," *JNSL* 26 (2000): 181–93; van Wolde, "Sentiments as Culturally Constructed Emotions."

14:9c[54]   Direct, 3
אני כברוש רענן
I [am] like a leafy juniper,[55]

---

54. Two potential metaphors are omitted here. Hosea 14:8a (ישבו ישבי בצלו) is sometimes understood as a metaphor for God, switching the third-person suffix to a first-person one: "They shall again live beneath *my* shadow" (*BHS*; NRSV). There is no evidence in the versions to support this change (*BHQ*, 73*). The context (14:6b–8) uniformly contains third-person verbs and suffixes referring to future Israel, thus favoring the MT's third-person suffix in 14:8a (e.g., NJPS). For further justification, see Tully, *Hosea*, 349. The MT's third person could still refer to tree-Yahweh's shade (see 14:9c). Eidevall prefers to embrace this ambiguity as the author's or redactor's intentional "'double exposure' effect" (*Grapes in the Desert*, 217). Tg. Neb. interprets as the shade of the Anointed One/Messiah. The second is 14:9b: אני עניתי ואשורנו ("[It was] I who answered, who bent down to look [after you]"). The metaphoricity of this clause is suggestive though indefinite. If the verb שור retains its concrete sense of "to look at from a bent position" (*HALOT*, 1449–50; see Akkadian *šurru*), it presupposes a physical body. The phrase is therefore metaphorical, denoting Yahweh's expression of concern for Israel. While ancient Israelites may have imagined God to have a body in some way (Sommer, Smith), it is irrelevant for the metaphor identification procedure criteria whether a reader recognizes the metaphoricity of an expression (Steen et al., "Pragglejaz in Practice," 175). See Benjamin D. Sommer, *The Bodies of God and the World of Ancient Israel* (Cambridge: Cambridge University Press, 2011); Smith, *Where the Gods Are*, 13–30. In its present context, the phrase denotes God's tender care for Israel. See Wolff, *Hosea*, 237; Jackie Naudé, "שׁור," *NIDOTTE* 4:71. Even if metaphorical, it does not add much new to a picture of Yahweh (see 11:1–4).

55. ברוש has been identified as a juniper (most commonly; e.g., NIV), cypress (NASB, NJPS, NRSV; Dearman, *Book of Hosea*, 335), cedar, pine tree (HCSB), or fir tree. For the latter, see Andersen and Freedman, *Hosea*, 643; K. Arvid Tångberg, "'I Am like an Evergreen Fir, from Me Comes Your Fruit': Notes on Meaning and Symbolism in Hosea 14:9b [MT]," *SJOT* 2 (1989): 81–93; Eidevall, *Grapes in the Desert*, 219. See Oestreich for a survey of the interpretive options (*Metaphors and Similes*, 192–95). I find it plausible that ברוש is *Juniperus phoenicea* (*HALOT*, 155). Regardless of the specific identification, it is a majestic, ever-flourishing tree that symbolizes provision (see 14:9d) and protection. Macintosh reads this passage so that the speaker shifts back and forth between Ephraim (lines a, c) and Yahweh (lines b, d), such that this metaphor is spoken by Ephraim (*Critical and Exegetical Commentary*, 576–81; also *BHQ* 73*; Tully, *Hosea*, 339, 350–52; Syr.; Tg. Neb.). He thinks identifying Yahweh as a tree carries too great a risk for idolatrous misinterpretations with Asherah (Macintosh, *Critical and Exegetical Commentary*, 577), but this is misguided (see Day, *Yahweh and the Gods*, 118). Others (e.g., Tully) consider the verse to be meaningless if spoken by Yahweh: "Has he *ever* had anything to do with [idols]?" asks Tully (*Hosea*, 350). I do not find this convincing, as Israel certainly thought he did, and Hosea has been at pains to correct their misperception.

14:9d   Direct, 3
ממני פריך נמצא
from me your fruit is found.

Compassion for the Orphan (14:4d)

Presumably this clause provides the reason that Israel can return to God, ask forgiveness, cease to trust in Assyrian power, and cease worshiping their handiwork (14:2–4c). Yahweh is the one who feels compassion for those who are weak and in need, such as the orphan. If the phrase—unique in the Bible—essentially suggests an emotion (sympathy), it may be fairly literally construed.[56] If, however, the verb connotes practical action in addition to emotion, it may suggest the more concrete instance of providing for the physical needs of an orphan.[57] The phrase can be understood as metaphorical in that it structures an abstract domain (God) in terms of a more concrete domain (a human meeting the practical needs of an orphan). The verb רחם, as commonly suggested, may connote distinctly motherly feelings of compassion (see רֶחֶם, "womb").

Israel was once Yahweh's own child (11:1). Even if they are no longer part of Yahweh's family (e.g., 1:9, 2:6, 9:15), they can return to Yahweh in confidence, knowing that Yahweh welcomes home the orphan (see 2:1, 25). This may imply a re-adoption of Israel (see 11:1), thereby inverting the last metaphor for God (14:1a–b) from father of a rebel to adopted father of an orphan.[58] Canonically, the term is significant in Yahweh's self-revelation to Moses (Exod 33:19, 34:6). Because רחם is, according to Horacio Simian-Yofre, "a fundamental element of Yahweh's nature,"[59] Israel can depend on this characteristic for his response when they repent. That is

---

56. This is the only Hebrew Bible occurrence of anyone having pity (רחם) on an orphan (יתום). Isaiah 9:16 is the only other Hebrew Bible occurrence of these two words, but the verb is negated. See also Exod 22:22–24, Deut 10:18, 24:17, Isa 1:17, 49:13. Psalm 68:6 calls God the "father of orphans" (אבי יתומים).

57. See, e.g., Deut 30:3, where it is parallel to "restore your fortunes" (ושב ... את שבותך). Conversely, to not have pity is to let die or suffer (e.g., Isa 9:16, 13:18, Jer 6:23, 13:14).

58. Light thinks Hos 14:4d pictures Yahweh as a father ("Theory-Constitutive Metaphor," 200).

59. H. Simian-Yofre, "רחם," TDOT 13:442.

4. Metaphors of Redemption 149

why the clause begins with "because" (אשר): it functions as the motivation for their preceding repentance.

Healer (14:5a)

This metaphor is the fifth and final use of the healing metaphor, and it inverts all prior occurrences (5:13, 6:1, 7:1, 11:3). Only here is there the long-awaited promise that Yahweh *will* heal them. Bernhard Oestreich argues that this pictures Yahweh as a father or king/leader.[60] While a parent image is possible in 11:3, it need not be so here. Oestreich argues that "no established profession of physicians existed in pre-exilic Israel."[61] Many people were associated with healing: parents, owners of animals, priests, prophets/diviners, kings, and more. The source domain cannot be specifically determined in this instance. Perhaps the metaphor should not be read primarily according to its precise source domain but for its literary implications in the book.

The object of their healing is משובתם: their turning away from Yahweh. The sum total of Israel's failures before Yahweh—their idolatry, political treachery, cultic and theological apostasy, ethical and social failures—are collectively characterized as a wound (see Jer 3:22).[62] The book repeatedly affirms that only Yahweh is capable of healing these wounds, of correcting these failures and setting Israel back on their feet. Healing therefore entails not only forgiveness[63] but restorative justice and transforming power. Whence comes this healing power?

Generous Love (14:5b)

This powerful phrase captivates commentators. It is an inversion of 9:15 and a return to the beginning of the relationship (11:1). Oestreich identifies this metaphor as that of adoptive love (Yahweh is a parent, presumably a father; perhaps this extends the metaphor of 14:4d), though the metaphor

---

60. Oestreich, *Metaphors and Similes*, 69–71, 84, 86.
61. Oestreich, *Metaphors and Similes*, 66. For healing in the ancient Near East, see p. 61 n. 114, above.
62. See Paul A. Kruger, "Yahweh's Generous Love: Eschatological Expectations in Hosea 14:2–9," *OTE* 1 (1988): 40.
63. Tg. Neb. Hos 14:9 identifies the "fruit" that only comes from Yahweh as the "forgiveness of their waywardness."

may also echo the marriage metaphor. He rightly claims that this metaphor adds an emotional emphasis and "makes the announced new beginning of Yahweh with His people emotionally plausible and attractive."[64]

What is new is the explicit identification of the *generosity* with which it is offered. נדב "describes the inner motivation of persons, that attitude or impulse or decision that moves them to act or speak" voluntarily.[65] These two words (אהבם נדבה) "represent a gesture of unconditioned grace."[66] Yahweh is not obligated to love them, but Yahweh freely chooses to lavish that love.[67]

Dew (14:6a)

This metaphor, too, is an inversion of previous instances that have drawn on the entailment of dew's transience (6:4, 13:3).[68] This instance highlights its association with life. Dew has a life-bringing capacity, as it is often the only precipitation for plants in certain areas and seasons.[69] This forms a natural transition into the following nine metaphors that portray Israel's flourishing in terms of plant life (14:6b–8). Yahweh, as dew (14:6a), is the cause of their subsequent flourishing (14:6b–8). The wordplay on the divine name (אהיה; see Exod 3:14, Hos 1:9) "states that what follows is essential to Yahweh's self-understanding."[70] Yahweh always has been and always will be their source of life.

---

64. Oestreich, *Metaphors and Similes*, 153. Light identifies the metaphor as that of a husband ("Theory-Constitutive Metaphor," 200).

65. Eugene Carpenter and Michael A. Grisanti, "נדב," *NIDOTTE* 3:31; see *HALOT*, 672; J. Conrad, "נדב," *TDOT* 9:220.

66. Fisch, *Poetry with a Purpose*, 155.

67. There is debate about the relationship between Israel's repentance and the giving of this love, which results in restoration. For further discussion, see Walker, "Metaphor of Healing," 152–66, and p. 189 n. 16, below.

68. It may also overturn the metaphor of the east wind in 13:15 (Eidevall, *Grapes in the Desert*, 214) and the lion metaphors of 5:14, 13:7 (Eidevall, *Grapes in the Desert*, 214 n. 39, citing Jeremias, *Prophet Hosea*, 172; see Mic 5:6–7).

69. See Wolff, *Hosea*, 236; Eidevall, *Grapes in the Desert*, 214; Seifert, *Metaphorisches Reden*, 236; Walker, "Metaphor of Healing," 174 n. 79; Benedikt Otzen, "טל," *TDOT* 5:323. Oestreich surveys interpretations (*Metaphors and Similes*, 169–89).

70. Walker, "Metaphor of Healing," 173 n. 78; see Charles D. Isbell, "The Divine Name אהיה as a Symbol of Presence in Israelite Tradition," *HAR* 2 (1978): 101–18; Yee, *Composition and Tradition*, 138; Fisch, *Poetry with a Purpose*, 144–45; Morris, *Prophecy, Poetry and Hosea*, 128–29; Sherwood, *Prostitute and the Prophet*, 248–51.

4. Metaphors of Redemption

This claim is underscored by the polemical nature of the metaphor.[71] Oestreich points out that Baal is said to have power over the elements but is never identified as dew or rain, so he rejects any Canaanite background or polemical purpose for this metaphor.[72] This is an overly strict view of what constitutes polemical appropriation.

The metaphor identifies *Yahweh's ability to give life to plants*, corresponding to the stock imagery of Israel flourishing as *plants* (Hos 14:6b–8).[73] It is significant that this aspect of Yahweh is identified using an image that is central to a fertility god's arena of control and responsibility, when source domains not associated with deities could have accomplished the same. In conjunction with the wordplay on the divine name, this suggests that the polemical claim of the metaphor is that Yahweh—*not Baal*—always has been and always will be their *exclusive* source of life (see 2:10, 14).

The Tree of Life and Its Fruit (14:9c–d)

This is the only place in the Old Testament that Yahweh is compared to a tree.[74] Some scholars therefore assume Ephraim must be the speaker in 14:9c, and hence the tree.[75] While the attribute "luxuriant" (רענן) is used almost entirely of trees in idolatrous contexts (Deut 12:2; 1 Kgs 14:23; 2 Kgs 16:4; 17:10; Isa 57:5; Jer 2:20; 3:6, 13; 11:16; 17:2, 8; Ezek 6:13; 2 Chr 28:4), this particular type of tree (ברוש) is never associated with idolatry in the Bible.[76] Nonetheless, it is commonplace to see Yahweh's appropria-

---

71. See the resources cited in Eidevall, *Grapes in the Desert*, 214 n. 36; Seifert, *Metaphorisches Reden*, 237; Walker, "Metaphor of Healing," 174 n. 80.

72. Oestreich, *Metaphors and Similes*, 183–84. Korpel argues otherwise, citing KTU 1.12.II.36–56 (*Rift in the Clouds*, 596). Notably, one of Baal's daughter is named "Dewy One" (*ṭly*); see *DULAT*, 876; John F. Healey, "Dew," *DDD*, 249–50.

73. Otzen, "טל," 327.

74. Wolff, *Hosea*, 237; Yee, *Composition and Tradition*, 138; Fisch, *Poetry with a Purpose*, 148; Seifert, *Metaphorisches Reden*, 241; J. Gordon McConville, "'I Am like a Luxuriant Juniper': Language about God in Hosea," in *Let Us Go Up to Zion: Essays in Honour of H. G. M. Williamson on the Occasion of His Sixty-Fifth Birthday*, ed. Iain Provan and Mark J. Boda (Leiden: Brill, 2012), 181.

75. See n. 55, above.

76. Oestreich, *Metaphors and Similes*, 208–9. This is contra Wolff's association of the "cypress" as a "holy tree" among Phoenicians (*Hosea*, 237). The polemic need not be against a sex cult (as supposed by Wolff) but generally against deities associated with trees (such as Asherah).

tion of the tree imagery here as polemical. Guy Couturier boldly claims, "It is obvious that the primary intention of its author is to deny idols any power of fertility. It is in this polemical context that all the elements of the oracle must be interpreted."[77] Far from conflating Yahweh with Asherah or any other deity, Yahweh is here "appropriating and absorbing the powers" of Asherah, particularly her perceived power over Israel's future fertility.[78] Judith Hadley is correct that the verse need not explicitly refer to or even allude to Asherah in order to make the point: Hosea may have "wanted to stress that Yahweh was able to function as a fertility deity in place of Asherah … [by] portray[ing] his fertility aspects as even more effective than those of Asherah, as he was a 'luxuriant tree, bearing fruit,' as opposed to a humanly constructed pole."[79] As Gerald Morris summarizes, "If Israel must worship the gods of Canaan, then 'I Will Be' [אהיה from 14:6a] will become the gods of Canaan."[80]

Oestreich views 14:9c and 14:9d as disjunctive. Because Oestreich claims that juniper (*Juniperus excelsa* in his view) do not bear fruit and are

---

77. Couturier, "Yahweh et les déesses," 245, my trans.

78. Keefe, "Hosea's (In)Fertility God," 29; similarly Seifert, *Metaphorisches Reden*, 241. On this verse see Manfried Dietrich and Oswald Loretz, *Jahwe und Seine Aschera: Anthropomorphes Kultbild in Mesopotamien, Ugarit und Israel–Das Biblische Bilderverbot*, UBL 9 (Münster: Ugarit-Verlag, 1992), 110–12, 173–81. The use of comparative כ may be significant in hedging against such conflation. As Korpel notes, "Nothing but a simile is meant" (*Rift in the Clouds*, 594; see Tångberg, "'I Am like,'" 91; Seifert, *Metaphorisches Reden*, 241; Keel, *Goddesses and Trees*, 56). Wyatt thinks this is unlikely ("Asherah," 103).

79. Hadley, *Cult of Asherah*, 76; see Wacker, "Traces of the Goddess," 237. Wellhausen emends the prior clause (אני עניתי ואשורנו) to אני ענתו ואשרתו in order to make the presence of Anat and Asherah explicit (*Die kleinen Propheten*, 20, 134). See discussions in Wolff, *Hosea*, 233; Frédéric Gangloff, "'Je suis son 'Anat et son 'Ašerâh' (Os 14,9)," *ETL* 74 (1998): 375–78. His emendation has not been widely adopted. Harper labels it "a freak of the imagination" (*Hosea*, 415). An intentional wordplay is possible without emendation. See John Day, "Asherah in the Hebrew Bible and Northwest Semitic Literature," *JBL* 105 (1986): 404–6; Wacker, "Traces of the Goddess," 224–27; Smith, *Early History of God*, 135–36. Day points out that among the eight parallels between Hos 13–14 and Isa 26–27, the Isaianic verse corresponding to Hos 14:9 explicitly mentions the *asherim*. See John Day, "A Case of Inner Scriptural Interpretation: The Dependence of Isaiah XXVI.13–XXVII.11 on Hosea XIII.4–XIV.10 [Eng. 9] and Its Relevance to Some Theories of the Redaction of the 'Isaiah Apocalypse,'" *JTS* 31 (1980): 315; Day, "Asherah," *ABD* 1:486. Frevel argues this is unlikely (*Aschera* 1:342–48).

80. Morris, *Prophecy, Poetry and Hosea*, 130.

4. Metaphors of Redemption

not tall enough to produce shade (see 14:8a), the two clauses cannot partake of the same image in his view.[81] Oestreich is mistaken, though. The *Juniperus* family can grow berries and be tall enough to shade an adult.[82] Hosea 14:9c and 14:9d should be read as partaking of a single metaphorical image. What is especially suggestive is that the berries of *Juniperus phoenicea* have been long used not for eating but primarily in traditional medicine.[83] Though present scholarship lacks proof, one wonders whether these traditional practices go back to Hosea's time and whether the tree imagery here is thereby suggestive of the healing metaphor in 14:5. Whereas Assyria (who could not heal, 5:13) was the means of God's punishment (13:7), God himself will be the means of healing (14:9d).

The temporal frame of this metaphor is ambiguous.[84] The sense seems to be as follows: "Your provision has always come from me, but now [i.e., in the future moment of this eschatological oracle] you will recognize and receive it as such." The metaphor suggests that throughout Israel's rebellion and Yahweh's judgment, Yahweh has constantly been the exclusive source of their provision and protection (see 5:13–14),[85] despite their not

---

81. Oestreich, *Metaphors and Similes*, 194–95.

82. Mirko Vidaković, *Conifers: Morphology and Variation*, rev. and expanded ed., trans. Maja Šoljan (Zagreb: Grafički Zavod Hrvatske, 1991), 227, 238–39; Aljos Farjon, *Monograph of Cupressaceae and Sciadopitys* (Surrey, UK: Royal Botanic Gardens, Kew, 2000), 287–94, 336–40. Contra Eidevall's claim that it is "probably pointless" to search for a specific tree that is coniferous, fruit-bearing, and tall enough for shade (*Grapes in the Desert*, 219).

83. Mohammad Sanad Abu-Darwish, Célia Cabral, and Lígia Salgueiro, "Juniperus Phoenicea from Jordan," in *Medicinal and Aromatic Plants of the Middle-East*, ed. Zohara Yaniv and Nativ Dudai, MAPW 2 (Dordrecht: Springer Netherlands, 2014), 241–52, esp. 247–48.

84. אני עניתי ואשורנו is perfective, but from the perspective of this future oracle could still refer to a time in Hosea's future. אני כברוש רענן lacks a verb and could be read as a present-tense predicate or a future due to the future frame of the context (GKC §141.f). In 14:9d, the Masoretic pointing (נִמְצָא) is commonly read as a *qatal* ("was found"), but the same pointing could be a participle, and therefore in the present tense or imminent future.

85. Yee, *Composition and Tradition*, 140; Couturier, "Yahweh et les déesses," 264; Eidevall, *Grapes in the Desert*, 219; Oestreich, *Metaphors and Similes*, 222–23; Nocquet, *Le "livret noir de Baal*," 287; McConville, "I Am like," 192. Eidevall and Oestreich suggest that the metaphor also depicts Yahweh as a king, because of the association of tree imagery with kings (Eidevall, *Grapes in the Desert*, 220; Oestreich, *Metaphors and Similes*, 215–18, 222–23).

recognizing Yahweh as such (see 2:10). Because Ephraim did *not* depend on Yahweh and acknowledge Yahweh as their provider, they experienced Yahweh as a predatory animal (13:4–8). They will yet experience Yahweh as the giver of all good things.[86] That Israel rejected Yahweh's provision has dishonored Yahweh's name,[87] but his honor will be restored as the people understand that their fruit comes from God. "Yahweh alone is 'the tree of life.'"[88]

Analyzing Their Interaction

Six points can be made pertaining to the interaction between metaphors in this cluster.

First, the collective contribution of the metaphors to a portrait of Yahweh can be briefly summarized. Yahweh's compassion (14:4d, 5a–b, 9b) compels him to heal (14:5a), provide for (14:6a, 9d), and protect (14:9c) Israel, resulting in Israel's flourishing (14:6b–8). The implicit polemic is that no other deity or nation is able to do this. Therefore, Israel should return to Yahweh and follow Yahweh alone (see 14:2–4).

Second, the relationship between the second and third metaphors is suggestive. The healing of their backsliding is followed by a phrase describing Yahweh's generous love (ארפא משובתם אהבם נדבה, 14:5a–b). The parallelism may have a focusing function, indicating the means of healing.[89] In other words, Israel may be healed *by love*. Divine love is the healing salve for Ephraim's "perpetual inconstancy."[90] Furthermore, the *means* of God's healing in 14:5b is the same as the *reason* Israel should repent in 14:4d: God loves. Whatever the relationship between Israel's

---

86. Seifert, *Metaphorisches Reden*, 235–42; Gregory Vall, "An Epistemology of Faith: The Knowledge of God in Israel's Prophetic Literature," in *Bible and Epistemology: Biblical Soundings on the Knowledge of God*, ed. Mary Healy and Robin Parry (Milton Keynes, UK: Paternoster, 2007), 39.

87. Haddox, "(E)Masculinity," 185–86.

88. Tångberg, "'I Am like,'" 92.

89. See Alter, *Art of Biblical Poetry*, 20, 31, 75–102. אהבם could be a *yiqtol* (Tully, *Hosea*, 345; so most English translations; LXX translates with a future [ἔσομαι]; Tg. Neb. with a prefix form [ארחימנון]), or a participle. If the latter, it is grammatically dependent on the finite verb (ארפא), further suggesting that love is the means of healing (Goldingay, *Israel's Faith*, 2:325).

90. Karl A. Plank, "The Scarred Countenance: Inconstancy in the Book of Hosea," *Judaism* 32 (1983): 353.

4. Metaphors of Redemption

repentance and restoration, God's compassion is both the divine means of healing and the basis of human motivation for seeking it. The use of רחם (14:4d) and the play on the divine name (14:6a) suggest that this is constitutive of Yahweh's character (see respective discussions above). Israel can trust that God will accept their genuine repentance, because this divine characteristic of compassion is fundamental to his being.

Third is the matter of the intervening plant-Israel metaphors and their implicit characterization of Yahweh.[91] An initial question concerns their source domain. It has been suggested that the language of the metaphors, which overlap significantly with the Song of Songs, evokes love-song imagery, suggesting that Israel is pictured as a wife and Yahweh as the husband in a restored marriage.[92] While reminiscent of such associations, the language can succeed apart from the marriage background. Both Hosea and Song of Songs partake of general imagery for beauty and flourishing.[93] Isaiah 27:6 uses similar imagery for Israel's flourishing "in that day."[94] As with other domains (e.g., marriage metaphors also used in political situations), I interpret this expression primarily in terms of the explicit source domain (flourishing nature), while recognizing that the metaphor's common usage in other contexts may evoke additional implications for its present context (a restored marriage relationship).

What then can be said about Yahweh? While Yahweh is not pictured as a farmer in every instance, the mentions of a garden or gardening practices (יחיו דגן)[95] and multiple plants regularly cultivated in the region (זית, olive tree; גפן, vine) suggest the possibility of this association. Additionally, Isa 27:2–6, which uses very similar language, explicitly identifies Yahweh as the owner/farmer of a vineyard. If this is the case in Hos 14, the flourishing of Israel in 14:6b–8 offers a tantalizing inversion of multiple previous metaphors that pictured Yahweh as frustrated, never getting what he intended

---

91. For a more extensive analysis of these metaphors than will be offered here, see Eidevall, *Grapes in the Desert*, 214–18.

92. See, e.g., Yee, *Composition and Tradition*, 138–40.

93. Eidevall, *Grapes in the Desert*, 213.

94. Day points out eight parallels (in the same order, with one exception) between Hos 13–14 and Isa 26–27 ("Case of Inner Scriptural Interpretation"; *Yahweh and the Gods*, 58–59, 122–24).

95. Lit. "they shall grow grain," though NRSV translates as "they shall flourish like a garden." See Robert B. Coote, "Hos 14:8: They Who Are Filled with Grain Shall Live," *JBL* 93 (1974): 161–73. Some of the images are of wild plants—e.g., the forests of Lebanon (assuming ellipsis for כלבנון [14:6c]) and perhaps the lily (כשושנה [14:6b]).

from Israel (7:8, 11, 16; 10:11). In the end Yahweh will get what he wants from the relationship: the plants will flourish as they should.

Furthermore, as dew, Yahweh is the *cause* of Israel's thriving. Robert Coote argues that 14:8 alludes to a "banquet of life" like Baal has in the Baal cycle.[96] He claims it is polemical, as much as to say, "Whatever Baal can do, the Lord can do better, including the throwing of a banquet of life through which Israel, filled with grain, shall live."[97] Even if one is not convinced by Coote's argument, the choice of burgeoning vegetation imagery for Israel implies that Israel's future is a result of Yahweh being the true storm god, capable of reliably bringing precipitation and fertility. This vision of the future is the ultimate subversion of Baal, for whom Israel no longer has need.

This leads to the fourth point: the high concentration of polemical metaphor appropriation in this passage. In addition to 14:6b–8, at least four other clauses are polemical. Baal was known for healing, which Yahweh appropriates (14:5a); Baal was associated with dew (14:6a); Yahweh, not Assyria, will look after Israel (14:9b);[98] and Yahweh, not Asherah, will be their tree of life (14:9c–d). Thus, four out of six metaphors for Yahweh (plus 14:9b) and all nine metaphors for Israel are on some level polemical appropriations, intended to overcome alterity between different perspectives.[99] Hosea thereby claims that "in YHWH all aspects of the Canaanite gods are united."[100]

The polemics point to the *purpose* of clustering at this stage, which is the fifth consideration. Clusters tend to occur in places central to the purpose of the discourse, "when some *intensive interactional work linked to the overall purpose of the discourse* is being carried out."[101] This unit has clustering, an unusually high rate of metaphor appropriation, *and* metaphor inversion.[102] That these three traits occur together at above-average

---

96. Coote, "Hos 14:8: They Who Are Filled," 171.
97. Coote, "Hos 14:8: They Who Are Filled," 173.
98. Contrast 14:9b with 13:7 and 14:4a; see Fisch, *Poetry with a Purpose*, 156.
99. See p. 26, above.
100. Korpel, *Rift in the Clouds*, 594.
101. Cameron and Stelma, "Metaphor Clusters," 134, emphasis added. See ch. 1 ("Why Metaphors Cluster"), esp. pp. 26–27, above.
102. For more on metaphor appropriation and inversion, see pp. 177–84 ("Culmination and Inversion in Hosea 14"), below.

rates suggests that this unit is making especially significant contributions to the rhetorical purpose of the discourse.

Presumably that rhetorical work is a final effort to convince the hearers that Yahweh is *worth* following. The polemics are designed to remove the *felt need* of the people for another deity.[103] The accusations and threats have been left behind and give way to wooing the people to Yahweh.[104] Rather than compelling them from behind with threats, this cluster draws them in with cords of love, as it were. Hosea heaps up metaphor after metaphor, hopeful image after hopeful image, inversion after inversion of previously negative images, and appropriation after appropriation of any competing deity's aspects in order to make the ultimate claim: Yahweh can do it all; it is worth following Yahweh. The metaphors "testify to the versatility of the one God and show that it is YHWH whom Israel always encounters, whether in prosperity or adversity [*Wohl und Wehe*], and that the people need no other god besides him."[105] Yahweh will meet their every need and desire, if they will but turn from other deities and nations to follow and obey him.[106]

Finally, it is significant that scholars have identified a few elements of this cluster, unlike previous clusters, as essential features of God's character. Such comments were noted pertaining to רחם (14:4d) and אהיה (14:6a). This suggests that the hopeful images of God's love and restoration of Israel in cluster 15 are nearer to the heart of Yahweh and resonate more profoundly with his essential nature than the images of judgment in most other clusters.[107]

Conclusion to Part 1

Part 1 has identified fifteen metaphor clusters, analyzed most metaphors individually, and then considered the interactions between metaphors within each cluster. Phenomena were noted such as overlapping entailments, shared or differing conceptual planes, the significance of shifting or

---

103. See Korpel, *Rift in the Clouds*, 593–94; Seifert, *Metaphorisches Reden*, 259–62; Keefe, "Hosea's (In)Fertility God," 23; McConville, "I Am like," 191–92.
104. Oestreich, *Metaphors and Similes*, 153.
105. Seifert, *Metaphorisches Reden*, 262.
106. Seifert, *Metaphorisches Reden*, 241, my trans.
107. See further ch. 9, esp. pp. 213–14 ("Passionate"), below.

consistent imagery, the appropriation of metaphors from Yahweh's rivals (whether nations or deities), emotional implications of the metaphors, and more. The question throughout has been, How do these metaphorical interactions contribute to the characterization of Yahweh? This was done over three chapters corresponding to the twice-repeated (Hos 4–11, 12–14) progression from indictment to sentencing to restoration. Israel's final and ultimate sentence was that of death (Hos 13), though there is hope for a resurrection on the other side of death (Hos 14).

This analysis of intracluster metaphor interactions ultimately is insufficient to paint a picture of God in Hosea. Just as important in Hosea are the interactions between clusters: the intercluster relationships that reuse, develop, invert, or otherwise play on other metaphors in the book. Part 2 builds on the textual analysis of part 1 to identify certain patterns of metaphor use across clusters, particularly patterns of divine emotion, metaphor inversion, and rhetorical purpose. Part 3 then synthesizes the textual analysis of part 1 and the literary analysis of part 2 into a theological portrait of God.

PART 2
Metaphor Patterns across Clusters

> Puzzling words and phrases have been rediscovered as parts of intricate patterns, each connection contributing to the book's meaning, not haphazardly scattered editorial leavings.... It is all the more unfortunate that the book has so frequently been regarded as slipshod rhetoric and all the more important that it be understood for what it is: a stark, full-length poem of inexhaustible power.
> —Gerald Morris, *Prophecy, Poetry and Hosea*

This study asks how the metaphors of Hos 4–14 characterize Yahweh. By "characterization" I mean "the representation of personages in such a way that they engage an audience's imagination, in essence causing us to entertain their existence as living individuals."[1] The reader experiences characterization in literature as a necessarily linear process given the nature of reading. "Reading a character becomes a process of discovery, attended by all the biblical hallmarks: progressive reconstruction, tentative closure of discontinuities, frequent and sometimes painful

---

1. Patrick, *Rendering of God*, 2; see further Meir Sternberg, *The Poetics of Biblical Narrative: Ideological Literature and the Drama of Reading*, ISBL (Bloomington: Indiana University Press, 1987), 321–41; Shimon Bar-Efrat, *Narrative Art in the Bible*, JSOTSup 70 (Sheffield: Almond, 1989), 47–92; Adele Berlin, *Poetics and Interpretation of Biblical Narrative* (Winona Lake, IN: Eisenbrauns, 1994), 23–42; Robert Alter, *The Art of Biblical Narrative*, 2nd ed. (New York: Basic, 2011), 116–17, 143–62. For views on the characterization of Yahweh in Hosea, see Brueggemann, "Recovering God of Hosea"; Keefe, "Hosea's (In)Fertility God"; Ehud Ben Zvi, "Reading Hosea and Imagining Yhwh," *HBT* 30 (2008): 43–57; Carolyn J. Sharp, "Interrogating the Violent God of Hosea: A Conversation with Walter Brueggemann, Alice Keefe, and Ehud Ben Zvi," *HBT* 30 (2008): 59–70; Mignon R. Jacobs, "YHWH's Call for Israel's 'Return': Command, Invitation, or Threat," *HBT* 32 (2010): 17–32.

reshaping in face of the unexpected, and intractable pockets of darkness to the very end."[2]

The isolated analyses of individual clusters in part 1 are thus insufficient for a characterization of Yahweh in Hos 4–14. Recall that mixed-metaphor clusters "connect and dynamize discourse." That is, they "extend, reject, limit or elaborate" previously used metaphors.[3] Putting all fifteen clusters in conversation is necessary. Part 2 therefore aims to take seriously the nature of Hosea as a literary work by analyzing the metaphoric interactions *across* clusters, accounting for similarities and differences. It observes patterns and developments across the metaphor clusters in as far as they characterize Yahweh. Depictions occur through a variety of means, spanning a spectrum of "explicitness and certainty, for conveying information about the motives, the attitudes, the moral nature of characters."[4] Such characterization can be implied or overt, and through actions or words.[5] The shame metaphors, for example, imply Yahweh's shame by virtue of association with unfaithful-wife-Israel, while Yahweh's hatred for Israel is overt in Hosea 9:15. Rarely is Yahweh overtly described as angry (e.g., 5:10, 8:5, 13:11; negated in 11:9, 14:5), but his actions—the consistency of images and threats of violent judgment—contribute to the portrayal of God's wrath. "Action is," after all, "the implementation of character."[6]

The following chapters presuppose, often without cross-reference, the conclusions of the cluster analyses in part 1. Cluster numbers are at times cited, and the reader is encouraged to revisit chapters 2, 3, and 4 for the interpretations of specific metaphors.

---

2. Sternberg, *Poetics of Biblical Narrative*, 323–24.
3. Kimmel, "Why We Mix Metaphors," 98.
4. Alter, *Art of Biblical Narrative*, 146.
5. Alter, *Art of Biblical Narrative*, 146.
6. Bar-Efrat, *Narrative Art*, 77; see Patrick, *Rendering of God*.

5
Affective Patterns

Hosea is often characterized as one of the most "passionate" prophets or books and the God of Hosea as viscerally emotive.[1] In Hosea, one sees deeper into the affective life of God than in perhaps any other book.[2] Indeed, "Hosea dares to take us inside that complex interior life of YHWH and thus to be exposed to a range of divine impulses not elsewhere available in Israel's ancient text."[3] Hosea 11:8–9, for instance, receives inordinate attention from biblical scholars and theologians alike. Occasionally, attention to divine emotion extends beyond obvious instances (e.g., 9:15) to include those implied by specific metaphors, such as God's disappointment in Hos 10:11 or his shame associated with Israel's promiscuity in Hosea 2 and 4. Yet there are emotive implications for metaphors in Hosea that have not been substantially investigated. Doing so is necessary for a more holistic picture of God.

While I cannot here present a comprehensive treatment of divine emotions suggested by Hosea's metaphors, I draw attention to five aspects

---

1. Yee, "Book of Hosea," 197; Keefe, *Woman's Body*, 220, says, "Hosea was indeed an angry man." A classic treatment is Abraham Heschel, *The Prophets* (New York: Harper & Row, 1962), 285–382; see also Walther Eichrodt, "'The Holy One in Your Midst': The Theology of Hosea," *Int* 15 (1961): 263; and the surveys in Leung Lai, "Hearing God's Bitter Cries," 32–33; Kakkanattu, *God's Enduring Love*, 1, 192–94.

2. The study of emotion within biblical scholarship has been limited until recently. See the breadth of works cited in Paul A. Kruger, "Emotions in the Hebrew Bible: A Few Observations on Prospects and Challenges," *OTE* 28 (2015): 395–420; Françoise Mirguet and Dominika Kurek-Chomycz, "Introduction: Emotions in Ancient Jewish Literature," *BibInt* 24 (2016): 435–41. For a recent broad array of essays on emotions in the Bible, see F. Scott Spencer, ed., *Mixed Feelings and Vexed Passions: Exploring Emotions in Biblical Literature*, RBS 90 (Atlanta: SBL Press, 2017). On human emotion and metaphor, see pp. 10–12, above.

3. Brueggemann, "Recovering God of Hosea," 6.

of the emotional life of Yahweh that are salient in the text yet that have not received substantial scholarly attention. This chapter also notes developments within Yahweh's emotional life.[4] The next chapter observes their inversions in Hos 14.

Yahweh's emotional portrayal occurs through a variety of means, spanning a spectrum of "explicitness and certainty, for conveying information about the motives, the attitudes, the moral nature of characters." Characterization can be implied or overt, and through actions or words.[5] The shame metaphors, for example, imply Yahweh's shame by virtue of association with unfaithful-wife-Israel. The language of love and hate, on the other hand, is explicit in Yahweh's words in Hos 9:15.

Actions also contribute to characterization. For instance, Yahweh is rarely overtly described as angry (e.g., 5:10, 8:5, 13:11; God's anger is negated in 11:9, 14:5), but the consistency of images and threats of violent judgment contributes to the portrayal of God's wrath. "Action is," after all, "the implementation of character."[6] Furthermore, imagery and actions can have a more powerful effect on hearers than direct literal speech. It is one thing for God to say "I am furious and I will judge you" and quite another to say "I will be like a lion, a lurking panther, a furiously bereaved bear who rips your chest open and tears you to pieces" (13:7–8).

Shame

Any reader of Hosea quickly notices divine anger as a prominent emotion. But metaphors nuance portraits in subtle ways. What gives rise to Yahweh's anger? This study suggests that underlying God's wrath is his experience of being hurt by those he loved. Such pain results in anger.

Recent scholarship recognizes the shame dynamic in the marriage metaphors of Hosea 1–3 but rarely that of the next two cycles of the book.[7] There are two ways in which shame surfaces in Hos 4–14. The first is its rhetorical strategy (the perlocutionary act) of eliciting shame in the hearers to provoke submission to Yahweh.[8] For example, Hosea humiliates the

---

4. For a visual depiction of the distribution of these emotions across Hos 4–14, see fig. A.1 in the appendix.
5. Alter, *Art of Biblical Narrative*, 146.
6. Bar-Efrat, *Narrative Art*, 77; see Patrick, *Rendering of God*.
7. See pp. 39–42, above, for a discussion of shame.
8. This is the main argument of Haddox, *Metaphor and Masculinity in Hosea*.

nation and its leadership by portraying them as a sexually promiscuous wife and as a male whore (4:15).[9]

The second way shame surfaces in these metaphors, and the focus of this section, is in their testimony to Yahweh's own experience of public shame through association with his promiscuous wife. Beyond Hos 1–3, Yahweh's shame is a prominent implication of clusters 1, 2, 6, 8, 9, 11, and 12 (i.e., about half of clusters). Notably, they occur in adjacent pairs of clusters. The first four derive from the domain of sexual promiscuity and the second three from the parent-child domain.

The humiliation in clusters 1 (Hos 4:10–16), 2 (5:1–7), 6 (6:10–7:1), and 8 (8:14–9:2) stems from the husband's experience within the marriage metaphor. In the social context of the ancient Near East, any sexual transgression (especially that of a woman) was contagious within the family unit, hence the husband's (Yahweh's) humiliation.[10] It was the (male) family members' responsibility to resolve their social shame. Such action could take the form of rejection, divorce, or, in the broader ancient Near East, violent punishment. Yahweh's response is pictured in the next cluster.

The narrative progress to cluster 9 (Hos 9:15–10:2) mirrors the standard pattern in the ancient Near East: sin, then shame, then action to remedy shame. Cluster 9 pictures a head of household disinheriting a family member, either a husband divorcing a wife or a father disowning a rebellious son. It was argued in chapter 3 that the latter is more plausible, hence Yahweh transitions from husband (cluster 8) to father (cluster 9). Socially, this would remedy any shame on the family.

Clusters 11 and 12 rewind the story. As an historical retrospective within the parent-child metaphor, cluster 11 (Hos 11:1–4) recounts how father-Yahweh was only ever good to son-Israel, yet Israel rejected the father. Though rarely noted by commentators, this experience would have shamed the father: the son has publicly humiliated him. But now Yahweh responds differently than in cluster 9. There, the solution was to reject the rebellious son. In cluster 12 (Hos 11:8–10), father-Yahweh vacillates, unsure of how to respond. The heart of God is warmed with affection for his wayward son (יחד נכמרו נחומי, 11:8). As argued in chapter 4, the coming punishment (11:5–7) will not be absolute (11:9). The relationship

---

9. Other metaphors may be associated with shame and result in ostracism; e.g., the illness metaphors in 5:13 (see Southwood, "Metaphor, Illness, and Identity").

10. Moon, *Hosea*, 41; see cluster 1.

is not over.[11] Judgment will be restrained and penultimate, motivated by a corrective and restorative intent. Hence, God's response to humiliation in cluster 12 is more tempered than that of cluster 9, suggesting an alternative possible trajectory for Israel's future. Perhaps the wife/son will not be utterly rejected. One awaits the conclusion of the story in the final cluster.

Betrayal

It is not surprising that rebellion and betrayal are consistent themes, given that most of Hos 4–14 is concerned with accusation and judgment. This is evident in the use of the lexemes בגד (5:7, 6:7), פשע (7:13, 8:1, 14:10), and מרה (14:1). The theme becomes even more apparent when one moves beyond lexical studies and considers the metaphors about Yahweh's emotional experience in response to betrayal.

Betrayal is implied in clusters 1, 2, 5, 6, 7, 8, 11, and 14 (i.e., over half the clusters). It is noteworthy and appropriate that six of the eight clusters related to betrayal occur in the accusation section of cycle 2.[12] The emotive impact varies between the metaphors. In the case of the suzerain metaphors, betrayal is a statement of fact, with little emphasis on emotion. But as an implication of the sexual promiscuity and parent metaphors, it testifies to a painful experience for Yahweh (see esp. 5:7 in ch. 2).

---

11. This punishment is not included as part of the metaphorical father/son story. Rather, it is described in literal descriptions of historical realities.

12. The accusation section of cycle 3 also highlights this theme, obliquely suggesting Yahweh's experience of betrayal or deception by Israel in Hos 12. Because there are no metaphor clusters for Yahweh in Hos 12, it is not analyzed in this project. Nonetheless, Israel's ancestor Jacob serves a metaphorical function. The chapter presents the deceptive and oppressive patriarch Jacob as an analogue to Hosea's Northern Kingdom. Just as their ancestor Jacob was deceptive in all his dealings (Hos 12:4–5, 8, 13), so Israel is deceptive in its dealings, whether with other nations or with God (12:1–2, 8–9). For a variety of recent views, see Erhard Blum, "Once Again: Hosea and the Pentateuchal Traditions," in *From Author to Copyist: Essays on the Composition, Redaction, and Transmission of the Hebrew Bible in Honor of Zipi Talshir*, ed. Cana Werman (Winona Lake, IN: Eisenbrauns, 2015), 81–94; Felipe Fruto Ramirez, "Are the Allusions to Jacob and Moses in Hosea 12 Late Insertions?," *Landas* 29 (2015): 119–43; Martin Schott, "Die Jakobpassagen in Hosea 12," *ZTK* 112 (2015): 1–26. I find Blum's account the most compelling. On the theme of Jacob's deceitfulness in Genesis, see John E. Anderson, *Jacob and the Divine Trickster: A Theology of Deception and Yhwh's Fidelity to the Ancestral Promise in the Jacob Cycle*, SLTHS 5 (Winona Lake, IN: Eisenbrauns, 2011).

As illustrated in table 5.1, the initial cluster uses the husband metaphor, while the final clusters use the father/parent metaphor. The interim witnesses an overlap of all three domains with gradual transitions. Rhetorically, the discourse begins and ends with the more personal, emotionally charged domains. Clusters 2, 7, and 8 are the only ones that use multiple metaphor domains to highlight Israel's betrayal.

Table 5.1: Clusters Involving Betrayal, according to Metaphor Domain

Cluster #	1	2	5	6	7	8	11	14
Husband	✓	✓		✓		9:1		
Suzerain		✓		✓	7:13; 8:1			
Father/Parent					7:12, 15?	8:14	✓	✓

All three domains involve two parties with mutual obligations. Marriage and political relationships depend on a covenant (the connection between betrayal and covenant is explicit in 6:7). A parent-child relationship does not but rests on natural parental obligations and socially assumed reciprocal obligations of submission and obedience on the part of the child.[13] In all three metaphor domains, when one party fails to meet their obligations, the relationship can be broken, so that the other party is free of any obligations.

The metaphoric interactions of cluster 1 (Hos 4:10–16), for example, raise the question of whether Yahweh's obligations still hold, if Israel has violated theirs. If wife-Israel has violated her commitment of fidelity to husband-Israel (4:10–15), (switching metaphors) is shepherd-Yahweh still obligated to feed sheep-Israel (4:16)?[14] In the suzerain metaphors, the suzerain can bring the curses of the covenant on the vassal.[15] Concerning the father/parent metaphors, 8:14 claims that Father-Yahweh has been faithful to his child, but son-Israel has forgotten his father. In Hosea, to forget (שכח) is to intentionally ignore or abandon, to "put out of mind."[16] Forgetting is active betrayal. Will Yahweh remain committed to his natural obligations to provide for his son after such heartless abandonment?

---

13. A covenant establishes "an elected, *as opposed to natural*, relationship of obligation" (Hugenberger, *Marriage as a Covenant*, 171, emphasis added).
14. See pp. 43–44, above.
15. See, e.g., in the immediate context of those metaphors: 5:7c; 6:5, 11a; 7:13, 16.
16. Goldingay's translation of שכח in Hos 8:14 (*First Testament*, 853).

God's anger, therefore, is not an irrational or vindictive rage. Anger is often a response to being hurt, as the object of God's affection has repeatedly spurned the divine care so faithfully offered. The power of these metaphors arises from the impactful embodied experiences their source domains evoke: a spouse's betrayal and a rebellious child's rejection are painful experiences, because they are the most intimate of human bonds. Yet these painful human experiences are inadequate pointers to the divine experience of the people's heartless response.

Though these texts raise the question of whether Yahweh will remain faithful to Israel (4:16), they do not provide an explicit answer. The intervening judgments suggest that Yahweh has had enough of this treatment. But then God vacillates (11:8). Yahweh explicitly affirms that he is *not* human (11:9) and does not respond to betrayal as humans do. The reader must await Hosea's final chapter for an answer.

Disappointment

God is disappointed and frustrated in the sense that he had expectations for Israel that they failed to meet. Scholars have noted this implication in certain metaphors (esp. Hos 10:11), but its presence in Hosea is more widespread.

Yahweh's disillusionment with Israel and the dissatisfaction of his purposes is a noteworthy feature of the middle of the discourse (clusters 7, 9, 10), with the exception of cluster 1 (specifically Hos 4:16).[17] These themes occur exclusively in cycle 2, mostly around the transition from accusation (4:1–8:14) to judgment (9:1–11:7).

Yahweh's disappointment is noted in at least three ways. These will be addressed beginning with the most indirect and moving to the most direct. The first set of metaphors that communicate God's dissatisfaction with Israel is those that picture Israel as useless, as deviant from its category. These do not directly testify to Yahweh's disappointment, but they portray Israel as a failed version of its kind; the connection to Yahweh comes later. The emphasis is not on willful disobedience but on Israel's failure to fulfill its purpose.

---

17. Disappointment is also a main feature of Hos 9:10. God was pleasantly surprised at finding Israel, but they turned away from Yahweh to the thing of shame. Hosea 9:10 is not part of a cluster and so is not analyzed in this study. See Eidevall, *Grapes in the Desert*, 147–52.

In cluster 7, examples include Israel as an unturned cake, burnt on one side and useless for eating (Hos 7:8); Israel as a witless dove, incapable of flying in a single direction (7:11); and Israel as the slack bow, useless for shooting an arrow (7:16). Their failure has to do with depending on other nations for security, implying that their intended purpose was to be a nation depending on Yahweh for safety and testifying to his sovereignty. In cluster 9, Israel is presented as a withering plant in five separate expressions. Farmer-Yahweh expected fruit (see 9:10), but this plant does not produce (פרי בלי יעשון, 9:16).[18] Once again, Israel is pictured as an exception to the norm, an ineffective version of its kind.

The second way metaphors witness to divine frustration is by emphasizing Israel's willful disobedience, as in Hos 4:16 (cluster 1). In a line of exquisite consonance, assonance, and rhythm, Israel is portrayed as a stubborn calf (כי כפרה סררה סרר ישראל) that refuses to comply with farmer-Yahweh's instruction.

The third and most explicit approach is to overtly describe the fact that Yahweh had plans for Israel that have not been realized. Hosea 10:11 (cluster 10) is the most explicit case, so it is unsurprising that scholars have noticed this aspect of the metaphor. Yahweh noticed a cow well-suited for certain tasks and intended to put that cow to good use. The metaphor testifies to Israel's "election to service."[19] Unfortunately, farmer-Yahweh did not get what he wanted from that cow.

Divine disappointment is often related to Israel's betrayal. Cluster 7 (Hos 7:8–8:1) is the only cluster that heavily emphasizes both disillusionment (7:8, 11, 16) and betrayal (7:13; 8:1). Clusters 9 and 10 focus on grievance and are bracketed by clusters highlighting duplicity (clusters 8 and 11). Cluster 1 includes a statement of Yahweh's frustration with Israel (4:16) but highlights betrayal through sexual promiscuity within the marriage metaphor (4:10–15). Sexual promiscuity within the marriage metaphor itself entails both betrayal and disappointment. Yahweh's displeasure in the marriage may be a subtle, secondary implication of the metaphor. Marriage begins with high expectations of a wonderful relationship (see, e.g., 2:16–17), which do not come to fruition and are replaced by dismay.

In summary, Yahweh had purposes in choosing Israel. The book underscores that God desires that Israel return to acknowledge and remain loyal

---

18. Further examples of useless Israel include 8:8–9; 10:1.
19. Wolff, *Hosea*, 185.

168   Hosea's God: A Metaphorical Theology

to Yahweh (e.g., 6:6), rather than to his adversaries (e.g., Baal and other deities, Assyria [e.g., 14:3]), and that Israel pursue an equitable society (10:12; 12:7). The call for Israel to *return* to Yahweh recognizes that they have failed to meet expectations. The cow refuses to plow, the plant fails to bear fruit, the bow is useless. This explains God's angry response and the consequent judgment. Will God ever get what he wanted from Israel? Will Israel ever fulfill the purpose for which it was chosen? One must wait until the final chapter for an answer.

Love and Hate

The arena of God's love and hate has drawn the most attention from scholars interested in the passionate language of Hosea. This section analyzes some of the dynamics between a few related metaphors within the clusters of Hos 4–14 and offers observations on their patterns and interactions.

Metaphors for God or Israel involving love or hate are found in clusters 8 (Hos 9:1), 9 (Hos 9:15), 10 (Hos 10:11), 11 (Hos 11:1-4), 12 (Hos 11:8), 14 (Hos 13:14), and 15 (Hos 14:5). Notably, they occur exclusively and pervasively in the second half of Hos 4–14.[20] There is considerable variety among these clusters. They may be summarized briefly, and in textual order, as follows: Israel *loved* the fees she received as an unfaithful wife (9:1), God the father *hated* and disowned the son Israel (9:15), cow-Israel *loved* threshing (10:11), God *loved* his son Israel (11:1), God's *compassion* is warmed (11:8), God's *compassion* is hidden from his sight (13:14), and God will *love* Israel freely (14:5). Hosea 14:5 is considered more fully below. Metaphoric expressions focusing on God's emotions are Hosea 9:15; 11:1(-4), 8; 13:14. The first two offer developed story lines; the second two profoundly depict divine affective motivations.

Most of the expressions have an obvious temporal horizon. The beginning of the relationship is pictured as ideal. At the exodus, God *loved* his son and created their relationship (11:1).[21] Also at the beginning, switching metaphors, Israel was a cow, which farmer-Yahweh noticed was well-fit for service (10:11). The cow apparently *loved* threshing; it was not resentful. Subsequently, in the wilderness (9:10, 13:5-6), Israel rejected God's initial

---

20. The only cluster from the second half of the book without a contribution to love and hate is cluster 13, though it is certainly an expression of God's wrath.

21. In Hosea, the exodus and subsequent wilderness period mark the ideal beginning of God's relationship with Israel (2:16-17; 9:10; 11:1; 12:10, 14; 13:4-5).

love. Significantly, Israel *never* loved or loves Yahweh in the book. Every use of אהב with Israel as a subject describes the nation's love of something *other than* their deity and incompatible with him.[22] Among the metaphor clusters, Israel is a prostitute who *loves* the fees she receives for her promiscuity (אהבת אתנן) rather than loving her proper husband Yahweh (9:1), and a heifer who *loves* to thresh (10:11). Outside metaphor clusters, Israel loved raisin cakes (ענבים, 3:1), ignominy (קלון, 4:18 [2x]), the "thing of shame" (בשת = Baal, 9:10; see 2:7, 9, 12, 14, 15), or oppression (לעשק, 12:8). Boda summarizes, "This contrast between Yahweh and his people reveals that the burning issue of the book of Hosea is the contrast between the passionate love of Yahweh for his people and the lack of response from those people."[23] God responds by disowning his son because of all Israel's evil at Gilgal (9:15). God will not continue to love them (לא אוסף אהבתם). He will drive the son from the house (מביתי אגרשם).

The temporal markers of the remaining two metaphors are much less clear. Indeed, 11:8 and 13:14 are the most challenging two verses regarding Yahweh's emotional life. They appear mutually exclusive, predicating opposite things of the same root (נחם). God's compassions both warm up (11:8) and are hidden from sight (13:14).

God asks questions of himself in 11:8a–d. His heart recoils (נהפך עלי לבי, 11:8e) in *response* to the questions, and 11:8e–f are resolutions to them. Hosea 11:8f (יחד נכמרו נחומי) uses a *qatal* verb, indicating the action is viewed as complete, as if God's affections become and stay tender when he considers what course of action to take with Israel. As argued in chapter 4, the verse indicates that God will still bring judgment on Israel for their transgression (11:5–7), but punishment will be tempered by compassion and does not end the relationship.

The *yiqtol* verb (יסתר) of Hos 13:14e, on the other hand, suggests the action is incomplete (in context, either an ongoing present reality or located in the future). The preceding four questions of Hos 13:14a–d indicate that the context of 13:14e is Yahweh deciding whether to inflict punishment or rescue from death. They are rhetorical questions to which the implied answer is in the negative. Rescue will not come. The *yiqtol* emphasizes the ongoing aspect of the hiddenness of compassion. Compassion is absent from the mental calculus of whether to inflict judgment on Israel.

---

22. The exception is 10:11, which is inverted in 4:16.
23. Boda, *Severe Mercy*, 295.

Since both 11:8f and 13:14e occur after four rhetorical questions, the difference between the two lines can be articulated in terms of the questions they answer. Hosea 11:8 asks about the *degree* of judgment: Will it be a total destruction (שׁחת), like Admah and Zeboiim? No. God's compassion will temper or restrain the degree of judgment. Hosea 13:14 asks about the *existence* of judgment: Will God rescue Israel from the incoming destruction (death)? No. God's compassion will not stop him from bringing destruction, to one extent or another. Hosea 11:8 debates the *degree* of punishment, while 13:14 considers whether to inflict it at all.

The different perspectives of these verses can be integrated as follows. God loved Israel in the beginning and hates them now due to their disobedience. His love tempers his punishment, while his sense of justice tempers his patience.[24] Said another way, God's justice is loving, and his love is just. "With Hosea, we should recognize that the answer does not lie in making a choice between the love and justice of God. It is not a question of either/or, but both/and. God is just, and God is love."[25]

Such an integration, however, risks robbing this textual world of its power and pathos to persuade. The book does not offer crisp, consistent theological summaries. The purpose is to awaken Israel to the dangers they face and provoke a return to Yahweh, as argued in chapter 7 below. Hosea employs shocking words and images to jolt the people out of their stupor.

A synthetic treatment of these two verses in isolation could give the false impression that they offer balance in near proximity. In truth, Hosea often proclaims a single divine aspect with vigor and offers no other aspect for parity.[26] The father, for example, is presented as justified in hating and disowning the son (9:15) without any mention of compassion in the near literary context. There is nothing within two chapters of that verse that offers a positive image of God. The presentation is univocally negative.

Like many prophetic books, the overwhelming majority of Hosea emphasizes justified judgment, impending violence, and punishment. God is capable of putting compassion out of mind so that it does not factor into his decision making for the immediate future of Israel. God is justified

---

24. The language of "tempering" or "restraint" is justified by 11:8f and 13:14e, which present נחם as mitigating or precluding what comes before, whether handing them over to total destruction like Admah and Zeboiim (11:8) or to total rescue (פדה, גאל [13:14]). See esp. Jeremias, *Die Reue Gottes*, 39, 110; Jeremias, *Prophet Hosea*, 145.

25. Carew, "Hosea," 1050.

26. See further the aspective approach in ch. 8 below.

in bringing judgment on Israel's flagrant rebellion. A few verses temper the absoluteness of that vision. While destruction is coming, it does not result in an absolute end. The destruction is restrained by love such that there is hope on the other side (11:8). Switching metaphors, the wife (Hos 2) or the son (9:15) can return home and be loved again. One must wait for the final chapter of Hosea to find out.

6
Literary Patterns

The individual metaphors of Hosea draw their power from the rich literary tapestry in which they are set. This chapter observes literary patterns in the use of metaphors across the book, including a shifting polemical strategy and an analysis of how the final chapter of Hosea gathers and inverts thematic and metaphoric threads. Scholars frequently notice Hosea's penchant for wordplay and reversal and how certain metaphors develop or reverse others.[1] Some instances were noted in the last chapter (e.g., on Hos 14:6 in relation to 1:9, 6:4, 13:3; or Hos 11:10 in relation to 5:14–15, 13:7–8). This chapter builds on such observations and focuses on patterns and metaphorical connotations that have not previously been sufficiently recognized. By way of introduction, a few broad patterns may first be noted.

First, there are interesting patterns in how the book repurposes and inverts metaphor source domains and applies them to different target domains. The source domain of dew (טל), for instance, refers to Israel's fickleness (6:4), then to Israel's transience in the face of exile (13:3). Finally, it is inverted into a hopeful image and applied to Yahweh's life-giving presence (14:6). Similar patterns are found in the water-related imagery, lion

---

1. In addition to the commentaries on relevant passages, see DeRoche, "Reversal of Creation in Hosea"; Jörg Jeremias, "Zur Eschatologie des Hoseabuches," in *Die Botschaft und die Boten: Festschrift für Hans Walter Wolff zum 70. Geburtstag*, ed. Jörg Jeremias and Lothar Perlitt (Neukirchen-Vluyn: Neukirchener, 1981), 217–34; Michael Lee Catlett, "Reversals in Hosea: A Literary Analysis" (PhD diss., Emory University, 1988); Fisch, *Poetry with a Purpose*, 136–57; Eidevall, *Grapes in the Desert*, 236–52; Morris, *Prophecy, Poetry and Hosea* (see esp. 148–51 for a list of over 70 puns); Haddox, *Metaphor and Masculinity in Hosea*, 144–57. Hosea often inverts Israel's traditions (for a brief survey, see Smith, "'Wilderness' in Hosea and Deuteronomy," 254–57) in its view that the end of Israel's story is a return to the beginning and in its nuanced use of שוב.

metaphors, and illness and healing that begin in the supercluster of 5:10–6:7: each source domain begins with negative connotations but becomes a picture of restoration.[2]

Second, source domains of metaphors for God vary in prominence over the course of the book; certain clusters favor certain domains. Sexual promiscuity and legal metaphors are most prominent at the beginning (clusters 1–2) and eventually trail off. The supercluster (clusters 3–5) uses source domains of destructive animals and presumed healing to contest what kind of storm god Yahweh will be for Israel. Clusters 6–7 involve mixed metaphors highlighting sexual promiscuity, Yahweh's disappointment, and Israel's betrayal. The final sexual promiscuity metaphors occur next, with father and shepherd metaphors (cluster 8), highlighting aspects of provision and fidelity. These give way to an extended use of the parental and farmer domains (clusters 9–12); in cluster 13, the shepherd becomes a predator; cluster 14 declares the hopeless finality of death; and in cluster 15, all the previous metaphors and their emotional implications converge in a grand set of hopeful reversals.

Third, the longest continuous stretches of Yahweh metaphors occur toward the end of the book (clusters 11, 13, 15), as if the urgency of Hosea's message were increasing.[3] Also toward the end of the book are the more overtly polemical appropriations of images and metaphors associated with other deities. These two points suggest a shift in the rhetorical strategy of the book.

Polemics and Metaphor Appropriation: A Shifting Strategy

Hosea's polemics, especially against Baal, have received much scholarly attention.[4] Yet there is no comprehensive analysis of Hosea's polemics

---

2. See Lancaster, "Wounds and Healing"; for more examples, see Morris, *Prophecy, Poetry and Hosea*, 101–31.

3. Cluster 7 is the longest cluster in terms of verses, but the cluster is primarily about Israel; the metaphors indirectly and intermittently concern Yahweh. Clusters 11, 13, and 15, on the other hand, involve longer *uninterrupted* stretches of strong metaphors that are more directly about Yahweh.

4. This study is primarily interested in the most prominent polemical category—namely, against other deities. See Kruger, "Yahweh and the Gods in Hosea"; Dearman, "Interpreting the Religious Polemics"; Ronald Scott Chalmers, *The Struggle of Yahweh and El for Hosea's Israel*, HMS 11 (Sheffield: Sheffield Phoenix, 2008); Anderson, *Monotheism and Yahweh's Appropriation*; Szabolcs-Ferencz Kató, *Jhwh: der Wettergott*

against deities, nations, and Israelite leaders. This section offers a modest contribution. Specifically, Hosea's antideity polemics evince a shift in strategy.[5]

Clusters 1, 5, 8, 10, 13 (perhaps), 14, and 15 involve polemical elements against other deities. Outside clusters, deity polemics occur at 4:17–19 (possibly), 9:10 (the "thing of shame," לבשת),[6] and much of Hos 13. Potential divine opponents include Baal (named in 2:10, 15, 18, 19; 11:2; 13:1; implied in 9:10; storm-god imagery appropriated in many places), Asherah (4:17–19?, 14:9), Mot (13:7–8, 14?), and perhaps El (ch. 13).[7] Baal is the primary divine opponent and the only one named.

An interesting pattern emerges among the polemics. Initial instances are overtly oppositional, simply denouncing those deities. For example, following Baal is like whoring (cluster 1). As such, Baal is characterized as the "other man," Yahweh's adversary. This direct antagonism continues through 9:10, where Baal is simply "shame" (בשת). The strategy then transitions

---

Hoseas? Der "ursprüngliche" Charakter Jhwhs ausgehend vom Hoseabuch, WMANT 158 (Göttingen: Vandenhoeck & Ruprecht, 2019). For more on Baal in Hosea, see p. 66 n. 133, above. Hosea also polemicizes against nations and Israel's leadership. Assyria is the key opponent (explicitly opposed in 5:13 and 14:4, though named frequently elsewhere. See Marvin A. Sweeney, "Hosea's Reading of Pentateuchal Narratives: A Window for a Foundational E Stratum," in *The Formation of the Pentateuch: Bridging the Academic Cultures of Europe, Israel, and North America*, ed. Jan C. Gertz et al., FAT 111 (Tübingen: Mohr Siebeck, 2016), 851–71; Zimran, "Notion of God"; Hamilton, "History among the Junipers," esp. 109–10. Egypt is frequently mentioned, but never polemically. For polemics against Israelites, see Margaret Diefenderfer Zulick, "Rhetorical Polyphony in the Book of the Prophet Hosea" (PhD diss., Northwestern University, 1994); Lyn M. Bechtel, "The Metaphors of 'Canaanite' and 'Baal' in Hosea," in *Inspired Speech: Prophecy in the Ancient Near East; Essays in Honor of Herbert H. Huffmon*, ed. Louis Stulman and John Kaltner, JSOTSup 378 (London: T&T Clark, 2004), 203–15; Haddox, "(E)Masculinity"; Haddox, *Metaphor and Masculinity in Hosea*; and, to a degree, Boshoff, "Who Let Grain, Grapes and Olives."

5. For a visual depiction, see fig. A.1 in the appendix.

6. בשת is widely recognized as a polemical substitute for בעל; see, e.g., 2 Sam 2:12, where Ishbaal, the son of Saul, is called Ishbosheth (see 1 Chr 8:33, 9:39); Jer 11:13, where בשת and בעל are in synonymous parallelism (see Day, *Yahweh and the Gods*, 81–83). On Hos 4:17–19, see p. 42 n. 47, above.

7. On 13:7–8, 14, see ch. 3, cluster 13. On 4:17–19, 14:9, see p. 33 n. 8, above, and on 14:9c–d. On Hos 13, see ch. 3, cluster 14. Chalmers argues that El is polemicized throughout Hos 11–13 (*Struggle of Yahweh and El*). See also Ronald Scott Chalmers, "Who Is the Real El? A Reconstruction of the Prophet's Polemic in Hosea 12:5a," *CBQ* 68 (2006): 611–30.

from head-to-head opposition to one of subversion by commandeering the imagery of Yahweh's rivals, beginning with cluster 10. Yahweh, *not Baal*, will bring rain, the metaphorical rain of deliverance (10:12). Yahweh, not El, is the supreme God overseeing that battle between Mot and Baal (cluster 14). Yahweh, not Baal, brings fertility and flourishing to Israel (cluster 15). Yahweh, not Asherah, is their tree of life (cluster 15).

This approach renders the opponents superfluous. The appropriation of imagery associated with other deities serves to absorb their powers into the constellation of Yahweh, exalting Yahweh as having a broader array of abilities than other deities. Michael Hundley summarizes this common dynamic in the ancient world:

> In a polytheistic context, a text does not often deny the existence of other gods or eliminate them. Rather, *to exalt a single deity, a text depicts that deity as co-opting the aspects of other deities.* Co-opting (some of) a deity's aspects in no way denies the existence of that god; instead that deity is no longer the exclusive bearer of the attribute, such that one need not access it [the deity] in order to access the attribute. As a result, when more than one god shares a function, *the less prominent deity may be forgotten because it is no longer necessary and thus effectively relegated to non-existent status.*[8]

Absorbing these abilities into Yahweh also undermines the people's felt need for those other deities. As Seifert summarizes,

> Apparently, the Israelites held that YHWH was incompetent in important areas of their life and felt therefore the need to turn also to other deities beyond him. That "Baalim" were worshiped *alongside YHWH*, indicates the problem of the limitations of one god. In the book of Hosea, it is easy to see how the metaphors ascribed functions to YHWH that the people at the time assigned to other gods. ... With Hosea himself, the ideas taken from the Canaanite region undergo an even greater change when they are integrated into the image of YHWH.[9]

It is Yahweh (the good husband), not Baal, who is the true provider of Israel's needs. The variety of metaphors for Yahweh "testify to the versatility of the one God and show that it is YHWH whom Israel always encounters,

---

8. Hundley, "Here a God," 99–100, emphasis added.
9. Seifert, *Metaphorisches Reden*, 259, emphasis original.

whether in prosperity or adversity [*Wohl und Wehe*], and that the people need no other god besides him."[10] As Morris remarks, "If Israel must worship the gods of Canaan, then 'I Will Be' [אהיה, 14:6] will become the gods of Canaan."[11]

Culmination and Inversion in Hosea 14

Hosea 14 is a master exemplar of artistic density and sophistication. All four negative divine emotions considered above are inverted (that is, all but love). With a single exception, every metaphor for God in this chapter is an inversion of prior uses.[12] Indeed, *virtually each word* within each expression is some kind of reversal. Eidevall thus describes 14:6–9 as "a final magnificent reversal of all reversals."[13] This is not to say that the chapter invalidates what came before;[14] it is to say that Israel's ultimate future will be an undoing of their past. Ephraim's destiny will be "not only a return from exile, but a return to the ideal beginning—to paradise."[15]

This section demonstrates how each image used for Yahweh in Hosea 14 is an inversion of something previous. It then shows how each of the four negative emotions of Yahweh identified above is inverted. It concludes with observations on the rhetorical and theological significance of these inversions.

Inverted Images

The first metaphor of cluster 15 is Hos 14:4d: אשר בך ירחם יתום. As the basis for the people's confidence that Yahweh will receive them when they repent, the image harks back to Hos 1–2. There are two elements to this

---

10. Seifert, *Metaphorisches Reden*, 262; see also 284.

11. Morris, *Prophecy, Poetry and Hosea*, 130; similarly, Korpel, *Rift in the Clouds*, 593–94.

12. Hosea 14:2–4 and 14:10 also involve inversions, but they do not involve metaphors for God and so are outside cluster 15. See Choon-Leong Seow, "Hosea 14:10 and the Foolish People Motif," *CBQ* 44 (1982): 212–24.

13. Eidevall, *Grapes in the Desert*, 242; see also Edwin M. Good, "The Composition of Hosea," *SEÅ* 31 (1966): 60–61; Nwaoru, *Imagery in the Prophecy*, 172–78.

14. Though some rabbis seemed to think it did (Pesiq. Rab Kah. 16:8).

15. Eidevall, *Grapes in the Desert*, 242; contra Andersen and Freedman, who write that "all the horror of the preceding judgements is *cancelled* by the ardour of this promise" (*Hosea*, 646, emphasis added).

reversal: God's having compassion and the imagery of the orphan. The verb רחם occurs in Hosea only here and in Hos 1–2 (1:6, 7; 2:6, 25). In the first three instances, Yahweh declares he will no longer have pity on the Northern Kingdom (1:6, 2:6), but he will on Judah (1:7). Within the restoration phase (2:16–25) of the first cycle (Hos 1–3), Yahweh declares that "on that day" (2:23) he will indeed have compassion on his child "No-Compassion" (ורחמתי את לא רחמה, 2:25). Mirroring that first restoration phase, this final restoration phase (14:2–9) of the final cycle (12:1–14:9) has the people confidently declare that Yahweh is the God to whom one can return in penitence and find a compassionate welcome. Unlike 6:1–6, where the people's assumption is rejected by Yahweh, here their convictions about Yahweh are confirmed in the next line (14:5a–b).

The second element of reversal in 14:4d relates to the orphan metaphor. In Hos 1–2, the people are characterized as a promiscuous woman and as her children, who are disowned (e.g., 1:9). Hosea 9:15 likewise shows Yahweh disowning his rebellious son, Israel. In the ancient world, women and children depended on a male for their protection and provision. To be disowned was to become an orphan, lacking the safety net of a male provider. In 5:7, the people are characterized as illegitimate children (בנים זרים); they *never* belonged to Yahweh. Yet in 14:4d, Hosea encourages Israel to confess their hope that even they—the orphan, the rebellious son, the children of infidelity—can once again return home to find mercy and acceptance by father-Yahweh. Hence 14:4d is a reversal of the passages saying Yahweh will not have compassion (רחם) on Israel, as well as a reversal of Israel's status of orphan (disowned son).

The second metaphor, ארפא משובתם (14:5a), inverts both of its elements: healing and apostasy.[16] In the beginning, Yahweh demonstrated his care for son/animal-Israel by healing, but Israel did not acknowledge that care (11:3). Subsequently, there have been no healers or saviors (5:13, 14; 13:4) and no healing, even at the hands of Yahweh (7:1). Here, for the first time,[17] God promises that Israel will be healed. Demonstrating the second element of inversion, healing has been impossible *precisely because of* their apostasy (5:4, 7:1, 11:7). Though beforehand the people were "hung up"

---

16. For other inversions in 14:5, see Macintosh, *Critical and Exegetical Commentary*, 569. The verb רפא is part of a larger set of wordplays on the name אפרים (Morris, *Prophecy, Poetry and Hosea*, 125–26).

17. In 6:1 the people assume that Yahweh will heal them, but they are misguided.

(תלואים) on their apostasy (משובה, 11:7), which kept them from returning to Yahweh (5:4), God now says that he will heal that apostasy.

The next metaphor is Hosea 14:5b, in which Yahweh declares אהבם נדבה. This plays on a variety of passages, as discussed in the last chapter. It inverts 9:15, where Yahweh disowns Ephraim, then says, "I will not continue to love them" (לא אוסף אהבתם). Three observations suggest that 14:5b envisions not merely a return to the past (when Yahweh loved his son, 11:1) but a step forward into a relationship envisioned in new images. First, the emphasis, as argued in chapter 4, is on Yahweh's free choice (נדבה) to love the people again. Second, Oestreich suggests that this metaphor envisions *adoptive* love.[18] Third, the orphan imagery of 14:4d may reverberate into this verse. This passage not only inverts past metaphors but advances them by picturing Yahweh extending mercy to and adopting orphan Israel.

Hosea 14:6 (אהיה כטל לישראל) involves several reversals. אהיה is a play on the divine name and an inversion of 1:9, where I AM (יהוה) says "I am not" (לא אהיה). The hope of Israel returns as I AM, "I will be" (אהיה). Second, "the dew of Israel's inconstancy [6:4] becomes the dew that causes their flourishing."[19] The dew that symbolizes Israel's rapid exile (13:3) now causes their renewed life in the land (14:6b–8). "Again, the context is radically altered. God offers to take Israel back, and this key word [*dew*], traveling through sorrow to anger to forgiveness is one of the many microcosms of the books."[20]

The collection of images for Israel's future flourishing (14:6b–8) also inverts at least three features in Hosea. To the extent that the imagery is suggestive of love poetry and renewed marital bliss, it is an inversion of the sexual promiscuity metaphors: the promiscuous wife is restored.[21] Husband and wife again fall in love and delight in each other. The imagery of agricultural flourishing is inversions of the curses that open the indictment of the second cycle, where the earth mourns and withers (4:3).[22] Finally,

---

18. Oestreich, *Metaphors and Similes*, 153.
19. Lancaster, "Wounds and Healing," 423.
20. Morris, *Prophecy, Poetry and Hosea*, 69.
21. See Morris, *Prophecy, Poetry and Hosea*, 114. Moughtin-Mumby acknowledges this textual strategy but questions whether it can be successful (*Sexual and Marital Metaphors*, 76–79, 260–68, 274–75).
22. See Moughtin-Mumby, *Sexual and Marital Metaphors*, 53–54.

the flourishing vegetation may invert the frustrated-farmer metaphors in which plant-Israel never grows and produces as it should.[23]

The penultimate metaphor, Yahweh as the luxuriant juniper (כברוש רענן, 14:9c), appears to be the single exception to reversal among the metaphors of Hos 14; it does not reverse any prior metaphor in Hosea.[24] Moreover, as noted in chapter 4, Hos 14:9c is the only place in Scripture that identifies Yahweh as a tree, underscoring the radically unique claim of this concluding metaphor for God.

The final metaphorical expression is 14:9d, where Yahweh declares that Israel's fruit comes from the Divine Juniper (14:9c). Fruit (פרי) has only been negative before Hos 14. Hosea 9:16 pictures Israel as a stricken plant that bears no fruit (פרי בלי יעשון). Two verses later, Israel is a ravaged vine with ravaged fruit (גפן בוקק ישראל פרי ישוה לו, 10:1). Finally, in a series of agricultural metaphors where the result of Israel's labor is wickedness and injustice, Israel eats the fruit of deception (אכלתם פרי כחש, 10:13). Hosea 14:9d, therefore, concludes the book of Hosea with the only positive use of פרי.[25] Israel enjoys good fruit only at the hands of Yahweh, their perpetual provider.

In cluster 15, therefore, *virtually every single word in every single metaphorical phrase* (with the exception of 14:9c) is an inversion of something prior. Yet it is not only metaphors that are turned upside down in Hos 14 but also Yahweh's emotions.

Overturned Emotions

Five emotional categories of Yahweh were identified above in chapter 5 as prominent elements of the metaphors in Hosea that are not always noted by scholars, namely, shame, betrayal, disappointment, and love/hate. All but love are overturned within the metaphors of cluster 15.

First, Yahweh's shame derived from his association with a promiscuous wife. Shame was contagious within the ancient Near Eastern household.[26]

---

23. See pp. 166–68 ("Disappointment"), above.

24. Literal trees are mentioned in 4:13.

25. MT Hos 14:3 has the people saying וּנְשַׁלְּמָה פָרִים שְׂפָתֵינוּ. Some interpret פרים (normally "bulls"; Tg. Neb.; Vulg.; NJPS) as "fruit" with an enclitic *mem* (LXX; Syr.; NRSV; see Macintosh, *Critical and Exegetical Commentary*, 561–65; Tully, *Hosea*, 342–43). This does not change the fact that fruit has only been negative before Hos 14—only that it might first be positive in 14:3 rather than 14:9d.

26. Moon, *Hosea*, 41.

The solution, therefore, is to remove the wife's shame, thereby dissolving the cause of the husband's shame. In the ancient Near East, this could be accomplished via divorce or punishment, even capital punishment. Hosea 14 presents a very different solution, observable on at least two levels, both within the Israel imagery of 14:6b–8. On the level of the flora metaphors, the plant is flourishing and life giving. These are images connoting honor, the opposite of the shameful imagery of the withering vine. Furthermore, these metaphors may be suggestive of a renewed marital relationship, one of love and delight. The shame is undone. The wife's honor, and therefore the husband's too, has been restored.[27] Switching metaphors again, Israel's healing (14:5) may also suggest the removal of the shameful stigmas associated with illness in the ancient Near East.[28] In sum, "salvation leads to the removal of shame."[29]

Second, Yahweh's sense of betrayal derived from Israel's turning to other things. God's people are "hung up" on turning away from Yahweh (תלואים למשובתי, 11:7). In 14:5, their turning away (משובה) is the object of Yahweh's healing. Their "constant inconstancy" is a wound healed by the balm of love.[30] Ephraim, once only capable of treason (5:4, 11:7), will no longer betray their God.

Third, the Lord was disappointed because the people failed to live up to God's intended purposes for them. This was especially evident in metaphors involving a farmer's animals and plants. In the agricultural imagery of 14:6b–8, this disappointment is overturned. Israel, pictured as a variety of plants, is thriving, finally bearing fruit. To the extent that Yahweh is the farmer, Yahweh finally receives the intended benefit from the land. God need no longer be disappointed. God's people finally live up to their potential, the reason for their election, and fulfill their purpose. To the extent that the imagery connotes marital bliss, it suggests that Yahweh need no longer be disappointed with his marriage.

Finally, the journey between love and hate not only comes full circle but also is transposed into a higher key. Yahweh's relationship with Israel began with love, but the predominant theme became God's wrath. In Hosea 14, though, Yahweh says that his anger has turned away from him (כי שב אפי ממנו, 14:5c). He now loves the people with "open-hearted gen-

---

27. Hadjiev, "Adultery, Shame, and Sexual Pollution," 223.
28. See Southwood, "Metaphor, Illness, and Identity," 230.
29. Hadjiev, "Honor and Shame," 334.
30. Plank speaks of "perpetual inconstancy" ("Scarred Countenance," 353).

erosity" (אהבם נדבה, 14:5b).[31] What is new here is the identification of God's love as extravagant, not calculated or in response to Israel's actions but spontaneous and resulting in "a gesture of unconditioned grace."[32]

Rhetorical and Theological Significance

At times, the metaphors of an opponent can be taken up and integrated into one's own speech as a means of overcoming alterity, as a means of reconciliation.[33] That does not happen in Hos 14. Virtually all of the book's metaphors reflect only one viewpoint—namely, Hosea's/Yahweh's.[34] Hosea 14 demonstrates not the reconciliation of two previously opposing view but the opposite: the *creation* of an alternative future. The metaphors of Hos 14 are in competition with those of Hos 4–13 (with the exception of 11:8–11). Yet they are not mutually exclusive or contradictory. They are differentiated by their temporal planes.[35] Those of Hos 4–13 reside on the temporal planes of the past, present, and near future. Hosea 14, as inferred from its parallel restoration section (2:16–25) of the first cycle (Hos 1–3), refers to the more distant future of "that day" (ביום ההוא, 2:18, 23).[36] The tension, then, is between two possible futures. One might assume, by the end of Hos 13, that the negative metaphors of Hos 4–13 will extend indefinitely into the future. Hosea 14 presents the alternative, heretofore unimaginable, final hope.

Just as the polemically appropriated metaphors of other deities were taken up, sometimes modified, and applied to Yahweh against an alternate worldview, so the metaphors of Hos 14 reject metaphors associated with a particular view of the ultimate future—namely, the assumption that the doom of Hos 4–13 continues without remedy forever. God's rage will flood over the people. Israel is wounded, sick, dying. God has disowned his son, Israel. God is disappointed in his crop. God will be like a lion and a moth. Yet Hos 14

---

31. Macintosh, *Critical and Exegetical Commentary*, 569.
32. Fisch, *Poetry with a Purpose*, 155.
33. See Cameron and Stelma, "Metaphor Clusters," 133–34, and p. 26, above.
34. Within the final form, Hos 6:1–3 is the only instance of another speaker (the people). They may be responding to Hosea's words in 5:8–15 in an attempt to overcome alterity. In Hos 6:4–6, their attempt is rejected. Hosea 5:8–6:6 is not an instance of reconciliation but of "metaphor competition" (see Hawley, *Metaphor Competition*).
35. See Kimmel, "Why We Mix Metaphors."
36. On the imagined future of Hos 14, see Hamilton, "History among the Junipers."

declares that these are *provisional* metaphors, witnesses to a temporary present and future reality. They do not represent Israel's ultimate future.

Hosea 14 presents a completely different view of Israel's final fate. It is crucial to recognize that this is *not* done using *new* metaphors. Metaphor clusters can function to "connect and dynamize discourse." They "extend, reject, limit or elaborate" *previously used metaphors*.[37] This is exactly what happens in Hos 14. To what end?

Hosea takes up the old metaphors of judgment and inverts, extends, limits, and/or elaborates them. Therein lies the theological significance of Hos 14's pattern of inversion. It does not reject Israel's present reality, or near future, or the vision of God presented in Hos 4–13. It affirms them as true *for a time*. The future involves a transition *through* those realities into a radically restored future. The terror of sin and the need for God's judgment are confirmed, but this is not the last word. Yahweh's love has the last word, as his disciplinary punishment is doled out and his people are finally restored. "Hosea's God is the one who brings hope and restoration out of the doom, punishment, and judgment of sin—not instead of it, but through it. Hosea does not always use new metaphors for restoration. Rather, the old realities of judgment and sin are transposed and refigured into images of hope."[38] This future will certainly obtain, because Yahweh accomplishes it.[39]

The multifaceted presentation of God in Hosea has long been the cause of discussion among biblical scholars and theologians. Yet the fact remains that

> the identity of the biblical God is not rigid or static. Rather, he is a persona whose identity emerges as dynamic, surprising and occasionally paradoxical, requiring of the reader a dialectical process of recognition. When a depiction borders on inconsistency, the interpreter must grasp it as a surprising manifestation of the one already known. When a depiction is polemical, the interpreter must recognize that the identity of Yahweh involves elements of paradox.[40]

This tension between the depictions of Yahweh in the present and in the distant future is a manifestation of Yahweh's most fundamental characteristics of mercy and justice (Exod 34:6–7).

---

37. Kimmel, "Why We Mix Metaphors," 98.
38. Lancaster, "Wounds and Healing," 424.
39. Hamilton, "History among the Junipers."
40. Patrick, *Rendering of God*, 59.

One may then wonder: For what purpose are these dynamic images deployed? Why retain tensive images, and why their grand inversion in Hos 14? It is these questions to which we next turn.

7
Rhetorical Patterns

Hosea has been characterized in such diametrically opposed ways as the quintessential prophet either of love or of doom.[1] Is Hosea fundamentally about mercy or judgment? The present analysis leads to the answer: neither. Or, perhaps, both. Both love and doom are included in the book, yet neither fully explains the prophetic oracles. Love and doom cohere in that both are subservient to the ultimate rhetorical purpose, namely, that of getting Israel to return to proper life before Yahweh. The claim that repentance is the goal of the book is not new; the present discussion focuses on the relationship between the call to repentance and the book's metaphors.

First, we must sketch an understanding of the term *repentance* in Hosea. The chapter then provides a brief survey of evidence that repentance is the goal of the oracles. Finally, the variety of rhetorical strategies by which Hosea's metaphors seek to provoke a return to Yahweh is explored. All three sections are representative, not exhaustive, given the breadth of primary and secondary material and limitations of space.

---

1. See Pesiq. Rab. 44:3; John F. Craghan, "Book of Hosea: A Survey of Recent Literature on the First of the Minor Prophets," *BTB* 1 (1971): 159. Using Hos 14:2–10 as an example, see the extensive surveys in Walker, "Metaphor of Healing," 152–66; see also ch. 4, cluster 15 above. Often those emphasizing doom (e.g., Marti, Wolfe, Stinespring) assume that the hopeful passages in Hosea are later additions (11:8–9 is an exception for Clements). See Ronald E. Clements, "Understanding the Book of Hosea," *RevExp* 72 (1975): 422. Others, while acknowledging redactions, claim that grace lies at the heart of the book and that this can originate with Hosea (e.g., see Eichrodt, "'Holy One in Your Midst,'" 263; Wolff, *Hosea*, xxx; Jeremias, *Prophet Hosea*, 20; Ben Zvi, *Hosea*, 97–98 [who claims the book originates among the literati of Persian Yehud; none of the book originates with a prophet Hosea in the eighth century]; Kakkanattu, *God's Enduring Love*, 193–94).

Toward a Definition of Repentance in Hosea

Admittedly the word *repentance* can be anachronistic. Readers often import foreign (esp. modern Protestant Christian) ideas of repentance into the ancient context of Hosea, emphasizing elements of individualism, regret, guilt, verbal confession, and internality, while minimizing elements of social context, ethics, cultic/ritual conformity, performative actions, externality, and obedience (esp. with regard to Hos 6:6). James Luther Mays, in his otherwise insightful commentary, is representative of this tendency to minimize ethics and ritual in repentance in favor of an internal and verbal construal of repentance. On Hos 14:2 he notes, "Hosea is categorically against the sacrificial approach to Yahweh (4.8; 5.6; 6.6; 8.13)." Instead, the prayer of 14:2–4 "is set over and against sacrifice *as an alternative.*" "Prayer is to be the means of their access to God," specifically through a "broken and contrite heart (Ps. 51.17)."[2]

This has been rightly critiqued,[3] and a more holistic and culturally appropriate construal of Hosea's call for return has emerged. Hoping to avoid anachronistic misunderstandings of repentance, this study understands the concept in Hosea to minimally suggest a primarily communal (re)turn to ethical, cultic, theological, and/or political conformity to a stipulated norm in a context of relational loyalty (e.g., a covenant).[4] This presupposes an at least implicit acknowledgment of the transgression of that norm.[5] While repentance certainly includes external, performative

---

2. Mays, *Hosea*, 186, emphasis added.
3. See esp. Lambert, *How Repentance Became Biblical*.
4. This understanding of repentance is consistent with the rest of the Hebrew BIble but reflects some of the specific nuances in Hosea. For broader surveys of repentance, see Mark J. Boda and Gordon T. Smith, eds., *Repentance in Christian Theology* (Collegeville, MN: Glazier, 2006); Mark J. Boda, *"Return to Me": A Biblical Theology of Repentance* (Downers Grove, IL: IVP Academic, 2015). On repentance in the prophets, see Carol J. Dempsey, "'Turn Back, O People': Repentance in the Latter Prophets," in Boda and Smith, *Repentance in Christian Theology*, 47–66; Boda, "Return to Me," 95–107; Gary E. Yates, "The Problem of Repentance and Relapse as a Unifying Theme in the Book of the Twelve," *Them* 41 (2016): 248–62. On ethical, cultic, theological, and/or political conformity, see Paba Nidhani De Andrado, "Ḥesed and Sacrifice: The Prophetic Critique in Hosea," *CBQ* 78 (2016): 47–67. On covenant, see Boda, *Severe Mercy*, 11. On anachronistic misunderstandings of repentance see Lambert, *How Repentance Became Biblical*, 6.
5. See Jeremiah Unterman, "Repentance and Redemption in Hosea," in *Society of Biblical Literature 1982 Seminar Papers* (Atlanta: Scholars Press, 1982): 541; Mark

7. Rhetorical Patterns

elements, its presentation in the Bible indicates it also involves aspects internal to the individual, though a modern scholar's ability to reconstruct those internal, culturally constructed experiences is limited.[6] Boda affirms that biblical repentance "involves several dimensions," namely,

> the behavioural (actual change in lifestyle and patterns of living), the affective (full engagement of internal orientation, all one's heart) and the verbal/ritual (oral declarations expression penitential desire whether in prayer or speech, including admission of sin and culpability, declaration of divine justice; various rites including sacrifice, fasting, sackcloth or baptism).[7]

Evidence for the Centrality of Repentance as a Rhetorical Goal

While the nature of Israel's repentance is debated, less contested is the claim that Israel's return to Yahweh is a primary goal of the book. At least six points support this claim. Because it is a common view that biblical prophets call for repentance, these points are presented briefly, with select representative examples and advocates.

First, a variety of passages call for acknowledging transgression, for religious and ethical reform, and for exclusive devotion to Yahweh, whether explicitly (10:12, 12:7, 14:2–4) or implicitly (e.g., 5:15, 7:14, 9:17, 10:2–3, 11:1–11).[8]

J. Boda, "The Priceless Gain of Penitence: From Communal Lament to Penitential Prayer in the 'Exilic' Liturgy of Israel," *HBT* 25 (2003): 54; Boda, *"Return to Me,"* 31. For the variety of metaphorical conceptions of such a transgression, see Lam, *Patterns of Sin*; see also Anderson, *Sin*.

6. See Kövecses, *Metaphor and Emotion*; van Wolde, "Sentiments as Culturally Constructed Emotions"; Schlimm, "Different Perspectives on Divine Pathos," 692–93. While Lambert offers an important corrective to modern eisegesis, Olson rightly denies Lambert's mutually exclusive binary options, affirming that *both* external action *and* internal experiences are important ("Emotion, Repentance, and the Question," 169–70, 172).

7. Boda, *"Return to Me,"* 31.

8. On 10:12, see Eidevall, *Grapes in the Desert*, 191. On 14:2–4, see Rudolph, *Hosea*, 249–50; Mays, *Hosea*, 185; Yee, *Composition and Tradition*, 135, 312. On 5:15, see Mays, *Hosea*, 92; Eidevall, *Grapes in the Desert*, 89–90; Macintosh, *Critical and Exegetical Commentary*, 214–15; Nwaoru, *Imagery in the Prophecy*, 73. Ben Zvi calls 5:15 the "interpretive key" to 5:1–7:2 (*Hosea*, 121). On 7:14, see Michael L. Barré, "Hearts, Beds, and Repentance in Psalm 4,5 and Hosea 7,14," *Bib* 76 (1995): 53–62. On

Second, the book's thrice-repeated indictment-judgment-restoration cycle (1:2–3:5, 4:1–11:11, 12:1–14:9) suggests that the final hopeful images are meant to draw Israel back to Yahweh and that repentance is a fundamental reason for the book's existence.[9]

A third reason is the use of the root שוב and corresponding wordplays, which Boda claims "reveals the priority of repentance to this prophet's message."[10] The prophetic hope is that Israel will finally say, "I will go and return [ואשובה] to my first husband, for it was better with me then than now" (2:9 NRSV; see 3:5).

While granting David Lambert's point that the nature of Israel's return has been misunderstood at times, a fourth consideration is that interpreters throughout history have recognized that some return to Yahweh is essential to the book's thought.[11]

Fifth, Walter Houston has argued that the perlocutionary effects of biblical prophetic words are both a sense of mourning over the declarations of judgment and prayers for mercy—with which repentance of a sort is consistent.[12]

9:17, see Rudolph, *Hosea*, 189; Macintosh, *Critical and Exegetical Commentary*, 382. On 10:2–3, see Gruber, *Hosea*, 408–13. Jacobs argues that the whole of chapter 11 is an implicit call to return, esp. 11:5 and 11:8 ("YHWH's Call," 18, 28).

9. Neef, *Heilstraditionen*; Yee, *Composition and Tradition*, 309–13; Yee, "Book of Hosea," 198; Sweeney, "Hosea's Reading," 856; Brian Gault, "Avenging Husband and Redeeming Lover? Opposing Portraits of God in Hosea," *JETS* 60 (2017): 489–509, esp. 504–5.

10. Boda, *"Return to Me,"* 95. The verb occurs 22 times in Hosea (2:9, 11; 3:5; 4:9; 5:4, 15; 6:1, 11; 7:10, 16; 8:13; 9:3; 11:5 [2x], 9; 12:3, 7, 15; 14:2, 3, 5, 8); the nominalized participle משובה occurs twice (11:7, 14:5). See, e.g., Jeremias, "Zur Eschatologie des Hoseabuches"; Yee, *Composition and Tradition*, 133; Eidevall, *Grapes in the Desert*, 241–42; Moughtin-Mumby, *Sexual and Marital Metaphors*, 57–58; Boda, *Severe Mercy*, 297–304, esp. 297–98.

11. E.g., see Tg. Neb. on Hos 14:5 (similarly Syr.; Rashi); Pesiq. Rab. 44:5: "All the Prophets call Israel to repentance, but none call like Hosea," trans. William G. Braude, *Pesikta Rabbati* (New Haven: Yale University Press, 1968); Pesiq. Rab Kah. 24; Theodoret of Cyrus, *Enarratio in Oseam Prophetam* (PG 81:1552–53); Erich Kurt Dietrich, *Die Umkehr: (Bekehrung und Busse) im Alten Testament und im Judentum bei besonderer Berücksichtigung der neutestamentlichen Zeit* (Stuttgart: Kohlhammer, 1936), 52; Rudolph, *Hosea*, 250; and the various entries in Koog-Pyoung Hong et al., "Hosea (Book and Person)," *EBR* 12:425–45. See n. 16, below.

12. Houston, "What Did the Prophets Think."

The sixth and final factor suggesting repentance is central to the purpose of Hosea is that repentance is essential to Hebrew Bible prophecy in general (see 2 Kgs 17:13; Jer 3:6–4:4; 18:7–11; Ezek 3:17–20; 18:21–23, 30).[13] Within the Book of the Twelve, "repentance, not pride, in the face of calamity and threat offers the only hope that YHWH will intervene to thwart, stall, stop, or repair a damaged people."[14]

A single book can "confound sense" by both inviting repentance and suggesting that repentance is impossible or that it is too late and God's judgment is fixed (see, e.g., Isa 6:9–10, 63:17, Jer 7:27–28, Amos 7:7–8, 8:1–3).[15] This seems to be the case in Hosea. The book simultaneously demands a return to God (10:12, 12:7, 14:2–4) and affirms that the people are incapable of returning to Yahweh (4:12, 5:4, 11:7).[16] "Sin has become so

---

13. On repentance in the prophets, see n. 4, above. On Jer 3:6–4:4, see Dempsey, "Turn Back, O People," 53–55.

14. James D. Nogalski, *The Book of the Twelve and Beyond: Collected Essays of James D. Nogalski*, AIL 29 (Atlanta: SBL Press, 2017), 193. See esp. Zech 1:2–4, Mal 3:7.

15. Julia M. O'Brien, "Metaphorization and Other Tropes in the Prophets," in *The Oxford Handbook of the Prophets*, ed. Carolyn J. Sharp (Oxford: Oxford University Press, 2016), 244; see also Morris, *Prophecy, Poetry and Hosea*, 74; Fisch, *Poetry with a Purpose*, 136–57; Landy, "Wilderness"; Yvonne Sherwood, "'Darke Texts Needs Notes': On Prophetic Prophecy, John Donne and the Baroque," *JSOT* 27 (2002): 47–74. This is especially true for preexilic prophets, who often recognize that the people must "undergo drastic punishment" in order to change, and for whom "revival must be a virtual resurrection of the dead." The prophets' goal may be to "plant seeds in the people that will grow in and after judgment" (Patrick, *Redeeming Judgment*, 163). See Mark J. Boda, "Repentance," *DOTPr*, 664–65, 668; Rolf Rendtorff, *The Old Testament: An Introduction*, trans. John Bowden (Philadelphia: Fortress, 1991), 220–21. For the view that some prophets such as Amos never intended to evoke repentance but only to declare inevitable judgment, see Childs, *Introduction to the Old Testament*, 409.

16. A complete analysis of the relationships between repentance and restoration, divine and human agency, and grace and obedience is beyond the scope of this work. For a history of interpretation since Wellhausen on the role of repentance in Hos 14:2–9 (the central passage on this question), see Walker, "Metaphor of Healing," 152–66. Walker summarizes that "virtually all scholars would agree that repentance and God's love are intertwined. They disagree on the precise emphasis of either pole" (162 n. 47). Prioritizing the need for repentance, esp. in 14:5, are, e.g., Tg. Neb.; Syr.; Vulg.; Rashi; Kimchi; Rudolph, *Hosea*, 251; Mays, *Hosea*, 185, 188; Yee, *Composition and Tradition*, 133; Davies, *Hosea* [1992], 299; Macintosh, *Critical and Exegetical Commentary*, 569. Many prioritize divine grace. Works since Walker's 1997 survey (who himself affirms the priority of grace: "Metaphor of Healing," 171–72, 187) include Eidevall, *Grapes in the Desert*, 242; Nwaoru, *Imagery in the Prophecy*, 179;

deeply habitual for Israel that repentance is not within their power."[17] This does not stop God from attempting to break into Israel's world of death with life-changing metaphors deployed in a variety of strategies. Perhaps one more provocative metaphor, grasping at the edge of language's ability to convey the divine reality, will catapult Israel into a heretofore unimagined world, one in which repentance becomes a possibility. "The challenge releases some urge to speak of God in elevated and shocking language."[18] Or perhaps all the metaphors and strategies will fail in the face of Israel's obstinacy, and Israel's only hope will reside in God's free choice to restore them apart from repentance (see Hos 14:5).

In sum, what unifies the metaphors of Hosea is not just grace or judgment alone. As Walther Eichrodt summarizes, "The real content of the theology of Hosea" is "the holy God exalted in his majesty above all human thoughts, who nevertheless strives in judgment and grace for the turning of his people to his saving love."[19]

Eight Strategies of Metaphor Deployment

While a variety of features serve this rhetorical goal, metaphors in particular are deployed using at least eight interlocking strategies.[20] The following strategies and their examples are representative, not exhaustive. The first three strategies push Israel back to Yahweh using negative consequences.

Daniël F. O'Kennedy, "God as Healer in the Prophetic Books of the Hebrew Bible," *HBT* 27 (2005): 99; Dempsey, "Turn Back, O People," 53 n. 6, 61; Kakkanattu, *God's Enduring Love*, 193; Boda, *Severe Mercy*, 302–4. Others claim the book does not provide a decisive answer as to the relationship between repentance and restoration (e.g., Craghan, "Book of Hosea," 161; Unterman, "Repentance and Redemption in Hosea," 548–49; Emmerson, *Hosea*, 162–63, who attributes this tension to two different editors; Catlett, "Reversals in Hosea," 273; Goldingay, *Israel's Faith*, 2:396). Hosea does not conclusively determine the relationship between restoration and repentance; it simply affirms the necessity of both. It closes by holding out the possibility of hope that Yahweh may "freely" love (אהבם נדבה) the people by his own choice apart from any action on their part (14:5), while simultaneously demanding their obedient return to Yahweh (14:2–4).

17. Vall, "Epistemology of Faith," 34.
18. Patrick, *Redeeming Judgment*, 201.
19. Eichrodt, "'Holy One in Your Midst,'" 273.
20. See the few strategies listed in Boda, *Severe Mercy*, 295; Jacobs, "YHWH's Call"; Patrick, *Redeeming Judgment*, 195.

The remaining approaches pull Israel by emphasizing the benefits of returning to Yahweh.

One of Hosea's most common strategies of using metaphors to procure repentance is to make direct threats against Israel. Hosea 7:12–13, for instance, uses metaphors as a threat of reprisal for Israel's political double-dealing: "When they go [to Assyria], I will spread my net over them; like a bird of the sky, I will bring them down; I will discipline them according to the report of their assembly" (7:12). These angry threats of death (e.g., 14:1) are intended to provoke repentance (14:2–4).[21] Judgment can also motivate a return to God *after* it has been meted out.[22]

Terrifying Israel is a second strategy, closely related to the first. The first emphasizes consequences of punishment; the second focuses on the emotional response.[23] Houston has shown how terrifying hearers is a prophetic rhetorical strategy for provoking repentance, and it surely was a common ancient strategy.[24] Consider the array of petrifying animals in 13:7–8 designed to provoke terror, or the images of 5:10–15 and 13:14–14:1, which end with implicit (5:15) or explicit (14:2–4) invitations to repentance.

A third function is that of shaming the hearers. This has been discussed at length and need not be repeated.[25] The sexual promiscuity metaphors (4:10–15, 5:3–4, 6:10, 8:9–10, 9:1) in particular function to shame Israel, with the hope of causing a return to submission to Yahweh.

The previous strategies push Israel back to Yahweh with negative consequences. But Hosea also woos Israel back with positive promises.[26] A fourth strategy seeks to draw Israel with attractive images of what life with

---

21. Jerome, *Commentaries on the Twelve Prophets* 2:257; Heschel, *Prophets*, 286; Houston, "What Did the Prophets Think."

22. See, e.g., Mays, *Hosea*, 185; Yee, *Composition and Tradition*, 81–82; Patrick, *Redeeming Judgment*, 160; Hos 5:2, 7:9, Isa 42:25.

23. Threats can terrify, but they can also provoke other responses—e.g., mourning (Houston, "What Did the Prophets Think").

24. Houston, "What Did the Prophets Think." Consider the suzerain curses on any would-be disloyal vassals, intended to terrify the vassals into submission, or the Assyrian war strategy of calculated atrocity, designed to terrify any potential rebellious city-states into submission by fear of the consequences.

25. See pp. 39–42 and 162–64 ("Shame"), above.

26. See מפתיה והלכתיה המדבר ודברתי על לבה in 2:16, leading to restoration in 2:17–25. See David J. A. Clines and David M. Gunn, "'You Tried to Persuade Me' and 'Violence! Outrage!' in Jeremiah XX 7–8," *VT* 28 (1978): 21.

Yahweh could be like. In cluster 15, Israel can find mercy as a runaway orphan accepted again into the house of father-Yahweh (14:4), receive healing and love (14:5), and become as a flourishing landscape, safe in Yahweh's protection and provision (14:6–9). Hosea's message is that these fruits are only found in Yahweh (14:9), not Baal, Assyria, Egypt, or any other alleged master. This restoration follows repentance (14:2–4).

Hosean metaphors can also instill confidence in Yahweh as a reliable deity, more powerful and dependable than Baal. Using this fifth approach, Hos 11:10 pictures Yahweh as the lion, victorious over all rivals, roaring in victory at the successful hunt. Under his banner the people *return* (והושבתים) to their land, trembling in awe at their powerful sovereign. This inspires confidence that Yahweh is capable and trustworthy.

A sixth strategy overtly *commands* repentance, metaphorically using verbs in the imperative mood. The sense of 10:12, for instance, is clearly a call for a return to Yahweh (ועת לדרוש את יהוה), yet all three imperative verbs are metaphorical. Yahweh demands that Israel sow (זרעו) righteousness, reap (קצרו) loyalty, and till (נירו) their metaphorical land so that the Lord might rain righteousness on them (וירה צדק לכם).

Seventh is the strategy of subversion, often via appropriation. "The power to create a new order by imposing a metaphor that 'redescribes reality,' Paul Ricoeur argues, is contingent on first 'creating rifts in an old order.'"[27] As Brueggemann notes, "First, the hated one must be ridiculed and made reachable, then she may be disobeyed and seen as a nobody who claims no allegiance and keeps no promises. The big house yields no real life, need not be feared, cannot be trusted, and must not be honored."[28] Before Israel can return to Yahweh, their grasp on their current idols must be weakened. Before claiming supremacy, Yahweh must undermine the power of competing sovereigns. This manifests initially as direct attacks on Yahweh's adversaries but eventually shifts to applying traits or abilities of competitors to Yahweh, rendering them unnecessary (see chs. 6 and 9 of this study).

Once alternatives have been unmasked as comparatively impotent, the old order can be replaced with a more powerful truth, a new vision of real-

---

27. Burkholder and Henry, "Criticism of Metaphor," 107, quoting Ricoeur, *Rule of Metaphor*, 22 (see also 197). For examples of this in Hosea, see Merryl Blair, "God Is an Earthquake: Destabilising Metaphor in Hosea 11," *ABR* 55 (2007): 1–12; Zimran, "Notion of God."

28. Brueggemann, *Prophetic Imagination*, 74.

ity. This eighth strategy is less a discrete strategy and more the cumulative result of all other strategies and every metaphor. Hosea's meta-strategy for metaphor deployment is to replace Israel's wrong understanding of reality with a right perception, resulting in right action. Macintosh suggests that Hosea "was greatly interested in the connection between thought and action and, above all, was convinced that wrong perceptions of reality, of the way things were, would lead inevitably to the demise and ruin of his people and nation."[29]

Metaphors are powerfully conducive to replacing faulty worldviews with a new reality given "the power of metaphor to *create a reality* rather than simply to give us a way of conceptualizing a preexisting reality."[30] Hosea constructs an alternative world in which Israel is to live and move and have their being.[31] In this metaphorical world, Yahweh is powerful and trustworthy, and can be relied on to compassionately receive a repentant Israel. Assyria and Egypt are exposed as weak protectors, while Yahweh is the only refuge (see 2:12, 5:14). Indeed, Yisca Zimran has persuasively argued that the Assyria-Egypt pairing in Hosea (7:11; 9:3; 11:5, 11; 12:2) functions as a kind of cipher for Israel's distance from Yahweh.[32] Baal is unmasked as a counterfeit provider, while Yahweh is proven to be the only true provider (see 2:10, 14:6–9).

New possibilities arise in this world. The metaphors enable the imagination to conceive of a novel set of plausible futures—"a world of possible impossibility"—and to generate fresh conceptions of God and therefore other visions of society and courses of human action.[33] In this new world,

---

29. Macintosh, "Hosea and the Wisdom Tradition," 125; see also Macintosh, *Critical and Exegetical Commentary*, xc.

30. Lakoff and Johnson, *Metaphors We Live By*, 144, emphasis added. See pp. 9–15 ("The Whole Power of Metaphor"), above.

31. For an argument similar to that presented below, see Cho, *Myth, History, and Metaphor*, esp. 33–38.

32. Zimran, "Prevalence and Purpose."

33. Brown, *Seeing the Psalms*, 215. On this imaginative function, see esp. Walter Brueggemann, *Theology of the Old Testament: Testimony, Dispute, Advocacy* (Minneapolis: Fortress, 1997), 68. See also Leo G. Perdue, *The Collapse of History: Reconstructing Old Testament Theology*, OBT (Minneapolis: Fortress, 1992), 264–98; Luke Timothy Johnson, "Imagining the World Scripture Imagines," *ModTheo* 14 (1998): 165–80; Avis, *God and the Creative Imagination*; Jonathan Kaplan and Robert Williamson Jr., eds., *Imagination, Ideology and Inspiration: Echoes of Brueggemann in a New Generation* (Sheffield: Sheffield Phoenix, 2015).

a return to Yahweh is finally possible and desirable. Through metaphors, Hosea confronts Israel with a choice of hitherto unknown possibilities for them to think, feel, and act.

The metaphorical world is a fundamentally *theological* vision. It is about what God is like and, consequently, what Israel is like.[34] This metaphoric theological vision is essentially a proper knowledge of God (דעת אלהים).[35] As Macintosh observes, "If false perceptions of the nation's God constituted the root cause of the sickness which raged within it, the antidote lay always to hand and it consisted of the correct understanding of ethical reality and of Yahweh who had defined and created it. The all-important phrase is, for Hosea, 'knowledge of Yahweh' (4.6; 6.3, 6)."[36] The intended result of embracing this metaphorical vision is that Israel will experience a new way of seeing themselves, their world, and their God because, "for the believer, getting to know Yahweh is getting to know one's world in its totality."[37] The sum of the eighth strategy is that in this new world, returning to God is the most logical, desirable, and beneficial course of action. Hence, knowledge of God *should* result in return to God.[38]

Summary

The coherence of Hosea's diverse metaphors becomes apparent in these eight strategies. The metaphors cohere in their rhetorical purpose of bringing Israel back to Yahweh. Metaphor theorists observe that "the most important thing to bear in mind" when analyzing the coherence of multiple metaphors "is the role of purpose."[39] It is furthermore significant that so many of Hosea's metaphors occur in clusters, since "metaphor clusters occur when some *intensive interactional work linked to the overall purpose of the discourse* is being carried out," such as presenting one's view

---

34. Brown, *Seeing the Psalms*, 214.
35. Eidevall interprets קחו עמכם דברים (14:3) as referring to the book of Hosea itself: "'Take (these) words.' The very words of this prophetical discourse could be used as a means to attain 'knowledge of God'" (*Grapes in the Desert*, 239). He furthermore postulates that, in an inversion of the ancient Near Eastern disappearing-deity motif, what the people "find out" in 14:9 is that which was lacking in the beginning (4:1): the knowledge of God (*Grapes in the Desert*, 252).
36. Macintosh, *Critical and Exegetical Commentary*, xcii.
37. Patrick, *Rendering of God*, 45.
38. See Dietrich, *Die Umkehr*, 53.
39. Lakoff and Johnson, *Metaphors We Live By*, 97.

to another who does not share it.[40] The overall purpose of the discourse of Hosea is to provoke a return to Yahweh. The metaphors are deployed according to eight interconnected strategies to serve this purpose, often clustering at textual locations central to this purpose.

This coherence of rhetorical purpose does not require metaphorical coherence based on a single conceptual or root metaphor, as some claim.[41] The driving force in Hosea's collection of metaphors is not consistency of domains but the desire to powerfully change Israel's perception and future. This is one of the "many ... rhetorical purposes" for which "strong motivations exist for interweaving different types of conceptual metaphor."[42] Consistent with its ancient context, there appears to be no concern regarding how a deity could be capable of both fierce violence and healing love. Both are communicated in the most extreme way, dialectically, to warn the audience of the severity of their peril and provoke repentance.[43]

Hosea does not aim for the logical precision or consistency of a philosopher, nor the atemporal metaphysical claims of a systematic theologian, but the rhetorical impact sought by a divinely inspired spokesperson, trying to make his point as forcefully as possible to pull his people back from the brink of destruction. Hans Walter Wolff summarizes, "As far as we know, never before had anyone dared to speak of God in this fashion. Subordinating all consideration of pious tradition and aesthetic sensitivities, the prophet sought to bear witness to Yahweh's awesome, overpowering strength and present action."[44]

Conclusion to Part 2

Part 2 has analyzed various themes and patterns found across the metaphor clusters of Hos 4–14. Chapter 5 identified five emotions as prominent across multiple clusters in Hosea, most of which are underrecognized by

---

40. Cameron and Stelma, "Metaphor Clusters," 134, emphasis added; see p. 26, above.

41. See pp. 203–5, below, esp. n. 23 there.

42. Kimmel, "Why We Mix Metaphors," 113. For a survey of other scholarly opinions on Hosea's motives for mixing metaphors, see Weiss, "Motives," 326.

43. See Hundley, "Here a God," 71.

44. Wolff, *Hosea*, xxv.

scholars: Yahweh's shame by association with Israel, Yahweh's sense of being betrayed by Israel, Yahweh's disappointment with Israel, and the vacillations between God's love and hate for Israel.

Chapter 6 concentrated on the literary nature of the book, recognizing patterns of metaphor development across the book. After briefly surveying some general patterns of metaphor deployment, a shifting strategy was identified in Hosea's polemics. The book transitions from directly opposing other deities to subverting them by appropriating aspects of their constellations (i.e., their associated imagery and abilities), thereby rendering those deities useless. Finally, Hos 14 was shown to be a comprehensive inversion of many of the book's previous metaphors. Virtually every word of every metaphor found in that metaphor cluster plays on or inverts a previous element of the book. Additionally, all four of Yahweh's negative emotions discussed in chapter 5 (all but love) are inverted in Hos 14, as God restores his and his wife's honor, Israel's infidelity is healed, Israel fulfills its purpose, and God freely and generously lavishes love on Israel. God is shown to be the sovereign Lord of all the universe, bringing life from death, restoration through judgment.

The present chapter examined the rhetorical goal and cohesion of the metaphors, arguing that their purpose is Israel's repentance. After defining repentance and surveying six considerations that suggest the centrality of repentance to the book, eight mutually inclusive strategies of metaphor deployment for provoking repentance were identified.

All that remains now is to tie together these disparate threads and initial probes into a coherent, metaphorically mediated vision of God in Hos 4–14.

PART 3
Who Do You Say That I Am?
A Metaphorical Theology of Hosea 4–14

> Never before had anyone dared to speak of God in this fashion.
> —Hans Wolff, *Hosea*

This project asks the question, Who is Yahweh as presented through the metaphors of Hos 4–14? Chapter 1 provided the frameworks by which to answer this question. Part 1 analyzed 103 metaphors for constructing an answer by investigating the internal metaphorical and poetic dynamics of fifteen metaphor clusters in Hos 4–14. Part 2 took initial steps toward synthesis, noting patterns and purposes among the metaphors. This final part brings together these various components to answer the study's driving question in two ways. Chapter 8 offers an aspect map of all of the metaphors studied in Hos 4–14. That is, it categorizes and organizes all 103 metaphors for God and identifies further statistical patterns to their deployment, all while resisting reductionism. In the next chapter, a five-fold characteristic portrait of Yahweh is derived from Hosea's metaphors. One characteristic, that of Yahweh's loyalty to Israel, is fundamental to all the others and to the metaphorics of the book.

8
An Aspective Constellation of Yahweh

The move from disparate metaphors to theological synthesis is justified by at least four observations. First, as shown repeatedly above and elaborated below, a multiplicity of metaphors does not necessitate a lack of coherence.[1] Second, ancient people also synthesized their concepts of deities, albeit differently from modern people. The mention of Baal or Ishtar or Marduk would likely have called to mind certain unique combinations of characteristics across wide spans of time and space; indeed, this is the nature of religious thought.[2] The same is, mutatis mutandis, likely true for Yahweh. Third, readers naturally and subconsciously do this with texts, and in general authors and editors presuppose in the very act of writing that readers will do the work of synthesizing.[3] Fourth, the book of Hosea welcomes a move to synthesis with its final verse: מי חכם ויבן אלה נבון וידעם. The implicit invitation is to consider and understand the holistic message of the book, including its metaphoric vision of Yahweh. "The text invites the reader to a way of life; it is a path that leads to understanding and to God."[4]

While the synthetic move may be justifiable, how can it be done? How should a synthetic interpretation be shaped by Hosea's proclivity toward multiplicity? With such a variety of metaphors, this could be an over-

---

1. For this claim from the perspective of metaphor theory, see, for instance, p. 23 n. 78, above, and p. 202, below. Chapter 7 emphasized rhetorical coherence, while ch. 9 will argue for a kind of theological coherence in the loyalty of God.

2. E.g., see Smith, *God in Translation*; Allen, "Splintered Divine"; Hundley, "Here a God"; Wilson-Wright, *Athtart*.

3. Jeffrey Stackert, "Pentateuchal Coherence and the Science of Reading," in Gertz et al., *Formation of the Pentateuch*, 253–68. Stackert makes a different deduction—namely, that one should therefore read *against* this inclination and seek the textual irregularities.

4. Garrett, *Hosea, Joel*, 282.

whelming prospect. Is God confused and conflicted in God's inner being?[5] Is there a transformation within God's own existence?[6] Does God's very being "lack coherence"?[7]

Introducing the Aspective Approach of the Ancient Near East

Eidevall understandably asks of the metaphoric diversity in Hosea, "How do you summarize a universe?"[8] One might answer, "With a constellation." A constellation results from what Hundley, following Emma Brunner-Traut, calls the "aspective approach" of ancient Near Eastern god-talk. With an appreciation of the ancient Near Eastern aspective approach, the metaphoric diversity of Hosea need not result in divine confusion or incoherence. Instead, patterns and consistent theological claims surface.

An aspective approach emphasizes the full articulation of each individual part of a subject without the felt need to synthesize, summarize, or systematize.[9] This tendency is motivated by the desire to ensure that each individual part of the whole is described in all of its fullness, resisting reductionism.[10] Scholars have noted this phenomenon, using various terminology, in areas as diverse as Egyptian math, literature, and visual art; Mesopotamian god-talk; structures of biblical poetry; ancient Near Eastern law codes; ancient Near Eastern iconography; and biblical wisdom literature.[11] Its opposite is the perspectival approach, more common in the

---

5. Weems, *Battered Love*; Brueggemann, "Recovering God of Hosea."
6. Janzen, "Metaphor and Reality."
7. Landy, "Wilderness," 46.
8. Eidevall, *Grapes in the Desert*, 2.
9. Emma Brunner-Traut, *Frühformen des Erkennens: Am Beispiel Altägyptens* (Darmstadt: Wissenschaftliche Buchgesellschaft, 1990), 8, 11; Brunner-Traut, "Epilogue: Aspective," in *Principles of Egyptian Art*, ed. Emma Brunner-Traut and John Baines, trans. John Baines, (repr. with revisions, Oxford: Griffith Institute, 1986), 421–48; Hundley, "Here a God," 69–70.
10. Hundley, "Here a God," 69, 71.
11. Egyptian math, literature, and visual art: Brunner-Traut, *Frühformen*. Mesopotamian god-talk: Hundley, "Here a God." Structures of biblical poetry: Grossberg, *Centripetal*. Ancient Near Eastern law codes: e.g., Raymond Westbrook, "Introduction: The Character of Ancient Near Eastern Law," in *A History of Ancient Near Eastern Law*, ed. Raymond Westbrook (Leiden: Brill, 2003), 1:20. Ancient Near Eastern iconography: Keel, *Symbolism*, 9–11. Biblical wisdom literature: Jutta Hausmann, *Studien zum Menschenbild der älteren Weisheit (Spr 10ff.)*, FAT 7 (Tübingen: Mohr Siebeck, 1995).

8. An Aspective Constellation of Yahweh

modern West, which prioritizes the need to articulate the synthesis of the whole, sometimes to the detriment of the parts.[12]

Within ancient Near Eastern aspective god-talk, Hundley identifies constellations of aspects associated with individual deities.[13] Aspects may include images, abstract qualities, heavenly bodies, metals, animals, numbers, and so forth. Each aspect may be more or less central to the conception of the deity, can change over time and across locations, and is usually associated with particular abilities of the deity. A deity's core aspects tend to be anthropomorphic.[14]

The *manner* of Hosea's presentation of Yahweh—diverse, vacillating images presented seemingly randomly at times—makes sense against this broader ancient Near Eastern background. Hosea is presenting various aspects of the deity without attempting to synthesize them.[15] Hosea's *motivation* for this mode of presentation is likely also consistent with the broader cultural pattern: to ensure that each individual aspect of Yahweh is articulated in its fullness.

The appropriateness of metaphor for an aspective approach to godtalk is striking. Both reflect the fact that no single image or aspect is sufficient to adequately reflect the divine reality. Both are suited to integrating diverse aspects of a complex reality. Both resist reductionism without semantic loss. Note the similarities between the following comments by Hundley on the aspective approach and Lakoff and Johnson on the nature of metaphors.

Hundley claims that

> ancient Near Easterners tend to focus on individual aspects and on representing those aspects in their fullness, often at the expense of the whole. In order to present the whole, especially when it is complex, they frequently amass and juxtapose various individual elements, most often without systematically attempting to fit those elements into a consistently articulated, all-encompassing organic unity.[16]

---

12. Brunner-Traut, *Frühformen*, 8; Hundley, "Here a God," 70.
13. Hundley, "Here a God"; see esp. 80–82.
14. Hundley, "Here a God," 81.
15. From a redactional perspective, scholars often recognize that the book does not appear to preserve original speech units but is organized according to themes and keywords (e.g., Rendtorff, *Old Testament*, 216).
16. Hundley, "Here a God," 69–70. For Brunner-Traut's treatment of Egyptian literature in this regard, see *Frühformen*, 145–54.

He continues, "When attempting to present the whole, they recognize that any representation is merely an approximation and thus pile on approximates in the hopes of approaching plenitude."[17]

One can almost hear an echo of this in the words of Lakoff and Johnson describing metaphor clusters:

> What may at first appear to be random, isolated metaphorical expressions ... turn out to be not random at all. Rather, they are part of whole metaphorical systems that together serve the complex purpose of characterizing the concept ... in all of its aspects, as we conceive them. *Though such metaphors do not provide us with a single consistent concrete image, they are nonetheless coherent and do fit together when there are overlapping entailments*, though not otherwise.[18]

Douglas Berggren thus affirms that "metaphor constitutes the indispensable principle for integrating diverse phenomena and perspectives *without sacrificing their diversity*."[19] This perfectly explains why metaphors, and clusters in particular, are so well-suited to an aspective approach and why both occur so prominently in Hosea. The aspective approach seeks to grasp the ineffable (one of Hosea's goals) through multiplicity rather than reductionism; so do metaphor clusters.

Hundley recognizes that "the Mesopotamians nowhere synthesize all of the parts into one cohesive whole." His article attempts to provide a theoretical basis for the modern scholar to do just that, while recognizing that this heuristic endeavor is nonetheless anachronistic, "a somewhat artificial undertaking."[20] It is this admittedly anachronistic and somewhat artificial project that is undertaken here.

The following treatment makes three modifications to Hundley's work. First, while Hundley recognizes diachronic changes and geographical diversity in a particular deity's constellations (he is summarizing how people across the ancient Near East over millennia conceive of deities), this constellation reflects the singular perspective of the final form of

---

17. Hundley, "Here a God," 71; see also Strawn, *Stronger Than a Lion?*, 272; Weiss, "From 'Mixed Metaphors,'" 127; O'Brien, *Challenging Prophetic Metaphor*, 176.

18. Lakoff and Johnson, *Metaphors We Live By*, 105, emphasis added; see also 95.

19. Douglas Berggren, "The Use and Abuse of Metaphor," *RM* 16 (1962): 237, emphasis added.

20. Hundley, "Here a God," 81, 69 n. 8; see also 71 n. 17.

Hosea.[21] Second, Hundley's constellations include anything associated with the deity, whereas the present constellation is limited to metaphors. Third, Hundley does not offer visualizations of the constellations; that is unique to this project.

An Aspective Constellation of Metaphors for God in Hosea 4–14

Figure 8.1 (p. 204, below) depicts one attempt at a coherent and comprehensive constellation of aspects of Yahweh found in the metaphor clusters of Hos 4–14.[22]

One of the major contributions of Hundley's work to metaphor studies in Hosea is the undermining of the perceived need of scholars to find a "root metaphor," a single metaphor that unites, underlies, or explains all other metaphors in the book.[23] This perceived need reflects a perspectival

---

21. One may grant that the book's production involved the contribution of multiple perspectives (authors/redactors/editors), but the final form as a singular book represents a single perspective. The one exception is Hos 6:1–3, which is the perspective of the cultic leaders, contrasted with Hosea's perspective. For details, see pp. 63–64 (esp. n. 122 there) and 72–77, above.

22. While including all metaphorical expressions studied here, no claim is made to being exhaustive or definitive for all metaphors in Hosea.

23. A root metaphor is "a model that holds together a variety of images" (Dearman, *Book of Hosea*, 11) or "a single metaphor around which a whole text revolves" (Morris, *Prophecy, Poetry and Hosea*, 135). Proposals for root metaphors of Hosea include "God is king" (Eidevall), "head of household" (Dearman), "teacher" (Ben Zvi), "healer" (Walker), or three motifs or metaphor networks, one for each cycle of the book, such as "husband, parent, husband" (Yee) or "husband, father, farmer" (Light, followed by Morris). See Eidevall, *Grapes in the Desert*, 231–32; Göran Eidevall, "Review of 'Metaphors and Similes for Yahweh in Hosea 14:2–9 [1–8]: A Study of Hoseanic Pictorial Language,'" *Bib* 81 (2000): 585; Dearman, *Book of Hosea*, 11, 44–50; J. Andrew Dearman, "YHWH's House: Gender Roles and Metaphors for Israel in Hosea," *JNSL* 25 (1999): 97–108; Ben Zvi, "Reading," 53–55; Walker, "Metaphor of Healing," 17; Yee, *Composition and Tradition*, 51; Light, "Theory-Constitutive Metaphor," 55, 63–65, 198–99; Morris, *Prophecy, Poetry and Hosea*, 135. Nonetheless, there is no consensus on a single "key" to the metaphorical cohesion of the book (Kelle, "Hosea 4–14," 356). Examples of biblical scholars comfortable with the diversity of metaphors and resisting this tendency toward reductionism include Landy, "Wilderness"; Brettler, "Incompatible Metaphors"; Andrea L. Weiss, "Making a Place for Metaphor in Biblical Theology," in *Methodological Studies*, vol. 1 of *Theology of the Hebrew Bible*, ed. Marvin A. Sweeney, RBS 92 (Atlanta: SBL Press, 2019), 127–39; Brent A. Strawn and Izaak J. de Hulster, "Figuring YHWH in

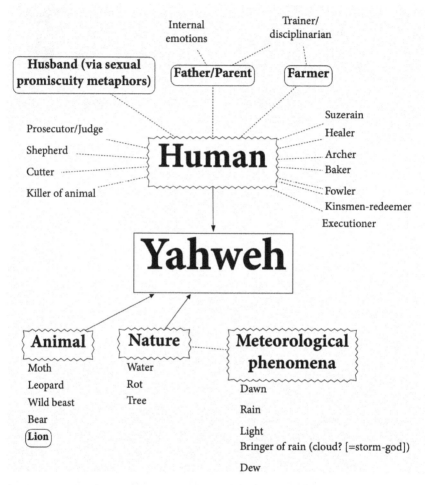

Fig. 8.1. A constellation of metaphors for Yahweh in Hosea 4–14

approach and does not take seriously the aspective nature of its divine presentation. It is noteworthy that scholars have proposed root metaphors that accord with certain significant metaphors in the book (e.g., husband

---

Unusual Ways: Deuteronomy 32 and Other Mixed Metaphors for God in the Old Testament," in *Iconographic Exegesis of the Hebrew Bible/Old Testament: An Introduction to Its Method and Practice*, ed. Izaak J. de Hulster, Brent A. Strawn, and Ryan P. Bonfiglio (Göttingen: Vandenhoeck & Ruprecht, 2015), 117–33.

and parent), yet never the most numerically prominent (i.e., the farmer).[24] Dearman's proposal of "head of household" is the broadest and may come closest of all root metaphor proposals to encompassing most metaphors domains.[25] Nonetheless, this constellation shows that *all proposed root metaphors constitute less than half of the metaphorical domains in the book.* None of the proposed root metaphors can account for the remaining metaphors used for Yahweh. Furthermore, the theoretical foundation for a root metaphor concept has been discounted by contemporary metaphor scholars,[26] and Hundley's work further justifies this from the perspective of ancient Near Eastern studies.

Some general observations about the distribution of metaphor domains and strengths across Hos 4–14 are in order before proceeding to their interpretive significance. Around 80 percent of metaphor clusters are in cycle 2 (Hos 4:1–11:11), with the remainder in cycle 3 (12:1–14:9). In terms of the three subsections within each cycle, 50 percent of metaphors are in the initial accusation subsections, with almost 40 percent in sentencing and a little over 10 percent in redemption subsections.

In terms of metaphor domains, the farmer metaphor is the most frequent (17 occurrences), followed closely by the parent/father domain (16), destructive animals (11; lion alone occurs 6 times), husband (10), healer (8), legal metaphors of prosecutor/judge (5), suzerain (4), shepherd (4), and disciplinarian (4).

In terms of metaphor strength, the metaphors studied split about evenly between category 3 (53 metaphors) and category 2 (46 metaphors), with only four category 1 metaphors. The total strength of metaphor domains[27] follows a very similar order to the prominence of domains. The farmer domain is the strongest (total domain strength of 40), followed by father/parent (39), destructive animal (30; lion alone is 15), husband (28), healing (17), suzerain (12), prosecutor/judge (11), shepherd (10), and

---

24. The one exception is Gary Light, who sees "husbandman" (i.e., farmer) as the "theory-constitutive metaphor" (i.e., root metaphor) of the third cycle of the book (Hos 12–14; see "Theory-Constitutive Metaphor," 198–99).

25. Dearman, *Book of Hosea*, 11, 44–50.

26. Scholars recognize that certain conceptual metaphors can be "nested" in a hierarchy (see, e.g., Kövecses, "Conceptual Metaphor Theory," 19–23), or that there can be systematicity among metaphors. See Stern, *Metaphor in Context*, 169–76; Lynne Cameron, Graham Low, and Robert Maslen, "Finding Systematicity in Metaphor Use," in Cameron and Maslen, *Metaphor Analysis*, 116–46.

27. That is, the sum of metaphor strengths of all expressions in a metaphor domain.

disciplinarian (7). Notable here is that the suzerain domain is judged to be much stronger than others (all four occurrences have a strength of 3), so its total domain strength is nearly twice that of disciplinarian, despite having the same number of occurrences.

There are 82 metaphorical expressions that picture Yahweh as a human, 11 as an animal, and 10 as features of nature (mostly meteorological, such as rain). A third of the metaphors are construed as subjectively positive images for Yahweh, with two-thirds being negative.[28] Within the positive metaphors, 46 percent refer to the past; only 9 percent could be interpreted as referring to the present, 26 percent refer to the future, and about 20 percent (i.e., 6:1–3) are presumed by the people but not necessarily shared by Hosea.

Beyond statistical distributions, a few observations on interpretive significance are apropos. First, consistent with Hundley's observations of deity constellations across Mesopotamia, Yahweh's constellation in Hosea has an anthropomorphic core. Approximately 80 percent of metaphorical expressions use some kind of anthropomorphic domain. Only 10 percent are theriomorphic, and 10 percent derive from nonanimal elements of nature, mostly meteorological phenomena (see fig. 8.1).

Second, particular metaphor domains are consistently, though not exclusively, associated with particular emotions of Yahweh and rhetorical strategies of the book.[29] This is evident in the three most prominent domains: husband, father/parent, and farmer. The husband metaphors, primarily manifest through metaphors of sexual promiscuity (e.g., clusters 1, 2, 6, and Hos 8:9–10), are frequently deployed to provoke shame in the (primarily male) recipients as well as testify to the indignation of husband-Yahweh, who is publicly shamed through association with wife-Israel. The father/parent domain is frequently used in contexts of historical retrospectives and demonstrations of Yahweh's past love and provision for child-Israel (e.g., most explicitly in cluster 11). Rhetorically, this indicts Israel's subsequent rejection of parent-Yahweh. As Jeremias summarizes, "In every act of love, benevolence, and 'healing,' demonstrating gratuitous [*grundloser*] affection, the father has met only constant rejection from the

---

28. A positive image is understood to be an image subjectively perceived to be a beneficial attribute of God (e.g., love). The image is positive even if it functions rhetorically in the passage in a "negative" way (e.g., 11:1–4, where God cared for Israel in the past, but this serves to indict Israel for subsequent betrayal).

29. See ch. 5 and pp. 190–94 ("Eight Strategies of Metaphor Deployment"), above.

son."³⁰ The farmer metaphors frequently express Yahweh's disappointment, also in contexts of historical retrospectives (e.g., clusters 9 and 10). Farmer-Yahweh had initial expectations for animal- or plant-Israel, expectations that Israel failed to meet.

Third, meteorological imagery is especially pronounced in certain places, attesting to the polemical nature of the book. It is no coincidence that this book, which so clearly names Baal as the divine opponent, applies to Yahweh so many images associated with a storm god.³¹ The polemical strategy changes over the course of the book, moving from denunciation to appropriation.³²

Fourth, Seifert claims that every theriomorphic metaphor always proclaims doom, and conversely that every metaphor of Yahweh's care for Israel is expressed using anthropomorphic imagery.³³ While the absolute nature of her claim cannot be sustained,³⁴ her point is instructive. The human and nature metaphors are mostly positive. Animals, on the other hand, almost always witness to the destructive power of Yahweh and are deployed as threats to provoke Israel's return to Yahweh. This makes the positive use of lion imagery in 11:10 (in the *redemption* stage of cycle 2) a rare exception to the pattern in Hosea.

This aspective constellation of Hos 4–14's 103 metaphors for God suggests that the diversity of the book's metaphors must be taken seriously. Fortunately, this is an increasingly common trend. A further step, not always taken in such discussions, is the articulation of a theology derived from these metaphors.

---

30. Jeremias, "Zur Eschatologie des Hoseabuches," 226, my trans.

31. Storm-god-associated images are not limited to meteorological imagery. See the discussions of 6:1–6 (esp. pp. 76–77), above (also Lancaster and Miglio, "Lord of the Storm"), and of Hos 13–14 in clusters 13–15.

32. See pp. 174–77 ("Polemics and Metaphor Appropriation: A Shifting Strategy"), above.

33. Seifert, *Metaphorisches Reden*, 254, 283. Eidevall also notices that certain metaphor domains are used for certain forms of speech; e.g., legal and sexual promiscuity metaphors are always negatively used for accusation (*Grapes in the Desert*, 226).

34. Hosea 11:10 is the only positive use of an animal metaphor. Seifert interprets 11:10 positively, so it is unclear how she sustains her blanket statement (*Metaphorisches Reden*, 217–27). Hosea 14:6, 9 include nonanthropomorphic restorative images for Yahweh (dew, tree, respectively), but she does not discuss them because she considers them to be post-Hosean (*Metaphorisches Reden*, 262).

9
A Character Portrait of Yahweh

The road from metaphor to theology is littered with pitfalls. Yet some kind of characterization is inevitable for any perception of divinity, ancient or modern. Yahweh is presented in Hosea as a being with changing emotions and thoughts, a personality, and a relational history with Israel. What follows is a description of five prominent divine characteristics that appear in the metaphors in Hosea.[1] One could identify six, or four, or one hundred, but these five are offered as some central themes among the metaphors that appear to me to arise from the present reading.[2]

Unknown, Yet Knowable, Yet Unknowable

The imagery of a book such as Hosea is not conducive to sharp delineations and clear categories. As a poetic composition full of metaphor, Hosea's pictures of Yahweh are prone to vague or changing boundaries, to the mysterious and apophatic. A metaphorical theology, therefore, must begin by acknowledging that Yahweh is genuinely knowable (hence the

---

1. For more on characterization, see pp. 159–62, above.
2. Rom-Shiloni raises important warnings to avoid anachronistic and Christian pietistic tendencies in assertions of divine "conceptions of anthropomorphism, spirituality, immanence, and transcendence." See Dalit Rom-Shiloni, "Hebrew Bible Theology: A Jewish Descriptive Approach," *JR* 96 (2016): 173. Consistent with her concerns, my interpretation of 6:1–6 affirms rather than rejects a "polemical, intra-HB discussion concerning divine presence and the extent of its involvement in human life (on the individual or collective levels)" (174), I have embraced anthropomorphic divine descriptions (175–76), and the first characteristic below appears to be the very essence of Rom-Shiloni's argument. Nonetheless, it seems inescapable to me that Hosea's God—while certainly immanent *and* transcendent, present *and* absent, personal *and* mysterious—is a *character* presented as having a kind of personality analogous to but different from (hence the use of metaphors) that of humans.

very existence of the communication) yet also beyond exhaustive knowing. This reflects, of course, the essence of metaphor, which genuinely communicates yet is beyond exhaustive literal translation; metaphor both illuminates and obscures.[3]

From Hosea's perspective, *Yahweh* has *known* Israel from the beginning (5:3, 13:5), yet that knowledge is never reciprocated.[4] The book *never* says that Israel has known Yahweh, whether in the past or present.[5] Israel's problem is that they *think* they know God. Israel *claims* to know God (8:2) and to be interested in pursuing such knowledge (6:3), but both contexts indicate these claims are untrue.[6] The emphasis throughout the book is that Israel has *never known* and still does *not know* God (2:10, 4:1, 5:4, 7:9, 11:3, all using negated ידע or דעת).[7] Because of this, Yahweh *knows* well their sin (5:3, 7:2, 8:13, 9:9) and has *made known* their coming punishment (5:9).

Hosea's burden is that this false or absent knowledge be replaced by true knowledge, and metaphors are the key to doing so. In order to replace Israel's faulty knowledge of Yahweh, their metaphors must first

---

3. O'Brien discusses the theological implications of this feature common to prophetic literature, including reflections from Morris, Sherwood, and others, in "Metaphorization and Other Tropes," 244, 253–55.

4. This monograph understands the "knowledge of God" in Hosea in a holistic sense: it has cognitive, affective, and ethical aspects. So Vall, "Epistemology of Faith"; M. Douglas Carew, "To Know or Not to Know: Hosea's Use of *ydʿ/dʿt*," in *The Old Testament in the Life of God's People: Essays in Honor of Elmer A. Martens*, ed. Jon Isaak (Winona Lake, IN: Eisenbrauns, 2009), 77–87; see also De Andrado, "Ḥesed and Sacrifice"; Seifert's discussion of "Becoming Acquainted with the Inaccessible God" (*Metaphorisches Reden*, 258–59).

5. Neither have they ever loved Yahweh (see p. 169, above).

6. Hosea 6:4–6 rejects the prayer of 6:1–3 as meaningless because of the people's fleeting loyalty. In 8:2 they claim, "We know you!" (ידענוך), yet they are condemned for covenant unfaithfulness (8:1; i.e., not knowing God), and rejecting "the good" (זנח ישראל טוב [8:3]; i.e., God). Hosea 9:7 is the only other passage in which Israel "knows" something, but it is an ironic indictment: they don't even recognize God's ways.

7. The *yiqtol* in 13:4 (ואלהים זולתי לא תדע) is challenging. If rendered as a preterite ("You have never known a [true] God but Me," NJPS), or with a present continuous aspect ("You know no God but me," NRSV), it would be the sole exception to the claim that Israel is never said to know God in the past or present. It should be understood according to the modal sense of the *yiqtol* form (*BHRG* §19.3.5.2, expressing an absolute prohibition [*BHRG* §19.3.5.1]; see NASB; Goldingay, *First Testament*, 856): Hosea 13:4 indicates that they *should* have known only Yahweh since Egypt.

be destabilized.[8] Hosea deploys at least two methods of destabilizing the old order: attacking the metaphors Israel uses and offering a multiplicity of perspectives on Yahweh in response to Israel's comparatively monolithic conception. The first method has been discussed at length and is not repeated here.[9] The second method merits further attention.

The variety of metaphors undermines the absolute certainty with which one holds certain beliefs about Yahweh. If God is revealed through *many* metaphors in Hosea, then it is only in the sum total of the mosaic of images that God can be rightly known, not the restricted set to which Israel holds.

Philosopher Ted Cohen, analyzing a Yom Kippur poem containing six pairs of metaphors for the relationship between God and God's people, claims there are two assumptions behind the poem: "The first is that there is nothing literal to be said [about God], and the second is that something must be said."[10] Or as Soskice says, "The task of saying the unsayable is aligned to that of knowing the unknowable."[11] Surely both statements could be said of Hosea's poetry as well. The author of the Yom Kippur poem, Cohen continues, has nothing literal to say:

> He will speak a metaphor. But he will not leave it at that, for there is the perilous possibility that the metaphor will be taken literally, or that it will be taken to exhaust what is to be said about God and God's relation to the people. And so he goes on, with metaphor after metaphor, each of them compelling *and each of them unsettling the others.* The search for more than one figure acknowledges the inadequacy of any one to exhaust what is to be said, and the multiplicity makes it impossible to fix on any one or two. *The speaker has an impossible task: to speak comprehensibly about something incomprehensible.* His response is to speak in every apt way he can conceive.[12]

This destabilizing multiplicity creates a rift in the old order. The "too muchness" of the mixed metaphors "communicates crucial data about

---

8. See Hosea's seventh rhetorical strategy, p. 192, above.

9. See pp. 174–77 ("Polemics and Metaphor Appropriation: A Shifting Strategy"), above, and pp. 215–17 ("The Exclusive Sovereign"), below.

10. Cohen, "Metaphor, Feeling, and Narrative," 233.

11. Soskice, *Metaphor and Religious Language*, 63.

12. Cohen, "Metaphor, Feeling, and Narrative," 234, first emphasis original, second emphasis added.

God even as that quality simultaneously functions to prohibit mastery of the divine Subject."[13] This undercuts Israel's assumption that their knowledge of Yahweh means they can control Yahweh for their benefit or that his responses are predictably beneficial for them (6:1–3). If knowledge is power, then the fact that Yahweh is beyond their complete knowing means he is beyond their control.

This unsettles Israel's self-identity, their understanding of Yahweh, and their possible futures. They are not who they thought they were; they do not actually know Yahweh. He is not who they thought he was, nor can they predict what he will be like. This throws into disarray Israel's assumptions about their future. The destabilizing vacillation is meant to keep the hearers/readers disoriented as the world as they know it is reorganized through prophetic speech.

Yet instability is not the only or final purpose of metaphor. They deconstruct in order to construct. Rifts are created in the old order for the purpose of replacing it with a new one. Hosea's metaphors also serve to convey genuinely new insight into the character of God, the nature of Israel's relationship with him, and Israel's options for their future. God *can* be known. Indeed, God desires and demands to be known—both by ancient Israel and all subsequent readers (6:6, 14:10).[14] This knowledge is profoundly mediated by metaphors. The very presence of the prophetic book, as an instance of divine communication to this unknowing people, testifies to the possibility of knowing God and to his impulse to be known. If God were absolutely unknowable, the book would not exist. Yet Hosea affirms that in the end, after Yahweh woos (מפתיה) Israel back and speaks to their heart (ודברתי על לבה, 2:16), Israel will finally know Yahweh in beautiful and holistic restoration (וידעת את יהוה, 2:22).[15] Metaphors are essential to both the unknown-ness and the known-ness of God.

---

13. Strawn and de Hulster, "Figuring YHWH," 132; see also Sherwood, *Prostitute and the Prophet*, 250–51.

14. See Garrett, *Hosea, Joel*, 282; Reinhard Gregor Kratz, "Erkenntnis Gottes im Hoseabuch," *ZTK* 94 (1997): 17; Bernard Gosse, "L'influence du livre des Proverbes sur le livre d'Osée, en relation avec les livres de Jérémie et d'Isaïe," *OTE* 28 (2015): 114; Lim and Castelo, *Hosea*, 224.

15. See Clines and Gunn, "You Tried," 21; Moughtin-Mumby, *Sexual and Marital Metaphors*, 254–55. Within the metaphor, this "knowing" has the quality of restored sexual intimacy in marriage. See, e.g., Macintosh, *Critical and Exegetical Commentary*, 85; Sweeney, *Twelve Prophets* 1:36; van Wolde, "Sentiments as Culturally Constructed Emotions," 18; contra Andersen and Freedman, *Hosea*, 283–84.

Passionate

Passionate conveys the idea that Yahweh is *not* portrayed as disinterested or halfhearted.[16] Rather, everything Yahweh thinks and feels, he experiences fully and strongly. For God, the opposite of love is not hatred or wrath but indifference.[17] It is because God loves Israel that the deity is presented as *anything but indifferent*. It is surely the case that *all* of God's characteristics and experiences, positive or negative, are expressed in full volume, whether God's love, justice, anger, wrath, shame, joy, sense of betrayal, loyalty to Israel, frustration, or other emotions. There is no middle ground or rational detachment for Yahweh in Hosea. Hosea suggests that human emotions pale in comparison to the intensity of God's.

One question has surfaced repeatedly throughout this project: What is the relationship between God's love and anger? Just as human beings act in ways that may be more or less central to who they are, Goldingay distinguishes between "dominant" and "secondary" aspects to God's personality. He claims that judgment is a secondary personality trait of God.[18] Lamentations 3:33 notes that God does not afflict from his heart (לא ענה מלבו). This is why judgment can at times be described as God's "strange deed" (זר מעשהו, Isa 28:21). It is expressed in the face of human rebellion and injustice, but it is not a natural aspect of Yahweh's personality. Yet affliction and punishment do not bring him joy the same way that love and loyalty do (Jer 9:23, Hos 6:6, Mic 7:18).[19] Israel's hope, therefore, lies in that he will not retain his anger forever (Ps 103:9; see also Ps 30:6, Isa 54:1–10) but will rejoice over them with singing (Zeph 3:17). As James Nogalski observes, "The fact that almost every book in the Twelve ends

---

16. This reflects the contemporary usage of the word *passion*, meaning strong emotion without implying negativity, rather than the older notions that entail *sinful and uncontrolled* activities or desires (common in the New Testament) or "drunkenness of the mind, an agitation of the soul devoid of reasoned purpose, operating blindly" (Heschel, *Prophets*, 224).

17. Anthony C. Thiselton, *The Hermeneutics of Doctrine* (Grand Rapids: Eerdmans, 2007), 573.

18. Goldingay, *Israel's Faith*, 2:165–66. Crucially, is it not justice that is secondary but judgment and, by implication, anger. Also on God's personality, see Blumenthal, *Facing the Abusing God*, 11–20; Patrick, *Rendering of God*, 37–40, 46–60.

19. Though see Deut 28:62–63, in which God delights (שוש) to bring both deliverance and destruction, depending on the people's obedience.

with hope for a better future contributes to this sense that YHWH desires mercy over judgment."[20]

Historically Engaged

Hosea draws substantially on Israel's historical traditions, perhaps more than any other prophet.[21] Indeed, "it is quite remarkable how thoroughly Israel's history is embedded in Hosea's proclamation."[22] Hosea's historical interests extend into the metaphors as well. Seifert goes so far as to claim that "virtually every Hosean metaphor for God is directly related to history—past, present, or future."[23] Israel's metaphorical adoption happened at the historical exodus tradition (Hos 11:1; see also Exod 4:22). Their metaphorical marriage began in the historical exodus and wilderness traditions (Hos 2:17). It was also in the wilderness that God was pleasantly surprised at finding a treasure like Israel, yet also where Israel first became detestable through idolatry (9:10). God disowned Israel in relation to a historical tradition concerning Gilgal (9:15). Hosea even stretches back to the time of the patriarchs. Hosea 12 uses Jacob "to lay bare Israel's present deceit against God and neighbor" and to call them to return to Yahweh (12:7).[24] Furthermore, Hosea, like all the prophets, envisions God's present and future metaphorical responses in historical terms. God will act within history, using Assyria (10:6; 11:5, 11), to destroy Israelite society as they know it, like a wild animal (e.g., 5:14–15, 13:7–8).

This emphasis on God's involvement in Israel's past, present, and future illustrates that Hosea does not know an abstract or uninvolved deity. Hosea's use of metaphor is tightly tied to Israel's lived experience through time, suggesting continuity of relationship between Israel and Yahweh. Hosea speaks metaphorically of the singular deity who worked in Israel's past, is speaking and active in their present, and will judge and restore in their future. Israel's entire temporal existence is understood in

---

20. James D. Nogalski, "God in the Book of the Twelve," in O'Brien, *Oxford Handbook of the Minor Prophets*, 113.

21. See, e.g., Daniels, *Hosea and Salvation History*; Holt, *Prophesying the Past*; Patrick, *Redeeming Judgment*, 208.

22. Wolff, *Hosea*, xxvi.

23. Seifert, *Metaphorisches Reden*, 262, my trans. The single exception she acknowledges is 14:6–9, though she views this passage as "post-Hosean."

24. Wolff, *Hosea*, xxvi. See Hos 2:1, Gen 22:17, 32:13.

relation to Yahweh. Furthermore, Else Holt suggests that the historical traditions are undergirded by Yahweh's demands for exclusivity and the knowledge of God.[25]

This is neatly encapsulated in the extended mixed-metaphor story of 13:4–8, which includes metaphors for God's early provision, Israel's subsequent betrayal that extends into their present forgetfulness, and imminent judgment.[26] Conveniently, the passage also demonstrates Holt's two pillars of Hosea's use of historical traditions: the demand for exclusivity (ואלהים זולתי לא תדע ומושיע אין בלתי, v. 4) and the knowledge of God (ואלהים זולתי לא תדע, v. 4, על כן שכחוני, v. 6). It also demonstrates that there is continuity of relationship between Yahweh and Israel, though admittedly not the kind of relationship that Israel would desire (since the passage ends in punishment). Nonetheless, Yahweh has not entirely abandoned Israel.

Additionally, the use of history is a rhetorical device used to stir Israel's memory and provoke a return to Yahweh. See, for example, the analysis of cluster 10 (Hos 10:10–12) in chapter 3, where biblical memory is the actualization of the past in the present to chart a course for the future.[27] Seifert rightly concludes that "For Hosea himself [as opposed to the 'post-Hosean' 14:6–8, 9], the metaphors visualize the God of history: they teach us how to understand and explain the present as an encounter with the God of the past and make it clear how Israel's future will also be decided by him."[28] Israel's future remains in the hands of the same deity who has guided their past and now speaks to them in the present. Whether they learn from these historical retrospectives and change their behavior in the present determines which future God will bring on them.

The Exclusive Sovereign

Two of the consistent themes that have surfaced in this study are the polemical function of metaphors and the technique of appropriating the metaphors of other nations and deities. Sometimes these coincide so that a given metaphor is both appropriated and polemical. Chapter 6 argues that there is a shifting pattern over the course of the book in this regard:

---

25. Holt, *Prophesying the Past*, 140.
26. Seifert also points out that the cipher of "Egypt" in Hos 11 connects Israel's past, present, and future (11:1, 5, 11; see *Metaphorisches Reden*, 262).
27. A phrase borrowed and modified from Arthurs, *Preaching as Reminding*.
28. Seifert, *Metaphorisches Reden*, 262, my trans.

metaphors begin as straightforwardly polemical but gradually move toward being polemically *appropriated*. In cluster 1, Baal is denounced without metaphor appropriation as the direct opponent of Yahweh—the "other man." By Hos 13–14, however, Yahweh is appropriating the metaphors of El, Mot, Baal, and Asherah, annexing all of their abilities for himself. Yahweh's rival deities and kingdoms must first be denounced and rendered impotent. The metaphor must first "break an old categorization"—only then can new worldviews be built on "the ruins of their forerunners."[29]

These and other features demonstrate that Yahweh demands to be the exclusive sovereign over Israel. *Yahweh* is the one who liberated them from slavery in Egypt—apart from whom they should have known no other deity (13:4). *Yahweh* is the one who adopted them in that moment, thereby creating the relationship (11:1). *Yahweh* is the one who showered them with good instructions for life with him (8:12), though they defied them all (8:1, 12). *Yahweh* made a covenant with Israel, though they sought international alliances "incompatible with devotion to the deity."[30] *Yahweh*, not Assyria, is the lion who is the sole power that governs Israel (5:14–15) and leads them into restoration (11:10); other "forces have no bearing on Israel's fate."[31] Through these and other metaphors, Yahweh has declared the right to be Ephraim's sole devotion.

Yahweh brooks no rivals. No other claimants to the throne, no other aspirants to rule, none other who demand Israel's loyalty will be tolerated—not Assyria, not Baal, nor any other imposter. As a jealous husband, a metaphor that "states Yahweh's claim of exclusiveness,"[32] Yahweh knows that there can be only two in this relationship. Any third party is an intruder who distorts the relationship between Yahweh and his people. Similarly, in the metaphor of God as suzerain to Israel, "the point seems to be: 'you can only be loyal to one overlord.'"[33]

Rivals will be cut down by direct attack or rendered useless by Yahweh appropriating their potential benefits for Israel. Yahweh has "effectively relegated to non-existent status" all competitors so that they "may be

---

29. Ricoeur, *Rule of Metaphor*, 197; see Hosea's seventh rhetorical strategy on p. 192, above.
30. Eidevall, *Grapes in the Desert*, 234.
31. Zimran, "Notion of God," 165.
32. Wolff, *Hosea*, xxvi.
33. Eidevall, *Grapes in the Desert*, 234.

forgotten."[34] Every strategy is deployed in Hosea's usage of metaphors in order to make the point: only Yahweh will do for Israel. The metaphors convey "that the people need no other God besides him."[35]

Exclusivity is at the heart of the relationship Yahweh has created. Yahweh has been exclusively faithful in this *monogamous* relationship. He longs to have that reciprocated.[36] Indeed, the very covenant that forms their relationship is associated with a complex of ideas "characterized by notions of reciprocity."[37] Yet despite Yahweh's love for the people, Hosea never once says the people have loved Yahweh. This contrast is, in Boda's words, the "burning issue" of the book.[38] Yahweh's commitment is what holds open the door to the possibility of reciprocation.

Committed to Israel

I have demonstrated above the futility of attempting to isolate a root metaphor. Is there anything, then, that holds these metaphors together? I answered above that the discourse's rhetorical purpose of provoking a return to Yahweh held the metaphors together. But there is also a common theological foundation. The fundamental theological reality that unites all of the metaphors is that *Yahweh is committed to Israel*. He does not give up on them. The relationship appears in jeopardy at many points (e.g., 9:15, 17; 13:1–14:1), but in the end (2:16–25, 3:4–5, 11:10–11, 14:2–9) Yahweh is still there, loyal to his people. In other words, God's commitment reflects

---

34. Hundley, "Here a God," 100.
35. Seifert, *Metaphorisches Reden*, 262, my trans.
36. Katrin Zehetgruber argues from a redactional perspective that reciprocity is central to the original message of Hosea. See Zehetgruber, *Zuwendung und Abwendung: Studien zur Reziprozität des JHWH/Israel-Verhältnisses im Hoseabuch*, WMANT 159 (Göttingen: Vandenhoeck & Ruprecht, 2020). That Hosea's God is genuinely relational is also self-evident. In Hosea, God genuinely *responds* to and is *affected* by God's people. Seifert notes, "Hosea's ominous metaphors for God do not show YHWH in and of himself to be a god of destruction; they do not teach timeless and suprahistorical truths about the nature of God, but in a concrete historical moment they allow YHWH to be recognized as the living God, who alone is to be feared" (*Metaphorisches Reden*, 182, my trans.). As Dale Patrick observes, "The God whom we meet in Scripture ... enacts his identity in interaction with human beings.... He is known in relation, not isolation; in interaction, not in eternal essence" (*Rendering of God*, 63).
37. Olyan, "Honor, Shame, and Covenant Relations," 217.
38. Boda, *Severe Mercy*, 295.

covenantal fidelity, חסד. What Jeremias rightly says of the whole book is especially true of its metaphors: "For Hosea, the incomprehensible thing about this God remains that he cannot forsake his stubborn people, even if they do not want to have anything to do with him."[39] This is consistent with the whole Book of the Twelve, which "creates a dynamic portrait of a deity who continues to work on behalf of people who repeatedly turn their backs on YHWH."[40]

This is not a root metaphor or a substitutionary, reductionistic approach to metaphor. It is a theological foundation that gives rise to Hosea's diverse metaphoric characterization of Yahweh. The following pages demonstrate that divine commitment undergirds the previous four characteristics; each metaphor cluster in Hosea 4–14 arises from this fundamental theological theme; fidelity is a necessary presupposition in many of the metaphor source domains chosen for Yahweh; and it coheres with the rhetorical purpose of the discourse—namely, Israel's repentance.

The Other Four Divine Characteristics as Manifestations of Yahweh's Commitment

The first four divine characteristics articulated above cohere in that they all arise from the fifth: God's loyalty to Israel.

Divine revelation and hiddenness, the first characteristic, is a manifestation of Yahweh's commitment in two ways. The first is that God still desires and demands to be known. *Because* Yahweh remains in relationship with the people of Israel, he sends a prophet to speak to his people and reaffirm his desire that his people know him. The very presence of the prophet in their midst is a sign that Yahweh still wants to engage.

Second, the vacillation among the metaphors reflects a profound divine self-claim. In Exod 3:14 (אהיה אשר אהיה), God declares that he will be whatever he needs to be for his people at any given time.[41] While

---

39. Jeremias, *Hosea*, 20, my trans.; see Childs, *Introduction to the Old Testament*, 382. Scholars have especially noted this in regard to Hos 11 (see discussion in ch. 4 above; Macintosh, *Critical and Exegetical Commentary*, 436; Wolff, *Hosea*, 193).

40. Nogalski, "God in the Book of the Twelve," 114.

41. This is not offered as an exhaustive explanation of the phrase אהיה אשר אהיה but as one implication. For initial discussions of views, see Brevard S. Childs, *The Book of Exodus: A Critical, Theological Commentary*, OTL (Louisville: Westminster John Knox, 1974), 60–64; Van der Toorn, "Yahweh," 913–16; William H. C. Propp, *Exodus*

Yahweh is constant in his basic characteristics (see Exod 34:6–7) and his dominant personality traits, these manifest in a variety of different ways at different times and in different circumstances.[42] Multiple metaphors are necessary because (note the variations on the divine name) sometimes God deems it necessary, for instance, to be a kind farmer (ואהיה להם כמרימי על לחיהם, Hos 11:4), other times a devouring lion (ואהי להם כמו שחל, 13:7), other times refreshing dew (אהיה כטל לישראל, 14:6).[43] Inherent in God's self-revelation is the presupposition that he will be or do whatever is necessary to exercise his commitment to Israel and establish his purposes through them and actualize the covenantal promise that "you shall be my people, and I will be your God" (see 1:9, 2:25).

The second characteristic, that God is passionate, is a clear manifestation of God's commitment to Israel in a variety of ways. For one, God would not have such strong emotions if he were disinterested or uncommitted as to the nature of his relationship to Israel. It is precisely the depth of God's loyalty to Israel that gives rise to the strength of his emotions in the book.

Some divine passions and decisions—for example, that God hates and rejects Israel (9:15, 17)—appear to challenge the claim that God's loyalty undergirds his passions. On further reflection, however, one finds that it is precisely this emotional variety that reflects God's ultimate commitment.

As Dale Patrick notes, a character must be *relatively* consistent in biography and emotional comportments, and as Shimon Bar-Efrat notes, the character must be sufficiently complex to be believable.[44] Within the metaphorical world of Hosea, God takes on human personae such as father or husband. Such a relationship sometimes brings conflicting sentiments, from the most profound love to the deepest pain and anger. For a

---

1–18: A New Translation with Introduction and Commentary, AB 2 (New Haven: Yale University Press, 1999), 204–5 (who understands the phrase as I do above); W. Ross Blackburn, *The God Who Makes Himself Known: The Missionary Heart of the Book of Exodus*, NSBT 28 (Downers Grove, IL: InterVarsity Press, 2012), 34–50; T. Desmond Alexander, *Exodus*, AOTC 2 (London: Apollos, 2017), 87–89, 100–101.

42. On dominant personality traits, see pp. 213–14 ("Passionate"), above. On Exod 34:6–7 in relation to Hosea, see Dearman, *Book of Hosea*, 379–82. On the stability and "disjunction" of Yahweh's character, see Brueggemann, *Theology of the Old Testament*, 229–313, 359–72, 400–403.

43. For further discussions on Hosea's plays on the divine name, see p. 150, esp. n. 70 there.

44. Patrick, *Rendering of God*, 46; Bar-Efrat, *Narrative Art*, 91.

characterization of God as a human spouse or parent to be believable and rhetorically effective, it must reflect a realistic range of emotions as understood from human experience. A flat or emotionally detached depiction of Yahweh, lacking such strong feelings, would not be a believably committed character or carry the rhetorical force of this more complex depiction.

All these emotions find a believable place within the context of a committed relationship. Yahweh remains committed to Israel and his purposes for them while temporarily not loving them and disowning them (מביתי אגרשם, 9:15). In God's view, a period of discipline is necessary for the continuation of this relationship. Discipline therefore is an *expression* of God's commitment to the continuation of the relationship. Israel is disowned (9:15) in the hope that the orphan will come back (see 14:4 in ch. 4 above). Ultimately, even rejection (9:17) and death (13:1, 14) will be reversed by the God who remains steadfastly loyal to this relationship (14:5-9).[45] In the final analysis, God does *not* perpetually hate Israel, and God does *not* in fact abandon or reject them forever. Though they are temporarily like chaff carried away by the wind in exile (13:3), God restores them to relationship (reaffirming the covenantal formula in the eschatological time of 2:25). Though he hates them for a moment (9:15), he ultimately loves them generously (14:5). The end of each of the three cycles in Hosea pictures God in continued relationship with Israel (2:16-25 and 3:4-5, 11:10-11, 14:2-9).

The third divine characteristic, that of God as historically engaged, is perhaps the most obvious manifestation of God's enduring loyalty to Israel. Put simply, that God has been and will be engaged (saving, providing, indicting, judging, punishing, restoring) in Israel's past, present, *and future* is a clear witness to his enduring devotion to the nation.

Fourth and finally, God's commitment is expressed through his demand for exclusive loyalty. That is, Hosea's polemics and metaphoric appropriation demonstrate that God *expects Israel to reciprocate his commitment*. As articulated above, it is because Yahweh has been faithful to his end of the monogamous covenant that he fights for and demands Israel's exclusive devotion. God is not passively resigned to the failings of his people. Nor does one find in Hosea a statement that Yahweh is a jealous God. Rather, one sees Yahweh in action as a loyal partner who fights, through the prophetic word, for the allegiance of his people. God

---

45. See pp. 177-84 ("Culmination and Inversion in Hosea 14"), above.

confronts the imposters and woos his people back (2:16) *because he is committed to them.*

Fifteen Metaphor Clusters as Manifestations of Yahweh's Commitment

Given the quantity of material, the following is by necessity a brief survey, demonstrating how at least one major feature of each cluster is an expression of God's fidelity to Israel.

Especially in cluster 1, Yahweh is ashamed of Israel's behavior. Because Yahweh has publicly committed himself to this nation (as a husband to a wife), he is associated with the shame of their infidelity. This is also apparent in the sexual promiscuity metaphors of cluster 8 (8:14–9:2), associated further with the commitment of a father to a child.

Divine frustration (e.g., cluster 1; esp. cluster 10) also evinces God's commitment. Because Yahweh has committed himself to using Israel for his purposes and providing for their needs, he is frustrated by their stubborn refusal to cooperate (4:16).

Cluster 2 (5:1–7) manifests Yahweh's commitment to Israel through his disciplinary action (מוסר, 5:2), which does not end the relationship but seeks to correct Israel's errant path. Hosea 5:7b takes the sexual metaphors of cluster 1 a step further: Israel has been sexually unfaithful to husband-Yahweh to the point of bearing illegitimate children (בנים זרים ילדו); yet, even in the face of public shame, God remains loyal to Israel.

Cluster 4 (6:1–3) is the sole exception in contributing to *Hosea's* view of Yahweh's commitment to Israel, because it constitutes the viewpoint of Israel's cultic representatives.[46] Nonetheless, even Israel's cultic representatives assume that Yahweh will be faithful to Israel, though they have different ideas about what that entails. The two clusters bracketing this one (clusters 3 and 5) are retorts to Israel's leadership showing that Yahweh's commitment to Israel is not, at least in the short term, always a positive thing for God's people (as they assume). His is also a commitment to his *covenant* with Israel, and that can mean bringing covenant curses.

Cluster 3 (5:10–15) demonstrates Yahweh's commitment in that his retributive judgment manifests his covenantal obligations to Israel, namely, the curses of the covenant for disobedience (also cluster 13). Loyalty to the covenant is loyalty to the relationship. Cluster 5 (6:4–6) is similar. Because

---

46. See pp. 63–64, above.

of Yahweh's commitment to the very covenant Israel has betrayed (6:7), a verdict of judgment is necessary (6:5c). In cluster 6 (6:10–7:1), Judah is also implicated in judgment (6:11). Though God still wills their good through healing (7:1), the relationship must for now consist of threshing (6:11). Similarly in cluster 7 (7:8–8:1), Israel has transgressed "my" covenant (יַעַן עָבְרוּ בְרִיתִי, 8:1c) and revolted against "my" instruction (וְעַל תּוֹרָתִי פָּשָׁעוּ, 8:1d).

Cluster 9 (9:15–10:2) includes the passages that portray Yahweh as hating, disowning, rejecting, and no longer loving Israel (9:15, 17). These are admittedly some of the most challenging passages for the claim of Yahweh's fundamental devotion to Israel. Yet, as shown above, these are, from the perspective of human experience, understandable reactions to Israel's behavior that express a temporary change in the relationship. They do not have the last word on Israel's fate, and they are designed to provoke Israel to return to Yahweh in fidelity. They are superseded by Yahweh's ultimate actions in freely loving (14:5) and perhaps readopting (14:4) Israel.

Cluster 11 (11:1–4) emphasizes Yahweh's past loyalty and provision despite Israel's past infidelity (also cluster 13). Cluster 12 (11:8–10) emphasizes Yahweh's *desire* to express compassion and the positive aspects of covenant loyalty (11:8). It shows that God will execute judgment on Israel, but it will not be an absolute destruction. Rather, Yahweh demonstrates his commitment by restoring the relationship and returning the people to their land (11:10–11).

Cluster 14 (13:14–14:1), like cluster 9 (9:15–10:2), depicts temporarily giving Israel over to death. Yet this is not the antithesis of Yahweh's commitment to Israel. Instead, Yahweh is the one who can bring life after death. Because he is committed to Israel forever, he will resurrect the nation in the final cluster in order to continue the relationship and his purposes with them.[47]

Unlike any other, cluster 15 (14:4–14:9) demonstrates what Yahweh's final, unrestrained commitment to Israel will entail. Having raised Israel from the dead (see Hos 13), re-adopted them (14:4), and healed them (14:5a), he loves them generously (14:5b), causes them to flourish (14:6–8), and provides for all their needs (14:9d). Having passed through death, Yahweh's commitment to Israel is ultimately demonstrated in their fullness of life.

---

47. For a comparison of the compassion in 11:8 with the hiding of compassion in 13:14, see pp. 168–71 ("Love and Hate"), above.

Commitment as an Essential Entailment of Hosea's Three Most Common Metaphor Domains

It is noteworthy that the book's three most common metaphors for God (farmer, parent, husband)[48] have commitment as an essential entailment. A farmer has purposes for the usefulness of the animal but also certain obligations for provision. It is in the farmer's interest to be committed to the well-being of the animal. Obligation is presupposed, for instance, in the irony of the first farmer metaphor analyzed (4:16). A parent-child relationship, similarly, has certain mutual obligations. In the ancient world, these would primarily have consisted of the parent's (primarily father's) obligation to provision, and the child's obligation to respect and obedience.[49] Though neither the farmer-animal nor the parent-child relationship is formally covenantal, both presuppose a degree of commitment between parties—admittedly the latter more so than the former. The last of these most common metaphors, that of husband and wife, *is* covenantal and carries with it the strongest sense of *exclusive* commitment to the other party. It is this essential feature of the metaphor that makes it, along with the parent-child metaphor, a favorite among biblical literature in expressing the claim to mutual exclusivity in the Israel-Yahweh relationship. Without mutual commitment, there is no relationship as the prophet envisions it.

Commitment and Repentance

This study has made two claims regarding what holds the metaphors of Hosea together: Israel's repentance (ch. 7) and Yahweh's faithfulness (this chapter). How do the two relate?

The metaphors of Hosea genuinely cohere in both claims, but at different stages, as it were, of communication: origin and goal.[50] As just demonstrated, they cohere in their theological *foundation* in as far as Yahweh's commitment to Israel provides an essential trait, a starting point, for the source domain of many of the book's primary metaphors and is expressed variously in each cluster. They also cohere in their *purpose*

---

48. See p. 205, above.
49. See discussion of 8:14 on pp. 92–93, 96–97, above; Brettler, "Incompatible Metaphors," 112.
50. On discourse coherence, see p. 23 n. 78, above.

because Hosea deploys the metaphors to provoke a variety of responses in the audience for the ultimate purpose of repentance.

While rhetorical purposes can change depending on the context, the reality of Yahweh's devotion to Israel is unchanging. The latter underwrites the former. The theological fact of God's loyalty (to himself, to his covenant[s], to his people) is an unchanging reality that creates the very possibility of Hosea's chosen rhetorical purpose. Hosea can call for repentance *only because* God remains committed to his people. If God had decided to renounce his people because of their infidelity, then repentance would not be possible. If one is to return, one needs a place and a person to which to return. If the return is to Yahweh, Yahweh must remain accessible. Repentance is only possible for the people because God, who disappears (5:6, 15), nonetheless remains available to be found (14:9).[51]

Essential to the nature of Israel's return to Yahweh is the knowledge of God (דעת אלהים) and the expression of loyalty (חסד; e.g., 6:6, 12:7), traits currently absent among God's people (4:1). This provides an additional perspective from which to see the coherence of the foundation and purpose of the metaphors. It is because Yahweh knows Israel and remains committed to them (i.e., shows חסד) that he desires (6:6) and demands (10:12, 12:7) the same in return (i.e., the rhetorical purpose of the metaphors). This is the essence of Israel's return to Yahweh. Repentance is reciprocity.

Summary

We have seen that the metaphors for God in Hos 4–14 share a theological foundation: the presupposition that God remains committed to Israel. This is essentially an expression of covenantal loyalty, of חסד. As such, it reflects the most basic of Israel's declarations of the character of their God (Exod 34:6–7; see Hos 2:21) as well as the grounds for their own expression of reciprocated loyalty (חסד; e.g., Hos 6:6, 10:12, 12:7).

Yes, God expresses rage (e.g., Hos 5:10, 8:5, 13:11; passim). Yes, he declares he will no longer love them (9:15). Yes, he promises their temporary destruction (e.g., 9:17, 10:14–15, 11:5–6, 13:7–14:1; passim). Yes, he has given them over to death (13:14). But on the other side of death, God remains committed to his people, able and willing to raise them to

---

51. Eidevall, *Grapes in the Desert*, 248–52.

new life. His commitment to them makes repentance a possibility. In a sense, this reflects Brueggemann's summary of Yahweh's character: in God are combined "unlimited sovereignty and risky solidarity."[52] That God can remain faithful even in such risky solidarity, even when his human partners are so relentlessly unfaithful, is owing, according to Hos 11:9, to the distinction between creature and Creator. He is faithful, because "he is God, not a fickle human partner."[53] To be divine is to be loyal and faithful in the face of human betrayal.[54] Perhaps "the instinct to love, comfort and tolerate is nearer the heart of Yhwh than the instinct to act in rage."[55] Such fidelity may indeed be the "measure of God's deity and holiness."[56]

---

52. Brueggemann, *Theology of the Old Testament*, 268.
53. Duby, "'For I Am God,'" 165.
54. See Plank, "Scarred Countenance," esp. 354.
55. Goldingay, *Israel's Faith*, 2:164.
56. McConville, "Hosea, Book of," 349.

10
Conclusion: Faithful beyond Death

In this book I am interested in the question, Who is Yahweh according to the metaphors of Hos 4–14? This primary question raises other questions, such as how one is to respond to the apparently paradoxical nature of Hosea's diverse metaphors as they now remain in the final form, and why metaphors appear to group together in certain places in the discourse. Also curious is how and why Hosea's metaphors are deployed—what are the purposes and strategies that underlie their distribution and contents?

Regarding the questions of how Hosea's metaphors are deployed and how I have integrated them, it turns out that Hosea's divine metaphors cluster together at key rhetorical points in the discourse that are central to the book's purpose, such that their interactions are complex and multivalent. Drawing on recent metaphor research, chapter 1 developed an approach whereby one can identify those clusters and analyze the internal interactions between metaphors within each cluster. I also outline my understanding of the holistic power of metaphor—shaping cognition, affect, and volition—which shapes my reading of Hosea.

In part 1, I used this framework to analyze 103 divine metaphors among 15 clusters in Hos 4–14. Hosea is structured as a thrice-repeated legal movement from accusation to sentencing to redemption. Chapter 2 deals with metaphors of accusation, chapter 3 is on sentencing, and chapter 4 addresses the redemption clusters. All three chapters follow a similar process. Metaphors in the passage are identified and individually studied for their contribution to a portrait of Yahweh, and then the mutual interactions between metaphors within each cluster are considered (how they develop or contrast with one another). Part 1 thus provides the raw material on which the rest of the book builds.

Part 2 transitioned to analyzing intercluster metaphor interactions, seeking patterns among the exegesis of part 1. Regardless of its compositional process, the book of Hosea as it now stands provides abundant evidence of intentional literary shaping. Studying the metaphors in isolation is thus insufficient; a literary perspective that accounts for metaphorical development or reversal is necessary. Hence, while part 1 focused on *intra*cluster metaphor interactions, part 2 attends to *inter*cluster interactions. Part 2 concentrates on three salient patterns, crucial for discerning a holistic characterization of Yahweh among clusters: divine emotions, metaphor developments and inversions, and the rhetorical purpose of the metaphors.

To begin part 2, in chapter 5 I focused on Hosea's presentation of Yahweh's emotional life. I drew attention to five divine emotions that arise from the 103 metaphors under consideration, most of which have received little scholarly attention until recently. They are God's shame by virtue of association with Israel, God's emotional experience of betrayal, God's disappointment with Israel, and God's vacillating responses of love and hatred in Hosea. All five emotional experiences change over the course of the book and lead the reader to wonder what God's final response to Israel will be. In the first case, God is publicly shamed by public association with Israel's public unfaithfulness. As the book moves closer to its conclusion, God's response to public humiliation is tempered, such that one wonders whether Israel's fate might not be as bad as initially thought. Similarly, the passages describing Israel's betrayal of Yahweh suggest that they deserve the death sentence, until Yahweh vacillates (11:8), then states that he does not respond to betrayal the way humans do (11:9). How will he respond? The metaphors on disappointment likewise show that Yahweh had a purpose in choosing Israel, which they have since failed to realize. Is there hope that they might yet realize their purpose such that God will no longer be frustrated with them? Finally, the juxtaposition between God's love and hatred (9:15) for Israel raises the question of which will prevail, while certain key passages toward the end of the book give glimmers of hope that God's indignation will not burst the floodgates and destroy Israel. Thus, a consideration of these five emotions leaves the attentive reader on the edge of her seat, awaiting the book's conclusion. For this, we turn to chapter 6.

Chapter 6 attends to two key literary patterns: metaphorical polemics throughout the book and culmination and inversion in Hos 14. I argue that the book witnesses a change in strategy for the deployment of Hosea's polemical metaphors. The book begins with direct attacks on Yahweh's enemies and gradually transitions to appropriating the metaphors of Yahweh's enemies and applying them to Yahweh. In the beginning, Hosea's metaphors tend to be polemical in an overtly oppositional way. For

10. Conclusion: Faithful beyond Death 229

instance, following Baal is like whoring (cluster 1, Hos 4:10–16). As such, Baal is characterized as the "other man," Yahweh's overt adversary. But a gradual shift in the balance of strategy occurs, namely, toward metaphor *appropriation*. In the final cluster (Hos 14:4–9), it is Yahweh, not Baal, who brings fertility and flourishing, and Yahweh, not Asherah, who is the tree of life. It is as if Yahweh transitions to a strategy of "Anything you can do, I can do better." This strategy renders all of Yahweh's rivals not only inferior but unnecessary for Israel's life.

Chapter 6 also demonstrates that Hos 14 represents a crescendo of ultimate reversal to almost all that preceded it. This is not to say that Hos 14 undoes or renders void all the threats and sentencing that came before but that those things do not have the final say for Israel's future. I argue that virtually every single word of every metaphorical expression in Hos 14:4–9 is an inversion of some previous metaphor and that every divine emotion (except for love) is overturned. The end of Israel's story reverses all that came before. That is, even after death, there is life. The question remains: *Why* deploy the metaphors in this way?

Chapter 7 concerns the rhetorical purpose of the book, which is the desire to cause Israel to return—in a holistic sense—to Yahweh. Indeed, I contend that Hosean divine metaphors (even the whole discourse) cohere on the basis of this shared rhetorical purpose. After defining what I mean (and do not mean) by *repentance*, I very briefly surveyed six reasons for claiming that repentance is the rhetorical goal of the discourse. The real thrust of this chapter, though, comes in identifying eight distinct strategies for *how* Hosea deploys its metaphors for this purpose. In my view, the final strategy is the meta-strategy, or the cumulative results of all other strategies and all metaphors.

Hosea deploys hundreds of metaphors in a variety of ways (e.g., terrifying or wooing them, or subverting Yahweh's challengers) with the goal of provoking Israel to return to Yahweh *essentially by using metaphors to create a new reality*—a new social imagination, a new worldview—for Israel. This new reality is centered on a new picture of who their God is, because as far as Hosea is concerned, all of Israel's problems derive from their faulty understanding of Yahweh. Show them who Yahweh really is, so the thinking goes, and thereby Hosea can create a whole new society with a whole new set of possible—previously unthinkable—futures. The purpose of the varied and tensive metaphors is to destabilize Israel's perceptions of themselves and their deity and to recreate their worldview out of the ashes of the old in accordance with Hosea's proposed alternative, thereby procuring Israel's return to Yahweh. In other words, Hosea intends to change ancient Israelite society by changing their metaphors for God. Different divine metaphors may result in a different society.

These various emotional, literary, and rhetorical patterns discerned in part 2 are crucial contributions to a portrait of God in Hos 4–14. Their rhetorical purpose hinges on discerning Hosea's metaphorical depiction of Yahweh. Part 3 tied these threads together into a composite mosaic of God in order to answer the primary question driving this study. This involved synthesizing aspective and character portraits of the deity.

Chapter 8 introduced aspect theory through the works of Brunner-Traut and Hundley. An aspective approach is one that seeks to emphasize an adequate description of each aspect of a subject without concern to synthesize, summarize, or systematize. That is, an aspective approach seeks a full articulation of the *parts* without needing to account for the *whole*. Brunner-Traut and Hundley rightly claim that the ancient Near East reflects this kind of thinking in many ways, including in ancient Near Eastern god-talk. This is one explanation of why a book such as Hosea—which tends toward fragmentation rather than tight coherence of a modern Western variety—could be seen as viable in the ancient Near East. Any synthetic picture of Yahweh, therefore, must account for this fact and respect the variety of metaphors, resisting reductionism as did the ancient cultures from which the book arose.

I therefore emphasize the *variety* of all 103 metaphors studied in this book, considering how many source domains there are and what their cumulative metaphorical strength is in the book; how many are positive or negative metaphors; where the metaphors occur with respect to Hosea's three phases (accusation, sentencing, redemption); patterns between types of metaphors and their function in the text; and other such observations. One obvious conclusion is that no single image (a root or primary metaphor such as "husband" or "king") can account for all of Hosea's metaphors. In fact, the sum total of all proposed root metaphors that I have found accounts for less than half of all the metaphor domains used for God in Hos 4–14. Consistent with ancient Near Eastern divine portraits, Yahweh's metaphors are primarily anthropomorphic (about 80 percent). The most common domains are, in order, farmer, parent/father, and husband. Theriomorphic imagery of specifically *destructive* animals accounts for about 10 percent of the metaphors—when considered collectively, this is less than only the farmer and parent domains, and more common than the husband metaphor. Additionally, certain domains often align with

10. Conclusion: Faithful beyond Death

certain *uses*. The father/parent domain, for instance, is frequently used in contexts of historical retrospectives of Yahweh's past love and provision for child-Israel, while farmer metaphors usually witness to God's plans for Israel and subsequent disappointment.

A good portrait, though, does not simply present the physical data of its subject. It gives the viewer a feel for the character and internal life of its subject: their warmth or fear or anguish. Chapter 9 seeks to discern a characterization of Yahweh from the book's metaphors. While much could be and has been said about the character of Yahweh in Hosea, I have chosen to focus on five characteristics that arose from my study of the individual clusters (part 1) and the patterns among them (part 2). In answer to this book's primary question (Who is Yahweh in the metaphors of Hos 4–14?), I argue that Hos 4–14 metaphorically depicts a deity who is (1) unknowable yet knowable: the metaphors say something about Yahweh while simultaneously underscoring that he is beyond comprehensive knowing and therefore beyond Israel's ability to manipulate for their own benefit. This destabilizes their certainty in their own future, opening the possibility that they might return to Yahweh for security. Yahweh is also (2) emotionally engaged in Israel's life. One simply cannot walk away from the book of Hosea with the impression that God is aloof or indifferent regarding Israel's future and well-being; in everything he does, Hosea's deity is passionate. I argue as well that God's love is a primary personality trait, while God's anger is secondary to his personality. (3) God is deeply engaged in Israel's life, in the past, present, and future. Again, Israel does not know an abstract or uninvolved deity; their future remains in the hands of the same deity who has guided their past and now invites them to return in the present. Such historical engagement is driven by Yahweh's (4) demand for reciprocated allegiance as their sovereign. Yahweh claims to be the one who has always ruled over Israel, and he will tolerate no rivals for the devotion of his people. And finally, God (5) ultimately transcends Israel's lack of allegiance through unwavering loyalty to the people of Israel, even through and beyond death itself. Everything depends on this fifth characteristic of commitment.

Hosea's metaphors are deployed in order to provoke Israel's return to Yahweh by destabilizing and reinventing their worldview. At the core of Hosea's proposed new social imagination is a portrait of Yahweh centered on and arising from his fidelity to Israel. It is because Yahweh remains faithful to Israel through thick and thin that he expects a reciprocal kind of loyalty from Israel, one that does not fade away like the morning dew.

Chapter 9 thus argued that God's commitment to his people is what underlies the book's most prominent metaphor source domains (farmer, parent, and husband), all fifteen metaphor clusters identified in Hos 4–14, all four of the other divine characteristics I see arising from the metaphors (Yahweh's incomprehensible comprehensibility, passion, historical engagement with Israel, and sovereignty), and the rhetorical purpose of the book (getting Israel to return to Yahweh). God is in fact so loyal to Israel that they can trust him even through death (Hos 13) to bring them back to life on the other side (Hos 14). Thus, my central argument in this book is that the entire metaphorical portrait of Yahweh rests on and exists because of Yahweh's fidelity to Israel. Virtually everything in Hosea finds its raison d'être in Yahweh's enduring commitment to Israel.

In sum, the aim of this study is to discern a portrait of Yahweh from the diverse metaphors of Hos 4–14. It examines and integrates the 103 metaphors for God among 15 metaphor clusters in Hos 4–14 as an experiment in respecting the diversity of tensive metaphors while synthesizing a coherent divine characterization. In so doing, the project draws on resources from metaphor research, particularly the study of metaphor clustering, and develops a new approach to metaphorical theology that integrates this modern perspective on clustering with the ancient aspective approach to god-talk. My conclusion is that the metaphorical presentation of Yahweh in Hos 4–14 arises from and manifests God's unerring loyalty to Israel, even beyond death. The contributions of this volume to biblical studies are (1) methodological: a fresh *approach* to metaphorical theology; and (2) exegetical and theological: a fresh metaphorical theology of Hos 4–14. Contributing to metaphor research, it applies emerging metaphor cluster analysis to an ancient text (most such studies are currently on modern, mostly English, discourse). Additionally, examining Hosea's deployment of metaphors in light of their rhetorical purpose and theological content contributes to broader discussions on how *changing* metaphors (especially metaphors for God) can destabilize and reinvent a worldview and thereby perhaps reshape a society.

Appendix
Graphs of the Distribution of Divine Metaphors, Themes, and Emotions in Hosea 4–14

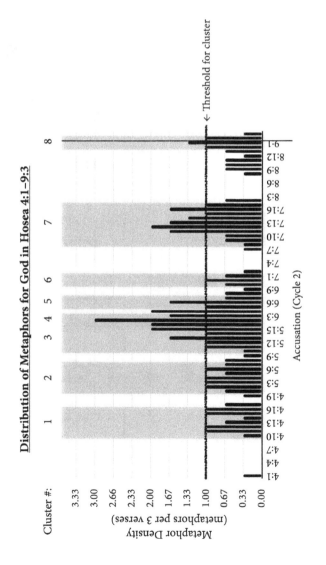

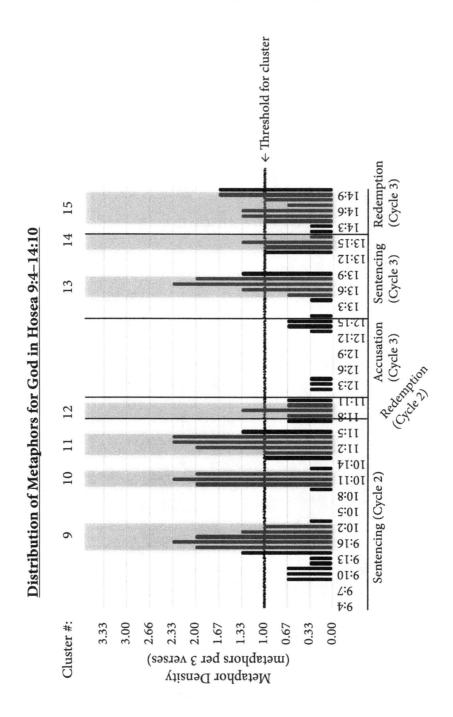

Bibliography

Aaron, David H. *Biblical Ambiguities: Metaphor, Semantics and Divine Imagery*. BRLAJ 4. Leiden: Brill, 2001.

Abma, Richtsje. *Bonds of Love: Methodic Studies of Prophetic Texts with Marriage Imagery (Isaiah 50:1-3 and 54:1-10, Hosea 1-3, Jeremiah 2-3)*. SSN. Assen: Van Gorcum, 1999.

Abu-Darwish, Mohammad Sanad, Célia Cabral, and Lígia Salgueiro. "Juniperus Phoenicea from Jordan." Pages 241-52 in *Medicinal and Aromatic Plants of the Middle-East*. Edited by Zohara Yaniv and Nativ Dudai. MAPW 2. Dordrecht: Springer Netherlands, 2014.

Adams, Karin. "Metaphor and Dissonance: A Reinterpretation of Hosea 4:13-14." *JBL* 127 (2008): 291-305.

Alexander, T. Desmond. *Exodus*. AOTC 2. London: Apollos, 2017.

Allen, Spencer L. "The Splintered Divine: A Study of Ištar, Baal, and Yahweh Divine Names and Divine Multiplicity in the Ancient Near East." PhD diss., University of Pennsylvania, 2011.

Alonso Schökel, Luis. *A Manual of Hebrew Poetics*. SubBi 11. Rome: Pontifical Biblical Institute, 1988.

Alt, Albrecht. "Hosea 5,8-6,6: Ein Krieg und seine Folgen in prophetischer Beleuchtung." Pages 163-87 in *Kleine Schriften zur Geschichte des Volkes Israel*. Vol. 2. Munich: Beck, 1953.

Alter, Robert. *The Art of Biblical Narrative*. 2nd ed. New York: Basic, 2011.

———. *The Art of Biblical Poetry*. Rev. ed. New York: Basic, 2011.

Andersen, Francis I., and David Noel Freedman. *Hosea: A New Translation*. AB 24. Garden City, NY: Doubleday, 1980.

Anderson, Gary A. *Sin: A History*. New Haven: Yale University Press, 2010.

Anderson, James S. *Monotheism and Yahweh's Appropriation of Baal*. LHBOTS 617. London: T&T Clark, 2015.

Anderson, John E. *Jacob and the Divine Trickster: A Theology of Deception and Yhwh's Fidelity to the Ancestral Promise in the Jacob Cycle*. SLTHS 5. Winona Lake, IN: Eisenbrauns, 2011.

Arnold, Bill T., and John H. Choi. *A Guide to Biblical Hebrew Syntax*. New York: Cambridge University Press, 2003.

Arnold, Patrick M. "Hosea and the Sin of Gibeah." *CBQ* 51 (1989): 447–60.

Arthurs, Jeffrey D. *Preaching as Reminding: Stirring Memory in an Age of Forgetfulness*. Downers Grove, IL: IVP Academic, 2017.

Assante, Julia. *Prostitutes and Courtesans in the Ancient World*. Edited by Christopher A. Faraone and Laura McClure. WSC. Madison: University of Wisconsin Press, 2006.

Austin, Benjamin M. *Plant Metaphors in the Old Greek of Isaiah*. SCS 69. Atlanta: SBL Press, 2019.

Austin, John L. *How to Do Things with Words*. 2nd rev. ed. Edited by James O. Urmson and Marina Sbisà. Cambridge: Harvard University Press, 1975.

Avis, Paul. *God and the Creative Imagination: Metaphor, Symbol and Myth in Religion and Theology*. London: Routledge, 1999.

Bar-Efrat, Shimon. *Narrative Art in the Bible*. JSOTSup 70. Sheffield: Almond, 1989.

Barré, Michael L. "Hearts, Beds, and Repentance in Psalm 4,5 and Hosea 7,14." *Bib* 76 (1995): 53–62.

———. "New Light on the Interpretation of Hosea 6:2." *VT* 28 (1978): 129–41.

Barrett, Lisa Feldman. *How Emotions Are Made: The Secret Life of the Brain*. Boston: Houghton Mifflin Harcourt, 2017.

Basson, Alec. "A Few Metaphorical Source Domains for Emotions in the Old Testament." *Scriptura* 100 (2009): 121–28.

Baumann, Gerlinde. *Love and Violence: Marriage as Metaphor for the Relationship between Yhwh and Israel in the Prophetic Books*. Translated by Linda M. Maloney. Collegeville, MN: Glazier, 2003.

Bechtel, Lyn M. "The Metaphors of 'Canaanite' and 'Baal' in Hosea." Pages 203–15 in *Inspired Speech: Prophecy in the Ancient Near East; Essays in Honor of Herbert H. Huffmon*. Edited by Louis Stulman and John Kaltner. JSOTSup 378. London: T&T Clark, 2004.

———. "Shame as a Sanction of Social Control in Biblical Israel: Judicial, Political, and Social Shaming." *JSOT* 16 (1991): 47–76.

Ben Zvi, Ehud. *Hosea*. FOTL. Grand Rapids: Eerdmans, 2005.

———. "Reading Hosea and Imagining Yhwh." *HBT* 30 (2008): 43–57.

Bergen, Robert D. "Calling Forth Yahweh's Curses: Hosea's Judgment of Israel in 8:1–10:15." *CTR* 7 (1993): 39–50.

Berggren, Douglas. "The Use and Abuse of Metaphor." *RM* 16 (1962): 237–58.

Bergmann, Claudia D. "We Have Seen the Enemy, and He Is Only a 'She': The Portrayal of Warriors as Women." *CBQ* 69 (2007): 651–72.

Berlin, Adele. *The Dynamics of Biblical Parallelism*. 2nd ed. Grand Rapids: Eerdmans, 2007.

———. "On Reading Biblical Poetry: The Role of Metaphor." Pages 25–36 in *Congress Volume: Cambridge, 1995*. Edited by John A. Emerton. VTSup 66. Leiden: Brill, 1997.

———. *Poetics and Interpretation of Biblical Narrative*. Winona Lake, IN: Eisenbrauns, 1994.

Bird, Phyllis A. *Harlot or Holy Woman? A Study of Hebrew Qedešah*. University Park, PA: Eisenbrauns, 2019.

———. "'To Play the Harlot': An Inquiry into an Old Testament Metaphor." Pages 75–94 in *Gender and Difference in Ancient Israel*. Edited by Peggy Day. Minneapolis: Fortress, 1989.

Black, Max. "More about Metaphor." Pages 19–41 in *Metaphor and Thought*. Edited by Andrew Ortony. 2nd ed. Cambridge: Cambridge University Press, 1993.

Blackburn, W. Ross. *The God Who Makes Himself Known: The Missionary Heart of the Book of Exodus*. NSBT 28. Downers Grove, IL: InterVarsity Press, 2012.

Blair, Merryl. "God Is an Earthquake: Destabilising Metaphor in Hosea 11." *ABR* 55 (2007): 1–12.

Blum, Erhard. "Once Again: Hosea and the Pentateuchal Traditions." Pages 81–94 in *From Author to Copyist: Essays on the Composition, Redaction, and Transmission of the Hebrew Bible in Honor of Zipi Talshir*. Edited by Cana Werman. Winona Lake, IN: Eisenbrauns, 2015.

Blumenthal, David R. *Facing the Abusing God: A Theology of Protest*. Louisville: Westminster John Knox, 1993.

Boda, Mark J. "The Priceless Gain of Penitence: From Communal Lament to Penitential Prayer in the 'Exilic' Liturgy of Israel." *HBT* 25 (2003): 51–75.

———. "Repentance." *DOTPr*, 664–71.

———. *"Return to Me": A Biblical Theology of Repentance*. Downers Grove, IL: IVP Academic, 2015.

———. *A Severe Mercy: Sin and Its Remedy in the Old Testament*. SLTHS 1. Winona Lake, IN: Eisenbrauns, 2009.

Boda, Mark J., and Gordon T. Smith, eds. *Repentance in Christian Theology*. Collegeville, MN: Glazier, 2006.

Booth, Wayne C. "Metaphor as Rhetoric: The Problem of Evaluation." Pages 47–70 in *On Metaphor*. Edited by Sheldon Sacks. Chicago: University of Chicago Press, 1979.

Bos, James M. *Reconsidering the Date and Provenance of the Book of Hosea: The Case for Persian-Period Yehud*. LHBOTS 580. London: Bloomsbury T&T Clark, 2013.

Boshoff, Willem. "Who Let Grain, Grapes and Olives Grow? Hosea's Polemics against the Yahwists of Israel." Pages 265–75 in *Religious Polemics in Context: Papers Presented to the Second International Conference of the Leiden Institute for the Study of Religions (LISOR) Held at Leiden, 27–28 April, 2000*. Edited by Theo L. Hettema and Arie van der Kooij. STR 11. Assen: Van Gorcum, 2004.

Botta, Alejandro F. "Hated by the Gods and Your Spouse: Legal Use of שנא in Elephantine and Its Ancient Near Eastern Context." Pages 105–28 in *Law and Religion in the Eastern Mediterranean: From Antiquity to Early Islam*. Edited by Anselm C. Hagedorn and Reinhard G. Kratz. Oxford: Oxford University Press, 2013.

Braaten, Laurie J. "Parent-Child Imagery in Hosea (Marriage, Legitimacy, Adoption, Disownment)." PhD diss., Boston University, 1987.

Braude, William G. *Pesikta Rabbati: Discourses for Feasts, Fasts, and Special Sabbaths*. 2 vols. New Haven: Yale University Press, 1968.

Brettler, Marc Zvi. "Incompatible Metaphors for YHWH in Isaiah 40–66." *JSOT* 23 (1998): 97–120.

Brown, William P. *Seeing the Psalms: A Theology of Metaphor*. Louisville: Westminster John Knox, 2002.

Brueggemann, Walter. "Preaching a Sub-version." *ThTo* 55 (1998): 195–212.

———. *The Prophetic Imagination*. 2nd ed. Minneapolis: Fortress, 2001.

———. "The Recovering God of Hosea." *HBT* 30 (2008): 5–20.

———. "Symmetry and Extremity in the Images of YHWH." Pages 241–57 in *The Blackwell Companion to the Hebrew Bible*. Edited by Leo G. Perdue. Malden, MA: Blackwell, 2001.

———. *Theology of the Old Testament: Testimony, Dispute, Advocacy*. Minneapolis: Fortress, 1997.

———. *Tradition for Crisis: A Study in Hosea*. Richmond, VA: John Knox, 1968.

———. "The 'Uncared for' Now Cared for (Jer 30:12–17): A Methodological Consideration." *JBL* 104 (1985): 419–28.
Brunner-Traut, Emma. "Epilogue: Aspective." Pages 421–48 in *Principles of Egyptian Art*. Edited by Emma Brunner-Traut and John Baines. Translated by John Baines. Reprint with revisions, Oxford: Griffith Institute, 1986.
———. *Frühformen des Erkennens: Am Beispiel Altägyptens*. Darmstadt: Wissenschaftliche Buchgesellschaft, 1990.
Bucher, Christina. "The Origin and Meaning of ZNH Terminology in the Book of Hosea." PhD diss., Claremont Graduate School, 1988.
Budin, Stephanie Lynn. *The Myth of Sacred Prostitution in Antiquity*. New York: Cambridge University Press, 2008.
Burkholder, Thomas R., and David Henry. "Criticism of Metaphor." Pages 97–115 in *Rhetorical Criticism: Perspectives in Action*. Edited by Jim A. Kuypers. LSPC. Lanham, MD: Lexington, 2009.
Butterworth, Mike. "נחם." *NIDOTTE* 3:81–83.
Cameron, Lynne. "Confrontation or Complementarity? Metaphor in Language Use and Cognitive Metaphor Theory." *ARCL* 5 (2007): 107–35.
———. "Metaphor and Talk." Pages 197–211 in *The Cambridge Handbook of Metaphor and Thought*. Edited by Raymond W. Gibbs Jr. New York: Cambridge University Press, 2008.
———. "Metaphors and Discourse Activity." Pages 147–60 in *Metaphor Analysis: Research Practice in Applied Linguistics, Social Sciences and the Humanities*. Edited by Lynne Cameron and Robert Maslen. London: Equinox, 2010.
———. "What Is Metaphor and Why Does It Matter?" Pages 3–25 in *Metaphor Analysis: Research Practice in Applied Linguistics, Social Sciences and the Humanities*. Edited by Lynne Cameron and Robert Maslen. London: Equinox, 2010.
Cameron, Lynne, Graham Low, and Robert Maslen. "Finding Systematicity in Metaphor Use." Pages 116–46 in *Metaphor Analysis: Research Practice in Applied Linguistics, Social Sciences and the Humanities*. Edited by Lynne Cameron and Robert Maslen. London: Equinox, 2010.
Cameron, Lynne, and Robert Maslen. "Identifying Metaphors in Discourse Data." Pages 97–115 in *Metaphor Analysis: Research Practice in Applied Linguistics, Social Sciences and the Humanities*. Edited by Lynne Cameron and Robert Maslen. London: Equinox, 2010.

Cameron, Lynne, and Juurd H. Stelma. "Metaphor Clusters in Discourse." *JAL* 1 (2004): 107–36.

Carew, M. Douglas. "Hosea." Pages 1013–26 in *Africa Bible Commentary: A One-Volume Commentary Written by Seventy African Scholars*. Edited by Tokunboh Adeyemo. Grand Rapids: Zondervan, 2006.

———. "To Know or Not to Know: Hosea's Use of *yd*ʿ/*d*ʿ*t*." Pages 77–87 in *The Old Testament in the Life of God's People: Essays in Honor of Elmer A. Martens*. Edited by Jon Isaak. Winona Lake, IN: Eisenbrauns, 2009.

Carpenter, Eugene, and Michael A. Grisanti. "נדב." *NIDOTTE* 3:31–32.

Carroll R., M. Daniel. "Hosea." Pages 213–305 in *The Expositor's Bible Commentary*. Vol. 8. Rev. ed. Edited by Tremper Longman III and David E. Garland. Grand Rapids: Zondervan, 2008.

———. "The Prophetic Denunciation of Religion in Hosea 4–7." *CTR* 7 (1993): 15–38.

Carver, Terrell, and Jernej Pikalo, eds. *Political Language and Metaphor: Interpreting and Changing the World*. RIPT 30. London: Routledge, 2011.

Cathcart, Kevin J., and Robert P. Gordon. *The Targum of the Minor Prophets*. Edited by Martin McNamara. ArBib 14. Collegeville, MN: Liturgical Press, 1997.

Catlett, Michael Lee. "Reversals in Hosea: A Literary Analysis." PhD diss., Emory University, 1988.

Chalmers, Ronald Scott. *The Struggle of Yahweh and El for Hosea's Israel*. HMS 11. Sheffield: Sheffield Phoenix, 2008.

———. "Who Is the Real El? A Reconstruction of the Prophet's Polemic in Hosea 12:5a." *CBQ* 68 (2006): 611–30.

Chapman, Cynthia R. *The Gendered Language of Warfare in the Israelite-Assyrian Encounter*. HSM 62. Winona Lake, IN: Eisenbrauns, 2004.

Charpin, Dominique. *La vie méconnue des temples mésopotamiens*. Paris: Les Belles Lettres, 2017.

Childs, Brevard S. *The Book of Exodus: A Critical, Theological Commentary*. OTL. Louisville: Westminster John Knox, 1974.

———. *Introduction to the Old Testament as Scripture*. Philadelphia: Fortress, 1979.

Chmiel, Jerzy. "Un kérygme prophétique ou une liturgie de repentance en Osée 6,1–6?" *AnCrac* 15 (1983): 99–104.

Cho, Paul K.-K. *Myth, History, and Metaphor in the Hebrew Bible*. Cambridge: Cambridge University Press, 2019.

Clements, Ronald E. "Understanding the Book of Hosea." *RevExp* 72 (1975): 405–23.

Clines, David J. A., and David M. Gunn. "'You Tried to Persuade Me' and 'Violence! Outrage!' in Jeremiah xx 7–8." *VT* 28 (1978): 20–27.

Cohen, Ted. "Metaphor, Feeling, and Narrative." *PL* 21 (1997): 223–44.

———. *Thinking of Others: On the Talent for Metaphor*. PMP. Princeton: Princeton University Press, 2008.

Conrad, J. "נדב." *TDOT* 9:219–26.

Cooper, Jerrold S. "The Job of Sex: The Social and Economic Role of Prostitutes in Ancient Mesopotamia." Pages 209–27 in *The Role of Women in Work and Society in the Ancient Near East*. Edited by Brigitte Lion and Cécile Michel. SANER 13. Berlin: de Gruyter, 2016.

Coote, Robert B. "Hos 14:8: They Who Are Filled with Grain Shall Live." *JBL* 93 (1974): 161–73.

Corts, Daniel P., and Kristina Meyers. "Conceptual Clusters in Figurative Language Production." *JPR* 31 (2002): 391–408.

Cottrill, Amy C. "A Reading of Ehud and Jael through the Lens of Affect Theory." *BibInt* 22 (2014): 430–49.

Couturier, Guy. "Yahweh et les déesses cananéennes en Osée 14,9." Pages 245–64 in *Communion et réunion: Mélanges Jean-Marie Roger Tillard*. Leuven: Leuven University Press, 1995.

Craghan, John F. "Book of Hosea: A Survey of Recent Literature on the First of the Minor Prophets." *BTB* 1 (1971): 145–70.

Crisp, Peter, Raymond Gibbs, Alice Deignan, Graham Low, Gerard Steen, Lynne Cameron, Elena Semino, Joe Grady, Alan Cienki, and Zoltán Kövecses. "MIP: A Method for Identifying Metaphorically Used Words in Discourse." *MS* 22 (2007): 1–39.

Cross, Frank Moore. *From Epic to Canon: History and Literature in Ancient Israel*. Baltimore: Johns Hopkins University Press, 2000.

Cruz, Juan. *Who Is like Yahweh? A Study of Divine Metaphors in the Book of Micah*. FRLANT 263. Göttingen: Vandenhoeck & Ruprecht, 2016.

Daniels, Dwight R. *Hosea and Salvation History: The Early Traditions of Israel in the Prophecy of Hosea*. BZAW 191. Berlin: de Gruyter, 1990.

———. "Is There a 'Prophetic Lawsuit' Genre." *ZAW* 99 (1987): 339–60.

Davies, Graham I. *Hosea*. NCB. Grand Rapids: Eerdmans, 1992.

———. *Hosea*. OTG 25. Sheffield: Sheffield Academic, 1993.

Day, John. "Asherah." *ABD* 1:483–87.

———. "Asherah in the Hebrew Bible and Northwest Semitic Literature." *JBL* 105 (1986): 385–408.

———. "Baal." *ABD* 1:545–49.

———. "A Case of Inner Scriptural Interpretation: The Dependence of Isaiah XXVI.13–XXVII.11 on Hosea XIII.4–XIV.10 (Eng. 9) and Its Relevance to Some Theories of the Redaction of the 'Isaiah Apocalypse.'" *JTS* 31 (1980): 309–19.

———. "Hosea and the Baal Cult." Pages 202–24 in *Prophecy and the Prophets in Ancient Israel*. Edited by John Day. LHBOTS 531. New York: T&T Clark, 2010.

———. *Yahweh and the Gods and Goddesses of Canaan*. JSOTSup 265. London: Sheffield Academic, 2002.

Day, Peggy. "The Bitch Had It Coming to Her: Rhetoric and Interpretation in Ezekiel 16." *BibInt* 8 (2000): 231–54.

———. "A Prostitute Unlike Women: Whoring as Metaphoric Vehicle for Foreign Alliances." Pages 167–73 in *Israel's Prophets and Israel's Past: Essays on the Relationship of Prophetic Texts and Israelite History in Honor of John H. Hayes*. Edited by Megan Bishop Moore and Brad E. Kelle. LHBOTS 446. New York: T&T Clark, 2006.

De Andrado, Paba Nidhani. "Ḥesed and Sacrifice: The Prophetic Critique in Hosea." *CBQ* 78 (2016): 47–67.

Dearman, J. Andrew. "Baal in Israel: The Contribution of Some Place Names and Personal Names to an Understanding of Early Israelite Religion." Pages 173–91 in *History and Interpretation: Essays in Honour of John H. Hayes*. Edited by M. Patrick Graham, William P. Brown, and Jeffrey K. Kuan. JSOTSup 173. Sheffield: JSOT, 1993.

———. *The Book of Hosea*. NICOT. Grand Rapids: Eerdmans, 2010.

———. "Interpreting the Religious Polemics against Baal and the Baalim in the Book of Hosea." *OTE* 14 (2001): 9–25.

———. "YHWH's House: Gender Roles and Metaphors for Israel in Hosea." *JNSL* 25 (1999): 97–108.

DeGrado, Jessie. "The Qdesha in Hosea 4:14: Putting the (Myth of the) Sacred Prostitute to Bed." *VT* 68 (2018): 8–40.

Dempsey, Carol J. *The Prophets: A Liberation-Critical Reading*. Minneapolis: Fortress, 2000.

———. "'Turn Back, O People': Repentance in the Latter Prophets." Pages 47–66 in *Repentance in Christian Theology*. Edited by Mark J. Boda and Gordon T. Smith. Collegeville, MN: Glazier, 2006.

DeRoche, Michael. "The Reversal of Creation in Hosea." *VT* 31 (1981): 400–409.

———. "Yahweh's *Rib* against Israel: A Reassessment of the So-Called 'Prophetic Lawsuit' in the Preexilic Prophets." *JBL* 102 (1983): 563–74.

Dietrich, Erich Kurt. *Die Umkehr: (Bekehrung und Busse) im Alten Testament und im Judentum bei besonderer Berücksichtigung der neutestamentlichen Zeit*. Stuttgart: Kohlhammer, 1936.

Dietrich, Manfried, and Oswald Loretz. "Baal RPU in KTU 1.108; 1.113 und nach 1.17 VI 25–33." *UF* 12 (1980): 171–82.

———. *Jahwe und Seine Aschera: Anthropomorphes Kultbild in Mesopotamien, Ugarit und Israel—Das Biblische Bilderverbot*. UBL 9. Münster: Ugarit-Verlag, 1992.

Donoghue, Denis. *Metaphor*. Cambridge: Harvard University Press, 2014.

Duby, Steven J. "'For I Am God, Not a Man': Divine Repentance and the Creator-Creature Distinction." *JTI* 12 (2018): 149–69.

Duhm, Bernhard. *Die zwölf Propheten, in den Versmassen der Urschrift übersetzt*. Tübingen: Mohr Siebeck, 1910.

Durand, Emmanuel. "God's Holiness: A Reappraisal of Transcendence." *ModTheo* 34 (2018): 419–33.

Ehrlich, Arnold B. *Randglossen zur Hebräischen Bibel*. Vol. 5. Leipzig: Hinrichs, 1912.

Eichrodt, Walther. "'The Holy One in Your Midst': The Theology of Hosea." *Int* 15 (1961): 259–73.

Eidevall, Göran. *Grapes in the Desert: Metaphors, Models, and Themes in Hosea 4–14*. ConBOT 43. Stockholm: Almqvist & Wiksell, 1996.

———. "Lions and Birds as Literature: Some Notes on Isaiah 31 and Hosea 11." *SJOT* 7 (1993): 78–87.

———. "Review of 'Metaphors and Similes for Yahweh in Hosea 14:2–9 (1–8): A Study of Hoseanic Pictorial Language.'" *Bib* 81 (2000): 583–85.

Emmerson, Grace I. "Fertility Goddess in Hosea 4:17–19." *VT* 24 (1974): 492–97.

———. *Hosea: An Israelite Prophet in Judean Perspective*. Sheffield: JSOT, 1984.

———. "Structure and Meaning of Hosea 8:1–3." *VT* 25 (1975): 700–710.

Erlandsson, Seth. "בגד." *TDOT* 1:470–73.

Fabry, Heinz-Josef. "נחם." *TDOT* 9:340–55.

Farjon, Aljos. *Monograph of Cupressaceae and Sciadopitys*. Surrey, UK: Royal Botanic Gardens, Kew, 2000.

Fisch, Harold. *Poetry with a Purpose: Biblical Poetics and Interpretation*. Bloomington: Indiana University Press, 1988.

Fitzgerald, Aloysius. *The Lord of the East Wind*. CBQMS 34. Washington, DC: Catholic Biblical Association of America, 2002.

Fontaine, Carole R. "Hosea." Pages 40–59 in *A Feminist Companion to the Latter Prophets*. Edited by Athalya Brenner. FCB 8. Sheffield: Sheffield Academic, 1995.

Frevel, Christian. *Aschera und der Ausschließlichkeitsanspruch YHWHs*. Vol. 1. BBB 94.1. Weinheim: Beltz Athenäum Verlag, 1995.

Gadamer, Hans-Georg. *Truth and Method*. 2nd rev. ed. Translated by Joel Weinsheimer and Donald G. Marshall. London: Continuum, 2004.

Galambush, Julie. *Jerusalem in the Book of Ezekiel: The City as Yahweh's Wife*. SBLDS 130. Atlanta: Scholars Press, 1992.

Gangloff, Frédéric. "'Je suis son 'Anat et son 'Ašerâh' (Os 14,9)." *ETL* 74 (1998): 373–85.

Gangloff, Frédéric, and Jean-Claude Haelewyck. "Osée 4,17–19: Un marzeah en l'honneur de la déesee 'Anat?" *ETL* 71 (1995): 370–82.

Garrett, Duane A. *Hosea, Joel*. NAC 19A. Nashville: Holman Reference, 1997.

Gault, Brian. "Avenging Husband and Redeeming Lover? Opposing Portraits of God in Hosea." *JETS* 60 (2017): 489–509.

Gibbs, Raymond W., Jr. "Metaphor, Language, and Dynamic Systems." Pages 56–69 in *The Routledge Handbook of Metaphor and Language*. Edited by Elena Semino and Zsófia Demjén. Abingdon: Routledge, 2017.

———. *Metaphor Wars: Conceptual Metaphors in Human Life*. Cambridge: Cambridge University Press, 2017.

———. "Why Do Some People Dislike Conceptual Metaphor Theory?" *CS* 5 (2009): 14–36.

Glenny, W. Edward. *Hosea: A Commentary Based on Hosea in Codex Vaticanus*. SeptCS. Leiden: Brill, 2013.

Glucksberg, Sam. *Understanding Figurative Language: From Metaphor to Idioms*. Oxford: Oxford University Press, 2001.

Goldingay, John. *The First Testament: A New Translation*. Downers Grove, IL: InterVarsity Press, 2018.

———. *Israel's Faith*. Vol. 2 of *Old Testament Theology*. Downers Grove, IL: IVP Academic, 2006.

Goldman, M. D. "The Real Interpretation of Hosea XI.3." *ABR* 4 (1954): 91–92.

Good, Edwin M. "The Composition of Hosea." *SEÅ* 31 (1966): 21–63.

———. "Hosea 5:8–6:6: An Alternative to Alt." *JBL* 85 (1966): 273–86.

Gordis, Robert. "Studies in Hebrew Roots of Contrasted Meanings." *JQR* 27 (1936): 33.

Gosse, Bernard. "L'influence du livre des Proverbes sur le livre d'Osée, en relation avec les livres de Jérémie et d'Isaïe." *OTE* 28 (2015): 113–20.

Gray, Alison Ruth. *Psalm 18 in Words and Pictures: A Reading through Metaphor*. BibInt 127. Leiden: Brill, 2014.

Green, Alberto R. W. *The Storm-God in the Ancient Near East*. BibJudStud 8. Winona Lake, IN: Eisenbrauns, 2003.

Greenstein, Edward L. "The God of Israel and the Gods of Canaan: How Different Were They?" Pages 47–58 in *Proceedings of the Twelfth World Congress of Jewish Studies: Jerusalem, July 29–August 5, 1997; Division A: The Bible and Its World*. Edited by Ron Margolin. Jerusalem: World Union of Jewish Studies, 1999.

Gregg, Melissa, and Gregory J. Seigworth. "An Inventory of Shimmers." Pages 1–25 in *The Affect Theory Reader*. Edited by Melissa Gregg and Gregory J. Seigworth. Durham, NC: Duke University Press, 2010.

Grondin, Jean. *Introduction to Philosophical Hermeneutics*. Translated by Joel Weinsheimer. New Haven: Yale University Press, 1997.

Groß, Heinrich. "Das Hohelied der Liebe Gottes: Zur Theologie von Hosea 11." Pages 83–91 in *Mysterium der Gnade: Festschrift für Johann Auer*. Edited by Heribert Roßmann and Joseph Ratzinger. Regensburg: Pustet, 1975.

Grossberg, Daniel. *Centripetal and Centrifugal Structures in Biblical Poetry*. SBLMS 39. Atlanta: Scholars Press, 1989.

Gruber, Mayer I. *Hosea: A Textual Commentary*. LHBOTS 653. New York: T&T Clark, 2017.

Habig, Brian C. "Hosea 6:7 Revisited." *Presb* 42 (2016): 4–20.

Haddox, Susan E. "(E)Masculinity in Hosea's Political Rhetoric." Pages 174–200 in *Israel's Prophets and Israel's Past: Essays on the Relationship of Prophetic Texts and Israelite History in Honor of John H. Hayes*. Edited by Megan Bishop Moore and Brad E. Kelle. LHBOTS 446. New York: T&T Clark, 2006.

———. *Metaphor and Masculinity in Hosea*. StBL 141. New York: Lang, 2011.

Hadjiev, Tchavdar S. "Adultery, Shame, and Sexual Pollution in Ancient Israel and in Hosea: A Response to Joshua Moon." *JSOT* 41 (2016): 221–36.

———. "Honor and Shame." *DOTPr*, 333–38.

Hadley, Judith M. *The Cult of Asherah in Ancient Israel and Judah: Evidence for a Hebrew Goddess*. UCOP 57. Cambridge: Cambridge University Press, 2000.

Hamilton, Mark W. "History among the Junipers: Hosea 14:2–10 as Metahistoriography." *BZ* 63 (2019): 105–16.

Harper, William R. *A Critical and Exegetical Commentary on Amos and Hosea*. ICC. Edinburgh: T&T Clark, 1905.

Harshav, Benjamin. *Explorations in Poetics*. Stanford, CA: Stanford University Press, 2007.

Hartsfield, Wallace. "Hosea." Pages 164–68 in *The Africana Bible: Reading Israel's Scriptures from Africa and the African Diaspora*. Edited by Hugh R. Page Jr., Randall C. Bailey, Valerie Bridgeman, Stacy Davis, Cheryl Kirk-Duggan, Madipoane Masenya, Nathaniel Samuel Murrell, and Rodney S. Sadler Jr. Minneapolis: Fortress, 2009.

Hausmann, Jutta. *Studien zum Menschenbild der älteren Weisheit (Spr 10ff.)*. FAT 7. Tübingen: Mohr Siebeck, 1995.

Hawley, Lance R. *Metaphor Competition in the Book of Job*. JAJSup 26. Göttingen: Vandenhoeck & Ruprecht, 2018.

Hayes, Katherine Murphey. *"The Earth Mourns": Prophetic Metaphor and Oral Aesthetic*. AcBib 8. Atlanta: Society of Biblical Literature, 2002.

Healey, John F. "Dew." *DDD*, 249–50.

———. "Mot." *DDD*, 598–603.

Hecke, Pierre van. "Conceptual Blending: A Recent Approach to Metaphor Illustrated with the Pastoral Metaphor in Hos 4,16." Pages 215–31 in *Metaphor in the Hebrew Bible*. Edited by Pierre van Hecke. BETL 187. Leuven: Leuven University Press, 2005.

———. "'For I Will Be like a Lion to Ephraim': Leonine Metaphors in the Twelve Prophets." Pages 387–402 in *The Books of the Twelve Prophets: Minor Prophets, Major Theologies*. Edited by Heinz-Josef Fabry. BETL 295. Leuven: Peeters, 2018.

Herrmann, Wolfgang. "Baal." *DDD*, 132–39.

Heschel, Abraham. *The Prophets*. New York: Harper & Row, 1962.

Hess, Richard S. *The Old Testament: A Historical, Theological, and Critical Introduction*. Grand Rapids: Baker Academic, 2016.

Hoffmeyer, Jeffrey H. "Covenant and Creation: Hosea 4:1–3." *RevExp* 102 (2005): 143–51.

Holt, Else K. *Prophesying the Past: The Use of Israel's History in the Book of Hosea*. JSOTSup 194. Sheffield: Sheffield Academic, 1995.

Hong, Koog-Pyoung, Karen Jobes, Timothy H. Lim, Isaac Gottlieb, Meira Polliack, Nehamit Pery, Joseph Davis, Martin Heimbucher, Theresa Krier, and Peter T. Chattaway. "Hosea (Book and Person)." *EBR* 12:425–45.

Hong, Seong-Hyuk. *The Metaphor of Illness and Healing in Hosea and Its Significance in the Socio-economic Context of Eighth-Century Israel and Judah*. StBL 95. New York: Lang, 2006.

Houston, Walter J. "What Did the Prophets Think They Were Doing? Speech Acts and Prophetic Discourse in the Old Testament." *BibInt* 1 (1993): 167–88.

Hubbard, David Allan. *Hosea*. TOTC. Downers Grove, IL: InterVarsity Press, 2009.

Hugenberger, Gordon P. *Marriage as a Covenant: Biblical Law and Ethics as Developed from Malachi*. BSL. Grand Rapids: Baker, 1994.

Humbert, Paul. "En marge du dictionnaire hébraïque." *ZAW* 62 (1949): 199–207.

Hundley, Michael B. "Here a God, There a God: An Examination of the Divine in Ancient Mesopotamia." *AoF* 40 (2013): 68–107.

Hutton, Jeremy, and Safwat Marzouk. "The Morphology of the tG-Stem in Hebrew and *Tirgaltî* in Hos 11:3." *JHS* 12 (2012): 1–41.

Ibn Ezra, Abraham ben Meïr. *The Commentary of Rabbi Abraham Ibn Ezra on Hosea*. Translated by Abe Lipshitz. New York: Sepher-Hermon, 1988.

Irvine, Stuart A. "Hosea." Pages 399–410 in *The Oxford Handbook of the Minor Prophets*. Edited by Julia M. O'Brien. New York: Oxford University Press, 2021.

———. "Relating Prophets and History: An Example from Hosea 13." Pages 158–66 in *Israel's Prophets and Israel's Past: Essays on the Relationship of Prophetic Texts and Israelite History in Honor of John H. Hayes*. Edited by Megan Bishop Moore and Brad E. Kelle. LHBOTS 446. New York: T&T Clark, 2006.

Isbell, Charles D. "The Divine Name אהיה as a Symbol of Presence in Israelite Tradition." *HAR* 2 (1978): 101–18.

Jacob, Edmond. "Osée." Pages 7–98 in *Osée, Joël, Abdias, Jonas, Amos*. CAT 11a. Neuchâtel: Delachaux & Niestlé, 1965.

Jacobs, Mignon R. "YHWH's Call for Israel's 'Return': Command, Invitation, or Threat." *HBT* 32 (2010): 17–32.

Janzen, J. Gerald. "Metaphor and Reality in Hosea 11." *Semeia* 24 (1982): 7–44.

Jeremias, Jörg. "Der Begriff 'Baal' im Hoseabuch und seine Wirkungsgeschichte." Pages 441–62 in *Ein Gott allein? JHWH-Verehrung und biblischer Monotheismus im Kontext der israelitischen und altorientalischen Religionsgeschichte*. Edited by Walter Dietrich and Martin A. Klopfenstein. Freiburg: Universitätsverlag, 1994.

———. *Der Prophet Hosea*. ATD 24/1. Göttingen: Vandenhoeck & Ruprecht, 1983.

———. *Die Reue Gottes: Aspekte alttestamentlicher Gottesvorstellung*. 2nd ed. BibThSt 31. Neukirchen-Vluyn: Neukirchener, 1997.

———. "'Ich bin wie ein Löwe für Efraim …' (Hos 5,14): … Aktualität und Allgemeingültigkeit im prophetischen Reden von Gott am Beispiel von Hos 5,8–14." Pages 75–95 in *"Ich will euer Gott werden": Beispiele biblischen Redens von Gott*. Edited by Norbert Lohfink. SBS 100. Stuttgart: Katholisches Bibelwerk, 1981.

———. "Zur Eschatologie des Hoseabuches." Pages 217–34 in *Die Botschaft und die Boten: Festschrift für Hans Walter Wolff zum 70. Geburtstag*. Edited by Jörg Jeremias and Lothar Perlitt. Neukirchen-Vluyn: Neukirchener, 1981.

Jerome. *Commentaries on the Twelve Prophets*. Edited by Thomas P. Scheck. Vol. 2. ACT. Downers Grove, IL: IVP Academic, 2017.

Johnson, Luke Timothy. "Imagining the World Scripture Imagines." *ModTheo* 14 (1998): 165–80.

Johnson, Mark. "Introduction: Metaphor in the Philosophical Tradition." Pages 3–47 in *Philosophical Perspectives on Metaphor*. Edited by Mark Johnson. Minneapolis: University of Minnesota Press, 1981.

———. "Metaphor: An Overview." Pages 208–12 in *Encyclopedia of Aesthetics*. Vol. 2. Edited by Michael Kelly. New York: Oxford University Press, 1998.

Joode, Johan de. *Metaphorical Landscapes and the Theology of the Book of Job*. VTSup 179. Leiden: Brill, 2018.

Kakkanattu, Joy Philip. *God's Enduring Love in the Book of Hosea: A Synchronic and Diachronic Analysis of Hosea 11:1–11*. FAT 2/14. Tübingen: Mohr Siebeck, 2006.

Kaplan, Jonathan, and Robert Williamson Jr., eds. *Imagination, Ideology and Inspiration: Echoes of Brueggemann in a New Generation*. Sheffield: Sheffield Phoenix, 2015.

Kató, Szabolcs-Ferencz. *Jhwh: der Wettergott Hoseas? Der "ursprüngliche" Charakter Jhwhs ausgehend vom Hoseabuch*. WMANT 158. Göttingen: Vandenhoeck & Ruprecht, 2019.

Keefe, Alice A. "Hosea." Pages 823–35 in *The Prophets: Fortress Commentary on the Bible Study Edition*. Edited by Gale A. Yee, Hugh R. Page Jr., and Matthew J. M. Coomber. Minneapolis: Fortress, 2016.

———. "Hosea's (In)Fertility God." *HBT* 30 (2008): 21–41.

———. *Woman's Body and the Social Body in Hosea*. JSOTSup 338. Sheffield: Sheffield Academic, 2001.

Keel, Othmar. *Goddesses and Trees, New Moon and Yahweh: Ancient Near Eastern Art and the Hebrew Bible*. JSOTSup 261. Sheffield: Sheffield Academic, 1998.

———. *The Symbolism of the Biblical World: Ancient Near Eastern Iconography and the Book of Psalms*. Translated by Timothy J. Hallett. Winona Lake, IN: Eisenbrauns, 1997.

Keel, Othmar, and Christoph Uehlinger. *Gods, Goddesses, and Images of God in Ancient Israel*. Translated by Thomas H. Trapp. Minneapolis: Fortress, 1998.

Kelle, Brad E. *Hosea 2: Metaphor and Rhetoric in Historical Perspective*. AcBib 20. Atlanta: Society of Biblical Literature, 2005.

———. "Hosea 4–14 in Twentieth-Century Scholarship." *CurBR* 8 (2010): 314–75.

Kim, Sungjin. "Is the Masoretic Text Still a Reliable Primary Text for the Book of Hosea?" *BBR* 28 (2018): 34–64.

Kimmel, Michael. "Why We Mix Metaphors (and Mix Them Well): Discourse Coherence, Conceptual Metaphor, and Beyond." *JP* 42 (2010): 97–115.

King, Andrew. "Did Jehu Destroy Baal from Israel? A Contextual Reading of Jehu's Revolt." *BBR* 27 (2017): 309–32.

King, Philip, and Lawrence Stager. *Life in Biblical Israel*. Louisville: Westminster John Knox, 2002.

Kitchen, Kenneth A., and Paul J. N. Lawrence. *Treaty, Law and Covenant in the Ancient Near East: Part 1; The Texts*. Vol. 1. Wiesbaden: Harrassowitz, 2012.

Korpel, Marjo Christina Annette. *A Rift in the Clouds: Ugaritic and Hebrew Descriptions of the Divine*. UBL 8. Münster: Ugarit-Verlag, 1990.

Kövecses, Zoltán. "Conceptual Metaphor Theory." Pages 13–27 in *The Routledge Handbook of Metaphor and Language*. Edited by Elena Semino and Zsófia Demjén. Abingdon: Routledge, 2017.

———. *Metaphor: A Practical Introduction*. 2nd ed. New York: Oxford University Press, 2010.

———. "Metaphor and Emotion." Pages 380–96 in *The Cambridge Handbook of Metaphor and Thought*. Edited by Raymond W. Gibbs Jr. New York: Cambridge University Press, 2008.

———. *Metaphor and Emotion: Language, Culture, and Body in Human Feeling*. Rev. ed. SESI 2. Cambridge: Cambridge University Press, 2003.

———. *Where Metaphors Come From: Reconsidering Context in Metaphor*. New York: Oxford University Press, 2015.

Kratz, Reinhard Gregor. "Erkenntnis Gottes im Hoseabuch." *ZTK* 94 (1997): 1–24.

Kreuzer, Siegfried. "Gott als Mutter in Hosea 11?" *TQ* 169 (1989): 123–32.

Kruger, Paul A. "A Cognitive Interpretation of the Emotion of Anger in the Hebrew Bible." *JNSL* 26 (2000): 181–93.

———. "The Divine Net in Hosea 7:12." *ETL* 68 (1992): 132–36.

———. "Emotions in the Hebrew Bible: A Few Observations on Prospects and Challenges." *OTE* 28 (2015): 395–420.

———. "On Emotions and the Expression of Emotions in the Old Testament: A Few Introductory Remarks." *BZ* 48 (2004): 213–28.

———. "Prophetic Imagery: On Metaphors and Similes in the Book Hosea." *JNSL* 14 (1988): 143–51.

———. "Yahweh and the Gods in Hosea." *JSem* 4 (1992): 81–97.

———. "Yahweh's Generous Love: Eschatological Expectations in Hosea 14:2–9." *OTE* 1 (1988): 27–48.

Kuypers, Jim A., and Andrew King. "What Is Rhetoric?" Pages 1–12 in *Rhetorical Criticism: Perspectives in Action*. Edited by Jim A. Kuypers. LSPC. Lanham, MD: Lexington, 2009.

Labahn, Antje, and Danilo Verde, eds. *Networks of Metaphors in the Hebrew Bible*. BETL 309. Leuven: Peeters, 2020.

Labuschagne, Casper J. "The Similes in the Book of Hosea." *OTWSA* 7 (1964): 64–76.

Lakoff, George. "The Contemporary Theory of Metaphor." Pages 202–51 in *Metaphor and Thought*. Edited by Andrew Ortony. 2nd ed. Cambridge: Cambridge University Press, 1993.

———. "The Invariance Hypothesis: Is Abstract Reason Based on Image-Schemas?" *CL* 1 (1990): 39–74.

———. "Mapping the Brain's Metaphor Circuitry: Metaphorical Thought in Everyday Reason." *FHN* 8 (2014): 1–14.

———. *Moral Politics: How Liberals and Conservatives Think*. 2nd ed. Chicago: University of Chicago Press, 2002.

———. "The Neural Theory of Metaphor." Pages 17–38 in *The Cambridge Handbook of Metaphor and Thought*. Edited by Raymond W. Gibbs Jr. New York: Cambridge University Press, 2008.

———. *The Political Mind: A Cognitive Scientist's Guide to Your Brain and Its Politics*. New York: Penguin, 2009.

Lakoff, George, and Mark Johnson. *Metaphors We Live By*. 2nd ed. Chicago: University of Chicago Press, 2003.

———. *Philosophy in the Flesh: The Embodied Mind and Its Challenge to Western Thought*. New York: Basic, 1999.

Lakoff, George, and Mark Turner. *More than Cool Reason: A Field Guide to Poetic Metaphor*. Chicago: University of Chicago Press, 1989.

Laldinsuah, Ronald. *Responsibility, Chastisement, and Restoration: Relational Justice in the Book of Hosea*. Carlisle: Langham Monographs, 2015.

Lam, Joseph. "Metaphor in the Ugaritic Literary Texts." *JNES* 78 (2019): 37–57.

———. "The Metaphorical Patterning of the Sin-Concept in Biblical Hebrew." PhD diss., University of Chicago, 2012.

———. *Patterns of Sin in the Hebrew Bible: Metaphor, Culture, and the Making of a Religious Concept*. New York: Oxford University Press, 2016.

Lambert, David. *How Repentance Became Biblical: Judaism, Christianity, and the Interpretation of Scripture*. Oxford: Oxford University Press, 2015.

Lancaster, Mason D. "Metaphor Research and the Hebrew Bible." *CurBR* 19 (2021): 235–85.

———. "Wounds and Healing, Dew and Lions: Hosea's Development of Divine Metaphors." *CBQ* 83 (2021): 407–24.

Lancaster, Mason D., and Adam E. Miglio. "Lord of the Storm and Oracular Decisions: Competing Construals of Storm God Imagery in Hosea 6:1–6." *VT* 70 (2020): 634–44.

Landy, Francis. *Hosea*. Readings. Sheffield: Sheffield Academic, 1995.

———. "In the Wilderness of Speech: Problems of Metaphor in Hosea." *BibInt* 3 (1995): 35–59.

Leeuwen, Cornelis van. "Meaning and Structure of Hosea X 1–8." *VT* 53 (2003): 367–78.

Leung Lai, Barbara M. "Hearing God's Bitter Cries (Hosea 11:1–9): Reading, Emotive-Experiencing, Appropriation." *HBT* 26 (2004): 24–49.

Light, Gary W. "Theory-Constitutive Metaphor and Its Development in the Book of Hosea." PhD diss., Southern Baptist Theological Seminary, 1991.

Lim, Bo H., and Daniel Castelo. *Hosea*. THOTC. Grand Rapids: Eerdmans, 2015.

Lindeman, Lisa M., and Lyn Y. Abramson. "The Mental Simulation of Motor Incapacity in Depression." *JCP* 22 (2008): 228–49.

Lindström, Fredrik. "'I Am God and Not Human' (Hos 11,9): Can Divine Compassion Overcome Our Anthropomorphism?" *SJOT* 29 (2015): 135–51.

Lohfink, Norbert. "Hate and Love in Osee 9:15." *CBQ* 25 (1963): 417.

Loon, Hanneke van. *Metaphors in the Discussion on Suffering in Job 3–31: Visions of Hope and Consolation*. BibInt 165. Leiden: Brill, 2018.

Low, Graham, and Zazie Todd. "Good Practice in Metaphor Analysis." Pages 217–29 in *Metaphor Analysis: Research Practice in Applied Linguistics, Social Sciences and the Humanities*. Edited by Lynne Cameron and Robert Maslen. London: Equinox, 2010.

Loya, Melissa T. "'Therefore the Earth Mourns': The Grievance of the Earth in Hosea 4:1-3." Pages 53–62 in *Exploring Ecological Hermeneutics*. Edited by Peter L. Trudinger and Norman C. Habel. SymS 46. Atlanta: Society of Biblical Literature, 2008.

Mácha, Jakub. "Metaphor in Analytic Philosophy and Cognitive Science." *RPF* 75 (2019): 2247–86.

Macintosh, Andrew A. *A Critical and Exegetical Commentary on Hosea*. ICC. London: Bloomsbury T&T Clark, 1997.

———. "Hosea and the Wisdom Tradition: Dependence and Independence." Pages 124–32 in *Wisdom in Ancient Israel: Essays in Honour of J. A. Emerton*. Edited by John Day, Robert P. Gordon, and Hugh G. M. Williamson. Cambridge: Cambridge University Press, 1995.

Macwilliam, Stuart. *Queer Theory and the Prophetic Marriage Metaphor in the Hebrew Bible*. Sheffield: Equinox, 2011.

Maier, Christl M. "Myth and Truth in Socio-historical Reconstruction of Ancient Societies: Hosea 4:11-14 as a Test Case." Pages 256–72 in *Thus Says the LORD: Essays on the Former and Latter Prophets in Honor of Robert R. Wilson*. Edited by John J. Ahn and Stephen L. Cook. LHBOTS 502. New York: T&T Clark, 2009.

Marti, D. Karl. *Das Dodekapropheton*. KHC 13. Tübingen: Mohr Siebeck, 1904.

Maslen, Robert. "Working with Large Amounts of Metaphor Data." Pages 180–94 in *Metaphor Analysis: Research Practice in Applied Linguistics, Social Sciences and the Humanities*. Edited by Lynne Cameron and Robert Maslen. London: Equinox, 2010.

Matthews, Victor H. "Honor and Shame in Gender-Related Legal Situations in the Hebrew Bible." Pages 97–112 in *Gender and Law in the Hebrew Bible and the Ancient Near East*. Edited by Bernard M. Levinson, Victor H. Matthews, and Tikva Frymer-Kensky. JSOTSup 262. Sheffield: Sheffield Academic, 1998.

Mays, James Luther. *Hosea: A Commentary*. OTL. Philadelphia: Westminster John Knox, 1969.

———. "Response to Janzen: 'Metaphor and Reality in Hosea 11.'" *Semeia* 24 (1982): 45–51.

McConville, J. Gordon. "Hosea, Book of." *DOTPr*, 338–50.

———. "'I Am like a Luxuriant Juniper': Language about God in Hosea." Pages 181–92 in *Let Us Go Up to Zion: Essays in Honour of H. G. M. Williamson on the Occasion of His Sixty-Fifth Birthday*. Edited by Iain Provan and Mark J. Boda. Leiden: Brill, 2012.

McFague, Sallie. *Metaphorical Theology: Models of God in Religious Language*. Philadelphia: Fortress, 1982.

McKenzie, John L. "Divine Passion in Osee." *CBQ* 17 (1955): 287–99.

McKenzie, Steven L. "Exodus Typology in Hosea." *ResQ* 22 (1979): 100–108.

Melnyk, Janet L. R. "When Israel Was a Child: Ancient Near Eastern Adoption Formulas and the Relationship between God and Israel." Pages 245–59 in *History and Interpretation: Essays in Honour of John H. Hayes*. Edited by M. Patrick Graham, William P. Brown, and Jeffrey K. Kuan. JSOTSup 173. Sheffield: JSOT, 1993.

Milgrom, Jacob. *Leviticus 1–16*. AB 3. New Haven: Yale University Press, 1998.

Miller, James E. "A Critical Response to Karin Adams's Reinterpretation of Hosea 4:13–14." *JBL* 128 (2009): 503–6.

Mirguet, Françoise. "What Is an 'Emotion' in the Hebrew Bible?: An Experience That Exceeds Most Contemporary Concepts." *BibInt* 24 (2016): 442–65.

Mirguet, Françoise, and Dominika Kurek-Chomycz. "Introduction: Emotions in Ancient Jewish Literature." *BibInt* 24 (2016): 435–41.

Moberly, R. Walter L. *Old Testament Theology: Reading the Hebrew Bible as Christian Scripture*. Grand Rapids: Baker Academic, 2013.

Moon, Joshua N. "Honor and Shame in Hosea's Marriages." *JSOT* 39 (2015): 335–51.

———. *Hosea*. AOTC 21. London: Apollos, 2018.

Moran, William L. "Ancient Near Eastern Background of the Love of God in Deuteronomy." *CBQ* 25 (1963): 77–87.

Morris, Gerald Paul. *Prophecy, Poetry and Hosea*. JSOTSup 219. Sheffield: Sheffield Academic, 1996.

Moughtin-Mumby, Sharon. *Sexual and Marital Metaphors in Hosea, Jeremiah, Isaiah and Ezekiel*. OTM. Oxford: Oxford University Press, 2008.

Mowinckel, Sigmund. "Drive and/or Ride in OT." *VT* 12 (1962): 278–99.

Mulder, Martin J., and Johannes C. de Moor. "בעל." *TDOT* 2:181–200.

Musolff, Andreas. "Metaphor and Persuasion in Politics." Pages 309–22 in *The Routledge Handbook of Metaphor and Language*. Edited by Elena Semino and Zsófia Demjén. Abingdon: Routledge, 2017.

Na'aman, Nadav. "The Book of Hosea as a Source for the Last Days of the Kingdom of Israel." *BZ* 59 (2015): 232–56.

Naudé, Jackie. "שׁור." *NIDOTTE* 4:71–72.

Neef, Heinz-Dieter. "Der Septuaginta-Text und der Masoreten-Text des Hoseabuches im Vergleich." *Bib* 67 (1986): 195–220.

———. *Die Heilstraditionen Israels in der Verkündigung des Propheten Hosea*. BZAW 169. Berlin: de Gruyter, 1987.

Nissinen, Martti. *Prophetie, Redaktion und Fortschreibung im Hoseabuch: Studien zum Werdegang eines Prophetenbuches im Lichte von Hos 4 und 11*. AOAT 231. Kevelaer: Butzon & Bercker, 1991.

———. *Prophets and Prophecy in the Ancient Near East*. WAW 12. Atlanta: Society of Biblical Literature, 2003.

Nissinen, Martti, and Risto Uro, eds. *Sacred Marriages: The Divine-Human Sexual Metaphor from Sumer to Early Christianity*. Winona Lake, IN: Eisenbrauns, 2008.

Nocquet, Dany. *Le "livret noir de Baal": La polémique contre le dieu Baal dans la Bible hébraïque et l'ancien Israël*. Geneva: Labor et Fides, 2004.

Nogalski, James D. *The Book of the Twelve and Beyond: Collected Essays of James D. Nogalski*. AIL 29. Atlanta: SBL Press, 2017.

———. *The Book of the Twelve: Hosea–Jonah*. SHBC. Macon, GA: Smyth & Helwys, 2011.

———. "God in the Book of the Twelve." Pages 103–16 in *The Oxford Handbook of the Minor Prophets*. Edited by Julia M. O'Brien. New York: Oxford University Press, 2021.

Nutkowicz, Hélène. "Concerning the Verb *śnʾ* in Judaeo-Aramaic Contracts from Elephantine." *JSS* 52 (2007): 211–25.

Nwaoru, Emmanuel O. *Imagery in the Prophecy of Hosea*. ÄAT 41. Wiesbaden: Harrassowitz, 1999.

O'Brien, Julia M. *Challenging Prophetic Metaphor: Theology and Ideology in the Prophets*. Louisville: Westminster John Knox, 2008.

———. "Metaphorization and Other Tropes in the Prophets." Pages 241–55 in *The Oxford Handbook of the Prophets*. Edited by Carolyn J. Sharp. Oxford: Oxford University Press, 2016.

Oestreich, Bernhard. *Metaphors and Similes for Yahweh in Hosea 14:2–9 (1–8)*. FSRT 1. Frankfurt: Lang, 1998.

O'Kennedy, Daniël F. "God as Healer in the Prophetic Books of the Hebrew Bible." *HBT* 27 (2005): 87–113.

———. "Healing as/or Forgiveness? The Use of the Term רפא in the Book of Hosea." *OTE* 14 (2001): 458–74.

Olson, Dennis T. "Emotion, Repentance, and the Question of the 'Inner Life' of Biblical Israelites: A Case Study in Hosea 6:1–3." Pages 161–76 in *Mixed Feelings and Vexed Passions: Exploring Emotions in Biblical Literature*. Edited by F. Scott Spencer. RBS 90. Atlanta: SBL Press, 2017.

Olyan, Saul M. *Asherah and the Cult of Yahweh in Israel*. SBLMS 34. Atlanta: Scholars Press, 1988.

———. "Honor, Shame, and Covenant Relations in Ancient Israel and Its Environment." *JBL* 115 (1996): 201–18.

Otis, Laura. *Banned Emotions: How Metaphors Can Shape What People Feel*. Oxford: Oxford University Press, 2019.

Otzen, Benedikt. "טל." *TDOT* 5:323–30.

Parpola, Simo. *Assyrian Prophecies*. SAA 9. Helsinki: Helsinki University Press, 1997.

Parpola, Simo, and Kazuko Watanabe. *Neo-Assyrian Treaties and Loyalty Oaths*. SAA 2. Winona Lake, IN: Eisenbrauns, 1988.

Patrick, Dale. *Redeeming Judgment*. Eugene, OR: Pickwick, 2012.

———. *The Rendering of God in the Old Testament*. OBT. Philadelphia: Augsburg Fortress, 1983.

Paul, Shalom M. "The Image of the Oven and the Cake in Hosea VII 4–10." *VT* 18 (1968): 114–20.

———. "The Shared Legacy of Sexual Metaphors and Euphemisms in Mesopotamian and Biblical Literature." Pages 489–98 in *Sex and Gender in the Ancient Near East: Proceedings of the 47th Rencontre Assyriologique*

Internationale. Edited by Simo Parpola and Robert M. Whiting. Helsinki: University of Helsinki Press, 2002.

Pentiuc, Eugen J., Gad Barnea, Étienne Méténier, and Łukasz Popko, eds. *Hosea: The Word of the Lord That Happened to Hosea*. BIT 3. Leuven: Peeters, 2017.

Perdue, Leo G. *The Collapse of History: Reconstructing Old Testament Theology*. OBT. Minneapolis: Fortress, 1992.

Petrie, Hugh G., and Rebecca S. Oshlag. "Metaphor and Learning." Pages 579–609 in *Metaphor and Thought*. 2nd ed. Edited by Andrew Ortony. Cambridge: Cambridge University Press, 1993.

Plank, Karl A. "The Scarred Countenance: Inconstancy in the Book of Hosea." *Judaism* 32 (1983): 343–54.

Propp, William H. C. *Exodus 1–18: A New Translation with Introduction and Commentary*. AB 2. New Haven: Yale University Press, 1999.

Pryce, Bertrand Casimis. "The Resurrection Motif in Hosea 5:8–6:6: An Exegetical Study." PhD diss., Andrews University, 1989.

Rad, Gerhard von. *Old Testament Theology*. Translated by David M. G. Stalker. Vol. 1. New York: Harper & Row, 1962.

Ramirez, Felipe Fruto. "Are the Allusions to Jacob and Moses in Hosea 12 Late Insertions?" *Landas* 29 (2015): 119–43.

———. "A Love like a Morning Mist: Hosea 5:15–6:6." *Landas* 27 (2013): 101–35.

———. "The Parable of the Heifer in Hosea 10:11–13." *Landas* 28 (2014): 101–13.

Rendtorff, Rolf. *The Old Testament: An Introduction*. Translated by John Bowden. Philadelphia: Fortress, 1991.

Richelle, Matthieu. "Structure littéraire et interprétation en Osée 4." *RB* 121 (2014): 5–20.

Ricoeur, Paul. "Biblical Hermeneutics." *Semeia* 4 (1975): 29–148.

———. "The Metaphorical Process as Cognition, Imagination, and Feeling." *CI* 5 (1978): 143–59.

———. "Poetry and Possibility." Pages 448–62 in *A Ricoeur Reader: Reflection and Imagination*. Edited by Mario J. Valdéz. Toronto: University of Toronto Press, 1991.

———. *The Rule of Metaphor: Multi-disciplinary Studies of the Creation of Meaning in Language*. Translated by Robert Czerny. Toronto: University of Toronto Press, 1981.

Roberts, Rabbi Matis. *Trei Asar: The Twelve Prophets; A New Translation with a Commentary Anthologized from Talmudic, Midrashic, and Rabbinic Sources*. Vol. 1. Brooklyn, NY: Mesorah, 1995.

Rogers, Nancy Louise. "Poetic Revelation: The Relationship between Parallelism and Metaphor in Biblical Hebrew Poetry." PhD diss., Fordham University, 2010.

Römer, Thomas. *The Invention of God*. Translated by Raymond Geuss. Cambridge: Harvard University Press, 2015.

Rom-Shiloni, Dalit. "Hebrew Bible Theology: A Jewish Descriptive Approach." *JR* 96 (2016): 165–84.

Rudolph, Wilhelm. *Hosea*. KAT 13/1. Stuttgart: Mohn, 1966.

Sander, David, and Klaus Scherer, eds. *Oxford Companion to Emotion and the Affective Sciences*. SAS. Oxford: Oxford University Press, 2009.

Schlimm, Matthew R. "Different Perspectives on Divine Pathos: An Examination of Hermeneutics in Biblical Theology." *CBQ* 69 (2007): 673–94.

Scholz, Susanne. "Reading the Minor Prophets for Gender and Sexuality." Pages 299–312 in *The Oxford Handbook of the Minor Prophets*. Edited by Julia M. O'Brien. New York: Oxford University Press, 2021.

Schott, Martin. "Die Jakobpassagen in Hosea 12." *ZTK* 112 (2015): 1–26.

Schüngel-Straumann, Helen. "God as Mother in Hosea 11." *TD* 34 (1987): 3–8.

Scurlock, JoAnn. *Sourcebook for Ancient Mesopotamian Medicine*. WAW 36. Atlanta: SBL Press, 2014.

Seifert, Brigitte. *Metaphorisches Reden von Gott im Hoseabuch*. FRLANT 166. Göttingen: Vandenhoeck & Ruprecht, 1996.

Sellin, Ernst. *Das Zwölfprophetenbuch: Hosea–Micha*. KAT 12/1. Leipzig: Deichert, 1929.

Semino, Elena, and Zsófia Demjén, eds. *The Routledge Handbook of Metaphor and Language*. Abingdon: Routledge, 2017.

Seow, Choon-Leong. "Hosea 14:10 and the Foolish People Motif." *CBQ* 44 (1982): 212–24.

Sharp, Carolyn J. "Interrogating the Violent God of Hosea: A Conversation with Walter Brueggemann, Alice Keefe, and Ehud Ben Zvi." *HBT* 30 (2008): 59–70.

Sherwood, Yvonne. "'Darke Texts Needs Notes': On Prophetic Prophecy, John Donne and the Baroque." *JSOT* 27 (2002): 47–74.

———. *The Prostitute and the Prophet: Hosea's Marriage in Literary-Theoretical Perspective*. LHBOTS 212. Sheffield: Sheffield Academic, 1996.

Siebert-Hommes, Jopie. "'With Bands of Love': Hosea 11 as 'Recapitulation' of the Basic Themes in the Book of Hosea." Pages 167–73 in *Unless Some One Guide Me … Festschrift for Karel A. Deurloo.* Edited by Janet W. Dyk, Piet J. van Midden, Klaas Spronk, Geert J. Venema, and Rochus Zuurmond. ACEBTrSup 2. Maastricht: Uitgeverij Shaker, 2001.

Simian-Yofre, Horacio. "רחם." *TDOT* 13:437–54.

Smith, Cooper. "The 'Wilderness' in Hosea and Deuteronomy: A Case of Thematic Reappropriation." *BBR* 28 (2018): 240–60.

Smith, Duane Andre. "Kinship and Covenant in Hosea 11:1–4." *HBT* 16 (1994): 41–53.

Smith, Mark S. *The Early History of God: Yahweh and the Other Deities in Ancient Israel.* 2nd ed. Grand Rapids: Eerdmans, 2002.

——— . *God in Translation: Deities in Cross-cultural Discourse in the Biblical World.* Grand Rapids: Eerdmans, 2008.

——— . *The Origins of Biblical Monotheism: Israel's Polytheistic Background and the Ugaritic Texts.* New York: Oxford University Press, 2003.

——— . *Where the Gods Are: Spatial Dimensions of Anthropomorphism in the Biblical World.* New Haven: Yale University Press, 2016.

Sommer, Benjamin D. *The Bodies of God and the World of Ancient Israel.* Cambridge: Cambridge University Press, 2011.

Soskice, Janet Martin. *Metaphor and Religious Language.* Oxford: Clarendon, 1985.

Southwood, Katherine. "Metaphor, Illness, and Identity in Psalms 88 and 102." *JSOT* 43 (2018): 228–46.

Spencer, F. Scott, ed. *Mixed Feelings and Vexed Passions: Exploring Emotions in Biblical Literature.* RBS 90. Atlanta: SBL Press, 2017.

Spronk, Klaas. *Beatific Afterlife in Ancient Israel and in the Ancient Near East.* AOAT 219. Neukirchen-Vluyn: Neukirchener, 1986.

Stackert, Jeffrey. "Pentateuchal Coherence and the Science of Reading." Pages 253–68 in *The Formation of the Pentateuch: Bridging the Academic Cultures of Europe, Israel, and North America.* Edited by Jan C. Gertz, Bernard M. Levinson, Dalit Rom-Shiloni, and Konrad Schmid. FAT 111. Tübingen: Mohr Siebeck, 2016.

Stark, Christine. *"Kultprostitution" im Alten Testament? Die Qedeschen der Hebräischen Bibel und das Motiv der Hurerei.* OBO 221. Göttingen: Vandenhoeck & Ruprecht, 2006.

Staubli, Thomas. "Disgusting Deeds and Disgusting Gods: Ethnic and Ethical Constructions of Disgust in the Hebrew Bible." *HBAI* 6 (2017): 457–87.

Steen, Gerard J. "Deliberate Metaphor Theory: Basic Assumptions, Main Tenets, Urgent Issues." *IP* 14 (2017): 1–24.

———. "Identifying Metaphors in Language." Pages 73–87 in *The Routledge Handbook of Metaphor and Language*. Edited by Elena Semino and Zsófia Demjén. Abingdon: Routledge, 2017.

Steen, Gerard J., Ewa Biernacka, Aletta G. Dorst, Anna Kaal, Clara I. López Rodríguez, and Trijntje Pasma. "Pragglejaz in Practice: Finding Metaphorically Used Words in Natural Discourse." Pages 165–84 in *Researching and Applying Metaphor in the Real World*. Edited by Graham Low, Zazie Todd, Alice Deignan, and Lynne Cameron. HCP 26. Amsterdam: Benjamins, 2010.

Steen, Gerard J., Aletta G. Dorst, J. Berenike Herrmann, Anna Kaal, Tina Krennmayr, and Trijntje Pasma. *A Method for Linguistic Metaphor Identification: From MIP to MIPVU*. CELCR 14. Amsterdam: Benjamins, 2010.

Stern, Josef. *Metaphor in Context*. Cambridge: MIT Press, 2000.

Sternberg, Meir. *The Poetics of Biblical Narrative: Ideological Literature and the Drama of Reading*. ISBL. Bloomington: Indiana University Press, 1987.

Stiebert, Johanna. *The Construction of Shame in the Hebrew Bible: The Prophetic Contribution*. LHBOTS 346. London: Sheffield Academic, 2002.

———. "Shame and Prophecy: Approaches Past and Present." *BibInt* 8 (2000): 255–75.

Stovell, Beth M. "'I Will Make Her like a Desert': Intertextual Allusion and Feminine and Agricultural Metaphors in the Book of the Twelve." Pages 37–61 in *The Book of the Twelve and the New Form Criticism*, edited by Mark J. Boda, Michael H. Floyd, and Colin M. Toffelmire. ANEM 10. Atlanta: SBL Press, 2015.

Strawn, Brent A. *What Is Stronger Than a Lion? Leonine Image and Metaphor in the Hebrew Bible and the Ancient Near East*. OBO 212. Göttingen: Vandenhoeck & Ruprecht, 2005.

Strawn, Brent A., and Izaak J. de Hulster. "Figuring YHWH in Unusual Ways: Deuteronomy 32 and Other Mixed Metaphors for God in the Old Testament." Pages 117–33 in *Iconographic Exegesis of the Hebrew Bible/Old Testament: An Introduction to Its Method and Practice*.

Edited by Izaak J. de Hulster, Brent A. Strawn, and Ryan P. Bonfiglio. Göttingen: Vandenhoeck & Ruprecht, 2015.

Stuart, Douglas. *Hosea–Jonah*. WBC 31. Grand Rapids: Zondervan, 2014.

Sweeney, Marvin A. "Hosea's Reading of Pentateuchal Narratives: A Window for a Foundational E Stratum." Pages 851–71 in *The Formation of the Pentateuch: Bridging the Academic Cultures of Europe, Israel, and North America*. Edited by Jan C. Gertz, Bernard M. Levinson, Dalit Rom-Shiloni, and Konrad Schmid. FAT 111. Tübingen: Mohr Siebeck, 2016.

———. *The Twelve Prophets*. Vol. 1. BerOl. Collegeville, MN: Liturgical Press, 2000.

Tångberg, K. Arvid. "'I Am like an Evergreen Fir, from Me Comes Your Fruit': Notes on Meaning and Symbolism in Hosea 14:9b (MT)." *SJOT* 2 (1989): 81–93.

Tauberschmidt, Gerhard. "Polysemy and Homonymy in Biblical Hebrew." *JT* 14 (2018): 29–41.

Taylor, Charles. *Modern Social Imaginaries*. Durham, NC: Duke University Press, 2003.

———. *A Secular Age*. Cambridge: Harvard University Press, 2007.

Thiselton, Anthony C. *The Hermeneutics of Doctrine*. Grand Rapids: Eerdmans, 2007.

Thistlethwaite, Susan Brooks. "Every Two Minutes: Battered Women and Feminist Interpretation." Pages 96–107 in *Feminist Interpretation of the Bible*. Edited by Letty M. Russell. Philadelphia: Westminster, 1985.

Tigay, Jeffrey H. "Israelite Religion: The Onomastic and Epigraphic Evidence." Pages 157–94 in *Ancient Israelite Religion: Essays in Honor of Frank Moore Cross*. Edited by Patrick Miller, Paul Hanson, and S. Dean McBride. Philadelphia: Fortress, 1987.

———. *You Shall Have No Other Gods: Israelite Religion in the Light of Hebrew Inscriptions*. HSS 31. Atlanta: Scholars Press, 1986.

Tilford, Nicole L. *Sensing World, Sensing Wisdom: The Cognitive Foundation of Biblical Metaphors*. AIL 31. Atlanta: SBL Press, 2017.

Todd, Zazie, and Graham Low. "A Selective Survey of Research Practice in Published Studies Using Metaphor Analysis." Pages 26–41 in *Metaphor Analysis: Research Practice in Applied Linguistics, Social Sciences and the Humanities*. Edited by Lynne Cameron and Robert Maslen. London: Equinox, 2010.

Toorn, Karel van der. "Prostitution, Cultic." *ABD* 5:510–13.

———. "Yahweh." *DDD*, 910–19.

Törnkvist, Rut. *The Use and Abuse of Female Sexual Imagery in the Book of Hosea: A Feminist Critical Approach to Hos 1–3*. AUUWR 7. Uppsala: Uppsala University Library, 1998.

Trotter, James M. *Reading Hosea in Achaemenid Yehud*. JSOTSup 328. Sheffield: Sheffield Academic, 2001.

Tully, Eric J. *Hosea: A Handbook on the Hebrew Text*. BHHB. Waco, TX: Baylor University Press, 2018.

Turner, Mark. "Aspects of the Invariance Hypothesis." *CL* 1 (1990): 247–55.

Underhill, James. *Creating Worldviews: Metaphor, Ideology and Language*. Edinburgh: Edinburgh University Press, 2013.

Unterman, Jeremiah. "Repentance and Redemption in Hosea." Pages 541–50 in *Society of Biblical Literature 1982 Seminar Papers*. Atlanta: Scholars Press, 1982.

Vall, Gregory. "An Epistemology of Faith: The Knowledge of God in Israel's Prophetic Literature." Pages 24–42 in *Bible and Epistemology: Biblical Soundings on the Knowledge of God*. Edited by Mary Healy and Robin Parry. Milton Keynes, UK: Paternoster, 2007.

Varela, Francisco J., Evan T. Thompson, and Eleanor Rosch. *The Embodied Mind: Cognitive Science and Human Experience*. Cambridge: MIT Press, 1991.

Varga, Somogy. "Embodied Concepts and Mental Health." *JMP* 43 (2018): 241–60.

Vidaković, Mirko. *Conifers: Morphology and Variation*. Rev. and expanded ed. Translated by Maja Šoljan. Zagreb: Grafički Zavod Hrvatske, 1991.

Vielhauer, Roman. *Das Werden des Buches Hosea: Eine Redaktionsgeschichtliche Untersuchung*. BZAW 349. Berlin: de Gruyter, 2007.

Wacker, Marie-Theres. *Figurationen des Weiblichen im Hosea-Buch*. HBS 8. Freiburg: Herder, 1996.

———. "Hosea." Pages 371–85 in *Feminist Biblical Interpretation: A Compendium of Critical Commentary on the Books of the Bible and Related Literature*. Edited by Luise Schottroff and Marie-Theres Wacker. Translated by Martin Rumscheidt. Grand Rapids: Eerdmans, 2012.

———. "Traces of the Goddess in the Book of Hosea." Pages 219–41 in *A Feminist Companion to the Latter Prophets*. Edited by Athalya Brenner. FCB 8. Sheffield: Sheffield Academic, 1995.

Wakely, Robin. "בגד." *NIDOTTE* 1:582–95.

Walker, Thomas Worth. "The Metaphor of Healing and the Theology of the Book of Hosea." PhD diss., Princeton Theological Seminary, 1997.

Ward, James M. *Hosea: A Theological Commentary*. New York: Harper & Row, 1967.
Watson, Paul Layton. "Mot, the God of Death, at Ugarit and in the Old Testament." PhD diss., Yale University, 1970.
Weems, Renita J. *Battered Love: Marriage, Sex, and Violence in the Hebrew Prophets*. Minneapolis: Fortress, 1995.
Weippert, Manfred. "Die Bildsprache der neuassyrischen Prophetie." Pages 55–93 in *Beiträge zur prophetischen Bildsprache in Israel und Assyrien*. OBO 64. Göttingen: Vandenhoeck & Ruprecht, 1985.
Weiss, Andrea L. "From 'Mixed Metaphors' to 'Adjacent Analogies': An Analysis of the Poetry of Hosea." Pages 109–27 in *Built by Wisdom, Established by Understanding: Essays on Biblical and Near Eastern Literature in Honor of Adele Berlin*. Bethesda: University Press of Maryland, 2013.
———. "Making a Place for Metaphor in Biblical Theology." Pages 127–39 in *Methodological Studies*. Vol. 1 of *Theology of the Hebrew Bible*. Edited by Marvin A. Sweeney. RBS 92. Atlanta: SBL Press, 2019.
———. "Motives behind Biblical Mixed Metaphors." Pages 317–28 in *Making a Difference: Essays on the Bible and Judaism in Honor of Tamara Cohn Eskenazi*. Edited by David J. A. Clines, Kent Harold Richards, and Jacob L. Wright. HBM 49. Sheffield: Sheffield Phoenix, 2012.
Wellhausen, Julius. *Die kleinen Propheten*. 4th ed. Berlin: de Gruyter, 1963.
Westbrook, Raymond. "Introduction: The Character of Ancient Near Eastern Law." Pages 1–90 in *A History of Ancient Near Eastern Law*. Vol. 1. Edited by Raymond Westbrook. Leiden: Brill, 2003.
Wijngaards, John. "Death and Resurrection in Covenantal Context (Hos 6:2)." *VT* 17 (1967): 226–39.
Wilson-Wright, Aren M. *Athtart: The Transmission and Transformation of a Goddess in the Late Bronze Age*. FAT 2/90. Tübingen: Mohr Siebeck, 2016.
Wolde, Ellen van. "Sentiments as Culturally Constructed Emotions: Anger and Love in the Hebrew Bible." *BibInt* 16 (2008): 1–24.
Wolff, Hans Walter. *Hosea*. Translated by Gary Stansell. Hermeneia. Philadelphia: Fortress, 1974.
Worden, Thomas. "The Literary Influence of the Ugaritic Fertility Myth on the Old Testament." *VT* 3 (1953): 273–97.
Wright, Christopher J. H. *The Mission of God: Unlocking the Bible's Grand Narrative*. Downers Grove, IL: IVP Academic, 2006.

———. *Old Testament Ethics for the People of God*. Downers Grove, IL: IVP Academic, 2013.
Wyatt, Nicholas. "Asherah." *DDD*, 99–105.
———. *Religious Texts from Ugarit: The Words of Ilimilku and His Colleagues*. Sheffield: Sheffield Academic, 1998.
Yates, Gary E. "The Problem of Repentance and Relapse as a Unifying Theme in the Book of the Twelve." *Them* 41 (2016): 248–62.
Yee, Gale A. "The Book of Hosea." *NIB* 7:195–297.
———. *Composition and Tradition in the Book of Hosea: A Redaction Critical Investigation*. SBLDS 102. Atlanta: Scholars Press, 1987.
———. "Hosea." Pages 299–308 in *Women's Bible Commentary*. 3rd rev. and updated ed. Edited by Carol A. Newsom, Sharon H. Ringe, and Jacqueline E. Lapsley. Louisville: Westminster John Knox, 2012.
———. *Poor Banished Children of Eve: Woman as Evil in the Hebrew Bible*. Minneapolis: Fortress, 2003.
Yoo, Yoon Jong. "Israelian Hebrew in the Book of Hosea." PhD diss., Cornell University, 1999.
Zehetgruber, Katrin. *Zuwendung und Abwendung: Studien zur Reziprozität des JHWH/Israel-Verhältnisses im Hoseabuch*. WMANT 159. Göttingen: Vandenhoeck & Ruprecht, 2020.
Zenger, Erich. "'Wie ein Löwe brüllt er …' (Hos 11,10): Zur Funktion poetischer Metaphorik im Zwölfprophetenbuch." Pages 33–45 in *"Wort Jhwhs, das geschah …" (Hos 1,1): Studien zum Zwölfprophetenbuch*. Edited by Erich Zenger. HBS 35. Freiburg: Herder, 2002.
Zimran, Yisca. "The Notion of God Reflected in the Lion Imagery of the Book of Hosea." *VT* 68 (2018): 149–67.
———. "The Prevalence and Purpose of the 'Assyria-Egypt' Motif in the Book of Hosea." *JSOT* 46 (2021): 3–23.
Zulick, Margaret Diefenderfer. "Rhetorical Polyphony in the Book of the Prophet Hosea." PhD diss., Northwestern University, 1994.

Ancient Sources Index

Hebrew Bible/Old Testament		20:5	36
		21:7	100
Genesis		21:9	36
13:10	142	21:14	100
14:2	142	22:13	100
14:8	142	26:14–39	85
19:13	142	27:29	85
19:14	142		
19:25	142	Numbers	
19:29	142	5:13	39
21:10	100	23:19	143
22:17	214	25:1–5	120
27:40	109	25:4	146
27:45	146	27:14	132
30:18	145	30:10	100
32:13	214		
34:4	39	Deuteronomy	
34:5	39	6:10–15	126
34:13	39, 145	7:8	86
43:8	66	8:7–20	126
		9:7	132
Exodus		9:26	86
3:14	150, 218	10:18	148
4:22	214	11:15–17	126
13:13	105–6	12:2	151
14:5	135	13:6	86
21:8	53	15:15	86
22:22–24	148	16:18	44
33:19	148	19:6	44
34:6	148	21:4	105–6
34:6–7	183, 219, 224	21:6	105–6
34:20	105–6	21:8	86
		21:15	101
Leviticus		21:18	132
5:8	106	21:18–21	100, 120

Deuteronomy (*cont.*)		15	101
21:20	132	15:29	143
21:22	44		
22:13	101	2 Samuel	
23:19	91	2:12	175
24:1–4	100		
24:3	101	1 Kings	
24:7	148	3:28	44
24:18	86	11:1–3	36
25:1	44	11:9–10	36
28:15–69	85	12:4–14	109
28:26	85	12:19	84
28:49	85	12:28–30	111
28:49–57	56	14:23	151
28:62–63	213	15:5	145
29:22–26	142		
29:23	142	2 Kings	
30:3	148	1:1	84
31:16	36	3:5	84
31:20	126	3:7	84
32:6	93	8:1	66
32:15–18	126	8:20	84
32:39	61	8:22	84
		10:28	67
Joshua		13:21	66
3:16	70	15:23–17:6	57
4:19	101	16:4	38, 151
4:23	145	17:10	151
		17:10–12	38
Judges		17:13	189
2:17	36	18:19	58
8:27	36	21:13	135
8:33	36	25:6	44
9:23	53		
11:2	100	1 Chronicles	
11:7	100	8:33	175
19–20	111	9:39	175
1 Samuel		2 Chronicles	
4:19	135	12:12	146
10:8	101	28:4	151
10:9	135		
13:4	101	Ezra	
13:8–9	101	10:14	146
14:33	53		

Ancient Sources Index

Job			
6:23	86	5:29–30	60
13:28	58, 60	6:9–10	189
14:12	66	7	57
14:14	66	9:11	146
30:15	135	9:16	146, 148
		9:20	146
		10:4	146
Psalms		10:15	69
9:16	82	11:9	60
25:3	53	12:1	146
29:12	58	13:18	148
30:6	213	17:5–6	78
31:5	82	23:17	36
35:7	82	23:17–18	91
37:6	71	24:16	53
39:12	59–60	26–27	152, 155
50:19	50	26:14	66
51:17	186	26:16	50
57:7	82	26:19	66
59:6	53	26:21	59
68:6	148	27:2	105
73:15	53	27:2–6	155
78:40	132	27:3	105
80:9–10	105	27:6	155
81:4	56–57	27:11	93
81:10	56	28:21	213
95:6–7	96	32:12	104
100:3	96	40:2	111
103:9	213	42:25	191
105:25	135	43:27	84
		46:5	98
Proverbs		49:13	148
1:2	50	51:8	60
24:18	146	51:13	92
29:8	146	53:5	50
		54:1–10	213
Ecclesiastes		54:5	92, 96
4:9	145	57:5	151
8:11	145	57:18	136
		60:5	135
Isaiah		63:17	189
1:2	84	66:3	105–6
1:17	148	66:24	84
5:1–7	105		
5:25	146		

Jeremiah		26:16	44
2:8	84	30:12–17	61
2:19–20	38	30:24	146
2:20	151	31:17	137
2:21	105	33:8	84
2:23	38	44:6	60
2:26–28	38	48:38	88
2:29	84	48:40	85
2:30	50	49:22	85
2:35	146	51:33	78
3:1–9	36		
3:6	151	Lamentations	
3:6–10	38	1:2	53
3:6–4:4	189	1:20	135
3:8	53	2:4	60
3:11	53, 55	3:33	213
3:13	38, 84, 151	3:42	84
3:20	53		
3:22	149	Ezekiel	
4:8	146	2:3	84
5:11	53	3:17–20	189
5:24	110	5:15	50
6:15	39	6:13	151
6:23	148	12:13	81
7:12	59	15:2–6	105
7:20	60	16	36
7:27–28	189	16:8	109
8:12	39	16:31	91
9:23	213	16:31–32	37
10:24	143	16:34	91
11:13	175	16:41	91
11:16	151	17:6	104
12:6	53	17:6–10	105
12:10	105	17:20	81
13:7	88	18:8	44
13:10	88	18:11	39
13:14	148	18:21	78–79
13:25	145	18:21–23	189
15:8	140	18:30	189
17:2	151	19:10	104
17:8	151	19:10–14	105
18:7–11	189	20:13	132
18:8	78	21:36	60
23:20	146	23	36
26:11	44	23:5	36

Ancient Sources Index

23:11–12	36	3:1	37, 169
32:3	81	3:3	37
44:22	100	3:4–5	217, 220
		3:5	31, 188
Daniel		4	6, 38, 46, 48, 161
9:16	146	4–11	36, 158
10:8	135	4–13	182–83
		4–14	2–6, 19, 22, 27–30, 38–39, 61, 66, 138–39, 159–60, 162, 164, 168, 195–97, 203, 205, 207, 218, 224, 227, 230–32
Hosea			
1–2	67, 177–78		
1–3	6, 30, 33, 37–38, 143, 162–63, 178, 182		
1:2	37, 54, 93–94	4:1	29, 31, 40–41, 46–49, 71, 85, 194, 210, 224
1:2–3:5	29, 188	4:1–2	31
1:6	178	4:1–3	46, 54
1:7	31, 178	4:1–5:7	48
1:9	148, 150, 173, 178–79, 219	4:1–8:14	29, 89, 92, 124, 166
2	37, 95, 118, 161, 171	4:1–11:11	29–30, 46, 89, 92, 108, 118, 129, 188, 205
2–3	144		
2:1	148, 214	4:2	37, 47
2:4	31, 37, 46–47, 49	4:2–10	6
2:6	37, 148, 178	4:3	47, 179
2:7	37, 92, 95–96, 169	4:5	31, 51, 70
2:9	96, 169, 188	4:6	54, 70–71
2:9–10	41, 95	4:7	40
2:10	95, 126, 151, 154, 175, 193, 210	4:8	186
2:11	188	4:9	21, 134, 188
2:11–15	43	4:9a	49
2:12	56, 108, 169, 193	4:10	41, 45, 56
2:14	56, 94–96, 151, 169	4:10–11a	4
2:14–15	96	4:10–15	22, **32–42**, 52, 100, 165, 167, 191
2:15	54, 95, 126, 169, 175		
2:16	191, 212, 221	4:10–16	**31–44**, 163, 165, 229
2:16–17	167–68	4:10–19	32, 34, 88
2:16–25	178, 182, 217, 220	4:10a–b	35
2:17	214	4:10c–11a	31, 35, 40
2:17–25	191	4:10c–11c	33
2:18	95–96, 134, 175, 182	4:11	31
2:19	125, 175	4:12	35–36, 39, 51, 93–94, 189
2:20	47	4:12c	31, 35, 52
2:21	224	4:12c–d	33, 36
2:21–22	48	4:12d	31, 36
2:22	54, 212	4:13	36, 38, 180
2:23	178, 182	4:13–14	33–34, 36
2:25	148, 178, 219–20	4:14	32, 36, 87

Hosea (cont.)

4:15	31, 35–36, 39, 43, 163
4:15a	31, 52
4:16	17, 32, **42–43**, 96, 165–67, 169, 221, 223
4:16a	21, 32
4:16b	32
4:17	38, 42–43
4:17–19	33, 42, 175
4:18	36, 40, 169
4:19	35, 42
5	46
5:1	38, **46–50**, 54–55
5:1d	44, 49
5:1–5	46, 48, 55
5:1-6	55
5:1–7	**44–57**, 163, 221
5:1–7b	56
5:1–7:2	187
5:2	17, **50–51**, 55, 110, 191, 221
5:2b	44, 46
5:3	37, 39, 46, **51–52**, 77, 210
5:3a	54
5:3c–d	45, 51–52
5:3–4	38, 53–55, 191
5:3b–4a	54
5:4	21, 37, 39, 46, **51–52**, 54, 79, 133, 178–79, 181, 188–89, 210
5:4b–c	45, 51
5:5	31, 38, **46–50**, 51, 54–55, 81
5:5a	45, 49
5:6	21, 55, 61, 68, 81, 186, 224
5:6a	57
5:6c	57
5:7	38, **52–54**, 55, 57, 60, 71, 108, 132, 164, 178
5:7a	45, 53–55
5:7b	46, 53–55, 221
5:7c	55–56, 165
5:8	57, 85
5:8–15	68, 182
5:8–6:6	6, 57, 72, 182
5:9	210
5:10	11, 160, 162, 224
5:10a	60
5:10b	57, 60
5:10–15	**57–63**, 68, 72, 191, 221
5:10–6:5	6
5:10–6:7	**57–77**, 81, 174
5:12	1, 21, 59–61
5:12a	58
5:12b	58
5:12–14	72
5:13	57–58, 61, 88, 127, 149, 153, 163, 175, 178, 187
5:13–14	129, 153
5:13–6:2	78
5:14	1, 59–61, 131, 138, 150, 178, 193
5:14a	59
5:14–15	21, 57, 61, 63, 138, 173, 214, 216
5:14b–15a	59–60
5:15	55, 59, 63, 68, 130, 188, 191, 224
5:15a	59, 61
6:1	61, 63, 149, 178, 188
6:1b	64
6:1c	64
6:1–2	68
6:1–3	2, **63–69**, 71–72, 76, 113, 182, 203, 206, 210, 212, 221
6:1–3a	65
6:1–6	178, 207, 209
6:2	22, 65
6:2a	65
6:2–3	4
6:2b–6:3a	65
6:3	68–69, 110, 210
6:3b	65
6:3c	65
6:3d	65
6:4	64, 71, 111, 150, 173, 179
6:4–6	63–64, 72, 76, 182, 210, 221
6:5	68, 71, 165
6:5a	69
6:5b	70
6:5c	4, 49, 70, 222
6:5–7	**69–77**
6:6	64, 71, 168, 186, 212–13, 224

6:7	31, 47, 53, 68, 71, 85, 101, 132, 164–65, 222		7:13c	**85–86**, 138
			7:13c–d	80
6:7a	70–71		7:13d	138
6:7b	70–71		7:13–16	84
6:7–10	70		7:14	84, 187
6:7–7:16	89		7:14a	62
6:8–10	54		7:15	84, 89, 110, 165
6:10	4, 37–39, 77–78, 191		7:15a	80, 83
6:10a	89		7:15a–b	**83–84**
6:10–7:1	**77–79**, 163, 222		7:15b	80
6:11	31, 78, 188, 222		7:16	**86–88**, 89, 156, 165, 167, 188
6:11a	77, 165		7:16b	80
6:11b	77–78		8:1	31, 47, 54, 71, 83, 88–89, 132, 164–65, 167, 210, 216
7:1	78–79, 149, 178, 222		8:1b	84
7:1a	77, 86		8:1c	80, 84–85, 222
7:1a–c	77–78		8:1c–d	**84–85**
7:2	56, 79, 210		8:1d	80, 85, 222
7:4	37		8:1–14	39, 92, 95
7:4–7	86		8:2	42, 54, 62, 79, 210
7:8	79, **86–88**, 89, 156, 167		8:3	210
7:8a	88		8:5	11, 160, 162, 224
7:8–16	88		8:6	38
7:8–8:1	**79–90**, 167, 222		8:8	56, 88, 108
7:9	56, 87–88, 191, 210		8:8c	88
7:10	61, **81**, 88–89, 188		8:8–9	88, 167
7:10a	49, 79, 81		8:8–14	56
7:11	61, 81, **86–88**, 89, 127, 156, 167, 193		8:9	37, 61, 88, 95–96
			8:9a	88
7:11a	87		8:9b	88
7:11a–b	79		8:9–10	38, 62, 191, 206
7:11b	82, 87–88		8:10	56
7:11d	79		8:12	51, 71, 83, 216
7:11–12	137		8:13	56, 93, 108, 186, 188, 210
7:12	20–21, 110, 165, 191		8:14	54, 56, 92–93, 96, 102, 165, 223
7:12a	**81–83**, 88–89		8:14a	91, **92–93**
7:12a–b	79		8:14–9:2	**91–97**, 163, 221
7:12b	89		9:1	37–38, 92–96, 165, 168–69, 191
7:12c	79		9:1b	91, **93–94**
7:12d	80, **83–84**		9:1c	91, **94–95**
7:12–13	191		9:1d–2	94
7:13	83–84, 88–89, 101, 131–33, 164–65, 167		9:1–9	39, 94–95, 99
			9:1–11:7	29, 92, 99, 107–8, 166
7:13–15	89		9:2	92, 96
7:13a	**84–85**		9:2a	92, **95–96**
7:13b	79–80			

Hosea (cont.)
- 9:2b — 95, 97
- 9:3 — 56, 94, 97, 188, 193
- 9:4 — 31
- 9:7 — 210
- 9:9 — 210
- 9:9–10 — 54
- 9:10 — 95, 102–5, 112, 120, 125, 133, 166–69, 175, 214
- 9:10–17 — 99
- 9:11–14 — 102
- 9:12 — 102
- 9:13 — 103–4
- 9:14 — 102
- 9:15 — **99–102**, 105, 120, 131–33, 148–49, 160–62, 168–70, 178–79, 214, 217, 219–20, 222, 224, 228
- 9:15b — 97, 101
- 9:15d — 97, 99
- 9:15d–e — 99
- 9:15e — 97, 99, 101
- 9:15f — 100
- 9:15–10:2 — **97–108**, 163, 222
- 9:16 — 88, 99, **102–5**, 107, 167, 180
- 9:16a — 97
- 9:16b — 97, 102
- 9:16c — 97
- 9:16e — 102
- 9:17 — **99–102**, 105, 187–88, 217, 219–20, 222, 224
- 9:17a — 101
- 9:17c — 97, 99, 101
- 10 — 6
- 10:1 — 88, 99, **102–5**, 107, 167, 180
- 10:1a — 98, 107
- 10:1a–b — 103–4, 107
- 10:1b — 98
- 10:1c–f — 103–4
- 10:1–2 — 111
- 10:1–8 — 99
- 10:1–15 — 110
- 10:2 — 1, 56, 99, 105
- 10:2a — 105
- 10:2b — 108
- 10:2c — 98, **105–7**
- 10:2–3 — 187–88
- 10:5 — 111
- 10:5–6 — 99
- 10:6 — 58, 88, 111, 127, 214
- 10:7 — 70
- 10:8 — 110–11
- 10:9 — 110–12, 133
- 10:10 — 4
- 10:10a — 108, **110–12**, 114–15
- 10:10–12 — **108–115**, 215
- 10:11 — 11, 31, **112**, 114–15, 156, 161, 166–69
- 10:11a — 109, 114
- 10:11b — 109, 114
- 10:11c — 109
- 10:11c–e — 114
- 10:11d — 109
- 10:11d–e — 109
- 10:11e — 110
- 10:12 — 61, 103, 110, 113–15, 145, 168, 176, 187, 189, 192, 224
- 10:12a–d — 113
- 10:12e — 110, **113–14**, 115
- 10:13 — 61, 111, 180
- 10:14–15 — 224
- 10:15 — 69–70, 111–12
- 11 — 118, 135, 188, 215, 218
- 11–13 — 175
- 11:1 — 1, 80, 118–23, 137, 148–49, 168, 179, 214–16
- 11:1a — 116
- 11:1b — 116
- 11:1–2 — 122
- 11:1–3 — **119–21**, 141
- 11:1–4 — 83, 112, **116–124**, 139, 147, 163, 168, 206, 222
- 11:1–8 — 122
- 11:1–9 — 137
- 11:1–11 — 187
- 11:2 — 4, 120, 123, 133, 175
- 11:2a — 120–21
- 11:2a–b — 116, 120
- 11:2c–d — 118, 120, 123
- 11:3 — 119, 121–23, 149, 178, 210
- 11:3a — 116

11:3b	4, 116	12:3	29, 31, 46–47, 49, 188
11:3c	117	12:4–5	164
11:3–4	117, 119, **121**–22	12:5	125
11:4	1, 121–22, 124, 219	12:7	21, 62, 113, 145, 168, 187–89, 214, 224
11:4a–b	123		
11:4aA	117	12:8	169
11:4aB	117	12:8–9	164
11:4b	117	12:10	80, 168
11:4c	118	12:11	69
11:5	122, 188, 193, 214–15	12:14	80, 168
11:5–6	224	12:15	188
11:5–7	118, 122, 137, 141, 163, 169	13	129–30, 135, 158, 175, 182, 222, 232
11:6	56, 118, 122		
11:7	79, 133, 178–79, 181, 188–89	13–14	134, 152, 155, 207, 216
11:7–8	120, 122	13:1	125, 134, 175, 220
11:8	11, 133, 135, 137–38, 140, 142–43, 163, 166, 168–70, 188, 222, 228	13:1–2	125
		13:1–14:1	29, 126, 130, 217
11:8a–d	111, 136–37, 169	13:2	128
11:8e	135, 137–38, 169	13:3	23, 150, 173, 179, 220
11:8e–f	137, **138**, 169	13:4	80, 85, 126, 129, 131, 210, 215–16
11:8f	131, 136, 138, 170		
11:8–9	132, 140, 145, 161, 185	13:4–5	168
11:8–10	**135–45**, 163, 222	13:4–6	128
11:8–11	29, 115, 118, 140, 142, 182	13:4–8	154, 215
11:9	122, 137, 140–43, 160, 162–63, 166, 188, 225, 228	13:5	124, 210
		13:5–6	126, 168
11:9a	141–42	13:5–8	96, 118, **124–129**
11:9a–b	142	13:6	54, 124–25, 215
11:9b	142	13:7	150, 153, 156, 219
11:9c–d	143	13:7a	125
11:10	21, 31, 128, 136–37, **138–39**, 173, 192, 207, 216	13:7b	125, 127
		13:7–8	21, 23, 125, 134, 138, 162, 173, 175, 191, 214
11:10a–b	136		
11:10b–c	137	13:7–14:1	224
11:10c–d	136	13:8	56
11:10–11	136, 142, 145, 217, 220, 222	13:8a	125
11:11	139, 193, 214–15	13:8b	125
12	164, 214	13:8c	125
12–14	30, 158, 205	13:8d	125
12:1	31	13:9–10	129
12:1–2	164	13:10	124
12:1–15	29	13:11	160, 162, 224
12:1–14:9	29–30, 46, 126, 129, 178, 188, 205	13:12–14	134
		13:14	124, 129, 131, 133–34, 136, 168–70, 175, 178, 220, 222, 224
12:2	47, 88, 193		

Hosea (cont.)
    13:14a   129
    13:14a–b   **131**, 133
    13:14a–d   169
    13:14b   129–30
    13:14c–d   124, 130, 134
    13:14e   130, **131-32**, 133, 169–70
    13:14–14:1   **129-34**, 191, 222
    13:15   128, 134, 150
    14   6, 135, 145, 155, 158, 162, **177-84**, 196, 228–29, 232
    14:1   131, 164, 191
    14:1a   133
    14:1a–b   130, **132-33**, 148
    14:1b   133
    14:1c–e   132
    14:2   21, 51, 186, 188
    14:2–3   62
    14:2–4   113, 145, 154, 177, 186–87, 189–92
    14:2–4c   148
    14:2–9   29–30, 178, 189, 217, 220
    14:2–10   185
    14:3   168, 180, 188, 194
    14:4   62, 175, 192, 220, 222
    14:4a   156
    14:4d   145, **148-49**, 154–55, 157, 177–79
    14:4–9   118, **145-57**, 222, 229
    14:5   61, 78, 145, 153, 160, 162, 168, 178, 181, 188–90, 192, 220, 222
    14:5a   145, **149**, 154, 156, 178, 222
    14:5a–b   154, 178
    14:5b   146, **149-50**, 154, 179, 181, 222
    14:5c   146, 182
    14:5–9   144, 220
    14:5–10   145–46
    14:6   1, 145, 173, 177, 179, 207, 219
    14:6a   146, **150-51**, 152, 154–57
    14:6b   155
    14:6c   155
    14:6–8   22, 215, 222
    14:6–9   177, 192–93, 214
    14:6b–8   145–47, 150–51, 154–56, 179, 181
    14:8   156, 188
    14:8a   147, 153
    14:9   17, 145, 152, 175, 192, 194, 207, 215, 224
    14:9b   147, 154, 156
    14:9c   147, 151–54, 180
    14:9c–d   **151-54**, 156, 175
    14:9d   147–48, 152–54, 180, 222
    14:10   51, 84, 132, 164, 177, 212

Joel
    2:23   110
    4:12–14   78
    4:16   139

Amos
    1:3   84
    1:6   84
    1:9   84
    1:11   84
    1:13   84
    2:1   84
    2:4   84
    2:6   84
    3:14   84, 106
    4:11   142
    5:12   84
    5:24   60
    7:7–8   189

Jonah
    3:9   146

Micah
    1:3   59
    1:7   91
    5:6–7   150
    7:18   213

Nahum
    1:3–5   28
    2:3   98
    2:11   98

Habakkuk		Dead Sea Scrolls	
2:14	60		
		4Q78	125
Zephaniah			
3:11	84	4Q82	110
3:17	213		
		4Q167	71
Zechariah			
1:2–4	189	Rabbinic Works	
1:13	136		
		b. Sanhedrin	
Malachi		38b[2]	70
2:11	53		
2:14	53	Lamentations Rabbah	
2:16	53	4.1	70
3:7	189		
		Pesiqta Rabbah	
Ancient Near Eastern Texts		44:3	185
		44:5	188
ARM			
13.23.9–10	81	Pesiqta Rab Kahana	
		16:8	177
COS		24	188
1.86	128		
1.103	68	Targum of the Prophets	
1.153	61	Hos 5:5	45
2.114C	109	Hos 5:7	56
2.118A	109	Hos 8:1	85
2.118E	109	Hos 9:1	95
2.119B	109	Hos 10:2	105
4.51	127	Hos 11:2	116
		Hos 11:2–3	117
		Hos 11:4	121
EA		Hos 14:5	154, 188
257	109	Hos 14:9	147, 149
KTU			
1.4.VIII.17–20	128	Early Christian Writings	
1.5.I.12b–15a	128		
1.10.I.10	68	Theodoret of Cyrus, *Enarratio in*	
1.12.II.36–56	151	*Oseam Prophetam*	188
1.17.VI.30	68		
1.21.II.6	68	Greco-Roman Literature	
		Aristotle, *Poetics*	
		1457b	13

Aristotle, *Rhetoric*
  1404b–1411b   13

Modern Authors Index

Aaron, David H.   35, 38
Abma, Richtsje   37, 67
Abramson, Lyn Y.   13
Abu-Darwish, Mohammad Sanad   153
Adams, Karin   34
Alexander, T. Desmond   219
Allen, Spencer L.   66, 199
Alonso Schökel, Luis   76
Alt, Albrecht   57
Alter, Robert   16, 154, 159–60, 162
Andersen, Francis I.   30, 33, 35, 37, 46–47, 53–54, 59–60, 62, 68, 71, 78, 98–99, 105, 108–112, 119, 130, 136–37, 140, 142, 147, 177, 212
Anderson, Gary A.   13, 187
Anderson, James S.   68, 174
Anderson, John E.   164
Arnold, Bill T.   59
Arnold, Patrick M.   111
Assante, Julia   33–34
Austin, Benjamin M.   7
Austin, John L.   13–14
Avis, Paul   20, 193
Bar-Efrat, Shimon   159–60, 162, 219
Barré, Michael L.   66–67, 187
Barrett, Lisa Feldman   11, 13
Basson, Alec   11, 60, 146
Baumann, Gerlinde   41–42
Bechtel, Lyn M.   40, 175
Ben Zvi, Ehud   4–5, 30, 35, 46, 63, 69, 100, 102, 110, 118–19, 122, 136, 146, 159, 185, 187, 203
Bergen, Robert D.   102
Berggren, Douglas   202
Bergmann, Claudia D.   87

Berlin, Adele   16, 159
Bird, Phyllis A.   33–37, 40
Black, Max   20, 50–51, 59
Blackburn, W. Ross   219
Blair, Merryl   192
Blum, Erhard   164
Blumenthal, David R.   41, 213
Boda, Mark J.   37–39, 63, 169, 186–90, 217
Booth, Wayne C.   13
Bos, James M.   4–5
Boshoff, Willem   76, 175
Botta, Alejandro F.   100–102
Braaten, Laurie J.   100, 117, 119–20, 122
Braude, William G.   188
Brettler, Marc Zvi   92–93, 96, 203, 223
Brown, William P.   10, 193–94
Brueggemann, Walter   1, 14–15, 26, 47, 61, 140–41, 159, 161, 192–93, 200, 219, 225
Brunner-Traut, Emma   200–201, 230
Bucher, Christina   32
Budin, Stephanie Lynn   34
Burkholder, Thomas R.   4, 13–14, 192
Butterworth, Mike   138
Cabral, Célia   153
Cameron, Lynne   11, 14, 16–19, 22, 25–26, 156, 182, 195, 205
Carew, M. Douglas   141, 170, 210
Carpenter, Eugene   150
Carroll R., M. Daniel   63–64, 140, 143
Carver, Terrell   14
Castelo, Daniel   54, 67, 70, 98–100, 104, 212
Cathcart, Kevin J.   45, 56, 85, 95

Catlett, Michael Lee	173, 190	*Eidevall, Göran (cont.)*	
Chalmers, Ronald Scott	174–75	68–69, 71, 78, 81–83, 85–89, 99–102,	
Chapman, Cynthia R.	87	104, 106, 109, 111–12, 117, 119, 121,	
Charpin, Dominique	34	124, 132, 136, 139, 146–47, 150–51,	
Childs, Brevard S.	33, 189, 218	153, 155, 166, 173, 177, 187–90, 194,	
Chmiel, Jerzy	67	200, 203, 207, 216, 224	
Cho, Paul K.-K.	7, 193	Ehrlich, Arnold B.	50
Choi, John H.	59	Emmerson, Grace I.	33, 85, 101, 136,
Clements, Ronald E.	185	142, 190	
Clines, David J. A.	191, 212	Erlandsson, Seth	52–54
Cohen, Ted	10, 12, 211	Fabry, Heinz-Josef	124, 138, 144
Conrad, J.	150	Farjon, Aljos	153
Cooper, Jerrold S.	34, 39	Fisch, Harold	47, 61, 63, 69, 124, 127,
Coote, Robert B.	155–56	129, 144, 150–51, 156, 173, 182, 189	
Corts, Daniel P.	25	Fitzgerald, Aloysius	129
Cottrill, Amy C.	10, 12	Fontaine, Carole R.	40
Couturier, Guy	146, 152–53	Freedman, David Noel	30, 33, 35, 37,
Craghan, John F.	185, 190	46–47, 53–54, 59–60, 62, 68, 71, 78,	
Crisp, Peter	18	98–99, 105, 108–112, 119, 130, 136–	
Cross, Frank Moore	85, 131	37, 140, 142, 147, 177, 212	
Cruz, Juan	4	Frevel, Christian	33, 146, 152
Daniels, Dwight R.	46, 117–18, 214	Gadamer, Hans-Georg	24
Davies, Graham I.	66, 71, 86, 92–94,	Galambush, Julie	33
101, 106–7, 112, 129, 146, 189		Gangloff, Frédéric	33, 152
Day, John	65–68, 129, 134, 146–47,	Garrett, Duane A.	63, 199, 212
152, 155, 175		Gault, Brian	188
Day, Peggy	33, 62	Gibbs, Raymond W., Jr.	4, 9, 18
De Andrado, Paba Nidhani	186, 210	Glenny, W. Edward	32, 54–55, 92, 98–
Dearman, J. Andrew	32–33, 37, 41–	99, 101, 112, 117, 124, 129	
42, 46, 53–54, 65, 67, 80, 83, 86–88,		Glucksberg, Sam	10
93–94, 99, 103, 105–6, 117, 119, 124,		Goldingay, John	45, 88, 129, 134, 144–
128–29, 147, 174, 203, 205, 219		45, 154, 190, 210, 213, 225	
DeGrado, Jessie	31, 33–35	Goldman, M. D.	119
Demjén, Zsófia	7	Good, Edwin M.	48, 59, 63, 72, 177
Dempsey, Carol J.	41, 186, 189–90	Gordis, Robert	104
DeRoche, Michael	46, 173	Gordon, Robert P.	45, 56, 85, 95
Dietrich, Erich Kurt	188, 194	Gosse, Bernard	212
Dietrich, Manfried	68, 152	Gray, Alison Ruth	23–24, 38
Donoghue, Denis	1	Green, Alberto R. W.	67, 134
Duby, Steven J.	140, 143, 225	Greenstein, Edward L.	66
Duhm, Bernhard	50	Gregg, Melissa	24
Durand, Emmanuel	143	Grisanti, Michael A.	150
Eichrodt, Walther	161, 185, 190	Grondin, Jean	24
Eidevall, Göran	xi, 6, 21, 30–32, 35–	Groß, Heinrich	144
37, 42, 46–48, 51, 53–54, 58–63, 66,		Grossberg, Daniel	30, 200

Modern Authors Index

Gruber, Mayer I.   4–5, 30, 32, 34–35, 38–39, 43, 45, 48, 51–52, 54–56, 62–63, 66, 69–70, 77, 80, 86, 88, 92–95, 98, 101, 104, 111, 124, 129–30, 136, 188
Gunn, David M.   191, 212
Habig, Brian C.   70
Haddox, Susan E.   17, 39–42, 60–61, 82, 87, 104, 154, 162, 173, 175
Hadjiev, Tchavdar S.   39–41, 181
Hadley, Judith M.   146, 152
Haelewyck, Jean-Claude   33
Hamilton, Mark W.   5, 61, 175, 182–83
Harper, William R.   64, 80, 99, 152
Harshav, Benjamin   8, 32, 114, 123
Hartsfield, Wallace   144
Hausmann, Jutta   200
Hawley, Lance R.   24, 182
Hayes, Katherine Murphey   47
Healey, John F.   128, 151
Hecke, Pierre van   44, 139
Henry, David   4, 13–14, 192
Herrmann, Wolfgang   68, 99
Heschel, Abraham   161, 191, 213
Hess, Richard S.   44
Hoffmeyer, Jeffrey H.   47
Holt, Else K.   101, 214–15
Hong, Koog-Pyoung   188
Hong, Seong-Hyuk   61
Houston, Walter J.   62, 188, 191
Hubbard, David Allan   86, 92, 99–100, 103, 105–6
Hugenberger, Gordon P.   47, 165
Hulster, Izaak J. de   203, 212
Humbert, Paul   98
Hundley, Michael B.   26, 176, 195, 199, 200–203, 230
Hutton, Jeremy   116
Ibn Ezra, Abraham ben Meïr   45, 55, 69, 80, 98, 105, 110, 130
Irvine, Stuart A.   5, 30, 67, 127, 130
Isbell, Charles D.   150
Jacob, Edmond   63, 106, 110, 136
Jacobs, Mignon R.   159, 188, 190
Janzen, J. Gerald   135, 145, 200

Jeremias, Jörg   30, 32–33, 48, 50, 54, 56–58, 63, 67, 69, 81, 84, 87, 88, 91–92, 94–95, 99, 108, 110, 112–13, 124, 136, 144, 146, 150, 170, 173, 185, 188, 206–7, 218
Jerome   2, 110, 191
Johnson, Luke Timothy   193
Johnson, Mark   7, 10, 13–14, 23–26, 193–94, 201–2
Joode, Johan de   8
Kakkanattu, Joy Philip   117–19, 121, 136–37, 139, 142, 161, 185, 190
Kaplan, Jonathan   193
Kató, Szabolcs-Ferencz   174
Keefe, Alice A.   34, 37–38, 41, 67, 104, 152, 157, 159, 161
Keel, Othmar   56, 59, 69, 81–82, 128, 139, 152, 200
Kelle, Brad E.   5–6, 14, 36–37, 57, 67, 100, 203
Kim, Sungjin   4
Kimmel, Michael   24–27, 72, 160, 182–83, 195
King, Andrew   13, 67
King, Philip   85
Kitchen, Kenneth A.   85, 87, 94, 126
Korpel, Marjo Christina Annette   66, 68, 128–29, 151–52, 156–57, 177
Kövecses, Zoltán   7–8, 11, 13, 17, 23–24, 187, 205
Kratz, Reinhard Gregor   212
Kreuzer, Siegfried   119
Kruger, Paul A.   5, 16–17, 39, 67, 83, 146, 149, 161, 174
Kurek-Chomycz, Dominika   161
Kuypers, Jim A.   13
Labahn, Antje   23
Labuschagne, Casper J.   5, 17, 43
Lakoff, George   4, 7–10, 12–14, 17, 23–26, 193–94, 201–2
Laldinsuah, Ronald   29
Lam, Joseph   13, 17, 19, 21, 130, 187
Lambert, David   62, 64, 186
Lancaster, Mason D.   6–8, 63, 68, 71, 76, 174, 179, 183, 207

Landy, Francis   1, 29, 48, 58, 61, 63, 69, 124, 129–30, 189, 200, 203
Lawrence, Paul J. N.   85, 87, 94, 126
Leeuwen, Cornelis van   98–99, 106–7
Leung Lai, Barbara M.   137–38, 144, 166
Light, Gary W.   30, 148, 150, 203, 205
Lim, Bo H.   54, 67, 70, 98–100, 104, 212
Lindeman, Lisa M.   13
Lindström, Fredrik   143
Lohfink, Norbert   100–101
Loon, Hanneke van   7–8
Loretz, Oswald   68, 152
Low, Graham   14, 23, 205
Loya, Melissa T.   47
Mácha, Jakub   7, 9
Macintosh, Andrew A.   5, 15, 31–33, 37, 43, 45, 47–51, 53–54, 56, 58–59, 62–64, 66, 69–71, 76–77, 79–80, 87–88, 91–95, 98–99, 101, 103–5, 108, 110–13, 116–18, 121–26, 129–31, 135–37, 140, 144–48, 178, 180, 182, 187–89, 193–94, 212, 218
Macwilliam, Stuart   42
Maier, Christl M.   34
Marti, D. Karl   105, 110, 136
Marzouk, Safwat   116
Maslen, Robert   17–19, 22–23, 26–27, 205
Matthews, Victor H.   40
Mays, James Luther 5, 30, 32, 53–54, 58–59, 62, 66, 70, 81, 85–86, 93–95, 99, 104, 109–10, 113, 117, 119–20, 135, 144, 186–87, 189, 191
McConville, J. Gordon   104, 144, 151, 153, 157, 225
McFague, Sallie   14
McKenzie, John L.   140–41
McKenzie, Steven L.   47
Melnyk, Janet L. R.   119–20
Meyers, Kristina   25
Miglio, Adam E.   63, 68, 71, 76, 207
Milgrom, Jacob   62
Miller, James E.   35
Mirguet, Françoise   101–2, 135, 161
Moberly, R. Walter L.   143

Moon, Joshua N.   35–36, 38, 40–41, 48, 54, 56, 63, 65, 98, 106, 113, 125, 129, 140, 144, 163, 180
Moor, Johannes C. de   99
Moran, William L.   62
Morris, Gerald Paul   30, 104, 118, 124, 150, 152, 159, 173–74, 177–79, 189, 203
Moughtin-Mumby, Sharon   5, 14, 17, 35–37, 42, 45–46, 52–53, 94, 104, 179, 188, 212
Mowinckel, Sigmund   109
Mulder, Martin J.   99
Musolff, Andreas   14
Na'aman, Nadav   5
Naudé, Jackie   147
Neef, Heinz-Dieter 47, 71, 118, 124, 188
Nissinen, Martti 38, 48, 71, 116, 119–20, 122
Nocquet, Dany   67, 153
Nogalski, James D.   48, 99, 122, 189, 214, 218
Nutkowicz, Hélène   101
Nwaoru, Emmanuel O.   62, 76, 120, 177, 187, 189
O'Brien, Julia M.   189, 210
Oestreich, Bernhard   17, 145–47, 149–53, 157, 179
O'Kennedy, Daniël F.   121, 190
Olson, Dennis T.   62–63, 187
Olyan, Saul M.   39, 47, 146, 217
Oshlag, Rebecca S.   9
Otis, Laura   12
Otzen, Benedikt   150–51
Parpola, Simo   61, 81, 85, 119–20
Patrick, Dale   139, 142, 159–60, 162, 183, 189–91, 194, 213–14, 217, 219
Paul, Shalom M.   87
Pentiuc, Eugen J.   37, 53, 58, 110
Perdue, Leo G.   193
Petrie, Hugh G.   9
Pikalo, Jernej   14
Plank, Karl A.   154, 181, 225
Propp, William H. C.   218
Pryce, Bertrand Casimis   65–66, 68

Modern Authors Index

Rad, Gerhard von 137
Ramirez, Felipe Fruto 63, 113–14, 164
Rendtorff, Rolf 189, 201
Richelle, Matthieu 46
Ricoeur, Paul 10, 13, 16–17, 192, 216
Roberts, Rabbi Matis 98
Rogers, Nancy Louise 16
Römer, Thomas 72
Rom-Shiloni, Dalit 209
Rosch, Eleanor 13
Rudolph, Wilhelm 58, 66, 81, 98, 101, 106, 109–10, 113, 117, 129, 136, 146, 187–89
Salgueiro, Lígia 153
Sander, David 11
Scherer, Klaus 11
Schlimm, Matthew R. 20, 187
Scholz, Susanne 42
Schott, Martin 164
Schüngel-Straumann, Helen 119
Scurlock, JoAnn 61
Seifert, Brigitte 19, 21, 33, 36, 48, 54, 58–59, 61–64, 67, 69, 72, 91–92, 94–95, 112, 117–22, 125, 129, 135–36, 143–44, 150–52, 154, 157, 176–77, 207, 214–15, 217
Seigworth, Gregory J. 24
Sellin, Ernst 105, 110
Semino, Elena 7
Seow, Choon-Leong 177
Sharp, Carolyn J. 159
Sherwood, Yvonne 41, 150, 189, 212
Siebert-Hommes, Jopie 118
Simian-Yofre, Horacio 148
Smith, Cooper 70, 173
Smith, Duane Andre 119
Smith, Gordon T. 186
Smith, Mark S. 66, 111, 128–29, 147, 152, 199
Sommer, Benjamin D. 147
Soskice, Janet Martin 7–8, 10, 13, 17, 20, 143, 211
Southwood, Katherine 61, 163, 181
Spencer, F. Scott 161
Spronk, Klaas 66
Stackert, Jeffrey 199
Stager, Lawrence 85
Stark, Christine 34, 36
Staubli, Thomas 39, 77
Steen, Gerard J. 7–9, 14, 17–20, 42, 147
Stelma, Juurd H. 16, 22, 25–26, 156, 182, 195
Stern, Josef 9, 16, 205
Sternberg, Meir 159–60
Stiebert, Johanna 39–40
Stovell, Beth M. 8
Strawn, Brent A. 26, 59–60, 126–28, 139, 202–3, 212
Stuart, Douglas 47, 78, 85–87, 98, 100, 102, 105–7, 109–13, 124, 130–31, 143
Sweeney, Marvin A. 32, 35, 37, 48, 54, 71, 85–86, 94, 98, 100–101, 108–11, 119, 124, 127, 134, 175, 188, 212
Tångberg, K. Arvid 147, 152, 154
Tauberschmidt, Gerhard 98
Taylor, Charles 4
Thiselton, Anthony C. 213
Thistlethwaite, Susan Brooks 41
Thompson, Evan T. 13
Tigay, Jeffrey H. 67
Tilford, Nicole L. 8
Todd, Zazie 14, 23
Toorn, Karel van der 34, 72, 218
Törnkvist, Rut 41
Trotter, James M. 5
Tully, Eric J. xi, 30–31, 45, 53–55, 57–58, 64–65, 77–80, 86–87, 91–95, 97–99, 101–3, 105–110, 112, 116–18, 120, 124, 126, 129–30, 135, 137, 139, 142, 145, 147, 154, 180
Turner, Mark 7, 24
Uehlinger, Christoph 69, 128
Underhill, James 14
Unterman, Jeremiah 186, 190
Uro, Risto 38
Vall, Gregory 154, 190, 210
Varela, Francisco J. 13
Varga, Somogy 13
Verde, Danilo 23
Vidaković, Mirko 153

Vielhauer, Roman 146
Wacker, Marie-Theres 33, 37, 41, 119, 152
Wakely, Robin 53–55
Walker, Thomas Worth 30, 61, 121, 146, 150–51, 185, 189, 203
Ward, James M. 129, 133
Watanabe, Kazuko 61, 81, 85
Watson, Paul Layton 66, 129, 133
Weems, Renita J. 36, 39, 41, 200
Weippert, Manfred 119
Weiss, Andrea L. 24, 26, 195, 202–3
Wellhausen, Julius 107, 110, 136, 146, 152
Westbrook, Raymond 200
Wijngaards, John 67
Williamson, Robert, Jr. 193
Wilson-Wright, Aren M. 66, 199
Wolde, Ellen van 102, 141, 146, 187, 212
Wolff, Hans Walter 5, 30, 32–33, 36, 39, 43–45, 47, 51, 54, 56, 58–60, 63, 66, 69, 71, 80, 84, 86–89, 91–92, 101, 105–113, 116–19, 122–24, 126, 128–30, 135–36, 144–47, 150–52, 167, 185, 195, 197, 214, 216, 218
Worden, Thomas 113, 134
Wright, Christopher J. H. 15, 85
Wyatt, Nicholas 119, 128, 152
Yates, Gary E. 186
Yee, Gale A. 36, 40, 42, 63, 110, 122, 150–51, 153, 155, 161, 187–89, 191, 203
Yoo, Yoon Jong 5, 91, 116
Zehetgruber, Katrin 217
Zenger, Erich 139, 143
Zimran, Yisca 21, 60, 62, 175, 192–93, 216
Zulick, Margaret Diefenderfer 175

CPSIA information can be obtained
at www.ICGtesting.com
Printed in the USA
JSHW022233180723
44871JS00008B/22